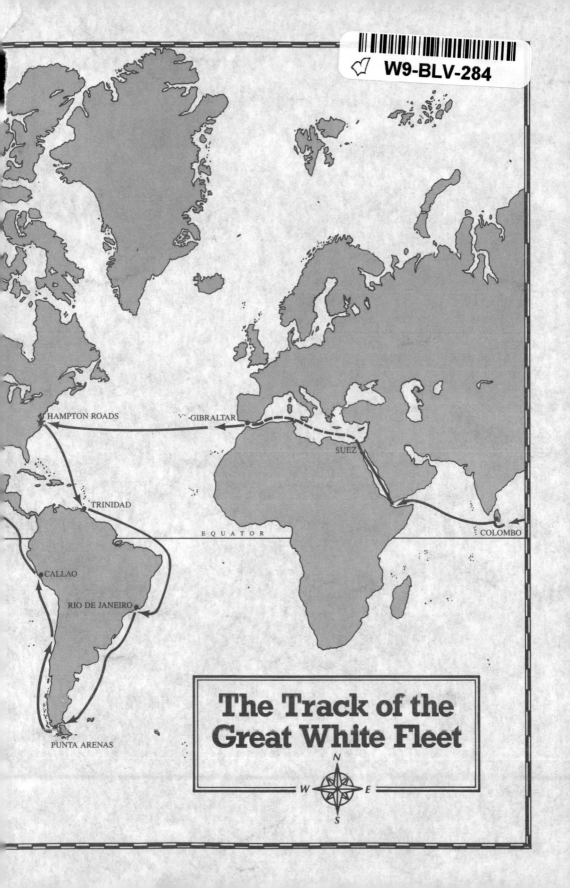

HAMPTON ROADS · GIBRALTAR

SUEZ

TRINIDAD

EQUATOR

COLOMBO

CALLAO

RIO DE JANEIRO

PUNTA ARENAS

The Track of the Great White Fleet

N

W E

S

Teddy Roosevelt's Great White Fleet

■

TEDDY ROOSEVELT'S
GREAT WHITE FLEET

James R. Reckner

NAVAL INSTITUTE PRESS ■ ANNAPOLIS, MARYLAND

Copyright © 1988
by the United States Naval Institute, Annapolis, Maryland

Title page painting: *United States Fleet in the Straits of Magellan on the Morning of February 8, 1908,* by Henry Reuterdahl. Courtesy of U.S. Naval Academy Museum.

Library of Congress Cataloging-in-Publication Data

Reckner, James R., 1940–
    Teddy Roosevelt's Great White Fleet / James R. Reckner.
      p.   cm.
    Bibliography: p.
    Includes index.
    ISBN 0-87021-697-X
    1. United States. Navy—Cruise, 1907–1909. 2. United States—History, Naval—20th century. 3. United States—Military relations—Japan. 4. Japan—Military relations—United States. 5. Voyages around the world. 6. Roosevelt, Theodore, 1858–1919.
    I. Title.
    VA58.R43   1988
    359′.00973—dc19

                  88-23054
                  CIP

Book design by Bea Jackson

Printed in the United States of America

2 4 6 8 9 7 5 3

This work is dedicated to my wife, Middy,
and also
to the enlisted men of the Great White Fleet

Contents

Preface

In the early months of 1907 American relations with Japan reached a crisis point. The quickening flow of Japanese immigrant labor had raised the concern of American workingmen on the West Coast and triggered discriminatory measures in California. Underlying the obvious fear of labor competition was apprehension about Japanese military prowess. Japan, recently victorious in land and sea battles against Russia, was viewed by many as a distinct military threat to the virtually defenseless West Coast and Hawaii. The possibility, however remote, that the Japanese government might take military action in response to California's discriminatory regulations rapidly transformed the immigration problem into a war scare. Historians of later generations examining this period of Japanese-American relations have concluded that the situation in 1907 was less serious than originally thought. Despite this historical hindsight, it is difficult to deny that at the time Americans perceived a crisis and reacted accordingly.

While actively seeking to resolve the problem of Japanese immigration and West Coast reactions to it, President Theodore Roosevelt ordered the implementation, for practice purposes, of a number of measures recommended by the Joint Board of the army and navy. These included the deployment of the entire battleship fleet—the U.S. Atlantic Fleet—to the Pacific. The voyage that followed, the world cruise of the Great White Fleet, has taken its place in American history as the single most significant naval event of the Roosevelt administration. But this assessment falsely suggests that the Far East was a preeminent naval concern. In reality, the navy's preoccupation with the defense implications of the war scare of 1907 was quite short-lived, a brief distraction from the traditional concentration on events in the Caribbean and Europe.

Indeed, an appreciation of this Caribbean/Atlantic orientation is critical to understanding the full significance to the navy of the American rapprochement with Japan, formalized by the Root-Takahira Agreement of November 1908. American leaders, naval officers in particular, were convinced that Germany under the kaiser represented the greatest threat to peace. The need to resolve difficulties with Japan, important for further development of bilateral relations, assumed even greater global significance because rapprochement would permit continued concentration of the battleship fleet in the Atlantic, an advantage that amply compensated for America's weak position in the Pacific. American distrust of German motives, kindled in Samoa in the 1880s and nurtured at Manila Bay in 1898, had been sustained by the Venezuela blockade of 1903 and Germany's threatening position regarding Morocco in 1905–6. As Seward W. Livermore has so well explained, most American naval deployments from 1903 to 1913 were in the direction of Europe, which reflected a continuing Anglo-French bias.[1]

Though from the more skeptical perspective of today, the Progressive Era's intensely emotional patriotism and the common belief that the United States was predestined to loom large on the world stage seem difficult to credit, these sentiments were real and forceful aspects of the American scene. Few would have argued with Theodore Roosevelt's claim that the United States had "no choice" as to whether it would "play a great part in the world." The only decision open to Americans, Roosevelt contended, was whether they would play that part "well or ill."[2]

Americans were unabashed in waxing poetic over the glory of the fleet and its cruise. Some Europeans decried such demonstrative pride, but whether they were critical or supportive of the cruise, the shifting of American naval power to the Pacific forced them to reappraise the balance of power in that ocean.

An account of the cruise of the Atlantic battleship fleet, later known as the Great White Fleet, forms a large part of the work that follows. And what a cruise it was! Unprecedented in many respects, including distance steamed and number of ships participating, the cruise commanded the world's attention. For the people of host ports it provided a unique entertainment opportunity, the significance of which they were quick to grasp. Indeed, the arrival of sixteen gleaming white- and buff-colored first-class battleships was the event of a lifetime. One million people lined the shores of the Golden Gate to welcome the fleet to San Francisco; half a million gathered in Sydney; hundreds of thousands turned out in other ports.

A remarkable air of innocence surrounds contemporary attitudes toward the fleet and its cruise. This is understandable. The world would enjoy six more years of naval pageantry and splendor before the horrors of unrestricted submarine warfare and ever-mounting casualty lists from the trenches in France extinguished a generation's romantic conceptions and preoccupation with things military. But that disillusionment lay in the future. In 1908 naval parades were applauded without reservation; few fears were expressed about the battleship cruise, and people along the route, particularly those in remote places never before visited by a great fleet, gladly surrendered themselves to the festivities.

The cruise was a highly successful exercise in national public awareness. It greatly expanded popular understanding of American foreign relations and defense considerations, particularly in regard to the Pacific Basin. In every corner of the nation it promoted public knowledge of, interest in, and sympathy for the navy.

PREFACE

But this generated increased public scrutiny of the Navy Department for most of the fourteen months the fleet was away, which brings up an important but often neglected theme related to the cruise: the sensational, often acrimonious, debates over ship design and naval organization.

One is confronted throughout this account with a basic contradiction. Although often cited as proof of the efficiency of the navy and its bureau system, the cruise never actually tested materiel and organizational deficiencies against which navy reformers campaigned. Battleship design errors such as incorrectly placed armor belts and unsafe ammunition hoists, as well as the fragmented authority of the bureau system that perpetuated these errors, were left unexamined. Primarily an exercise in extended peacetime cruising and naval diplomacy, the battleship cruise tended to mask the navy's defects and thus, at least superficially, to diminish the strength of the reform argument.

What the American public saw was the successful completion, with few apparent difficulties, of the longest fleet cruise ever undertaken by any navy. That ships of the fleet might not have been properly designed as a result of faulty organization within the Navy Department, that the navy lacked the essential logistic support of a healthy merchant marine, and that senior officers of the fleet were too old and, despite their advanced age, too inexperienced in high command—these were fine points often ignored in favor of the pomp and ceremony, the orations and ovations, that attended the battleships as they proceeded on their great voyage.

I would like to acknowledge the support and assistance of the University of Auckland, New Zealand, particularly the late Professor L. J. (Jim) Holt, who provided me with the initial encouragement to undertake this work, and Professor P. N. Tarling, who read numerous early drafts, offered incisive comment, and gave valued guidance.

In the United States, Mr. John S. Stone kindly authorized the use of Surgeon Eugene P. Stone's diary. Mr. Stanley Kalkus and Mr. John Vajda of the Navy Department Library extended every courtesy and assisted me in the use of the library's unique collection of works. Rear Admiral John D. H. Kane, director of Naval History, Captain David A. Long, executive director of the Naval Historical Foundation, and Rear Admiral Robert P. Hilton all gave valuable encouragement. Chaplain Commander Lawrence Martin lent advice, books, and moral support, as did D. J. Crawford of the History and Museums division of the U.S. Marine Corps.

Dr. Dean C. Allard of the Naval Historical Center deserves special acknowledgment for his encouragement over many months of correspondence, for his assistance in locating materials, and for his constructive criticism of an early draft of this work. My thanks also to Mrs. Nancy Miller of the Naval Historical Center, who assisted me during research, and to Richard A. Von Doenhoff of the National Archives for his generous contribution of time, effort, and enthusiasm.

Admiral Jose T. Merino, commander in chief of the Chilean navy, and Dr. Mateo Martinić of the Patagonia Institute in Punta Arenas, Chile, provided primary materials on the fleet visit to Chile.

PREFACE

Finally, I must acknowledge the support of my wife and children, who found themselves captive participants in my pursuit of the Great White Fleet and who yet managed to retain their sense of humor. Without their understanding and support, completion of this work would have been impossible.

To all of the above I owe anything of quality in the work that follows; the burden of any errors of omission or commission, however, remains with me.

Teddy Roosevelt's Great White Fleet

∎

ONE

The Pacific Challenge

During the fifteen years before America's Atlantic Fleet sailed on its world cruise, the balance of power shifted dramatically in the Pacific. Between the Sino-Japanese (1894–95) and Russo-Japanese (1904–5) wars the most significant strategic development in this ocean was the strengthening of Japan's armed forces, particularly its navy.

One of the terms of the Treaty of Shimonoseki, virtually dictated to China by a victorious Japan in 1895, was the cession to the latter of Port Arthur, a strategic port on China's Liaotung Peninsula. Subsequent intervention by Russia, Germany, and France forced Japan to retrocede it to China. Russia eventually took control of the port, replacing China as the Japanese army's primary strategic enemy. With a view toward isolating Russia in Manchuria, the Japanese government authorized the doubling of its army and navy in 1896. This triggered a series of responses from European powers with interests in the Far East. To counterbalance Japanese warship construction, the Russians, following commencement of their extraordinary naval program of 1898, dispatched all their newly built battleships and cruisers to the Far East. Britain, with its extensive interests in China, felt compelled to match this buildup despite pressing commitments in waters nearer home. When, in January 1901, the Russian navy deployed two additional battleships to the Far East, the British Admiralty could no longer keep up with Russia's commitment. Only one British battleship was sent, from the Mediterranean Fleet; no more could be spared.[1] With their naval resources seriously overextended, British diplomats unsuccessfully sought to rationalize their defense commitments through a rapprochement with Germany and then with Russia. Having failed in these efforts, Britain turned toward Japan.

Complicating British considerations was the rapid growth of other European navies, particularly those of France and Germany. An atmosphere of mutual suspicion had strained Anglo-French relations since the Fashoda incident of 1898. By the turn of the century the French navy was searching for an effective deterrent against the Royal Navy. In 1900 France concentrated its battle fleet in the Mediterranean and adopted an energetic naval construction program; in 1901, following a ten-year lapse, it reinstituted its annual Atlantic-Mediterranean fleet maneuvers.[2] During the next two years of these exercises an active offensive was assumed against the British fleets—a development noted with concern by the Admiralty.[3]

The growth of German naval strength during this period was equally significant, for its thrust was specifically anti-British. The 1898 *Flottengesetz,* or naval law, with its commitment to the construction of a first-class navy, has been characterized as "the point of no return" in the movement toward single-power domination of the European continent; it virtually assured British rivalry and resistance.[4] German naval aims expanded significantly when on 14 June 1900 the Reichstag, influenced by Britain's distraction with the Boer War and mindful also of the military requirements of intervention in the Boxer Rebellion in China, approved a second *Flottengesetz* that doubled the size of the authorized fleet.[5]

Thus the British government, as it began active consideration of an alliance with Japan toward the end of 1901, received strong Admiralty support. The First Lord of Admiralty, Lord Selborne, succinctly summarized the strategic situation, observing that if the Royal Navy was defeated in the North Atlantic or the Mediterranean, no amount of superiority in the Far East would alleviate the situation. If, however, the Royal Navy was victorious in the North Atlantic and the Mediterranean, even disasters in the Pacific would matter little.[6] As the Selborne memorandum clearly showed, considerations of security nearer home, in the wake of the unprecedented naval expansion of European continental powers, drove Britain to reduce the potential for conflict in peripheral areas. This was accomplished, first and foremost, through an alliance with Japan, signed 30 January 1902, which gave the two countries overwhelming naval superiority in the Far East.

The period 1902–4 saw significant naval developments in Europe. The Admiralty firmly identified the threat to British interests posed by the new German navy, while French naval strength declined precipitously as a result of the policies of the radical-socialist minister of marine, Camille Pelletan. The Anglo-French entente of 1904 finally removed France's navy as a threat, thereby permitting the Royal Navy to reduce strength in the Mediterranean and reinforce the Home Fleet, Britain's answer to a rapidly growing German High Sea Fleet.

The appointment in 1904 of Admiral Sir John Fisher (later Admiral of the Fleet Lord Fisher of Kilverstone) as First Sea Lord set the stage for a bold attempt to rationalize the disposition and composition of the Royal Navy. Fisher pursued an unswerving policy of confronting Germany by concentrating capital ships in the Narrow Seas. He also scrapped large numbers of units with marginal combat capabilities and energetically campaigned for the single-caliber main-battery battleship. When the first such unit, HMS *Dreadnought,* was commissioned in 1906, it signaled the beginning of a new era in naval armaments competition.

As Europe's new naval balance established itself, Russo-Japanese relations deteriorated. The Anglo-Japanese alliance had reduced the possibility of European intervention in China in support of Russia, while the naval preponderance achieved through the alliance gave Japan an opportunity to challenge Russian control of the Liaotung Peninsula.

Japan opened hostilities on 9 February 1904 with an unannounced naval attack on the Russian fleet at Port Arthur. The Russian navy's strategic deployment as two independent fleets, one in the Baltic and the other in Pacific waters, enabled the numerically inferior Japanese to engage and defeat their enemy in detail. The Russian Baltic Fleet, under Admiral Zinovy Rodzhestvensky's command, rushed to the Pacific to relieve the forces at Port Arthur. After a lengthy voyage plagued by engineering and logistic problems, particularly supplying coal, the ill-prepared and demoralized fleet reached the theater of war. Although Russia's stronghold at Port Arthur had already fallen to the Japanese, Rodzhestvensky received orders to continue to Vladivostok. He was intercepted in the Strait of Tsushima, where his ships were annihilated by Admiral Togo's fleet.

Following that battle, the British Committee for Imperial Defense was presented with a new "naval strengths" estimate showing that allied naval forces in the Far East were "preposterously strong."[7] Using figures from this report, the Admiralty argued that the five British battleships maintained in Far Eastern waters in accordance with secret naval agreements concluded at the time of the signing of the original alliance should be brought home. Later negotiations resulted in the deletion of all naval and military references from the ten-year treaty renewal, which was signed in London on 12 August 1905.

Subsequently the reason for British adherence to the alliance completely changed. From 1902 to 1905 it had provided mutual security against Russia; from 1907 onward, following Britain's entente with Russia and Russian rapprochement with Japan, the alliance limited the possibility of Anglo-Japanese rivalry in the Far East as it grew increasingly apparent that Britain's most pressing need was to concentrate naval strength in Europe. In effect, Britain became a captive of its own alliance.

Thus by 1907, after a tumultuous decade, the international naval scene had altered significantly. Developing industrialization on the European continent had encouraged ambitious naval expansion schemes that challenged British naval superiority. The Russian navy had risen dramatically only to be destroyed at Tsushima; the French navy had shown steady and credible development but declined rapidly after 1902 and, following the entente with Britain in 1904, ceased to represent a threat to the Royal Navy. Reflecting the effectiveness and strength of Germany's industrialization, the kaiser's navy alone in continental Europe continued a program of energetic expansion. The 1898 *Flottengesetz*, with its systematic outline for naval expansion, had been extended and enlarged by new resolutions in 1900 and 1906. Further expansion authorized in 1908 and 1912 would boost Germany to second place, after England, in the naval competition.

One important result of these developments was European withdrawal from the Pacific and from the waters of the western hemisphere. Russian forces in the Pacific had been reduced to a level of impotence little altered until the 1970s, and Britain, adhering to the recommendation of the Committee for Imperial Defense, removed its five battleships from that ocean.

The extent of British withdrawal was not general knowledge until December 1907, when Captain Alfred Thayer Mahan reported that by May 1908 eighty-six percent of the Royal Navy's battleship strength would be concentrated in or near home waters.[8] The vast Pacific had become a power vacuum. Rivalry in home waters had canceled the potential of either Britain's navy or Germany's to influence events in this distant body of water.

Indeed, by 1905 the Royal Navy's superiority, the foundation of British power since the conclusion of the Napoleonic wars in the nineteenth century, had become conditional. Although the navy continued to maintain a "two-power standard," the First Sea Lord's preoccupation with Germany restricted the practical application of Britain's overwhelming strength to European waters so long as the High Sea Fleet remained intact. In the western hemisphere British interests had become dependent on the cooperation of the United States, for British planners had abandoned any prospect of establishing naval superiority there in the event of war with that country. More important, Britain's superiority in the Pacific was now conditional, relying on the naval strength of its ally, Japan, in any future conflict.

America's strategic policy between 1898 and 1907 reflected growing influence in Asia. When the United States gained an imperial foothold in the Pacific in 1898, businessmen thought that Oriental markets were poised on the threshold of unprecedented growth. Exploitation of their vast commercial potential, although it would prove largely illusory, provided a motive for territorial and naval expansion at the turn of the century. Perceived commercial opportunity and the requirements for defense of insular possessions helped to shape American foreign policy in the Pacific region and influenced the evolution of naval plans and requirements.

The outbreak of hostilities with Spain in May 1898 resulted in congressional authorization of ambitious shipbuilding programs (1898–1900) that included eight new battleships.[9] A second burst of naval authorizations came after the assassination of President McKinley in September 1901 propelled Theodore Roosevelt to the presidency. Characteristically, Roosevelt pursued his naval program with vigor and determination. In his first annual message to Congress he declared no part of his policy was more important than naval expansion.[10]

Among the most ardent and uninhibited navalists of the period was Democratic Congressman Richmond Pearson Hobson, a retired naval captain. In an article published in 1902 Hobson called for the construction of a navy second to none, suggesting as a goal one greater than the aggregate of all the other great fleets of the world. Emphasizing the nation's burgeoning population, industrial productivity, natural resources, and rapidly expanding commercial interests, Hobson concluded his appeal with a combination of Social Darwinism, patriotic bombast, and prophecy not uncommon in this ebullient period of American history: "The finger of fate is pointing forward. America will be the controlling World power, holding the sceptre of the sea, reigning in mighty beneficence with the guiding principle of a maximum of world service. She will help all the nations of the earth. Europe will be saved by her young off-spring grown to manhood."[11]

Despite such strong nationalistic appeals, the movement for greater naval expansion faced growing and influential opposition. Nevertheless, Roosevelt achieved significant results in his drive to expand the navy, gaining congressional authorization for ten additional battleships in the next four years.[12] By March 1905 he had apparently decided that further growth was unnecessary, an idea first mentioned to Major General Leonard Wood, military commander of the Philippines, toward the end of the Russo-Japanese War.[13] In the months that followed Russia was soundly defeated by the Japanese and the Anglo-Japanese alliance was renewed for an additional ten years. Shortly afterward, Secretary of War William H. Taft visited Japan, where, in discussions with Premier Katsura, he was assured that Japan did not have designs in the Philippines. Taft, in turn, expressed the opinion that Japanese suzerainty over Korea was a logical result of the Russo-Japanese War.[14] His recognition of that suzerainty amounted to little more than an acknowledgment of the facts of life in the postwar Orient. Although events would soon obscure the fact, in July 1905 there were no apparent major conflicts in Japanese-American interests, a situation that made it easy for Katsura to propose an informal alliance between Japan, Great Britain, and the United States. Taft responded that no alliance was possible without Senate assent, but added that the United States would act along with the two powers as if it were under treaty obligation.

Having essentially "cleared his yardarms" in Asia by acknowledging realities that the United States lacked the military power and political will to alter, and by emphasizing the unity of American, British, and Japanese interests, Roosevelt may well have felt secure enough to propose the reduction in battleship building as a concession to growing domestic opposition to further naval expansion. He made the decision public in his fifth annual message to Congress on 5 December 1905. To achieve the reduction, Roosevelt announced, it would be necessary only to add one battleship per year to replace superseded or outworn vessels.[15]

The timing of this decision proved singularly unfortunate, for the immediate future brought noteworthy technological advances in battleship design and construction. The *Dreadnought*'s launching in 1906 revolutionized battleship construction. This single-caliber main-battery prototype lent her name to an era of entirely new naval construction demands. Within the next three years nearly seventy dreadnoughts would be ordered throughout the world as navies sought to either redress the imbalance created by their competitors' acquisition of these ships or alter an existing balance of regional power.

The *Dreadnought*'s advent and the great worldwide increase in shipbuilding appropriations it generated would in itself have been sufficient cause for President Roosevelt to reverse his policy and add to the American battle fleet a reasonable number of dreadnoughts. Declining relations with Japan offered another compelling reason. The unity of interests expressed in the Taft-Katsura discussions of 1905 had proved ephemeral. As Japan extended its influence into Manchuria, concern grew amongst American businessmen and diplomats that the Open Door was being closed to U.S. commercial interests.

Further, continuing immigration of Japanese laborers to the West Coast kindled fear on the part of American workers that cheap Oriental labor would displace them. Efforts to have Japanese immigrants excluded from the United States were dismissed by Roosevelt as sheer foolishness,[16] but his pronouncement did not keep anti-Japanese fervor from igniting into a virtual war scare. In 1906 the San Francisco School Board enacted a regulation requiring all Japanese students to attend a segregated school set aside for "Mongolians," an objectionable regulation Roosevelt exerted strong pressure to have removed. At the same time he sought to reach an amicable settlement with Japan in regard to the immigration of laborers. Under the terms of the resulting "Gentlemen's Agreement"—actually a series of agreements—the Japanese government would restrict the issuance of passports to laborers while the school board would desist from implementing its segregation regulations. This development notwithstanding, in May 1907 anti-Japanese tensions flared, resulting in riots in San Francisco and other West Coast cities. Tension was aggravated by a yellow press that played on racial fears and indulged in irresponsible speculation concerning the possibility of war with Japan.

Although in retrospect it is not difficult to discount the gravity of this scare, many contemporaries, lacking information available to the modern historian, considered the situation to be serious. In June and July even the more respectable newspapers ran articles pronouncing war imminent—articles by admirals, generals, missionaries, and politicians. War was an impending reality in the eyes of many Americans, and the precipitate decline in Japanese-American relations offered ample reason for the president to abandon his nonexpansion program and support more ambitious battleship construction.

One other event pushed him in this direction. Early in 1907 delegates from the world's naval powers met at the Hague in an attempt to limit the size and number of warships. In this mission they were totally unsuccessful. The conference, rather than producing an agreement on limitation, devoted most of its time to developing rules for naval warfare. This failure ensured the continued and rapid production of dreadnoughts the world over.

Naval expansion after the war with Spain generated lively debate over the battle fleet's disposition. The problem of strategy was complicated in this period before construction of the Panama Canal by the great distance between America's Atlantic and Pacific coasts and by Mahan's generally accepted dictum of concentration of forces. This "law" of naval strategy had been most impressively confirmed when the Russian navy, divided into two fleets for the protection of Russia's Baltic and Pacific coasts, had been defeated in detail by a numerically inferior enemy. America's strategic dilemma was, and remained until World War II, the need to provide for a naval defense in the Atlantic and the Pacific with a force that was adequate for the protection of only one.

Before 1906 strategic planners had focused on the Atlantic and the Caribbean. The Joint Board of the Army and Navy had concluded, and the secretaries of the navy and war agreed, that hostilities in the Philippines were most likely to result not from Japanese aggression but from European infringement of the Monroe Doctrine—that is, a European squadron might descend on American bases in the Philippines while staging a simultaneous attack in the Caribbean or some other area of the western hemisphere. Such a conclusion was the natural outgrowth of America's experience in the recent war against Spain when, in a secondary operation, Commodore Dewey attacked Spanish forces in the Philippines.

American perception of German imperial ambitions in the Caribbean and South America and Dewey's encounter with the commander of the kaiser's squadron at Manila Bay in 1898 combined to create a healthy suspicion of Germany. It was identified as America's most probable enemy, and senior officers recommended assigning highest priority to planning for war with that country even before the first meeting of the newly formed General Board in 1900. Development of War Plan Black, to counter German aggression in the western hemisphere, began in the first year of the board's existence.

Concern over German intentions tended to identify American interests more with those of Britain. This gave freedom of movement to the United States and made the battleship fleet's world cruise possible. The Anglo-German naval confrontation had become so intense that by 1906 Germany ceased active planning for operations in the western hemisphere and placed full emphasis on the pending battle in the Narrow Seas.[17] After the Royal Navy withdrew from the western hemisphere and Asian waters, leaving them open to more direct influence by other naval powers, Germany had to limit the scope of its naval operations as well, for concentration of force by one antagonist dictated concentration of force by the other. Thus as long as Anglo-German rivalry continued, keeping the western hemisphere free of any significant European presence, the Atlantic battleship fleet could temporarily transfer to the Pacific without bringing any significant threat to the Atlantic coast.

The strategic situation in the Pacific, from the American point of view, had changed dramatically following the Russo-Japanese War. Japan's growing naval strength, the proven prowess of its armies, and domestic attitudes in both Japan and the United States contributed to the emergence of that country as America's potential enemy in the Pacific. The American navy reappraised its deployment policies and decided, in the summer of 1906, to replace the battleship squadron in Asian waters with an armored cruiser squadron. With the altered naval balance and the removal of European battleships, armored cruisers, so the reasoning went, would be sufficient to impress the Chinese yet speedy enough to avoid destruction at the hands of the Japanese.[18]

However, the General Board reviewed the overall strategic situation again, in April 1907, and concluded that the primary threat still came from Europe. In the event of war with a European power, concentration of the battle fleet in the Atlantic would be critical. The prospect of hostilities with European navies in the East was considered unlikely after the redeployment of their battleships from that region—a cogent reason for the continued concentration of the entire battle fleet on the Atlantic coast.

The board reaffirmed the principle of fleet concentration in the event of war with Japan, but felt that for a base it would be better to use Subic Bay, if it were completed, rather than the Atlantic. Even so, the board observed, the navy had to be prepared for trouble with European nations in the defense of the Monroe Doctrine, making total concentration in Pacific waters unwise. The board concluded with an equivocation worthy of the Delphic oracle: "Concentration is the true principle and no departure from this rule should be seriously considered."[19]

The changed Asian scene also called for a reexamination of plans for the development and defense of the navy's Philippine base. The earlier premise, that hostilities in the Philippines would be a spinoff of some European act violating the Monroe Doctrine and hence would develop into a limited naval conflict, was no longer valid. Now it was possible that hostilities would involve a sustained Japanese land campaign. The army somewhat belatedly discerned great similarities between the topographies of Subic Bay and Port Arthur, concluding that a land attack in strength would render the navy's favored port indefensible with any force likely to be made available to it. Therefore, while temporary measures were put in hand for the defense of Subic Bay, the army pressed for, and eventually won, approval for its own plan to concentrate forces in and around Manila Bay; it would serve as America's defensive position, holding Japanese forces at bay while awaiting the arrival of the battleship fleet from the Atlantic.

The army and navy's inability to agree on a Philippine base led Roosevelt to push funding for the development of Pearl Harbor. In this effort he enjoyed considerable success, obtaining an initial congressional authorization of one million dollars for the project. By the time the battleship fleet actually reached the Pacific Coast in May 1908, the basic decisions that would guide and also limit America's Pacific defense posture over the next three decades had already been made.

TWO

An Important Change of Naval Policy

At the height of the Japanese-American crisis of 1907, the president left Washington and took up residence at Sagamore Hill, his home in Oyster Bay, Long Island. Perhaps to show the public that the crisis concerned him less than it did some sectors of the press, his secretary announced that the vacation would be his longest at Sagamore Hill since becoming president.[1] But although Roosevelt consistently held the prospect of war with Japan to be remote, it would have been out of character for him not to consider the military implications of the situation and take measures to increase preparedness. In fact, while Roosevelt was vacationing at Oyster Bay, officers of the General Board and the army's General Staff kept busy. On 14 June the president had asked Assistant Secretary of War Robert Shaw Oliver to inform him of the Joint Board's plans in case of trouble between the two countries. For the navy the problem was complex. Contingencies had been studied since the preceding year, when strains in the traditional *entente cordiale* with Japan had prompted planners to reconsider America's defense position in the Pacific.[2] The military's view was that, as a result of Japan's naval and military strength, the United States in any future conflict would be forced to adopt a defensive posture in the Pacific while assembling and dispatching the Atlantic Fleet to that ocean.[3]

Responding to the president's query, the Joint Board provided a set of plans and also proposed a number of preparatory naval and military measures, including a recommendation that the full American battleship fleet be assembled and sent to the Orient as soon as possible.[4] Their report was forwarded to Roosevelt, who then requested that army and navy representatives come to Oyster Bay to discuss them.[5]

The administration may well have wished this sensitive report to remain confidential. However, on 19 June the *New York Herald,* with a prescience reflecting access to inside sources, reported rumors that the General Board was "seriously considering" sending a force of battleships to the Pacific.

The meeting took place at Oyster Bay on 27 June 1907, in an environment completely dominated by Roosevelt. Present were Secretary of the Navy Victor H. Metcalf, Postmaster General George von Lengerke Meyer, Captain Richard Wainwright of the General Board, and Colonel W. W. Wotherspoon, acting president of the Army War College.

Discussion was informal and lasted about an hour and a half. The president opened by saying that while he did not believe war would break out, he concurred in the Joint Board's recommendations. Concerning specific navy actions, he directed Secretary Metcalf to arrange immediate shipment of a large supply of coal to Subic Bay. Additionally, certain advance base materials, including coastal defense guns, were to be moved from Cavite, near Manila, to Subic Bay, the guns mounted for temporary defense of the base there. As for the disposition of the fleet, the four armored cruisers then in Asian waters would return immediately to the U.S. Pacific Coast; monitors and gunboats remaining on the Asiatic station would be concentrated at Subic Bay. Finally, Roosevelt wanted the entire battleship fleet transferred to the Pacific sometime in October.

This last directive elicited further discussion. The president, in the first of many such statements, emphasized that the transfer should be considered a training exercise. A question arose about the number of battleships to be sent, to which Roosevelt replied, all of them. "If the Navy had fourteen ready, he wanted fourteen to go; if sixteen, eighteen, or twenty, he wanted them all to go." Metcalf, wondering if he could announce the fleet transfer, was given permission.[6] Then the discussion turned to preparatory actions to be taken by the army.

The Oyster Bay decisions did not long remain secret. On 1 July they were leaked to the press, with the *New York Herald* once again on the inside track. It reported that President Roosevelt had "determined upon an important change of American naval policy," the main feature being the transfer of sixteen battleships and two armored cruisers to the Pacific; Rear Admiral Robley D. Evans would be in command and would take the ships via the Strait of Magellan.[7] This and similar disclosures in other papers elicited prompt denials from the White House.[8]

Any initial concern the administration might have felt over Japan's reaction to the fleet transfer was allayed by Ambassador to the United States Viscount Aoki, who told reporters that his country did not regard the move as an unfriendly act.[9] In any case, the following day Roosevelt released a statement implying that plans for the pending cruise of the fleet were far less advanced than they actually were. "There is no intention of sending a fleet at once to the Pacific," he stated. "For the last two years the Administration has been perfecting its plans to arrange for a long ocean cruise of the battleship fleet, when a sufficient number of warships are gathered." It might only be to the Mediterranean or to South America, he suggested, and scheduling was still quite flexible. The decision whether the fleet would remain in the Atlantic or go to the Pacific would "be determined simply as a matter of routine in the management and drill of the navy." Roosevelt concluded with an assertion that America's relations with the world had never been more peaceful, and should the fleet be sent to the Pacific it would "possess no more significance than the further fact that three or four months later it would be withdrawn from the Pacific." Neither event would be anything more than ordinary navy routine.[10] This equivocal statement was followed a few hours later by a much more categorical announcement by Secretary Metcalf, issued from his home in Oakland. He stated without reservation that "eighteen or twenty of the largest battleships would come around Cape Horn on a practice cruise, and would be seen in San Francisco Harbor."[11]

Reasons for the administration's denial of early leaks concerning the cruise remain somewhat obscure. Perhaps the intention was to permit Metcalf to make the official announcement in California, as Roosevelt had promised. A rationale might also be found in the domestic political situation. The presidential statement was a masterpiece of obfuscation. Leaving all options open, it tended to defuse potential opposition. Metcalf's announcement, however, promised in definite terms that the Pacific Coast, the region most threatened by the Japanese crisis, would soon receive the naval presence it craved. In effect, the administration had skillfully maneuvered to turn popular interest in the navy into solid support for the government's plan. At the same time, those inclined to argue against the cruise were faced with an evasive presidential statement—the only "official" government position—and therefore lacked a base upon which to build opposition.

This less than frank method of announcement left people guessing the real reason for the cruise. Its military purpose remained secret. From the beginning Roosevelt chose to emphasize that it would be a good drill. Press and public, however, were quick to discern a wide range of reasons for a cruise to be ordered at that specific time. Depending upon one's viewpoint, it either promised to benefit the navy and the nation or it threatened to plunge America into an easily avoidable war with Japan—at the very least stoking the insatiable fires of naval aggrandizement. A number of papers such as New York's *Sun* and *Nation* opposed a cruise and the many political and diplomatic complications they feared would arise from it. On the whole, though, reaction to the announcement was expansive, almost euphoric. The usually sedate *New York Times* waxed enthusiastic over "this notion of having the pick and flower of the American navy perambulate the South American continent. . . ." The fighting force, the paper continued, "will traverse those erst mysterious and defying waters with almost as much confidence as they might traverse the Atlantic Coast of their own country from Bar Harbor to Key West."[12]

That such a cruise would also have significance for America's hemispheric foreign policy there was little doubt. Circumnavigation of South America was hailed as a proclamation to the republics there that the United States could maintain the Monroe Doctrine.[13]

The tenor of President Roosevelt's references to the cruise throughout the month of July can best be described as one of increasing determination. The original decision of 27 June to send the fleet to the West Coast may have been tentative, the basic route and itinerary not yet determined; but events in July apparently confirmed, in his mind, the necessity of the cruise. The war scare continued to rear its head. That month the yellow press broke out again in hysteria, and immigration statistics for May and June 1907 indicated that despite the Gentlemen's Agreement, Japanese immigration to the United States had shown a marked increase over the same period in 1906. Opposition from the chairman of the Senate Naval Affairs Committee further hardened the president's resolve. A report from Acting Secretary of the Navy Newberry describing Senator Eugene Hale's efforts to block the departure of the fleet by threatening to withhold additional funds for coal elicited a sharp response from Roosevelt.[14] After condemning Hale's actions, he stated categorically that the fleet would go to the Pacific. Newberry was ordered to submit the alternative plans for the cruise as soon as possible.[15]

These he forwarded to the president on 7 August. Three routes had been considered: by way of the Suez Canal, the Cape of Good Hope, and the Strait of Magellan. Rear Admiral Evans, fleet commander in chief, and Rear Admiral Brownson, chief of the Bureau of Navigation, preferred the Strait of Magellan. But Evans was prepared to transit the hazardous strait only during the summer months, when there would be the greatest amount of daylight to facilitate navigation. This, as William R. Braisted has pointed out, carried "the ominous implication that the fleet could hasten to the relief of the Philippines, in accordance with the Joint Board's plans, during only three months of the year."[16]

With the Navy Department's initial planning and itinerary recommendations in hand, the president called a meeting with Acting Secretary Newberry and Rear Admirals Brownson and Evans at Oyster Bay on 23 August. They reviewed the strength and disposition of the world's major navies and discussed them in relation to the cruise.[17] Toward the meeting's end Roosevelt confirmed that sixteen battleships would be sent to San Francisco via the Strait of Magellan, but left the return route to be decided on later.[18]

Roosevelt's decision to conduct the cruise was based on the recommendations of the Joint Board. The State Department had not been represented at planning meetings and no diplomatic input had been requested. The whole set of measures, of which the cruise was but one, had been ordered for military reasons. The subject, however, continues to excite some academic debate, as a result to no small extent of conflicting justifications offered by Roosevelt himself.

The president's annual address to Congress, delivered on the eve of the fleet's departure from Hampton Roads, emphasized that the only way officers and men could learn to handle the fleet in wartime was to "have them practice under similar conditions in time of peace."[19] In his autobiography he wrote that his prime purpose was "to impress the American people" and "stimulate popular interest and belief" in the navy.[20] He further muddied the waters by suggesting in a letter of 1911 that he had begun to detect a "slight undertone of veiled truculence" in the Japanese government's attitude about developments in California. "It was time for a show down," the president wrote. "I had great confidence in the fleet."[21]

What seems apparent, when reexamining in chronological order the many statements and speculations concerning the reasons for the cruise, is that they continued to evolve as planning for it progressed. That it was necessary to the development of naval war plans remained secret. This explains why the president did not mention it in his correspondence and subsequent writings. Also apparent in the record is the significant fact that the itinerary of the cruise from Hampton Roads to Magdalena Bay, Mexico, was determined exclusively by naval planners.

Once definitely decided on, the cruise suggested a whole range of further objectives that could be realized along with the military one. By the time the fleet actually left Hampton Roads, many of the nonmilitary reasons proposed by Roosevelt, the experts, and the press held a degree of validity. Nevertheless, that it was still the military aspect that retained highest priority during the voyage to the Pacific Coast is suggested by the navy's declining, despite strong diplomatic pressure, an invitation to have the battleships call at an Argentine port.[22] Indeed, the only concession the navy made was to have the fleet pass through the harbor of Valparaiso without stopping, and therefore without losing any time in the scheduled transit from Punta Arenas, Chile, to Callao, Peru.

It is possible, reviewing State and Navy Department records, to discern three phases during which different factors influenced the planning and execution of the cruise. In the first, encompassing the voyage from Hampton Roads to Magdalena Bay, the Navy Department maintained complete control of the cruise, and it assumed dimensions entirely compatible with an exercise designed to determine how quickly and efficiently the Atlantic Fleet could be transferred to the Pacific. As mentioned, the itinerary was determined exclusively by the Navy Department, and with naval goals in mind. This explains the frequent administration assertions during the latter half of 1907 that the cruise was intended primarily as an exercise.

A second, albeit minor, phase involved planning for the fleet's visit to the Pacific Coast. Congressmen, city officials, and local men of influence sought to modify this portion of the itinerary for the benefit of their constituents or local communities. With the General Board's overall plans completed, the secretary of the navy proved more amenable to these requests for modifications which, in addition to giving the navy wider publicity on the West Coast, might also reap domestic political benefits for the administration.

In arrangements for the return voyage to the Atlantic Coast, the third phase, the navy's desires were largely subordinated to the administration's foreign policy objectives and to one overriding domestic consideration: the fleet had to return to home waters before Roosevelt left the White House.

Thus the cruise, first and foremost an exercise of a naval war plan, evolved into a tool of domestic public relations: it would popularize the navy. Only after the test of its military capabilities was completed did foreign policy considerations assume preeminence in determining the fleet's course. The first half of the cruise was an exercise in naval contingency planning; the second half, an exercise in naval diplomacy, at home and abroad. Understanding these changing priorities is essential to understanding the "reasons" for the cruise.

Finally, as for its timing, the natural tendency is to explain this exclusively in the context of American relations with Japan, but it is possible that the battleship construction program itself was more important. President Roosevelt briefly alluded to it when he suggested, in July 1907, that for the previous two years the administration had been "perfecting its plans to arrange for a long ocean cruise of the battleship fleet, when a sufficient number of warships are gathered."[23] The years 1906 and 1907 saw the final fruition of the battleship authorizations made in the early years of Roosevelt's first term. Between 19 February 1906 and 1 July

1907 ten battleships joined the fleet, while three others were nearing completion. The ten newly completed ships, all predreadnought designs, formed the backbone of the fleet transferred to the Pacific. By 1 July 1907 "a sufficient number of warships" had been assembled. From a purely military standpoint, the navy had finally achieved sufficient strength to consider seriously a sustained exercise for the fleet.

Such a cruise would be valuable for testing fleet and infrastructure capabilities. Having built a battleship fleet and concentrated it on one coast, the navy had to know whether it could move from coast to coast and arrive prepared to fight. After its long voyage from the Baltic, the Russian fleet had reached Tsushima in exceedingly poor condition, a lesson that impressed on American naval planners the need for a considerable period of maintenance and repair on the Pacific Coast before the fleet would be ready for possible combat operations.

It might be argued that although the Japanese-American crisis provided the rationale for the cruise, U.S. naval expansion after the Spanish-American War made it feasible and the general strategic situation made it desirable. Whether fleet expansion gave birth to deteriorating relations with Japan in order to justify the cruise remains only intriguing supposition; that the existence of a strong and modern battle fleet significantly affected President Roosevelt's attitude toward that country when the crisis did arise is abundantly clear from his correspondence.[24]

The president's definitive statement of 23 August failed to silence the skeptics. Many naval officers, aware that West Coast facilities could not support a major fleet, doubted that the ships would actually go to the Pacific. Some suggested the cruise was largely the product of "congressional bluff": if it was canceled because of a lack of support facilities, then there would be a popular uproar forcing Congress to vote sufficient funds to develop them.[25]

A review of the existing support infrastructure on the Pacific Coast suggests that healthy skepticism was justified. The postwar distribution of naval dry-dock facilities had been determined primarily by the partisan political considerations of the Senate Naval Affairs Committee. Most new naval shipyards were located within the constituencies of the more influential committee members; only two dry-dock facilities had been built on the Pacific Coast.[26] The General Board, Admiral of the Navy George Dewey told Secretary Metcalf, found the lack of docking and repair facilities on the Pacific Coast to be one of great seriousness.[27]

The Mare Island Naval Shipyard, near San Francisco, could not be reached by battleships because of a shallow approach channel. Despite this some thirteen million dollars had been spent on improvements in the decade since the war,[28] prompting the *New York Times* to comment, as the fleet was preparing to sail, that the Mare Island dry dock might as well be in China.[29] Channel limitations notwithstanding, Mare Island was in the process of receiving a new dry dock with dimensions sufficient to admit the largest battleships—dimensions including a depth over the sill considerably greater than the depth of the access channel! The dock, under construction since 1900, had originally been scheduled for completion by 20 December 1907 but was delayed on account of an unstable foundation.[30]

Only the Puget Sound Navy Yard at Bremerton, Washington, could dock modern battleships, and at the time it was repairing the battleship *Wisconsin* and reconstructing the old battleship *Oregon*.[31] Rear Admiral Burwell, commandant at Bremerton, received rush orders to complete these repairs—orders that only highlighted the severe shortage of facilities.[32] Commenting on the state of Pacific Coast dry docks, a British technical journal observed that it "needs but a glance . . . to convince one of their utter inadequacy."[33] Ironically, given this situation, the largest dry dock facility on the Pacific Coast, the civilian-owned San Francisco Drydock Company's Hunter's Point dock, had been closed and was being dismantled as a result of successive losses in battleship construction.[34] Only through personal intervention by President Roosevelt was the dock reopened.[35]

Beyond these scant West Coast facilities lay even more meager ones on the unfortified American islands of Hawaii and Guam and in the Philippines. Congressional reluctance to distribute appropriations in accordance with the navy's actual needs in the continental United States—where there were constituencies and therefore discernible domestic political advantage in getting a share of the wealth—has already been noted. Navy requests for appropriations to fortify coaling stations and dry docks in the insular possessions had largely been ignored.

That sector of the public opposed to the cruise raised alarms over the misguided notion that it was Roosevelt's intention to keep the fleet in the Pacific and then demand the construction of a replacement fleet for the Atlantic.[36] Practical constraints ruled out such a development. The American navy, with its facilities concentrated on the Atlantic Coast, could provide only short-term support for a fleet on the Pacific Coast. In order to remain in fighting trim, the fleet had to return to the Atlantic. With some justification the *New York Times* concluded that the cruise was a warning to the United States. It demonstrated the absolute necessity of developing the navy's Pacific bases so that the fleet would not have to rely on "good fortune to get through a crisis with inadequate facilities."[37]

An even more pressing problem confronted the Navy Department: supplying the prodigious amount of coal ships would consume en route to the Pacific. The need for a fleet of dedicated naval colliers had been illustrated in the Spanish-American War when Commodore Dewey, faced with a shortage of bunker coal at Hong Kong on the eve of hostilities, managed to secure his fuel supply only by purchasing a British collier with a cargo of coal already on board. A more immediate lesson had been provided by the ill-fated and much-delayed voyage of the Russian fleet under Admiral Rodzhestvensky.

Drawing lessons from the Russo-Japanese War, Rear Admiral George Melville, a former chief of the Bureau of Equipment—the bureau responsible for all aspects of fleet coal support—commented that strong as the navy was for defensive purposes, it was weaker than generally realized for conducting distant military-naval operations. He attributed this to the lack of a strong merchant fleet. The conclusions to be drawn from Russia's experience seemed quite plain to Melville. The navy, he argued, should build auxiliaries, at the same time not significantly increasing the number of warships in the fleet. The bulk of expenditures in the immediate future, Melville suggested, should be dedicated to shipbuilding facilities, access channels, naval stations, and a fleet of large fast colliers. "But little reliance should be placed upon fixed coaling stations, since in time of war most of these stations might prove as much a menace as an aid to a naval fleet. By keeping the coal afloat there would always be fuel available for immediate transportation."[38]

This was sound, if visionary, advice. Although the Navy Department consistently sought congressional authorization for the construction of fleet colliers, they were viewed as adjuncts to the main building program. Conventional naval thought remained fixed on battleships and coaling stations; in the annual naval appropriation debates requests for colliers were consistently sacrificed for more battleships. By 1907 only two mission-designed fleet colliers had been authorized and neither was completed. The greatly expanded battleship force lacked the dedicated collier support that would ensure its mobility.

This deficiency could to some degree have been corrected by an active merchant marine on which the government might rely for logistic support in time of war. But federal regulations required exclusive use of American-built ships and American crews, and Congress had displayed a marked reluctance to subsidize the additional expenses compliance with these regulations incurred. As a result, the American merchant marine had experienced a long period of decline; by the first decade of the century it was moribund.

The significance of fuel requirements did not escape President Roosevelt. Writing to Acting Secretary of the Navy Newberry on 17 August 1907, Roosevelt directed him to start work on coal arrangements immediately, warning that the Bureau of Equipment's efforts in this respect would receive his personal attention.[39]

By the end of August the itinerary to San Francisco had been worked out and Secretary Newberry let it be known publicly that the fleet would make five coaling stops: Trinidad, Rio de Janeiro, Punta Arenas, Callao, and Magdalena Bay. He estimated the fleet would require 125,000 tons of coal; in addition to coal from bunkers and that available at Magdalena Bay, some 100,000 tons would have to be shipped to the fleet in transit.[40]

Following this announcement, the press published reports saying that the administration would need an additional appropriation for the coal.[41] Responding to this claim, Newberry maintained that the entire supply for the trip to San Francisco could be met from existing appropriations.[42] The press continued to express skepticism, about the cruise as a whole and particularly about coal procurement. President Roosevelt effectively terminated the debate when on 26 September he let it be known "that if American coal cannot be procured he [would] get foreign coal, and if American ships cannot be chartered to transport what the navy colliers cannot carry, he [would] charter foreign colliers."[43]

To encourage the use of American ships, Roosevelt offered to award coal-carrying contracts to American colliers if their bids did not exceed foreign bids by more than fifty percent.[44] When bidding closed on 2 October, no major American shipping company had tendered because of an inability to procure return freights from the Pacific.[45] Therefore on 12 October the Navy Department contracted for thirty foreign ships and eight naval colliers to carry coal for the trip to San Francisco.[46]

This should have been sufficient to confirm Roosevelt's determination to go through with the cruise despite congressional opposition. In a speech at Vicksburg during his tour of the South in late October, he answered criticism that he was exceeding Congress's appropriation for coal. The government had enough money to get the fleet to the Pacific, he told the crowd. If the appropriation was exhausted by then, another would have to be made to bring the fleet home.[47] This was in keeping with Roosevelt's general approach to problem solving. But to Congress it was a gratuitous insult, one more episode in the souring of relations between that body and the chief executive, and though minor, it would contribute in its own way to the bitter debates over Roosevelt's naval appropriations bill in the months ahead.

The significance of the battle fleet's dependence on foreign-flag colliers to ensure its mobility generated larger-scale discussion as well. Undoubtedly, as noted German naval critic Graf Ernst von Reventlow pointed out in an interview after the fleet left Hampton Roads, the most interesting technical aspect of the cruise was providing coal for such a large fleet over such a prolonged period. If, he warned, the American navy had to continue relying on England for colliers, that country could use the fact to advantage when any complications arose between America and Japan.[48] Though von Reventlow's reason for exposing the weakness of the American position undoubtedly lay in Anglo-German rivalry and the almost too obvious German desire to strain America's friendship with England, his logic regarding the fleet's fuel supply was inescapable. The primary motivation behind the cruise was to exercise an aspect of a plan to be implemented in the event of war with Japan. Britain was joined with Japan in a military alliance the terms of which, from 1905 on, required it to assist that country in case of war against a single power. Yet most of the logistic support for the American Fleet as it exercised a war plan against Japan was entrusted to the British merchant marine.

Americans tended to discount the possibility that, should England have to choose between Japan and the United States in a future conflict, those oft-invoked Anglo-American racial, cultural, and economic ties, not to mention strategic considerations vis à vis Germany, would be disregarded in favor of treaty commitments with Japan. But the formal British commitment to Japan remained, and statements of loyalty surfaced fairly regularly in the British press.

Inevitably, the lack of American colliers supplied yet another argument to opponents of further naval expansion. Dependence on foreign colliers, they argued, indicated a serious gap in the existing fleet's capabilities, one that should be corrected before further funds were expended on Theodore Roosevelt's dreadnoughts. Senator Hale, opposing the administration demand for four battleships in 1908, summarized collier requirements for a circumnavigation of South America and observed that, had the countries controlling colliers withdrawn them, the battleship fleet, "magnificent as it is, would be helpless . . . , as useless as 'a painted ship upon a painted ocean.' "[49]

As the coal situation was being publicly examined, senior officers of the Navy Department closely followed the fleet's progress around South America, while at sea, flag and commanding officers coped with the practical problems of providing the battleships with fuel. Doubtless all involved would have heartily agreed with Rear Admiral Melville, who five years earlier had written, "Coal, or the want of it, is the life or death of a fleet."[50]

THREE

Did You Ever See
Such a Fleet?

The battleships of the Atlantic Fleet carried out their normal routine in summer of 1907. Fleet activity, much to the chagrin of admirals and commanding officers, focused on the Jamestown Exposition, which opened near Norfolk on 26 April 1907. The fleet remained anchored at Hampton Roads, hosting foreign warships and serving as an important attraction for the poorly organized and financially troubled exposition until mid-May, when all but one division of four battleships departed for northern waters. The fleet returned to Hampton Roads for a presidential review on 10 June 1907 but by mid-July it was once again in northern waters, where for a month individual units conducted target practice off Cape Cod.[1] The battleships returned to Hampton Roads in late August for the exposition's closing, after which the entire battleship fleet except for the *Alabama* put to sea for full battle maneuvers. This was the first opportunity the fleet, reorganized on 30 June 1907, had had to conduct maneuvers as a unit. A short upkeep period in home ports followed before the ships gathered once more off Cape Cod for six more days of maneuvers in mid-September. Then the battle fleet dispersed to home yards to make final preparations for the long cruise.[2]

The fleet's armored cruisers moved in an equally deliberate manner. The Atlantic Fleet's two new ones, the *Washington* and *Tennessee,* had already sailed to Bordeaux to represent the United States at the Exposition of Steam Navigation Centennial before the Oyster Bay conference. This cruise was completed on schedule, the ships returning to the United States on 6 August to begin preparations for an October transfer to the Pacific Fleet. By the end of September the cruisers now under the command of Rear Admiral Uriel Sebree and designated the Special Service Squadron—or, popularly, the Pathfinder Squadron—were ready to proceed following the scheduled course of the battleships.[3] Sebree was directed to keep complete logs of his voyage and to forward copies from each port to Rear Admiral Evans and the Navy Department.

On 12 October, after coaling and receiving additional supplies and ammunition at Hampton Roads, the Special Service Squadron sailed for the Pacific where, with the armored cruisers *California* and *South Dakota,* it would form the Second Division of the U.S. Pacific Fleet under Admiral Sebree.[4]

The "immediate" return of the armored cruiser division in Asiatic waters, ordered by President Roosevelt at the Oyster Bay conference, did not materialize. Any sense of urgency Washington might have felt regarding the Japanese situation was not shared by officers of the Pacific Fleet's First Division, then in Chinese waters. Its four new armored cruisers—the *West Virginia* (flagship), *Colorado, Maryland,* and *Pennsylvania*—under the command of Rear Admiral James H. Dayton, had visited Kobe and Yokohama at the end of May. At the latter port high officials of the Imperial Japanese Navy had cordially received the ships, and the senior officers had been granted an audience with the Japanese emperor.[5]

By mid-June the division was at Chefoo (Zhifu), China, conducting its annual battle practice. On 1 July Acting Secretary of the Navy Newberry issued orders for Admiral Dayton to proceed to the Pacific Coast. Newberry told him that the directive was not a "political condition" but a "tactical order" that would unite his division with the Second Division under Sebree.[6] Dayton therefore continued the normal exercise schedule while planning a routine return voyage via Yokohama and Hawaii.[7] The division sailed for Cavite in the Philippines to coal and take on stores toward the end of July.[8] There, in accordance with cabled instructions from Washington, they landed all the cruisers' mining outfits and Gatling guns to augment the base defenses at Subic Bay.[9]

At no time between the end of June and the first week of August had the Navy Department queried Dayton's proposed route for the return voyage. This seems remarkable in light of the department's concern over the Japanese situation; Yokohama was the most reasonable coaling stop in the course of a great circle navigation route from the Philippines to Hawaii. Furthermore, the U.S. Navy maintained a small coal stockpile in that port from which Dayton could draw if necessary.

Lacking any specific guidance, Dayton had the navy collier *Alexander* loaded at Cavite and dispatched to Yokohama. At 5:00 A.M. on 10 August the armored cruiser division set sail, following the collier's track.[10] The ships were ninety miles north of Cavite when Dayton received a terse directive from Washington to proceed directly to Honolulu without calling in Japan.[11] By this time it was too late to alter the schedule; the *Alexander* was in Yokohama, there was no coal available at Guam, and the distance to Hawaii was too great for an uninterrupted voyage.[12] The Navy Department therefore reluctantly agreed to the Yokohama visit.[13] Despite department concerns, the cruiser division's visit to Yokohama was free of incident, and on 22 August, after a five-day stay, the ships sailed for Hawaii. There they arrived on 2 September, well over two months after Roosevelt had ordered them home.[14]

Although the Navy Department's confidential correspondence with Admiral Dayton indicated increasing concern over the delay, strategic redeployment of this significant portion of the navy's Pacific force was carried out in a manner unlikely to cause public questioning. Cruiser movements, rather than being masked in the secrecy normally attending preparations for war, were announced on 8 August, as was the Navy Department's plan to form a second armored cruiser division in the Pacific Fleet.[15] Similarly, the movements of Atlantic Fleet battleships were highly publicized, with particular emphasis on their nonmilitary nature. It would have been difficult for the Japanese to discern hostile intent in either of these announcements, and indeed there is little evidence to suggest that they felt threatened.

By the beginning of December 1907 the navy's eight armored cruisers were in the eastern Pacific, while preparations for the departure of the battleship fleet and its supporting units were nearing completion in the main naval bases at Boston, New York, Philadelphia, and Norfolk. The torpedo-boat destroyer flotilla, which was to transfer to the Pacific at the same time as the battleship fleet, left Norfolk Navy Yard on 1 December, moved into Hampton Roads to compensate compasses, and on the following morning set out for San Francisco. A separate itinerary had been developed for the destroyers because they lacked the range necessary to complete the longer legs scheduled for the battleships.[16]

The first battleship to complete her dockyard preparations sailed from the New York Navy Yard in Brooklyn on the second day of December, en route to the fleet rendezvous in Hampton Roads. As the *Louisiana* got under way and steamed out through the East River, New York's tugs and ferry boats "gave her a rousing send-off."[17]

Popular attention naturally focused on the pending formal farewell when the fleet would depart Hampton Roads, but most of the battleship crews said goodbye to their families in late November and early December as the big ships completed fitting out at their home ports. On 1 December there were six battleships in New York, then still the "home" of the navy. The biggest crowds ever to be entertained in that city's navy yard thronged around the officers and men of the fleet on the last Sunday it was "at home."[18]

By 9 December all sixteen battleships had headed south, where the gathering in Hampton Roads quickly captured the attention of the nation. As they arrived the battleships took up precise positions, corresponding to the standard steaming formation known as line of squadrons: two parallel lines of eight battleships, anchored with the squadron flagships, *Connecticut* and *Minnesota,* near Old Point Comfort and the mouth of Hampton Roads. With the fleet there, Fort Monroe and the Chamberlin Hotel in Hampton became the center of its social life.

The fleet assembled at Hampton Roads to complete preparations for departure—specifically, to coal ships to their maximum capacity and take on additional ammunition and stores. But social engagements soon overshadowed these mundane tasks. The calendar for "Navy Farewell Week," filled with receptions, luncheons, balls, and other entertainments, culminated on Friday, 13 December, with a grand ball at the Chamberlin Hotel in honor of Admiral Evans and the officers of the fleet. This formal occasion called for evening dress "B" uniform, with white waistcoat and gold-laced trousers.[19] The upper crust from Norfolk, Richmond,

Baltimore, Washington, and other eastern cities turned out, and the ball was judged a success despite unfavorable weather.[20]

While officers attended social functions and enlisted men enjoyed final nights ashore at Portsmouth and Norfolk, other personnel were being subjected to an extreme and irrational display of injustice. In the preceding decade Asian men had joined the navy to work exclusively as officers' cooks and servants. They performed their tasks well. With the strain in American relations with Japan, however, many officers questioned the advisability of continued employment of Japanese nationals. One particularly influential voice was that of Rear Admiral Albert S. Barker. Barker had commanded a special service squadron of two battleships and seven auxiliaries that had cruised from the Atlantic to Manila in 1898–99, the most significant U.S. fleet movement in recent years. Admiral Dewey, in response to a request for Barker's views on planning the battleship cruise and on war with Japan, received a lengthy plea that all Japanese be transferred to home stations or discharged.[21] Fleet officers shared his unreasoning fear that these loyal servants, through "self-sacrificing" actions, might cripple the fleet on the eve of any action against the Imperial Japanese Navy. That was the opinion expressed by one of the fleet commander in chief's staff officers to the president's naval aide, Lieutenant Commander William Snowden Sims.[22]

About the time Sims received this advice, a decision was taken to remove all Japanese from departing battleships. The Navy Department denied it with a disingenuousness difficult to credit. Admiral Evans, "high naval authorities" reported, was taking a large number of additional men to crew ships of the Pacific Fleet. To make room, men with little service time left, and less efficient long-term men, were being put ashore. "In these two classes there are some Japanese," but they did not "include by a good many" all the Japanese messmen in the fleet.[23] In fact, some sixty were transferred to the receiving ship *Hancock* at Brooklyn and an additional twelve to the *Franklin* at Norfolk—virtually all the Japanese in the fleet.[24] Although this action undoubtedly offended those who had loyally served the navy for many years, all obeyed their orders. One young Japanese, despondent over the treatment he had received, attempted suicide by drowning.[25]

The decision to remove the messmen, unquestionably an injustice, must be viewed as but another manifestation of broader public fear. Although tension in Japanese-American relations had been considerably reduced since its peak in mid-summer, otherwise responsible Americans reported as suspicious virtually any action by a Japanese living in the United States or its possessions. While the fleet was in Hampton Roads, an official of a small community nearby apprehended a Japanese whom he said he saw making sketches of Fort Monroe. The matter attracted considerable interest. The man, it was speculated, had hoped to procure the plan of Fort Monroe and observe the ships of the Atlantic Fleet.[26] Such was the atmosphere of suspicion that no one seriously questioned the Japanese need to risk detection by covertly gathering information on Fort Monroe, a defensive installation nearly fifteen thousand miles from the Imperial Japanese Navy's base at Yokosuka. Discovery of this latest "plot" may well have confirmed, in many minds, the correctness of the decision to remove Japanese crew members as potential fifth columnists.

Weather posed a greater threat to the fleet's successful sendoff. A series of winter gales and blizzards had lashed the East Coast during the first two weeks of December. On Saturday, 14 December, barely forty-eight hours before the scheduled presidential review and departure, there was "half a gale blowing in the Hampton Roads, rain falling in torrents, and a regular storm raging beyond the Capes."[27] Then on Sunday evening, the fleet's last day in home waters, the weather cleared. Next day dawned to brilliant skies.

At 8:00 A.M. the morning colors ceremony was conducted and the ships "full dressed" to honor President Roosevelt.[28] A few minutes later the presidential yacht *Mayflower* hove into sight, and at a signal from the flagship all sixteen battleships rendered a simultaneous twenty-one-gun salute to the chief executive. The *Mayflower* continued into the Roads, received a second salute from Fort Monroe, and then proceeded down the column between the First and Second Squadrons. The ships were impressively turned out, rails manned, bands playing, marine detachments paraded. Roosevelt, moved by the scene, paced rapidly up and down the *Mayflower*'s deck exclaiming to Secretary Metcalf and his other guests over the grandeur of the scene: "Did you ever see such a fleet? Isn't it magnificent? Oughtn't we all feel proud?"[29]

As the *Mayflower* came to anchor captains' gigs and admirals' barges made their way toward her carrying senior officers to a final meeting with the president. In accordance with navy custom, Rear Admiral Evans boarded first, followed by admirals and then commanding officers.[30] President Roosevelt took time to speak personally to each and pose with them for photographers. And, not forgetting the enlisted men, he had the coxswain of the *Louisiana*'s gig report aboard. He shook the man's hand, introduced him to Mrs. Roosevelt, and asked him to extend a personal farewell to the crew.

Toward the end of the reception, Roosevelt drew Evans aside and spent a few minutes in animated conversation with him. The details of that discussion were never fully disclosed, but it seems that among other things the president authorized him to advise the fleet of their ultimate destination. Rear Admiral Charles M. Thomas, second in command of the fleet, also spoke privately with Roosevelt. To Thomas, Roosevelt emphasized the need to maintain a constant state of readiness, though he did not anticipate trouble. Thomas assured him that the fleet was prepared for any eventuality, and added, apparently alluding to the destruction of the battleship *Maine* in 1898, "Mister President, there will be no surprise this time." In response, the president smiled and said, "I'm sure of that."[31]

As admirals and captains returned to their ships, the *Mayflower* got under way and steamed slowly out of the Roads, turning south toward Cape Henry and the open sea. Battleship anchors were already at short stay in anticipation of departure. At 10:00 A.M. the *Connecticut* hoisted a signal ordering squadrons to weigh anchor in succession. When the signal was hauled down, the First Squadron immediately weighed. Its eight battleships, whose bows had swung to landward with the ebbing tide, slowly hauled around to seaward and, issuing dense columns of black smoke from their stacks, started to move out of Hampton Roads. Ships of the Second Squadron, timing their movements to complement those of the First, got under way and fell in astern of the leading squadron, forming an impressive single column of sixteen first-class battleships. They gathered way, led by the *Connecticut,* and passed the crowded Chamberlin and Old Dominion wharves close aboard to port. There the flagship's band played "Auld Lang Syne," whose words "should old acquaintance be forgot" provoked "thundrous 'No's' from the multitude on shore."[32]

The *Mayflower* preceded the battleships to the Tail of the Horseshoe, a shoal at the mouth of the Chesapeake Bay, and anchored to review the departing fleet. After clearing Old Point Comfort, the battleships quickly positioned themselves four hundred yards apart in a precisely aligned three-mile-long column. As each one passed the *Mayflower,* its rails were once again manned, officers paraded in full-dress uniform, and a final twenty-one-gun salute was fired to the commander in chief. By the time the *Kentucky,* last battleship of the Fourth Division, had passed in review, Roosevelt was apparently overcome with emotion. At this point the *Mayflower* was scheduled to proceed up the Chesapeake Bay to Washington, but the president couldn't resist a desire to prolong the departure, and so his yacht accompanied the fleet past the Virginia Capes to the open sea. "When last seen . . . the ships were clear of Cape Henry and standing to the southward in the imposing single column in which they left the roadstead. The *Mayflower* was abreast of the Admiral's ship and apparently as much bent on the Pacific cruise as the rest of the fleet."[33]

The battleship fleet's departure triggered foreign press speculation about the significance of the event, much of which was published in U.S. newspapers. American correspondents, summarizing the pronouncements of various European newspapers and interviewing people of note in the naval world, presented their readers with a kaleidoscope of conflicting evaluations. British commentators, forced to reconsider U.S. strength, were divided on the cruise: some tended to view it as an enlightened emulation of naval policies pursued by Great Britain in the preceding century, while others saw it as a crude and untimely flexing of American muscle. In the latter category were the *Sunday Observer,* which called it a "bluff and an indiscretion, . . . a profound mistake," the *Evening Standard* (a "Brobdingnagian expedition"), and the *Globe* ("a piece of American bombast quite unworthy of [Japan's] notice").[34] British papers that adopted a less hostile attitude emphasized the increasing importance of the Pacific in American strategic thinking. And the *Daily News* suggested the expedition would "justify itself as an enormous advertisement, while the American shipyards work day and night to replace the departing battleships."[35] British views tended to reflect the concerns of a nation allied with Japan, a nation long accustomed to naval supremacy and now confronted with the visible evidence of their loss of that supremacy in the Pacific.

German newspapers quite understandably viewed the development in a different light. The military expert of the *Berliner Tageblatt* welcomed it as "the greatest naval experiment ever undertaken by any nation in time of peace."[36] Other reports from Berlin addressed themselves to the technical experience the fleet would gain in planning and executing the cruise.[37]

Reaction from Russia, eagerly sought, was predictable in view of that country's recent experience with Japan. A week before the departure, *Novoe Vremya* reported war was unavoidable "because both these countries are new, have never known defeat, . . . want the overlordship of the Pacific. . . ."[38] The fleet's departure was hailed by the same paper as "the best guarantee of peace, by checking the elation of the Oriental nations."[39]

In Japan, press reaction was reported as uniformly friendly. *Jiji Shimpo,* an independent paper with wide circulation in intellectual and business circles, refused to entertain the idea "even for one moment . . . that the purpose of the trip was to threaten Japan. Should the American Fleet visit these shores," the paper concluded, "it will be given a most cordial reception worthy of the special friendship between Japan and the United States."[40] On the following day an enterprising American correspondent obtained similarly friendly statements from Foreign Minister Count Hayashi Tadasu, Navy Minister Admiral Baron Saitō Makato, Privy Councillor Viscount Kaneko Kentarō, Regent of Korea Prince Itō Hirabumi, and Premier Marquis Katsura Tarō.[41]

While the press busily canvassed world leaders for opinions and debated the "true significance" of a cruise, the fleet was getting on with its job.

FOUR

In Erst Mysterious
and Defying Waters

After Roosevelt's final salute off the Tail of the Horseshoe on 16 December, the battleships continued past the Virginia Capes and the fleet exercise area then known as the Southern Drill Ground, heading south under ideal conditions. Three days later, in calm seas under a blue sky, they were riding "as steady as a church."[1] These conditions continued and temperatures steadily rose, making the seven-day voyage to the first port of call ideal for shaking down. Many of the ships were newly commissioned, with relatively inexperienced crews; all had received large drafts of recruits fresh from training centers just before sailing. There had been considerable shifting of battleship commanding officers to ensure that only the "younger" captains, those with no less than four years before statutory retirement at age sixty-two, would hold command during the cruise.[2] One of the division commanders, Rear Admiral Charles Stillman Sperry, recently returned from Europe where he had served as one of the American delegates to the second Hague Convention, had just assumed command of the Fourth Division.[3]

When his fleet gained the open sea Admiral Evans ordered a shift from the single column that had so impressed crowds ashore. The main value of the single column was the freedom of maneuver it provided individual ships navigating in restricted waters. But the fleet's two standard steaming formations were line of divisions and line of squadrons. In the former, the four division flagships steamed abreast of each other with the three remaining ships of each division following in the wake of their respective flagships; in the latter, more frequently used, the fleet formed two columns behind the squadron flagships. These two formations kept the fleet in a reasonably compact mass, more rapidly responsive to flag signals than the single column and more easily maneuvered as a unit.

Stations were maintained with ships only four hundred yards apart mainmast to mainmast, providing endless exercise for the development of watch officers' station-keeping skills. The process of daily maneuvering as a unit would eventually instill in the fleet a sense of unity hitherto lacking and reaffirm what British Admiral Sir John Fisher had to say: "Confidence is a plant of slow growth. Long and constant association of ships of a fleet is essential to success."[4]

Although there had been much speculation about the possibility of war with Japan and some talk that the fleet would return home via the Suez Canal, no official statement had been issued concerning the fleet's ultimate destination.[5] To the actual participants, the departure of the fleet on 16 December 1907 was an undertaking full of uncertainty. Therefore they were pleased when, just after dinner on the first night at sea, Admiral Evans signaled that after a short time on the Pacific Coast, they would return to the Atlantic via the Suez Canal.[6] The admiral's choice of wireless telegraph to transmit this message to the fleet had unexpected repercussions. As a result of atmospheric conditions that extended the effective distance of radio transmission, his words were picked up ashore and subsequently published in the nation's newspapers. Evans's unanticipated gaffe elicited an immediate presidential denial.[7]

On 20 December he sought to limit the impact of his statement, reporting that it was only his *personal* belief that the Navy Department intended to send the fleet home via the Suez Canal late the following summer or fall. Even this modified statement drew an immediate denial by Secretary Metcalf, who responded that although the topic had been discussed, a decision had not yet been reached and would not be for some time.[8] The official position remained simply that the fleet was proceeding on a practice cruise to San Francisco; the return route was yet to be determined. This conservative stance betrayed some of the planners' uncertainty over the success of the voyage. Such a lengthy one was risky from the materiel point of view. The recent experience of Russia's fleet under Admiral Rodzhestvensky being the only precedent, planners considered it likely that some ships would need major repairs by the time the fleet reached San Francisco. In case difficulties developed en route to San Francisco, the cruise might have to be quietly ended there, and that could only be done if no further objectives had been publicly announced.

Not fully appreciated at the time of Evans's unintended leak were the implications of the rapidly expanding ship-to-shore communications capabilities that allowed it to happen. With the fleet commander's greatly increased ability to communicate over long distances came an increase in the distance at which higher authorities might exercise control over the fleet from ashore. The commander would now have to align his public announcements with the administration's foreign policy goals. But more importantly, the traditional independence of naval commanders at sea would be restricted.

The wisdom of cautious publicity became apparent as the battleships continued their southerly transit. On 20 December the *Kentucky* experienced the first of the fleet's engineering casualties and fell out of formation for two hours to effect repairs.[9] Two hours later the *Illinois* temporarily drew out of formation with an engineering problem.[10] Later that day, as the fleet approached Puerto Rico from the north, the *Illinois* was detached to proceed ahead to the small American-controlled island of Culebra to land an ill crew member; the *Missouri* was sent to San Juan on a similar mission.[11] The two battleships rejoined the fleet as it entered the Caribbean Sea through the Virgin Passage on 21 December. The trip to Trinidad was briefly delayed the following day when a sailor on the *Alabama,* who had died of pneumonia and spinal meningitis, was buried at sea.[12]

By mid-afternoon of 23 December the fleet made landfall on the mountainous coast of Venezuela as the battleships covered the last few miles to Port of Spain.[13] The column of ships passed through the Dragon's Mouth, entrance to the Gulf of Paria on which Port of Spain is located, and conducted an elaborate maneuver as they approached the city.[14] Not until after sunset did the fleet actually anchor, and therefore the customary gun salutes were not exchanged with the authorities ashore.

Admiral Evans's formal call on the British governor, Sir Henry Moore Jackson, had been scheduled for the following morning, and no liberty was granted before that.[15] In the morning a British army colonel called on Evans to say that the governor wished to return the admiral's official call at the Queen's Park Hotel rather than on board the flagship, as normal protocol dictated.[16] Jackson's reluctance meant Evans had to extend his stay ashore. Despite a clean bill of health in the weeks preceding the fleet's departure, the admiral was suffering from rheumatic gout and had to be supported by two aides as he made the trip ashore with Admirals Thomas, Sperry, and Emory to pay his respects. "They were met at the wharf with a guard of honor, composed of policemen, and the Constabulary band played our national air while the officers were entering their carriages."[17] That was the extent of the British ceremonial reception.

American Consul William Handley concluded that the governor had acted as though he were under instructions from the British government to be courteous but not enthusiastic. The governor had objected to the business community's plans to hold a ball during the visit, saying he was planning to give one. The businessmen reluctantly canceled their entertainment; subsequently the governor canceled his, without explaining himself. Handley reported that the incident had caused local comment. Some people attributed the poor reception to the "bad impression created by the Swettenham-Davis incident in January [1907], others to the English-Japanese alliance."[18]

Governor Jackson may well, in Handley's opinion, have acted like a man under instructions, but no documentary evidence has been found to support that opinion. It is possible that the governor, who had recently returned from London, received verbal instructions from the Colonial Office, but they probably would have reflected that office's concern about the West Indies rather than British hostility born of the Anglo-Japanese Alliance. Two related events shaped Colonial Office policy in the West Indies in 1907: the afore-mentioned Swettenham-Davis affair and reduction of the Royal Navy presence in the Caribbean. The Swettenham-Davis affair began on 15 January 1907 when an earthquake and fire killed hundreds of people and caused extensive property damage in Jamaica.[19] Rear Admiral Davis, then in command of two battleships and a destroyer at Guantanamo Bay, Cuba, rushed to the scene of the disaster.[20] Ignoring normal protocol, which required a gun salute to the colony's flag, Davis immediately landed sailors and marines and commenced humanitarian assistance. Such a course of action seemed reasonable under the circumstances, but he failed to take into account the attitude of the colonial governor. Sir Alexander Swettenham, brother of the famous colonial administrator Sir Frank Swettenham, was well known for his anti-American bias. Theodore Roosevelt had earlier characterized him as "a rather rare individual, an old school tory with the old school tory tendency to dislike everything American."[21] Thoroughly rattled, Swettenham took exception to Admiral Davis's failure to salute the flag. He demanded prompt U.S. withdrawal, even though the need of assistance was abundantly apparent. Swettenham then dispatched an intemperate letter condemning as unwarranted the American intervention, thus stirring an unseemly international incident that received wide and often heated publicity in the press of both nations and resulted in Swettenham's resignation.[22]

The Swettenham affair caused considerable ill-will and exposed a more serious problem: the reduction of Royal Navy presence in the West Indies. Had sufficient British naval strength been maintained in the region, England's most important possession there would not have been subjected to the "indignity" of requiring American assistance. In a confidential Cabinet memorandum dated July 1907, the Colonial Office opposed the navy's policy of maintaining but one ship to cover the vast area between Bermuda and British Guiana.[23]

By December the Swettenham affair had cooled, but as Handley's report suggested, it was not yet forgotten in the British West Indies. The battleship fleet's visit to Port of Spain was America's first large-scale, official trip to the British West Indies since that unfortunate incident. While some contemporaries attributed Britain's apparent indifference to long familiarity with visits from Royal Navy ships, including HMS *Dreadnought* the previous year, more probably it masked grave concern over Britain's lack of naval presence.[24] The remarkably large American fleet of sixteen first-class battleships, six destroyers, four auxiliaries, and three naval colliers further highlighted this shortage—there wasn't one Royal Navy ship on hand to fly Britain's white ensign.

Not all sins of omission were British. On 24 December, the first full day the fleet was in port, Britain's senior military officer in Trinidad invited 250 American naval officers to a reception. Only the four admirals and their aides showed up. Admiral Thomas later discovered that the invitation had been circulated to each battleship, but no officers were ordered to attend, so none went.[25] From this it may safely be concluded that no small amount of indifference also existed on the part of American officers. To prevent such a recurrence, a certain number of officers was ordered to attend every scheduled social function for the remainder of the cruise. But undoubtedly the unattended reception did little to encourage a friendly reaction from British officialdom.

International considerations and "official indifference" notwithstanding, the fleet visit to Trinidad had been arranged with one goal in mind: to restock supplies of fuel that had been depleted during the 1,800-mile voyage from Hampton Roads, in anticipation of the longest leg of the voyage, the 3,400-mile trip to Rio de Janeiro. Each battleship consumed approximately ninety tons of coal per day when steaming at ten knots. In addition to coal consumed by destroyers, fleet auxiliaries, and colliers, the fleet required about 1,500 tons of coal a day. The Bureau of Equipment had contracted for five colliers to provide coal at Trinidad, and the admirals and commanding officers were undoubtedly pleased when they received an early wireless report that all five had arrived at Port of Spain in advance of the fleet.[26]

Coaling commenced on the morning of 24 December. The process called for all hands, including officers. Enlisted men dressed in worn-out uniforms saved specially for the occasion, and some donned outrageously nonregulation items such as civilian hats and loud ties, this being about the only time such informality was permitted, even encouraged, to sustain crew morale during an onerous task. The ship's band, mustered on the quarterdeck, played ragtime music to keep the work going at a lively pace. Men labored in shifts in the hold of the collier, filling 800-pound bags of coal that were then winched across to the battleship, there to be emptied into various bunkers.

Coaling ship was exceedingly hot and decidedly unpopular. Not even when the last bag of coal had been hoisted aboard was the job done; in the course of coaling a pall of black dust settled over collier and battleship alike, sifting into virtually every corner and requiring a complete scrubdown afterwards. It was a time- as well as energy-consuming task, and with the exception of Christmas Day, granted as a full holiday, the labor continued for the duration of the visit.

On the final day the battleship *Ohio* was coaling from the Norwegian collier *Fortuna* when a crew member discovered half a stick of dynamite in the black chunks. The news was immediately passed to the commanding officer, Captain Bartlett, who personally carried the dynamite to Admiral Evans. Although the discovery was unsettling, it was by no means unprecedented and did not indicate the work of saboteurs or anarchists. The broken stick of dynamite in the *Ohio*, like one discovered in the *Rhode Island* a few months earlier, was believed to come from blasting charges that had failed to detonate when the coal was being mined. After the *Rhode Island* incident the Navy Department had issued strict orders that all coal must be thoroughly inspected. The discovery in the *Ohio* was probably a result of this instruction. Following Bartlett's visit, Evans issued orders for the fleet to further tighten up its method of checking coal.[27]

When their ships were not coaling or at sea compensating compasses, officers and special first-class libertymen were permitted ashore. The enlisted men found little in the way of organized entertainment in Port of Spain; many passed up the fifty-minute boat ride and remained on board. For those who took liberty the most popular pastimes seemed to have been riding trolley cars and playing baseball in the Savannah, a park in the center of town.[28] Missing in all the surviving accounts of the visit is any sense of significant personal contact between sailors and the people of Trinidad—the sort of contact made during almost all subsequent port visits throughout the cruise.

Christmas was a day when most of the men turned their thoughts toward home, or at least shared in the Christmas spirit with shipmates. Crew members gathered elaborate sprays of greenery from ashore and decorated their ships with a "peace on earth'' theme, which choice newspaper correspondent Franklin Matthews found somewhat incongruous.[29] The morning was devoted, by and large, to opening presents and reading special Christmas letters thoughtfully provided by loved ones before the fleet left home. In the afternoon there were athletic events, including boat races between enlisted crews and baseball games ashore, while in the *Minnesota* a reception was held for the officers of the fleet. That evening individual wardrooms and other messes enjoyed the traditional Christmas dinner and gift giving, and a party of officers made its way around the fleet carolling at each wardroom in turn. These "homespun" entertainments, along with smokers, minstrel shows, and concerts, were a normal part of the social life of the fleet. In this era before radio, television, and video, the American bluejacket was quite capable of devising his own entertainment, being much less reliant on the shore for diversion than his modern-day counterpart. Boxing, boating, baseball, singing, and vaudeville filled a large portion of his spare time, at sea and in port.

Even as the fleet celebrated Christmas at anchor off Port of Spain, the torpedo-boat destroyer flotilla was getting under way for the next port of call.[30] These diminutive, black-hulled ships had actually sailed for Para, Brazil, before the battleships arrived at Port of Spain, but the *Lawrence* experienced a relatively minor engineering problem shortly after leaving port and the flotilla commander, Lieutenant Hutchison Cone, decided his ships should return to Trinidad while repairs were made. Those completed, the flotilla got under way again on 24 December. In making a dashing fourteen-knot departure, the flotilla flagship *Whipple* picked up the anchor chain of the collier *Fortuna* with her port screw and came to a sudden stop. The *Lawrence,* next in line, was unable to stop and collided with the *Whipple,* sustaining light damage. Divers quickly cleared the *Whipple*'s screw, but the accident further delayed the departure. On Christmas morning, four days behind schedule, the flotilla fired a salute to Admiral Evans's flag and, carefully avoiding the *Fortuna,* again set out for Para.[31]

Following Christmas the battleships continued coaling, with liberty granted daily to crews of ships not engaged in the task. Stores opened for business after Boxing Day, most of the men taking the opportunity to mail thousands of postcards and to buy Panama hats, pets, and other souvenirs. As correspondent Matthews reported, they also patronized the saloons, but their behavior ashore was generally dignified and no incidents came to the attention of the police.[32] In recognition of this, and in contrast to his earlier behavior, Governor Jackson sent Evans a message congratulating him on the irreproachable conduct of his men.[33]

Coaling continued until departure day, 29 December. Admiral Evans had originally intended to get under way at 8:00 A.M., but the *Maine,* the ship with the greatest appetite for coal and one of the smallest bunker capacities, held things up.[34] She being the last ship to coal, her crew worked down to the bottom of the collier, where they had to dig the black fuel from pockets and corners and between limbers in the holds.[35]

At 4:00 P.M. Evans hoisted the signal for the battleships to weigh anchor and within minutes the fleet was once again under way, regaining the open sea through the Dragon's Mouth.[36] They steamed along the northern coast of Trinidad on an east-southeasterly course, then followed the northern coast of Brazil en route to Cape St. Roque, the easternmost point of South America. The routine of battle drills in the morning and signal and other drills in the afternoon was quickly reestablished.

New Year's Eve fell on the third day after the departure from Trinidad. This was announced in the traditional manner, with sailors parading through their ships dressed in bizarre costumes and playing music on homemade or hastily improvised instruments. This was another activity that amused sailors in the era before packaged entertainment replaced individual initiative, but as an interruption of shipboard routine it paled in comparison with what happened four days later when the fleet crossed the equator.[37] According to custom, as ships approached it King Neptune and his retinue boarded each ship and summoned all those who had not previously visited his domain to present themselves at court. A mock ceremony followed, in which initiates mustered before the court and were accused of such sins as knowing more about haystacks than seaweed. Then they received a mock shaving of the hair and were ducked in a pool specially erected for the event. Frivolous though it may seem to those not familiar with the traditions of the sea, this ceremony served a practical purpose; it raised the self-esteem of newly initiated sailors. Today it is still followed and revered.[38]

The New Year's celebration and equator crossing received unprecedented publicity, but a more significant story was already developing in the fleet. The day before its departure Admiral Evans publicly announced that it would reach Rio de Janeiro on the evening of Friday, 10 January 1908.[39] In determining that schedule his staff had calculated the distance from Trinidad to Rio de Janeiro as 2,900 nautical miles. Midway through the trip Admiral Thomas noted that the actual distance was at least 3,300 miles, concluding that "somebody must have blundered egregiously."[40] Furthermore, a series of minor breakdowns along the coast of Brazil required a drop in speed of a knot or two so that the beleaguered ships could keep up.[41] An adverse current, increased coal consumption, and heightened concern over fuel supplies also slowed progress.[42] In any case, many of the older ships with smaller bunkers lacked sufficient fuel reserves for increased speed; the fleet would have to steam at an economical ten knots, making a late arrival at Rio unavoidable.

When the dimensions of the fuel problem became apparent, stringent measures were adopted to reduce coal consumption. Ships with acute problems such as the *New Jersey* were ordered to steam at the most economical rate, were relieved of the requirement to maintain surplus steam, and were shifted to the rear of their divisions, where because they did not have to keep station accurately they would burn a bit less coal. In the *Illinois,* which, after the *Alabama,* had the smallest bunker capacity of the fleet, freshwater bathing was forbidden and electric lighting restricted.[43] Admiral Thomas reviewed the consumption statistics and recorded with some understatement that Evans must have been getting a "little nervous over the coal efficiency of the *Alabama, Illinois,* and *New Jersey.* It would be *awful* to be compelled to tow those ships into port."[44] The situation took a turn for the worse two days later when Captain William Southerland of the *New Jersey* reported that an inspection of the bunkers had uncovered a shortage of eighty tons of coal. Thomas concluded that unless firing efficiency improved and sea conditions grew more favorable, the *New Jersey* would run out of coal two hours before reaching Rio.[45]

The ships of Rear Admiral Charles Sperry's Fourth Division, the four oldest of the fleet, had the smallest bunker capacity and therefore departed Hampton Roads under the strictest orders to economize. The Fourth Division's *Illinois,* with a bunker capacity seven hundred tons less than the *New Jersey*'s, nevertheless through careful measures now looked as if she would reach Rio unassisted. Sperry was scathing in his evaluation of Captain Southerland's dilemma, characterizing as "frantic gabble" his reports concerning the *New Jersey*'s coal consumption.[46]

On 7 January the fleet rounded Cape St. Roque, the easternmost point of South America. With a current now favoring the fleet, the ships began to make good about 10.6 knots. Admiral Thomas estimated that the *New Jersey* could reach Rio with a narrow reserve of forty-five tons of coal.[47]

The breakdowns, the adverse current, and the navigational plotting error forced a revision of the fleet's estimated time of arrival, which was moved from Friday 10 January to Sunday 12 January. This new schedule was threatened by additional breakdowns, a man-overboard alarm in the *Missouri,* and the sudden appearance in the midst of the fleet of an unlighted barkentine.[48]

FIVE

The Birthday of the Fleet

Of all South American countries, Brazil perhaps had most reason to welcome the fleet. By the beginning of the twentieth century other South American republics had become firmly oriented toward Europe both commercially and culturally. But a preference for Brazilian coffee had made the United States the largest single consumer of Brazil's major export product, and the balance of trade was very much in the southern country's favor. The largest state in South America, with a Portuguese-speaking population that set it apart from its Spanish neighbors, Brazil tended to identify with the United States.[1] As one Brazilian newspaper put it, "The two colossi of the New World have [had] between them many points of contact and notions of sympathy . . . since our Republican Revolution of 1817."[2] News of the fleet's visit to Rio had been received enthusiastically, and preparations to entertain the guests were well in hand before they reached Trinidad.[3]

The fleet's revised arrival date of 12 January was well known in Rio de Janeiro, but the precise hour had not been announced.[4] On Sunday thousands of people were ready to welcome the ships between 8:00 and 9:00 A.M. The time was more accurately fixed when the fleet was reported at 8:30 off Cape Frio, some seventy miles away. Though it could not be expected in port before mid-afternoon, when a Brazilian naval escort put to sea at 9:30 to greet and escort the fleet, large crowds had gathered along the length of the Beira Mar.[5]

As the fleet approached the Guanabara Harbor the Brazilian escort joined it. The cruiser *Barroso* fired a fifteen-gun salute, giving Admiral Evans the honors normally accorded a vice admiral, and then fell in with the formation for the last few miles.[6] The flagship *Connecticut* passed Fort Villagagnon, southern guardian of the harbor entrance, and fired a twenty-one-gun salute to Brazil. While this was in progress, the fleet passed over the bar and through a mass of civilian sightseeing craft. The Brazilian coastal battleship *Floriano* fired a thirteen-gun salute to Admiral Evans's flag, and the *Connecticut* drew abeam of the German cruiser *Bremen,* which fired another salute to the admiral. After this the fleet anchored in line of divisions at 4:00 P.M.[7]

Then the official rounds began.[8] All flag and commanding officers assembled in the *Connecticut* to pay their respects to the commander in chief. Joining them there were Brazil's minister of marine, the captain of the port, the American consul, the commandants of Brazilian naval divisions, civic authorities, and members of the official welcoming committee.[9] The initial spate of visits, which stood in sharp contrast to the stiff British reception at Trinidad, was but the opening act of a rapidfire succession of social engagements. All admirals and captains were required to follow a grueling schedule except for Admiral Evans, who by this point had become seriously ill. The next senior officer, Rear Admiral Charles M. Thomas, himself suffering from a weak heart, stood in for the commander in chief as Brazil's official guest for the duration of the visit.[10]

Rear Admiral William H. Emory, commanding the Second Division, complained of the rigors of making diplomatic rounds and the unsuitability of the navy's heavy formal uniform in the tropics: "The good Lord never inflicted such misery on a human being as He did upon me and those that accompanied me."[11] The program on 13 January, for example, required Admirals Thomas, Sperry, and Emory, along with sixteen battleship skippers, to call on the minister of marine in Rio de Janeiro. Afterward they repaired to Thomas's flagship, the *Minnesota,* to await the minister's return call. When that was over they traveled by boat and rail in full ceremonial uniform to the summer capital, Petropolis, some twenty-two miles from Rio. There they called on President Penna of Brazil and attended a banquet at the American ambassador's residence. Taking accommodations overnight at Petropolis, the senior officers boarded a train at 7:30 the following morning and reached their ships at about 11:00—just in time to set out for a luncheon hosted by the minister of marine at the top of Corcovado.

Maintaining such a schedule undoubtedly was tiring. Nevertheless, observing diplomatic protocol had long been an integral part of navy life in peacetime. That on this most important voyage the fleet was commanded by men clearly not equal to the task stands as a condemnation of the officer promotion system that allowed only sexagenarians to accede to high command.

In contrast to the marked lack of organized entertainment for the enlisted men at Port of Spain, here an extensive program had been tailored specially for them. A committee of American and British residents, headed by the American vice consul, established information and exchange bureaus and organized excursions to local attractions. Hearty participation by the British community—the "flags of Brazil and England and the United States were entwined," Franklin Matthews reported—must be seen as an effective rebuttal of the later suggestion that the British government had sought to dramatize its hostility toward the cruise.[12] Certainly if this had been the intention, pressure would have been brought to bear through His Majesty's diplomatic representatives to ensure that the British community did not assume such a prominent role in the fleet's reception.

Following a waterfront brawl the first night in port, the senior shore patrol officer temporarily curtailed liberty for the enlisted men. According to the *New York Times* the affair was no more than "a fight between drunken negroes and a few of the sailors from the American fleet," in which three sailors were wounded.[13] After an investigation liberty was reinstituted and the number of men permitted ashore the next day was doubled, to a total of four thousand.[14]

Not all was delightful diversion in Rio. While there, the fleet had to coal. Before 12 January all the contracted colliers had arrived, and coaling commenced on the thirteenth. As at Port of Spain, naval colliers provided most of the fuel, and here a valuable lesson in logistic support was learned. Those designated to provide coal for the fleet in Rio, like all naval colliers then in service, were acquired at the outbreak of the war with Spain in 1898 and had limited bunker capacity. Masters had ignored orders to preserve their cargoes intact by purchasing bunker fuel as necessary. Thus, to complete the relatively short haul to Trinidad, the colliers had used five hundred tons of cargo coal themselves, leaving the fleet short that amount.[15]

The problem, of course, increased in direct proportion to the distance at which the fuel support was required, resulting in a deficiency of 3,218.9 tons at Rio de Janeiro. This performance led Evans to report that the naval colliers' usefulness was "confined to the distribution of coal from coal depots at a short radius from the United States." He recommended to the Navy Department that it not employ naval colliers to carry coal to the Pacific Coast because they would probably burn a greater part of their cargo simply getting there.[16]

The significance of this state of affairs has generally been overlooked. It meant that during the remainder of its cruise the battleship fleet would be totally dependent on foreign tramp steamers for distant fuel support. It also meant that the American navy, through lack of colliers, would be unable to conduct combat operations far from its own bases. Given the continuing debate over which base to use, Subic Bay or Manila, the slow development of Pearl Harbor, and the meager facilities at Guam, any plan to defend America's Pacific possessions would require the support of neutral merchant shipping. The availability of shipping, in turn, would largely depend on the attitude adopted by Britain in any future conflict.

The two mission-designed naval colliers then under construction would not be so limited in range; however, the number of these ships eventually authorized for construction was so small that the problem of fuel support remained unresolved until the introduction of liquid fuels for general use.

There had been no shortage of doomsday prophets after the voyage was announced. Unfortunately Navy Secretary Metcalf displayed a remarkable inability to distinguish credible reports from nonsense, and when Admiral Sperry visited him before the fleet's departure he was evidently in a "blue funk."[17] A fortnight before the departure, the Navy Department had expressed concern over an anonymous report that the Japanese had purchased and equipped minelayers in Germany.[18] The naval attaché in Berlin laid this worry to rest, saying the report was false.[19]

THE BIRTHDAY OF THE FLEET

In no time a larger threat emerged in a report from Captain John C. Fremont, naval attaché in Paris. On 19 December, in a letter to Captain R. P. Rogers, chief of naval intelligence, Fremont forwarded news of a plot to inflict damage on the fleet in Rio. A separate letter named the alleged conspirators, while yet another disclosed information about Fremont's source, a "twenty-two-year old American of independent means" who was "absolutely trustworthy."[20] Two days later, his concern over the fleet's safety growing, Fremont cabled the essence of his report to Washington.[21] The navy secretary reacted swiftly, in a cable to Admiral Evans ordering him to take every precaution against injury to the fleet.[22] Secretary of State Elihu Root alerted the ambassador to Brazil, adding, though, the vital assessment that the information was "unverified and probably not worthy of much credence."[23]

Despite Secretary Metcalf's concern, senior officers of the fleet were unanimous in refusing to give credibility to the plot. After discussing Metcalf's messages with Evans, Thomas dismissed the whole affair as "bosh" and said that his opinion was shared by all the officers with whom he had spoken. The secretary had overreacted, he concluded.[24] In any case, possible precautions were limited. The repair ship *Panther* and the tender *Yankton* were dispatched early from Port of Spain to take measures to protect the fleet before its arrival in Rio de Janeiro.[25]

The plot took a new twist when Ambassador White in Paris cabled Secretary Root, who then informed the American ambassador to Brazil that the German steamer *Mainz*, which had been at Rio on 12–13 December, might have delivered mines for the conspirators.[26] A hurried investigation by the U.S. confidential treasury agent in Cologne led to the conclusion that the *Mainz* had carried materials "more or less used in the manufacture of explosives."[27] Investigation in Brazil, however, suggested that the alleged conspirators were reputable people and that the *Mainz*'s cargo had been purchased for legitimate purposes. The plot was discredited in Rio.[28]

The American ambassador reported that there would be no remission of vigilance in Brazil, and police and naval authorities continued to ensure that no calamity befell the fleet while it was in Brazilian waters. Their actions remained confidential until after the fleet's arrival. On 19 January Rio's chief of police announced that his force had uncovered a plot to dynamite the fleet and was even then seeking the leader, one Jean Fedher of Petropolis, and his accomplices, described as five Italians, one Canadian, and another German.[29]

The American media responded with disbelief. "It would be unmannerly to treat this revelation with levity," the *New York Times* editorialized, "but somehow we do not feel that our warships are going to be destroyed by Anarchists. You cannot destroy armor plate by oratory."[30] Reinforcing this assessment, the following day's edition carried a report from Paris that the original warning had been given little credence there, coming as it did from "a young man more or less given to romancing."[31] Although the plot, in this light, might have appeared ludicrous, no such details were provided to Admiral Evans. Indeed, with specific orders from the secretary of the navy to take every precaution, he had no option other than to treat the threat as real.[32]

This was not the only alarming rumor making the rounds at Rio. There were reports of Russian spies trailing the fleet around South America.[33] The French paper *Patrie* published under the banner "WHERE IS THE JAPANESE FLEET?" a report that it had been sighted off Hawaii.[34] Other sources offered dire warnings that the Japanese torpedo-boat flotilla would be waiting in ambush in the Strait of Magellan, ready to sink the fleet as it navigated those restricted waters.[35]

Private citizens wrote to President Roosevelt and an already distracted Secretary Metcalf. "A Friend of America" confided to Captain Rogers, chief of naval intelligence, that Japanese and German agents had planted grenades in the coal being delivered to the fleet at Rio; that two crew members in the battleship *Georgia* were leaking information to German and Japanese agents; that Japanese submarines were indeed within striking range of the Strait of Magellan.[36] Rogers reacted by reiterating to the naval attaché in Tokyo the need to report promptly any unusual movements of Japanese warships.[37]

While Roosevelt was skeptical of the reports, Secretary Metcalf, in response to talk of a Japanese submarine threat, authorized Evans to modify the itinerary of the torpedo-boat destroyers so they could escort the fleet through the Strait of Magellan.[38] In compliance, Evans issued orders to the destroyer flotilla commander indicating it was imperative that the flotilla arrive at Punta Arenas early in order not to delay movements of the main fleet.[39]

Meanwhile, the Japanese took an extraordinary step to assuage American fears. In an interview Japan's minister of marine revealed that daily reports of the disposition of his country's fleet were being handed to the U.S. naval attaché in Tokyo. Most emphatically he pointed out that no Japanese vessel was any nearer the Pacific coast than Yokosuka, that every battleship, torpedo boat, and submarine was either in Yokosuka, Kure, or Sasebo. This was confirmed by Commander John A. Dougherty, the American naval attaché.[40] No more categorical or definitive statement concerning the Imperial Japanese Navy's intentions was possible.

As phantom plots and curious international intrigues were being disclosed and discounted, the fleet itinerary became a source of diplomatic friction. The problem lay in a deep-seated hostility between Argentina and Brazil. The Rio Conference of 1906 and Secretary of State Root's visit to Buenos Aires during that conference had done much to improve Argentine-American and Brazilian-Argentine relations. But the "newborn glow of cordiality" was short-lived.[41] Less than a month later, Brazil signed contracts in England for the construction of three modern dreadnoughts.[42] In South America this development, clearly seen as a challenge to Argentina's naval supremacy, created new tensions between the two countries. It came at a time when opposition to further major naval expenditure made it politically inexpedient for Argentina to respond by placing a similar order, and it had a destabilizing effect, prompting Chile and Argentina to cancel their mutual non-aggression pact of 1902. By the terms of this agreement, both nations were to have limited their naval armaments for five years.[43]

In this context, Argentina felt some uneasiness over frequent and public demonstrations of friendship between the United States and Brazil. These included a Brazilian banquet in honor of the American delegation at the Hague Conference, a cordial reception at the White House of the Brazilian admiral and staff who participated in the Jamestown Exposition in 1907, and now the visit to Rio de Janeiro.[44] After its lengthy stay in Brazil, moreover, the fleet planned to skip Argentina and proceed to its scheduled visits in Chile and Peru. As in 1907, when Rear Admiral Sebree's armored cruiser Special Service Squadron visited Uruguay, Brazil, Chile, and Peru, but not Argentina, the citizens of that country felt snubbed.

The relatively shallow waters of the Rio de la Plata at Buenos Aires effectively prevented the battleships from visiting the Argentine capital, but as the fleet approached Rio de Janeiro, the U.S. chargé d'affaires in Buenos Aires cabled the State Department to ask whether the torpedo-boat flotilla would come. The minister of foreign affairs, he reported, had called him to his office to say that a "bad impression" had been produced by rumors that the destroyers would not visit, and to express his regret "that Brazil should be favored and Argentina slighted."[45] This telegram brought a rapid response. By 13 January the Navy Department had sent a cable directing the torpedo flotilla to visit Buenos Aires instead of Montevideo.[46]

This change of schedule did not reach the Argentine foreign minister before inaccurate translations of congratulatory messages passed between President Roosevelt and President Penna of Brazil. In response to Penna's message, received at the White House on the afternoon of 14 January, Roosevelt had immediately ordered the State Department to compose "a cordial and flowery response." This was a masterpiece of diplomatic wording; it said much but gave no specific commitment, alluding to the "long-continued and never to be broken amity and helpfulness" of the two republics.[47]

Before Roosevelt's telegram was published, the phrase "amity and helpfulness" was translated as *mutua ayuda,* or "mutual assistance." This loose rendering unleashed discussion in Rio's editorial pages about the possibility of a formal alliance and caused understandable concern in Buenos Aires.[48] News of the telegram, in its inaccurate Portuguese version, struck Argentine Foreign Minister Zeballos "like a bomb blast." He called the fleet's bypassing of Argentina an act of hostility and sent a message to the Argentine minister in Washington demanding that he obtain ship visits either to Buenos Aires or Bahia Blanca.[49] By the time Minister Portela presented his plea to Secretary Root, the torpedo flotilla's visit to Buenos Aires had already been approved.

At this point Evans's desire to have the torpedo flotilla escort the battleships through the Strait of Magellan intruded. The flotilla had originally been scheduled to arrive at Punta Arenas after the battleships entered the Pacific Ocean. Now, even though the flotilla was running behind schedule because of the difficulties at Port of Spain, it was ordered to arrive at Punta Arenas in sufficient time to coal and then escort the battleships on 7 February. This change raised new doubts about the Buenos Aires visit, which America's ambassador to Brazil communicated to Admiral Evans. Argentina, he warned, was anxious for definite word that the destroyers would visit Buenos Aires; Argentina's minister of foreign affairs would regard omission of a visit as "deplorable."[50] Confronted with a problem of obvious diplomatic importance, Evans held off a day, hoping for some guidance from the Navy Department, then decided in favor of the visit.[51]

With the Buenos Aires visit finally resolved, the fleet enjoyed the final days of entertainment in Rio before continuing southward. On Monday night Brazil's minister of foreign affairs, Baron do Rio Branco, hosted the final formal entertainment ashore. Next day was the last full day in port, and it was a busy one aboard the flagships *Connecticut* and *Minnesota*.

Foreign visits offered an ideal opportunity for systematic gathering of information on ports, their defenses, and also host navies. Marine Corps Major Dion Williams, the fleet intelligence officer, was also a specialist in base defenses. He pursued his intelligence assignment energetically, organizing teams of officers to assemble information in specific areas and supervising compilation of a report from each port. With disarming sincerity, Louis Maxfield, signal officer in the *Illinois,* reported to his mother that he had been assigned intelligence-gathering duties. "Please don't tell anyone that officers were detailed to do such things," he wrote, "because some people might think it wasn't . . . courteous . . . ."[52]

In addition to developing a campaign plan for the capture of Rio harbor, Major Williams, with Lieutenant Commander Ridley McLean, the fleet gunnery officer, and Artist-Correspondent Henry Reuterdahl, compiled a detailed report on the Brazilian navy. Reuterdahl, whose broad knowledge of naval affairs was widely acknowledged and respected, analyzed the caliber of Brazilian officers and enlisted men and speculated about the probable efficiency of the newly ordered dreadnoughts. In his view, the condition of its fleet units suggested the Brazilian navy wouldn't realize the full potential of those dreadnoughts. Expressing a view that doubtless would have caused further Argentine concern, Reuterdahl wrote that in the event of a war, the Monroe Doctrine being an issue, Brazil would become an ally of the United States. It was important, he concluded, to know that the new Brazilian fleet would be properly trained and proficient in gunnery and tactics.[53]

While the fleet's intelligence officers were completing their reports and discussing the shape of their war plan for Rio on board the *Connecticut,* Reuterdahl changed hats: the marine artist, who enjoyed good relations with Rear Admiral Thomas, decorated the flagship *Minnesota* with fountains and massive arrangements of greenery. On its final day in port the fleet was to return Brazilian hospitality with a reception whose guest list included virtually the entire diplomatic corps, local nobility, high society, and leaders of the American community in Rio de Janeiro.

In the early afternoon of 22 January, departure day, President Penna came down from Petropolis accompanied by the American ambassador and boarded the presidential yacht *Silva Jardin.* As the resplendent vessel approached the fleet its battleships fired a simultaneous twenty-one-gun salute. The presidential party boarded Thomas's flagship to take formal farewell of the fleet at 2:00 P.M.[54] Penna inspected the full-dressed battleships after reembarking on his yacht and then proceeded to Fort Villagagnon for a review. As the fleet made final preparations its Brazilian counterpart weighed anchor and made a circuit around the American battleships.

The fleet got under way at 3:30, just as a torrential rain enveloped the maneuvering fleets and scattered the multitude of sightseeing boats.[55] The battleships formed in column, reversing their order of entry, and fired a final salute to the Brazilian president as they steamed past Fort Villagagnon in lifting rain. After the ships crossed the bar and cleared the harbor, they smoothly formed line of divisions and settled into their sea routine for another long voyage.[56] Virtually the entire Brazilian navy, en route to the southern states for three months of training, followed the American fleet to sea. The graceful sail and steam cruiser *Benjamin Constant,* of Brazil's Division of Training Ships, was itself embarking on a world cruise for the training of midshipmen.[57]

So ended the visit to Rio de Janeiro. *A Noticia* heaped praise on the "youthful and orderly" enlisted men who embodied the spirit of their countrymen. The paper raised again the prospect of an American-Brazilian alliance and described the fleet visit in terms that could not fail to arouse Argentine fears. Rarely, it was suggested, does the work of statesmen in forging international friendship coincide so exactly with public sentiment, a job reinforced by the cordiality and good behavior of American sailors.[58]

The sleek, black-hulled torpedo-boat destroyers *Whipple, Truxtun, Lawrence, Hopkins, Hull,* and *Stewart,* under the command of Lieutenant Hutchison I. Cone, weighed anchor at 8:30 P.M. on 21 January and departed Rio for Buenos Aires.[59] After an uneventful voyage the flotilla arrived off that city in the early morning hours of the twenty-sixth. Despite stormy weather, the ships were watched by a multitude as a division of Argentine torpedo boats escorted them in.[60]

The Argentine government had planned to match Brazil's welcome. The commanding officers—five lieutenants and one ensign—found themselves showered with honors of the sort normally reserved for captains and admirals. Among other functions they attended a banquet given by the minister of marine and receptions hosted by the president and the American legation.[61] The young destroyer officers carried out their diplomatic duties admirably.

U.S. diplomats, on the other hand, handled theirs poorly. One blunder in particular had the effect of canceling benefits accrued when the navy rerouted its destroyers. Following the presidential reception in Buenos Aires, President Alcortes sent a congratulatory telegram to President Roosevelt, Foreign Minister Zeballos an equally congratulatory cable to Secretary of State Root.[62] As noted, similar messages from Brazil less than two weeks earlier had brought direct, effusive, highly publicized responses from Roosevelt and Root. President Alcortes and Minister Zeballos, however, were answered indirectly in a single cable sent from Root via Chargé Wilson, causing unnecessary offense.[63] Only when Argentina's minister of foreign affairs expressed "surprise and regret" that no replies had been received from Roosevelt and Root did the State Department hurry to repair the damage.[64] As Harold Peterson has suggested, such insensitivity undermined the goodwill created by Root's personal diplomacy of 1906.[65]

While the torpedo flotilla was being entertained in Buenos Aires, the battleship fleet continued south to Punta Arenas, its next coaling stop. That journey's highlight was yet another mark of courtesy extended by the Argentine government. As the battleship fleet steamed off the Rio de la Plata, the Argentine cruiser squadron—the armored cruisers *San Martin* and *Buenos Ayres* and the protected cruisers *Pueyrredon* and *9 de Julio,* under the command of Rear Admiral Hipolito Oliva— was at sea attempting a rendezvous. For several days overcast weather had complicated their efforts, but by the evening of 26 January the Argentine ships had succeeded in making contact. Rear Admiral Oliva exchanged courteous messages with Evans, then fell in astern of the battleships for the night.[66]

Next morning the American battleships formed a single column, and shortly after 8:00 the Argentine squadron began passing up the starboard side of the fleet, rails manned and bands playing "The Star-Spangled Banner." As the flagship *San Martin* drew abreast of the *Connecticut,* she hoisted the American flag and fired a seventeen-gun salute to Rear Admiral Evans, according him the honor reserved for a full admiral. The *Connecticut* returned the salute, hoisted Argentina's ensign, and fired a highly complimentary national salute of twenty-one guns. After a final exchange of messages the grey-hulled Argentine ships departed for home, leaving an impression of skill and professionalism that was much commented upon.[67]

Rear Admiral Sperry, in a report to Secretary Metcalf, took the opportunity to press for a policy decision concerning the paint on American warships. He discussed at some length the value of war colors in reducing the distance at which ships might be detected, but recognized that repainting them during the cruise would be impolitic, possibly even interpreted as a declaration of hostilities.[68]

The long hours of station keeping in formation had paid off. Now, Sperry reported, sixteen battleships which a few weeks earlier had been "perpetually backing and filling" to maintain their stations within the fleet were now "jogging along" in squares of four "as if they were tied together." Another noteworthy development on this third leg of the voyage was a marked reduction in the number of engineering casualties. Sperry attributed earlier problems to the fleet's proximity to navy yards, a situation in which responsibility for maintenance was divided between shipyards and ships' crews. This arrangement was "nothing less than the curse of the Navy." Now forced to rely on their own resources, and always under the flagship's scrutiny, the ships developed their own repair and maintenance potential. "In my opinion," Sperry wrote, "the fleet . . . will be in far worse condition after its next visit to a Navy Yard than it will be when it gets there."

The cumulative effect of these tactical and technical benefits that had eluded the fleet during routine operations in home waters was of greatest importance to the navy. "It is the birthday of the fleet," Sperry concluded, "and a Navy without a fleet is simply a mob of ships."[69]

SIX

Magnificent Marine Parade

Like Argentina, Chile in the decade 1898–1908 regarded the United States with some suspicion. Initially, it felt that the United States had greatly magnified the *Baltimore* incident of 1891 as a pretext for possible intervention in Chile's affairs.[1] America's rapid rise in the world was accompanied by what Chile interpreted as threatening events: U.S. involvement in the Venezuelan boundary dispute of 1895, the Spanish-American War, and the Panama "incident" in 1903.[2] Though Secretary of State Root's personal diplomacy at the 1906 Conference of American States and his subsequent visit to Chile did much to allay concern, Chileans remained guarded. Following a description of the U.S. ships departing Valparaiso and disappearing over the northern horizon, the magazine *Zigzag* asked, "Will they be destined to watch over the security of the young nations of America . . . ? Or [are] . . . they destined to be our perpetual ruin?"[3]

The selection of remote Punta Arenas rather than Valparaiso as the fleet's southern coaling stop was not, however, a reflection of the state of Chilean-American relations. Practical considerations had dictated the choice. Valparaiso's port in 1908 was little more than an open and unsheltered roadstead that had the added disadvantage of exceedingly deep water. It was only for lack of good anchorage area there that the fleet's visit to Punta Arenas had been arranged.

For this isolated frontier town of about fourteen thousand, the planned fleet visit, the only one to a Chilean port, would be a momentous event. Even before the fleet had anchored in Brazil the Chilean government decided to send a cruiser to the outpost with a special welcoming committee.[4] But the central government, unlike that of Brazil and Peru, expended little effort to provide entertainment for the fleet. The local business community itself made preparations, decorating the town and its buildings with Chilean and American flags, bunting, and greenery. The cruiser *Chacabuco,* flying the flag of Rear Admiral Juan M. Simpson and carrying U.S. Minister John M. Hicks, left Valparaiso on 22 January and anchored at Punta Arenas on the evening of the twenty-seventh.[5]

The small British cruiser *Sappho* anchored before the city on the evening of the thirtieth.[6] It seems reasonable to assume that her arrival was more than coincidence. To observe and report on the state of the U.S. fleet as it entered the Pacific was an entirely legitimate intelligence mission, one the Americans would understand. It did not imply hostility, nor were the British officers, as has been suggested, "coldly uncommunicative."[7] Indeed, the *Sappho*'s commanding officer, whom Sperry described as a good fellow, actively participated in social events.[8]

On 31 January the battleships reached Possession Bay, at the Atlantic entrance to the Strait of Magellan, and there anchored to await a favorable tide. "We seem to be at the end of the world," Signal Officer Louis Maxfield wrote. "South of us we can just see Tierra del Fuego, and a mile north is the most barren and desolate land you can imagine. . . ."[9] The fleet got under way at 3:30 the following morning to take advantage of a flood tide. Before noon, after passing through the first two narrows of the strait, the battleships arrived at Broad Reach, the bay on which Punta Arenas is located.[10]

As ships made their way toward the anchorage, thousands of people lined the town's beaches and wharves.[11] Commercial activity ground to a halt, and, observed the local paper, Puntarenese willingly went without lunch to witness the event.[12] The *Connecticut* paused, broke Chile's national ensign at the main, and commenced a twenty-one-gun national salute. The people on shore watched, and "as if moved by an invisible spring, they broke out in a single gigantic shout and vigorously waved their arms in the air."[13] A salute to Admiral Simpson's flag came next, then a salute to Evans from HMS *Sappho*.[14] Following this, the fleet anchored in line of squadrons.[15] Hardly had the *Connecticut* anchored when Admiral Simpson's chief of staff arrived on board to inform Evans that the admiral, ignoring protocol, would himself call on Evans to convey the welcome of the government and people of Chile.[16]

Punta Arenas looked stark after the tropical luxuriousness of Rio de Janeiro. The town was rather solidly built up for six or seven blocks from the waterfront, mainly with unpretentious single-story dwellings of brick or adobe that had corrugated iron roofing designed to withstand the rigors of subantarctic winters. Although the hills beyond were forested, land immediately around the town had been stripped of vegetation by a forest fire. For acres all one could see were the burnt trunks of once-green trees.

This did not deter inveterate sightseers. Because of the town's size liberty was restricted to officers and seventy special first-class libertymen from each battleship. As they came ashore they read a sign erected at the fleet landing by the local chamber of commerce: SPECIAL PRICES FOR THE NORTH AMERICAN FLEET. This was received with well-founded cynicism: prices had apparently been raised for the duration of the visit.[17]

The social calendar for the visit was considerably lighter than in Rio de Janeiro. Most notable was a "grandiose fiesta" on 2 February at the home of American Consul Moritz Braun, a man of considerable wealth, in honor of Minister Hicks and admirals and officers of the U.S. Fleet.[18] This and other evening affairs were reserved for officers. For the enlisted ranks Punta Arenas had little outside the traditional entertainments to offer. The main activities, once the town had been explored, consisted of long hikes into the hills surrounding the port and some ambitious hunting expeditions across the strait to Tierra del Fuego.[19]

The main reason for the port visit, of course, was to take on full bunkers of coal; the 2,374-mile trip from Rio de Janeiro had depleted fuel supplies, and the next leg would exceed 2,800 miles. The Bureau of Equipment had contracted for the delivery of twenty thousand tons in four foreign colliers, but when the fleet arrived there were only three waiting, with a combined cargo of about fifteen thousand tons. Admiral Simpson, Hicks reported, secured authorization from Santiago to offer the Chilean government's coal supply at Punta Arenas to Admiral Evans. Before it was necessary to deplete local supplies, however, the fourth collier, the *Towergate,* appeared, having sailed from Philadelphia on Christmas Day.[20]

Even with this arrival problems remained. In Trinidad six colliers had been employed over a six-day period; in Rio de Janeiro, five colliers over a nine-day period. Now in Punta Arenas the fleet had the services of three colliers for two days and four for four days. There weren't enough colliers to keep more than four ships busy at once, and so, pressed for time, men coaled day and night in an effort to complete the miserable process as rapidly as possible.

As the last ships received their coal, the final social functions were held ashore and afloat. Of these, the most significant, from an historic viewpoint, was a luncheon on board the *Chacabuco* for American petty officers. The event received only routine press, but following the death of Admiral Evans in 1912 it was recalled that on this occasion a marine from the *Louisiana,* drunk on a strong local wine called *pisco,* had struck a Chilean officer. The Chilean, according to the account, accepted apologies for this assault, whereupon the marine promptly knocked down another officer. According to a later account, "Americans . . . then overpowered the ruffian, dragged him to a launch, and clamped him in irons in the *Louisiana*'s brig." Captain Richard Wainwright, the story continues, awakened the bed-ridden Evans, who wrote a formal letter of apology to Admiral Simpson. Early the next morning Simpson called on Evans and agreed not to report the incident to the government.[21]

The truth of this story, which has become almost a permanent fixture in accounts of the cruise, is suspect. The American marine was a sergeant; the specific rank of the Chileans involved has been variously, but never specifically, reported.[22] Probably they were *suboficiales,* noncommissioned officers, and therefore the sergeant's peers in the naval hierarchy, the dinner being hosted by the *Chacabuco*'s petty officers. Striking any officer, particularly officers of high rank, was then— as now—a very serious offense in the navy, and discipline in the navy and marine corps in 1908 was harsh. "In those days," Archa Adamson recalled, "if you winked an eye you got the irons."[23] It is unlikely that the behavior described in the standard accounts of the incident would have warranted anything less than a general court-martial. Yet a review of marine corps muster rolls from the *Louisiana* reveals that the sergeant received only a letter of reprimand from the commander in chief for "drunk and disorderly behavior."[24] Thus it seems reasonable to conclude that we have embellished versions of what must have been a minor incident in which a marine sergeant became drunk and possibly struck one or two Chilean petty officers. Such an event on board a foreign warship in a foreign port would have been unfortunate, but most certainly not the "diplomatic catastrophe" described in modern accounts of the incident.[25] Rear Admiral Simpson reported that relations remained cordial during the affair.[26] In the final analysis, this appreciation seems closest to the truth.

During the visit a singularly fortunate alteration was made to the fleet's itinerary. The bed-ridden Evans, informed by Thomas that the people of Valparaiso "were simply wild to see our Fleet," and that Minister Hicks wanted to know if he would pass close to the entrance to Valparaiso Harbor, agreed whole-heartedly.[27] This diplomatic wisdom was reinforced when Secretary of State Root, perhaps mindful of the affront so recently suffered by Buenos Aires, acted immediately on a suggestion from Minister Hicks and sent a telegram in Roosevelt's name to President Pedro Montt of Chile thanking him for the fleet's warm reception.[28]

On the final evening in port Admiral Thomas, still acting on behalf of Evans, gave a dinner in the *Minnesota* honoring his Chilean hosts.[29] Ashore, an enormous crowd gathered on the wharf to witness the searchlight display put on by the ships of the fleet, which the local paper described as a fantastic spectacle.[30]

At about 11:00 P.M. on 7 February the fleet, preceded by the *Chacabuco,* got under way. This departure hour had been chosen so the ships would reach Cape Froward near dawn, allowing maximum daylight for navigation of the hazardous 140-mile stretch to Cape Pilar, where the Magellan Strait meets the Pacific Ocean. To transit the strait, the ships formed a single column four hundred yards apart, eight hundred between divisions. The *Chacabuco* continued to lead the fleet, while the destroyer flotilla, which had arrived at Punta Arenas on 4 February, provided escort. Three destroyers were stationed on either side of the column's head. All day the ships steamed through the grand, lonely landscape, making their way without incident. In late afternoon, as the fleet neared the Pacific end of the strait, the destroyers again parted. With a Chilean naval officer acting as pilot they continued north through the network of islands and channels, en route to Talcahuana, Chile, for a ten-day visit.[31]

One contemporary British writer touched on the strategic significance of this transit when he suggested that the first turn of the screws in the Pacific implied "a definite change of front" in American policy.[32] While those far removed from the scene could view developments on this large scale, weather conditions conspired to reduce the fleet's vision to the smallest possible. Thick fog settled over the ships as they debouched from the strait, creating difficulties that a generation accustomed to electronic navigational aids would find difficult to appreciate. The battleship fleet used three devices to maintain formation in fog: a steam whistle, searchlights, and a chip log. The ships had been assigned identifying letters of the Morse code. In fog, they sounded the letters sequentially, according to their position within the fleet. Each vessel also trained a searchlight aft to increase the distance at which it might be seen by the next ship in line, and towed a chip log, a spar with an upright board fastened to it, at a predetermined distance astern. The chip log threw up a spray easily visible to the next ship in line, facilitating the judgment of distance. These precautions had all been adopted within the preceding year.

Fog and overcast conditions lingered until 13 February as the battleships continued north along the Chilean coast. The *Chacabuco* left the fleet on the twelfth for a brief stop at Talcahuana, Chile, to coal and transmit messages to Valparaiso. On the thirteenth, after signaling confirmation of the fleet's arrival time, she returned with three Chilean destroyers to escort the fleet to Valparaiso.[33]

Having allowed time for delays due to heavy weather, which did not materialize, the fleet was now ahead of schedule and had to reduce speed to eight knots. En route, it encountered the old cruiser *Chicago* heading for Norfolk to be converted to a training ship. She had departed Valparaiso on 13 February after a four-day visit and was now on her way to Punta Arenas.[34] As the *Chicago* approached she proudly displayed her long homeward-bound pennant and fired salutes to Admirals Simpson and Evans.

Valparaiso was alive with excitement. Hotels were full but still people poured in from all parts of the country, an estimated quarter million.[35] As the hour of the fleet's arrival approached, they swarmed to the summits around the city.[36] President Pedro Montt and a large party of military officers, foreign diplomats, and wives were on board the training ship *General Baquedano,* lying at anchor to review the fleet.

At 11:30 the first plumes of smoke rose from below the horizon; stacks, then superstructures, and finally complete profiles hove into view as the fleet approached the port in single column. Each ship flew Chile's flag from the mainmast, the Stars and Stripes from the foremast and peak. Sun shone on the spotless white hulls. By the time they reached the southern arm of the harbor, it was apparent the Chilean public had turned out en masse to watch "the most magnificent marine pageant that has ever been seen in the Pacific Ocean, and, probably, in the whole world."[37] Chile's official sentiment was expressed by about five hundred Chilean sailors clad in white and arranged to spell the word *Welcome* against a high hill. Their message could be seen at a distance of two miles.

The fleet's maneuver in Valparaiso Harbor was a masterpiece of symmetry and timing. When the *Minnesota,* in the middle of the column, came abreast of the Point Angeles fort at the harbor's southern entrance, the ships fired a simultaneous twenty-one-gun salute to Chile.[38] By the time this was over the *Connecticut,* leading the column, had drawn abreast of the *General Baquedano.* With her rails manned by bluejackets, her marine guard paraded, her red-jacketed band played Chile's national anthem, and all hands saluted as she fired the first of sixteen twenty-one-gun salutes to President Montt before continuing her circuit of the harbor and heading out to sea. When she came abreast of the fort guarding the harbor's northern arm, the *Kentucky,* at the other end of the column, passed the southern fort inbound, completing a perfect crescent.[39]

This maneuver had been conducted at a speed of eight knots. After the *Kentucky* finished saluting President Montt, speed was increased to ten knots and on signal all ships simultaneously hauled down Chile's ensign from their mastheads. Admiral

Thomas, delighted with the flawless maneuver, bragged, "I can confidently assert that a more perfect exhibition of Marine Efficiency, power, and drill, has never been witnessed on this Earth at any time in the World's history." This was not "extravagant praise," he added, but a "fact, patent to all."[40]

After the fleet had disappeared over the northern horizon, the magazine *Zigzag* expressed reservations about the unprecedented display of power, noting that while the fleet advanced "serenely and majestically," the men in it did not even bother to think of how they might be regarded by the countries of South America.[41]

The fleet continued north for four uneventful days, with the now standard routine of morning and afternoon drills. Midshipman Maxfield reported the progress of a fleet-wide signal contest and complained heatedly about his captain's new order that all *Illinois* midshipmen spend ten hours a week studying radiotelegraphy and drawing a full plan of the ship's fire-control system.[42] In retrospect, this effort to teach midshipmen the navy's new technology appears progressive. Their complaint was that radiotelegraphy and fire control were not topics required for promotion to ensign, and thus distracted from the all-important examination preparations.

Five days after passing Valparaiso, twelve days out of Punta Arenas, the fleet was met by the Peruvian cruiser *Bolognesi,* assigned to escort it the last few miles to Callao.[43]

The general outline of the Peruvian plan to receive the U.S. fleet had been settled as early as December 1907 and was intended to reflect the warm relations between the United States and Peru.[44] America's minister to Peru, Leslie Combs, reported to Secretary of State Root early in December that although the government still had not paid off bills incurred on the occasion of his, the secretary's, visit in 1906, he feared the Peruvians would be led by their "sense of propriety, hospitality, and desire to display the good feeling existing between our countries, to an expense they can ill afford."[45] As a further indication of close ties, Peru had requested authorization to assign midshipmen to the U.S. fleet so they could learn from the Americans.[46] This request had been granted.

Peruvians followed the fleet's progress around South America with great interest, their sentiment subject to the occasional absurd rumor. Alleged activities of Japanese spies were constantly reported, and a suspect Japanese theatrical company had been imprisoned at the bidding, supposedly, of Minister Combs.[47]

When the battleships arrived on the morning of 20 February, clean and trim under a tropical sun, the people of Callao and Lima were ready for a show. The battleships did not fail them.[48] Entering port, they shifted from line of squadrons to line of divisions in a finely executed maneuver.[49] The arrival was accompanied by the normal round of salutes, including a fifteen-gun salute from the Peruvian ships in harbor according Rear Admiral Evans the honor normally rendered a vice admiral. As the ships completed their maneuver, the signal to anchor in present formation was hoisted, and after it was hauled down anchors hit the water, chains rattled as they paid out through hawsepipes, boat booms swung out, and colors rose on the after flagstaff of each ship.[50] Thomas recorded that, in his opinion, none of the ships was over ten or fifteen yards out of station when they anchored—a noteworthy feat of seamanship.[51]

Of the thousands of Peruvians that viewed the fleet's arrival from wharves, hinterlands, and water, the Americans seemed most impressed with those afloat. Great crowds turned out in everything from merchant steamers to rowboats, waving Peruvian and American flags and, according to one midshipman, shouting "*Viva los* Yankees."[52]

The five contracted colliers that had been awaiting the fleet were immediately called alongside by the First Division; the remaining ships, in response to the great change in latitude since the last port visit, spent the afternoon at sea swinging ship to compensate their magnetic compasses. Meanwhile the round of social engagements started up again in earnest. Here arrangements were complicated because most activities took place in Lima, some nine miles from Callao. Although Louis Maxfield commented on the mildness of the climate, Rear Admiral Emory found it unbearable, particularly at functions where special full dress uniform was required.[53]

One highlight of the visit was a gala banquet hosted by President Jose Pardo on his birthday—one he most conveniently shared with George Washington, 22 February. Each battleship was required to send ten officers and three midshipmen, and Rear Admiral Emory wrote that few would have attended otherwise.[54] But for this event orders could have been dispensed with; there were more volunteers than vacancies.[55]

The following afternoon President Pardo, who had been unable to receive Evans ashore because of the admiral's continued illness, visited the flagship *Connecticut*. He also initiated the now-standard complimentary messages between presidents.[56] Roosevelt's response to Pardo was prompt and most satisfactory from Peru's point of view; however, to some Americans it smacked of imperialism. It had included the decidedly unrepublican phrase "from me and my people," an unfortunate choice of words that American journalists used as proof of the president's "marked imperialistic and megalomaniac tendencies." In response to attacks Roosevelt maintained an uncharacteristic silence because, as he confided to his son, he had seen neither Pardo's message nor his own reply. The duty of drafting "one of the usual fatuous answers" had fallen upon Assistant Secretary of State Alvy A. Adee, who duly produced the suitably florid response and had Secretary of State Root sign it for the president.[57]

The central and unique event during this visit was a bullfight arranged for the fleet. Six bulls named in honor of the Americans were to be fought. President Pardo invited three thousand bluejackets and six hundred officers and had them carried to Lima in two special trains. The enlisted men, who marched from the railroad station to the bullring escorted by a Peruvian military band, took seats near the ring, while officers sat higher up in the *plaza de toros*.[58] After two or three fights the Americans decided that the bulls stood not a chance, and some were genuinely appalled by the cruelty of the sport. Robert Dunn, special correspondent for *Harper's Weekly* traveling with the fleet, made mention of bluejackets cheering loudly for the animals.[59] Some officers and a great many enlisted men departed halfway through the spectacle, fed up. The general consensus was that, while they were glad to have had this experience, it was not one they cared to repeat.[60]

Officers and men also availed themselves of the opportunity to see Lima's monuments: Pizarro's remains entombed in glass and the Senate chambers that had earlier been the site of the Inquisition.[61]

The behavior of the bluejackets, whose liberty expired at 8:00 P.M. daily, left little to be desired, and before the fleet departed Minister Combs cabled Secretary Root to express his admiration.[62]

As during previous port calls, on the last day the fleet returned local hospitality with a reception in the flagship. President Pardo and his ministers were regally entertained. Pardo, hoping to see the admiral, had the rare privilege of visiting for a few minutes with Evans in his quarters.[63]

Minister Combs received a welcome distinctly less warm. Throughout the visit his relations with senior officers of the fleet had been strained, a situation arising from his objection to the efforts of Evans's chief of staff, Captain Royal R. Ingersoll, to assert his commander in chief's authority even though Admiral Thomas was actually shouldering social responsibilities during the visit. Difficulties began at Combs's first encounter with Ingersoll, when the chief of staff requested that Combs, in Evans's name, invite the president to visit the fleet. Combs balked, saying the invitation should be delivered by the admiral personally.[64] As a result, Thomas delivered an invitation to dinner, but in Evans's flagship, where Ingersoll remained in charge of arrangements.[65] When Combs arrived in the *Connecticut* for dinner, he was surprised and deeply offended to find that he had been relegated to a position twentieth in seniority, below even Peruvian navy captains. The seating arrangement was an intentional snub, and in front of the president of Peru.[66]

A few minutes before 10:00 A.M. on departure day, 29 February 1908, the Peruvian cruiser *Almirante Grau* got under way flying the flag of President Pardo. She steamed through the fleet anchorage as, with all hands in full-dress uniform and rails manned, the American ships fired a simultaneous twenty-gun national salute to Peru. Then she moved to a position well outside the harbor and anchored.[67]

At 10:00 A.M. the divisions of the fleet got under way in sequence, forming a single column to pass in review before the president. The maneuver was slightly marred when a man from the *Georgia* jumped overboard. The *Georgia* had to sheer out of column to pick him up, while the next ship closed the gap. The *Georgia* recovered her lifeboat in time to take position at the rear of the column, and the fleet passed President Pardo as if nothing had happened.[68] Although he first thought the sailor involved was crazy, "on leisurely investigation," Rear Admiral Emory later reported, "it was found that the man's intention was to desert."[69]

The fleet continued without pause, shaping a course toward the open sea and the awaiting *Almirante Grau.* As individual ships passed her, rails were manned once again, marines presented arms, and bands played Peru's national anthem. After clearing the *Almirante Grau,* each ship opened up with a twenty-one-gun national salute.

Earlier, the tender *Yankton* had been dispatched on a rescue mission to search for an American merchant seaman, Fred Jeffs, who had been stranded in the Galapagos islands five months earlier, in October 1907.[70] The decision to send a ship had been publicly announced on 12 February by the Navy Department in response to a request from a prominent person in Connecticut who had interceded in Jeffs's case.[71] The *Yankton*'s thorough search proved fruitless, and the tender subsequently rejoined the fleet as it conducted an incident-free, 3,100-mile voyage to Magdalena Bay.[72]

Aboard the battleships gunnery officers were making full use of the time at sea drilling their men in final preparation for the annual record target practice.[73] The weather was fine and calm and the fleet steamed in line of squadrons, each day one squadron opening the distance between columns to about 8,000 yards by steering an oblique course. Thus battleships were positioned for range-finding exercises, measuring and recording the distance to their opposite numbers at two-minute intervals on signal from the flagship. The results were compared for accuracy at the end of each drill.[74]

In this manner the trip passed rapidly until, on 11 March, the battleships sighted the drab, barren mountains of Cape San Lucar.[75] They reduced speed in order to arrive at Magdalena Bay after daybreak on 12 March 1908.

Inhospitable though its surroundings might have been, Magdalena Bay itself, with over one hundred square miles of good anchorage ground, was perfectly suited to drills. The American navy had long wanted to get its hands on it.[76] The status of the bay had been the main topic during discussions held between Secretary of State Root and Mexican President Diaz in October 1907. Diaz recommended that his government grant the United States a five-year concession. The Mexican Senate, ever suspicious—with some reason—of American intentions, limited this to permission to maintain two colliers in the bay for a period of three years, "provided a like concession was made to the Government of Mexico by the United States."[77] Mexico remained particularly sensitive to any potential infringement of its sovereignty over Magdalena Bay and refused to allow the fleet to land marines for small arms practice. It also denied permission for the landing of any other armed parties, prohibited the hoisting of the American flag on shore, and stipulated that gunnery firing "not be directed toward the shore."[78]

Mexican sensitivities, however, were largely disregarded in Washington. Shortly after the fleet left Punta Arenas, Ambassador David E. Thompson forwarded a cable request that Mexico be informed of ports to be visited by the fleet and on what dates.[79] The response reported the fleet to be two days behind schedule and likely to arrive at Magdalena Bay on 17 March.[80] No further information was provided until the thirteenth, when Thompson cabled with understandable pique requesting permission to officially notify the Mexican government of the fleet's arrival, noting that Mexican newspapers were reporting it had reached Magdalena Bay on the twelfth, five days earlier than the Mexican government had been led to expect it.[81] Given that it had left Callao at 10:00 A.M. on 29 February and that the distance to Magdalena Bay is 3,100 miles, it would have been no feat to determine an arrival date of no later than 13 March. This change and its diplomatic significance should have been appreciated by the Bureau of Navigation by 29 February at the very latest; yet no evidence exists that anyone at the Navy Department ever calculated the time and distance factors or advised the State Department. Even Evans's wireless message to the Navy Department, sent in the early morning hours of 12 March, just before the fleet entered Magdalena Bay, failed to trigger an immediate notification of the State Department for transmission to Mexico.[82]

Now Mexico, which had planned to have the governor of Baja California meet the fleet in the gunboat *Tampico,* had to change arrangements at short notice. In view of this cavalier treatment, it would not be unreasonable if, once again, the Mexican government paused to reconsider the nature of its relationship with its powerful neighbor to the north.

Mexico's embarrassment, however, was swept aside by the momentous occasion of the successful completion of the first portion of the cruise. Accolades were showered on the fleet, and a "feeling of genuine satisfaction" prevailed in Washington. The accomplishment, the *New York Times* editorialized, "must silence the croakers for a long time" and put an end to the apprehension that had dogged the fleet since it left Hampton Roads.[83] Admiral Thomas expressed a similar sentiment, observing that it was *"in better condition for extended cruising than when we left Hampton Roads.* With the *greatest ease* we could continue on immediately to cruise around the world via the Suez Canal, stopping only to fill up with coal. . . ."[84]

Although the success pales in comparison with naval achievements later in the century, in 1908 it was remarkable, allaying fears about the ships' mechanical reliability and assuring naval planners that a fleet might undertake a lengthy cruise and arrive at its destination in battleworthy condition. For a nation struggling with the problem of defending two widely separated coasts, this conclusion was of great importance.

The day after the fleet's arrival Secretary Metcalf briefed President Roosevelt and his cabinet on the voyage. After hearing the report Roosevelt authorized Metcalf to announce that the fleet would begin its return journey around 6 July, traveling via Australia, Manila, and the Suez Canal.[85]

While the fleet's itinerary was being considered, more immediate matters occupied the attention of the men in the battleships. Colliers carrying coal to replenish depleted stocks awaited them, and quantities of timber had recently been left by the Pacific Fleet cruisers so that the battleships could build gunnery targets. The first few days at Magdalena Bay were occupied with coaling and preparing targets, laying out firing ranges, calibrating range-finding equipment, and conducting final prefiring drills for gun crews.

Gunnery practice, the annual graded shooting or "record practice," as it was then known, started for individual ships as soon as they had coaled and their targets and ranges were ready. The *Illinois* was one of the first to begin; she was finished by 18 March, and that day the *Rhode Island* commenced.[86] Upon completion, each ship conducted minelaying exercises as well as drills at clearing ship for action.[87] Ten days after arriving, ships were finishing up this work. Now it was time to conduct infantry drills in preparation for the parades scheduled in California.[88]

Before the fleet had reached Magdalena Bay Secretary Metcalf directed Evans to take the battleships on to San Diego, Santa Barbara, San Pedro, and Santa Cruz, arriving at San Francisco on 5 May.[89] The itinerary for these port visits was published on 17 March, and subsequent mails brought news of extensive preparations and elaborate receptions being planned.

At least one of the officers of the fleet was not looking forward to the California celebrations. Rear Admiral Robley D. Evans, the navy's senior officer on active duty and the last serving naval officer to have participated in the Civil War, announced on 14 March that for reasons of health he had asked to be relieved when the fleet reached San Francisco.[90] Evans had been wounded as a midshipman in the Union assault on Fort Fisher in 1865. A bullet entered his left leg, another shattered his right knee, and a third took off a toe and severely wrenched one of his ankles. Eventually he was returned to the active list, but he suffered pain for the rest of his life.[91]

Forty-two years after the assault on Fort Fisher Evans had risen to the highest seagoing position in the navy: commander in chief of the Atlantic Fleet. By this time his legs had developed painful rheumatism. Speculation in April 1907 that his health would force an early retirement was dismissed by him as "rot" invented by someone wanting to see him relieved.[92] Evans would not have had to look far for naval officers interested in seeing him retire. The General Board was displeased with his failure to exercise energetically their new battle plan during the Caribbean fleet exercise in spring of 1907.[93] Furthermore, the navy's inspector of target practice, Lieutenant Commander William S. Sims, had written at the time of the exercise that Evans had been, in the opinion of most in the fleet, "an almost complete failure" as commander in chief.[94]

As the battleships prepared for their long voyage there had been another spate of retirement rumors. According to the press Evans continued to treat them as a joke, but public assurances of the admiral's good health came suspiciously often. On the eve of the fleet's departure he was described as an "efficient survivor of the Civil War" who looked younger every day; in reality he was too ill to command the fleet effectively, and the president was familiar with his condition.[95]

Shortly after the departure Henry Reuterdahl surprised his host in the *Minnesota*, Rear Admiral Thomas, by commenting that it had been "touch and go" whether Evans would take the fleet to the Pacific. The subject had been discussed at a cabinet meeting, where it was decided that, though he was in no condition for the job, it would be better to let Evans remain "rather than run the risk of a newspaper sensation all over the country" by detaching him before the sailing of the fleet.[96] It is safe to assume that Roosevelt's awareness of Evans's condition was the reason he had taken the time to repeat last minute instructions to the second in command, Rear Admiral Thomas.[97]

Even before Evans's sortie ashore in Trinidad, Thomas had found him looking unwell.[98] Two days after the fleet left Trinidad, his condition deteriorated and he was forced to take to his bed.[99] As the voyage progressed his condition worsened. One night just before reaching Rio de Janeiro Evans, in great pain and depressed, experienced difficulty breathing; Captain Ingersoll feared he would not survive the night.[100] Thomas felt that Evans was in such bad shape that it was "criminal to himself and the Navy, and the fleet in particular," for him to continue to retain command.[101] Still Evans showed no inclination to step down. His retention of command resulted in a highly irregular arrangement that inevitably strained relations within the fleet's command echelon. Captain Ingersoll carried out all of the routine functions of the commander in chief except official duties ashore, the responsibility for which fell to Rear Admiral Thomas. Thus in essence, Thomas privately complained, three rear admirals had to follow the orders of a captain.[102]

Evans's condition remained little changed throughout the Rio visit and apparently further deteriorated during the trip to Punta Arenas. At this point Thomas decided that if there was no improvement by the day the fleet was scheduled to leave that port, he would assume command and involuntarily place Evans, now heavily drugged and continuing to suffer depression, on the sick list.[103] This plan was abandoned when Captain Ingersoll reported that Evans had improved enough to sit up in bed.[104] Evans remained very ill nonetheless and despite claims to the contrary in his autobiography, he played no role in navigating the fleet through the Strait of Magellan.[105]

It was under these conditions that Minister Combs forced the issue of Rear Admiral Thomas inviting the Peruvian president to visit the fleet. He concluded, quite correctly, that the problem arose from an anomaly in the command arrangements. In a separate confidential cable to Secretary Root he warned that Evans's "protracted . . . illness" was affecting the interests of the fleet. Furthermore, he reported, correspondents traveling with the fleet told him they had been suppressing the truth of the admiral's condition.[106]

Within the fleet, Evans's prolonged illness encouraged considerable speculation concerning future command arrangements. Rear Admiral Sperry had received the interesting intelligence from Ingersoll that when Evans finally stood down at San Francisco, Thomas, who was not scheduled to retire until October 1908, would also step aside.[107] Evans had publicly supported Sperry as his successor, and developments seemed favorable to his ambition.[108] He was not, however, content to let events unfold unassisted. His timely report to Secretary Metcalf on the fleet's progress was a calculated effort to publicize himself as the most logical candidate for the position of commander in chief, and he exerted indirect pressure through General Horace Porter.[109] Porter, a Civil War Medal of Honor recipient and influential Republican, had served as Roosevelt's ambassador to France and in 1908 was president of the Navy League. Sperry told him that he had written a lengthy report to Secretary Metcalf that might "attract attention."[110] To his wife he confided having said nothing of his aspiration to the secretary, but if General Porter should see Metcalf, he concluded, the report "might be a convenient basis for talk."[111]

As senior officers waited to hear from Washington, a rumor gained currency that Captain Wainwright of the *Louisiana* would be promoted and given command.[112] Thomas accepted this possibility philosophically, reporting that his early return home would "*more* than compensate for Teddy's insane 'penchant' for pushing young men to the front."[113] Sperry, however, panicked, dropped all pretense of subtlety, and asked General Porter to intercede for him.[114] The decision to appoint Sperry was finally taken on 17 March, though it was probably Roosevelt's intention all along that he should fill the top position.[115] Sperry was the next senior officer after Thomas and in that respect the logical candidate. The unusual interest Secretary Metcalf took in soliciting Sperry's views on the cruise before the fleet's departure strongly indicates that even then he was being considered for command. His case undoubtedly was assisted—if such assistance was necessary—by General Porter, and also by his conveniently timed cruise report, which got to Metcalf just as the nomination for command was being discussed.[116]

Evans's continued poor health led to the decision that he must leave the fleet at Magdalena Bay and undergo treatment at the Paso Robles hot springs, near San Luis Obispo, California, for which purpose the flagship *Connecticut* steamed north to San Diego on 30 March.[117] Though President Roosevelt had approved Evans's request for relief, it would not officially take effect until the fleet reached San Francisco.[118] He was in nominal command from his sick bed in Paso Robles; Thomas, still designated commander, Second Squadron, and senior officer present, performed all of Evans's duties, while Sperry, commander-in-chief designate, continued as commander of the Fourth Division. The latter privately complained about the situation, saying it inhibited him from getting on with the business of organizing the cruise.[119] This problem was resolved when Secretary Metcalf ordered Evans to have Sperry prepare an itinerary for the return cruise.

For another month command arrangements remained unsettled. Throughout April the nation received daily medical reports on Admiral Evans's condition, almost always optimistic, and Evans continued to maintain tenuous communications with Thomas whenever the fleet was in port.[120] Following Evans's relief in San Francisco, Thomas officially assumed command of the fleet. He held the position for less than a week, his assignment being only a token gesture in recognition of long service. Therefore it was mid-May before Sperry finally became commander in chief and the fleet command structure returned to normal.

SEVEN

Return to
God's Country

While the problems of succession to command occupied senior officers, individual battleship crews continued their record gunnery practice and drilled for the parades planned on the West Coast. The ships coaled once again, received a layer of paint to remove traces of rust, and were inspected by Rear Admiral Thomas. At 4:00 P.M. on 11 April the fleet steamed out of Magdalena Bay, with Thomas flying his flag on the *Connecticut*.[1]

As the 690-mile passage north progressed the men of the fleet grew jubilant over their return to home waters—"God's Country," or "*the* Country," as Louis Maxfield put it.[2] They followed the coastline and saw the monument marking the Mexican-American border. From that point on crowds lined the shore to see the fleet's arrival. Amid a flotilla of welcoming craft the battleships approached Coronado, California, a suburb of San Diego, and came to anchor off the imposing Hotel Del Coronado at 1:00 P.M. on 14 April, four months after their departure from Hampton Roads.

Despite advance publication of the entertainment schedule, the men were unprepared for the intensely effusive reception they received. Local boats delivered some thirty-three thousand oranges to the fleet, while another boat brought young women carrying armfuls of flowers. Although enlisted men were not granted liberty that first day, the officers who went ashore were overwhelmed. Like honored guests they descended a 700-foot pier specially built for the use of landing parties, and at its end they encountered large applauding crowds.[3] A carnival air hung over city streets that blazed with electric lights and beaches where red fires welcomed the fleet.[4]

The highlight of this visit came on 15 April when the naval brigade paraded. Sailors in sixty-four companies "with trousers reefed down in canvas leggings" and marines in sixteen companies marched for three miles through festive streets from the waterfront to City Park to receive the State of California's official welcome.[5]

While it was an impressive demonstration for the citizens of San Diego, for the men of the fleet it was like most parades, "hot, dusty and tiresome." The brigade had been landed in small boats after a ten-mile trip from the anchorage off Coronado. Including transit time to and from San Diego the ordeal took up more than ten hours, an inconvenience for which the warm reception helped to compensate.[6]

Parties of officers took automobile rides into the hinterlands of San Diego, covering a circuit of about seventy miles. The tourists were surprised at the interest taken in them by people along the route. At crossroads and ranch gates people gathered, in some places scattering roses over the road.[7] The fleet reception, in short, was beyond all expectation. It culminated with a ball for junior officers at the Hotel Del Coronado on Good Friday. The choice of date seemed in bad taste to some, but attendance was ordered and the event proved to be the most spectacular of any during the four-day visit.[8]

At 6:00 A.M. on Saturday, 18 April, the fleet got under way for the ten-hour trip to San Pedro. Despite the early hour people lined the beach again to see the battleships off. As they steamed north, keeping as close to the shore as navigation would permit, each successive vantage point along the coast was crowded with Californians anxious to view the passage of the fleet.[9] On arrival the beaches around San Pedro were swarming with people, more even than at San Diego, and to the men of the fleet it seemed as though all of Los Angeles had turned out.[10] The ships anchored for the night in a single column in the outer harbor. The next morning, Easter Sunday, protests from the Sunday Rest Association notwithstanding, the divisions would proceed independently to various Los Angeles ports—San Pedro, Long Beach, Santa Monica, and Redondo.[11]

In the meantime the fleet put on a searchlight show for the crowds before they made their way home. Many had to take an hour-long trolley ride back to Los Angeles. The public transportation system was overtaxed, the cars filling up rapidly but at the end of two hours hardly putting a dent in the crowd. As a result, some people chose to camp for the night on the bluff overlooking the harbor.[12]

Los Angeles's program of entertainment began on Monday, 20 April, with an elaborate plan to provide a full day's free entertainment for a quarter of the enlisted men on each of four successive days. On Thursday 250 officers were taken on auto tours of Los Angeles County. They left the city on the highway to Pasadena, where they enjoyed a feast at midday, and then proceeded to Hollywood, passing through extensive groves of orange, lemon, fig, and olive trees. Thousands of Civil War veterans cheered the officers as they passed through Sawtelle, and at Santa Monica virtually the entire population of the city was on hand to greet them. Next day the tour was repeated on a larger scale for 3,000 enlisted men.[13]

As departure day approached it was announced that the fleet would get under way at 5:00 A.M. on Saturday 25 April and that it would conduct maneuvers off Venice, Ocean Park, and Santa Monica before heading north to Santa Barbara. News of the planned display drew tens of thousands of people to Santa Monica, and as a result all accommodations were booked solid. Friday night, women and children slept on the beach or in the canyons outside the city. Others found space on the floor of City Hall. "The thousands who gathered at Venice whiled away the hours before daylight by dancing." When morning approached, men and women climbed rooftops and trees, risking life and limb to get a better view of the spectacle.[14] An estimated one hundred thousand people watched as the ships got under way at the appointed time and reunited in Santa Monica Bay. Unfortunately, just after maneuvers began fog closed in and they had to be abandoned.[15] With the final display aborted, ships once again shaped a northerly course, en route to their next port of call, Santa Barbara. The fog lifted before noon. Steaming close to the shore, the fleet completed its run and at 4:00 P.M. anchored in line of squadrons off Santa Barbara's State Street.[16]

A program of formal engagements had been organized for the officers—banquets and balls at the Potter Hotel, a reception in the extensive gardens of retired Rear Admiral Bowman H. McCalla's home, and a "flower battle."[17] The enlisted men, on the other hand, found little arranged for them. In sharp contrast to the visit to Los Angeles, the stay at Santa Barbara was marred by exorbitant prices for food and drink. Wives who had come to see their husbands in the fleet complained of unusually high hotel bills. Dissatisfaction boiled into violence when a restaurant owner overcharged two enlisted men. Word of the incident spread rapidly among the liberty party and crowds of sailors gathered in front of the restaurant, throwing stones. Windows and fixtures were broken and the owner and his employees fled. Men on shore patrol quickly dispersed the crowd, but discontent lingered. Santa Barbara was a bad liberty port for enlisted men, and after spending a short while there many took the train to Los Angeles or returned to their ships.[18]

The choice of final port visits before San Francisco had not been easy. Whereas San Diego, Los Angeles, and Santa Barbara were the major cities in their respective parts of the state, further north the navy had to cope with competing demands from local communities. San Luis Obispo, an inland city, insisted that the fleet stop for a day at Port Hartford so that its citizens might have the opportunity to entertain the men. The navy agreed only to conduct a parade "Valparaiso-style" through the bay on which the port was situated, without actually stopping. More seriously, Monterey and Santa Cruz had been in open competition for the attention of the fleet, a situation resolved by having it stay at Monterey for the first day of the visit, then dividing it between the two cities until the last day, when all the ships would visit Santa Cruz.[19]

By 4 May the full battleship fleet had assembled at Santa Cruz. At 1:30 P.M. the torpedo boat flotilla arrived after a stormy passage from San Pedro. That same day, further to the north, the eight armored cruisers of the Pacific Fleet entered San Francisco Bay after a three-day passage from Seattle.[20]

Early next morning the *Connecticut* went to Monterey to pick up Admiral Evans, who on the preceding evening had moved from his room at the Paso Robles health resort to accommodations on the special railway car *Sacramento,* which had been provided and specially decorated for his use. "I am a new man today," he claimed as he left Paso Robles. "Didn't I say I'd lead the fleet through the Golden Gate?"[21] The old admiral, unfortunately, was not a new man. Although he was on board the *Connecticut* for the naval pageant that unfolded the following day, he led the fleet in name only, remaining in his emergency cabin aft of the flag bridge. All orders issued came from Captain Ingersoll.

San Francisco, which had been the declared destination of the fleet since July of the preceding year, had been preparing for the long-awaited visit for some months, in conjunction with sister city Oakland drawing up a plan of lavish entertainment for the officers and men. Much of the money to finance this came from private subscriptions. Ironically, one of the largest donations, three thousand dollars, was presented to the reception committee by the Japanese community of San Francisco.[22]

San Francisco increased the magnitude of its welcome when it was announced that Secretary of the Navy Metcalf would review the fleet upon its arrival. A week later this was revised: the review would include all ships on the Pacific Coast.[23] With these plans fully publicized, the city drew as many as half a million visitors from throughout the West the first week of May. Railway officials estimated they had brought more than 300,000 people into the city in the forty-eight hours before the fleet's arrival. One correspondent reported that on the night of 5 May a huge red bonfire burned on the peak of Mount Tamalpais, signaling that the fleet had come to anchor off San Francisco. "That night began the greatest movement that the Pacific Coast had ever seen, and by daylight the entire country surrounding the bay was alive with people."[24]

The morning of the great day, as a mass of spectators gathered until both sides of the Golden Gate were "black with people, [and] all the way from Tamalpais round by the Marin shore was a great multitude," the fleet remained anchored about ten miles out to sea.[25] The battleships *Nebraska* and *Wisconsin* arrived that morning, bringing the total strength to eighteen battleships, six destroyers, and six auxiliaries. At 11:00 A.M., amidst patches of fog, the thirty ships got under way for the Golden Gate.

As they approached San Francisco the sun broke through and burned away the fog, revealing to the men of the fleet a huge WELCOME sign in fifty-foot-high white letters on the side of Telegraph Hill. The distance to shore decreased and they were amazed at the mass of bodies they beheld—an estimated one million people. Unhindered by small craft, all of which were kept well clear, the fleet steamed through the Golden Gate in perfect formation and received salutes from the army forts guarding the bay. The ships continued past Angel Island, where the Pacific Fleet lay with anchors at short stay. It joined the battleships when they approached, and the multitude on shore now saw the unprecedented spectacle of forty-six ships of the navy proceeding south through the bay, then reversing course. The flagship *Connecticut* fired a seventeen-gun salute to Secretary Metcalf as she passed the gunboat *Yorktown,* which flew his flag. Following this ceremony the ships anchored in three columns off San Francisco, flagships just to the east of the Oakland ferry route. Expressing the feeling that the review provoked, one spectator recorded, "Our hearts beat high with pride in our own country, and in the sure protection of its invincible strength."[26]

Immediately after the ships anchored, flag and commanding officers of both fleets made their way to the *Connecticut* to pay their respects to Admiral Evans, whose blue two-star flag flew for the last time from her truck. Shortly afterward, he went ashore to join his wife and daughter at the St. Francis Hotel.[27] Although he was supposed to review the fleet with Secretary Metcalf and participate in the change of command, his poor health interfered. Unknown to all, Evans had taken his final departure.

A massive naval and military parade was held the next day, 7 May. Landing brigades from both the Atlantic and the Pacific fleets were put ashore for the occasion. With over seventy-five hundred marines and bluejackets, they constituted the largest U.S. naval landing force ever to be fielded in peace or war up to that time. Admiral Evans, who had agreed to participate in the parade, shared the second carriage in the line of march with San Francisco's mayor and was warmly received by the thousands who lined the way.[28]

Next day the crowds had another spectacle in store. On a bay bathed in brilliant sunshine Secretary Metcalf formally reviewed the combined Atlantic and Pacific fleets from the *Yorktown*. She passed between the two columns of ships nearest Oakland—the Pacific Fleet's armored cruisers and the battleships of the Atlantic Fleet's Second Squadron—then came about and steamed between the First Squadron's battleships and the torpedo boat destroyers that lay inshore of the heavy ships. Throughout the review ships, their sides manned, their quarterdecks crowded with officers and marine guards, "kept up a roar of salutes" while red-coated bands played the national anthem.[29]

An official reception was hosted by the City of San Francisco at the St. Francis Hotel on the third night. During dinner Admiral Evans, wheeled into the room to make a farewell speech, attacked Henry Reuterdahl, who was present at the dinner, for his highly publicized criticism of defects in American battleship design and navy administration. In defense of the service, Evans emphasized the strength of its personnel. It is not "armor belts or waterlines that win battles," he claimed. "It is the men who shoot the straightest and hardest and can stand punishment the longest. If you have such men—and we have just that kind of stuff in our navy—it makes no difference whether the armor belts are of leather or wood, or eggshells, or anything else."[30] He concluded his last public speech as commander in chief with a plea for enlargement of the navy. Afterward he was wheeled back to his room.

But given crews of equal capability and motivation, armor belts and waterlines could indeed determine the outcome of a naval engagement. Admiral Evans's reluctance to address the substantive aspects of the criticism may be interpreted as tacit admission of the validity of Reuterdahl's arguments.

Even this brief appearance severely strained the old admiral, and on the advice of his physician he was confined to his room at the St. Francis. Next day his flag was hauled down for the last time and command of the fleet was transferred for a short interregnum to Rear Admiral Charles M. Thomas. At 6:20 P.M. Rear Admiral Evans and his family embarked on the Southern Pacific's special railway car *Sunset* and began the long journey east to Washington and retirement.[31]

EIGHT

Criminations and Recriminations

Deployment of the battleship fleet to the Pacific was the most highly publicized indication that the navy's operating forces had been reorganized. Beginning with the establishment of the North Atlantic Fleet in 1902, this reorganization had been marked by a progressive concentration of forces, primarily in the Atlantic. By the beginning of 1907 all of the navy's operational battleships had been assembled in a single fighting unit—the Atlantic Fleet.

Reorganization in the Pacific had not proceeded apace. The Asiatic Fleet and the Pacific Squadron continued independent operations until 27 February 1907. At that time the secretary of the navy issued an order to consolidate "under one administrative command . . . all cruising vessels in the Pacific Ocean."[1] A further adjustment was made at the time of the cruise: two modern armored cruisers were transferred from the Atlantic Fleet to the Pacific. Now the main battle formation of the Pacific Fleet, the First Squadron, consisted of two divisions of modern armored cruisers under the direct command of the fleet commander in chief.[2]

By the beginning of 1908 the navy's operating forces had achieved a reasonable degree of centralized control. Two fleet commanders in chief, Atlantic and Pacific, exercised direct command of all major seagoing forces, and the major combatants of both those forces were organized into reasonably homogeneous formations capable of maneuvering as tactical entities.

Such changes enjoyed no parallel in the navy's shore-based establishment. The system of administration, including development and maintenance of ships and shore stations through a number of bureaus charged with specific support functions, had been established by law in 1842 and had survived intact for six decades. The only concession to vast technological changes that had occurred during this period was the addition of several more bureaus.

The efficient maintenance and operation of a large and rapidly growing fleet required an unprecedented amount of coordination among technical bureaus and between those bureaus and line officers at sea. This, however, rarely occurred. Writing in 1909, Rear Admiral George W. Melville, in an unfortunate effort to justify the methods of the bureau system, stated that on matters of general naval policy he could not remember one time in his sixteen years as chief of the Bureau of Steam Engineering (1887–1903) that the eight bureau chiefs had been "called together as a body to discuss or settle anything." His opinion, furthermore, had never been asked on matters of navigation or strategy, and he "certainly never offered any suggestions on such subjects to the Secretary or any other official." He attended to his own duties and, "as a rule, every other Bureau Chief attended to his, each keeping clear of the other's work."[3] This state of affairs was far from that which Secretary of the Navy Abel P. Upshur had envisioned when in 1842 Congress was considering his reorganization plan. "These bureaus," he advised, "should be conducted in harmony each with the others. . . ."[4]

The need for closer coordination resulted in continuous debate over the most efficient arrangement for the organization of the Navy Department from the inception of the "New Navy" in the 1880s until World War I. Efforts at establishing a navy general staff to supervise and coordinate the bureaus ran into stiff opposition because, however efficient such a staff might have been, it threatened to encroach on the long-established territories of the bureau chiefs. Their positions of influence at stake, they raised the specious specter of loss of civilian control over the navy, claiming that reform plans, most notably the introduction of a general staff, would reduce the secretary of the navy to a mere figurehead to be manipulated by the chief of that staff.

Of equal importance, administrative reform threatened to interfere with the system of political patronage that influenced the allocation of naval appropriations. This system, jealously guarded by certain congressmen, was largely responsible for the navy's unsatisfactory shore-based support structure. "Naval administration as it is," one contemporary succinctly observed, "bears such an unusual crop of fat plums that strong pressure of public opinion will be required to force the politicians to relinquish their familiar requisites."[5]

As early as 1901 bureau chiefs had started receiving from a number of middle-rank officers a series of cogently argued criticisms of the nation's new battleships. The letters had been pigeonholed or otherwise discounted by the Navy Department, presumably because acceptance of their validity implied failure on the part of the bureaus responsible for alleged defects. The bureaucracy's unwillingness to act on criticism was inherent and undoubtedly exacerbated by professional rivalry between line and staff officers. Inaction, however, could not still the growing concern of a younger generation of officers who actually manned the ships.

One of the more vocal and articulate critics was William Snowden Sims, who later rose to fame as commander of U.S. Naval Forces in Europe during World War I. Assigned to the *Kentucky* following a tour of duty as naval attaché in Paris, which had familiarized him with the latest European designs, Lieutenant Commander Sims was appalled to find grave design errors in the nation's newest battleship. He sent a lengthy report to the Navy Department pointing out deficiencies.[6] Among other things, he severely criticized the turrets with their oversized ports and unprotected ammunition hoists, which permitted direct access to the magazines and thereby endangered the entire ship in the event of a turret explosion or fire.[7] His goal was to call the attention of the secretary of the navy to the inefficiencies of the Navy Department, that is, "how they could get so many fatal mistakes into the same ship."[8]

Sims's objections were shared by many senior officers. Rear Admiral Henry Clay Taylor had proposed the establishment of a navy general staff in 1900 as a method to channel the efforts of various bureaus, but in the face of opposition from Secretary of the Navy Long, he had modified his proposal and gained authorization for the establishment of a purely advisory body, the General Board. Further efforts to gain authorization for a general staff were blocked by the bureau chiefs, a conservative assistant secretary, and the chairman of the Naval Affairs Committee, Senator Eugene Hale.[9] Admiral Taylor was able to accept these setbacks with equanimity, for, as Daniel J. Costello has written, he was an "evolutionist when it came to naval administration." He knew that only through patience and perseverence would opposition to the general staff idea be overcome.[10]

After Taylor's sudden death in 1904 attitudes polarized. No officer enjoyed Dewey's complete support on the sensitive issue of reform; the Admiral of the Navy was reluctant to commit his famous name and the dignity of his office to additional new schemes. A reorganization plan proposed by Secretary of the Navy Bonaparte in 1906 encountered opposition from the bureaus and Senator Hale, sharing the fate of earlier reforms.[11] With the loss of Taylor's moderate, gradual approach to change and the failure of the 1906 effort, more insistent reformers saw no avenue within the establishment by which they might legitimately pursue their goal. The debate would have to go public.

Although the most publicized aspects of the summer of 1907 were the war scare and the decision to send the battleship fleet to the Pacific, this period was also noteworthy for a renewal of reform agitation and for acrimonious public criticism of the Navy Department. The opening salvo of the new round of debate was fired by *The Navy,* a magazine thought to reflect the views of some senior naval officers. The June 1907 issue highlighted defects in the battleships *Oregon, Kearsarge,* and *Kentucky,* claiming the main-turret gun ports to be oversized and the main guns therefore unprotected. Furthermore, armor belts had been incorrectly placed, turret ammunition hoists badly designed, and speeds in actual service never approached those reached on sea trials.[12] The Navy Department reaction to this well-intended criticism was to deny the defects and adopt the position maintained by the chief of the Bureau of Construction and Repair throughout the months of bitter debate that followed: the ships "had been built up to the best conception of the naval architects of the day." In fact, the department had been aware of defects for at least six years.[13]

The Navy resumed the attack in July, rebutting department statements and adding further detail to its charges of the preceding month. In reference, for example, to the huge gun ports in the *Kentucky* and *Kearsarge,* it reported that during the recent European cruise officers in those ships had attempted to conceal actual gun port size by building turret shutters of wood and painting them to look like steel.[14] This article elicited an unexpected response from the Navy Department. Rear Admiral Willard H. Brownson, chief of the Bureau of Navigation and acting secretary of the navy, acknowledged the defects but claimed they had now been corrected; the gun ports, for instance, were smaller in later battleships.[15] This partial admission led at least one opposition paper to infer the probability "that the rest of *The Navy*'s charges are well founded."[16] Where there's smoke, there must be fire.

Soon after, Captain Henry McCrea assumed command of the battleship *Georgia* in Boston and took his new command to sea for gunnery exercises. Later that day a powder charge ignited during a firing run for the aft eight-inch-gun turret, killing ten men and wounding eleven others. Among the fatalities was Lieutenant Caspar F. Goodrich, Jr., son of the commandant of the New York Navy Yard. After Evans Rear Admiral Goodrich was the seniormost officer on active duty.[17] The tragedy was but the latest in a series, the most costly of which had occurred on board the battleship *Missouri* in 1904. The *Georgia* explosion was finally attributed to "flareback," that is, burning particles from a charge that blew back through the gun and prematurely ignited the next charge.[18]

Public reaction to the *Georgia* incident fueled the debate over the safety of battleship turrets. *Scientific American* attributed the explosion to unnecessary haste, concluding that the underlying cause of all turret accidents was a tendency during target practice "to neglect certain rules of caution, in order to acquire that speed of loading which is essential to rapidity of fire and the scoring of the highest possible number of hits in a given time on the target."[19] This argument failed to take into account the certainty that should the guns ever be fired in anger, an even greater need for rapidity of fire would exist. Clearly a system would have to be developed for the automatic ejection of any material lingering in the guns from the previous charge at a speed greater than that attainable in the loading and firing cycle.

The turret debate occasioned further consideration of ammunition hoist designs. In each of the turret accidents of the previous few years, only good fortune or individual heroic action had saved the navy from greater tragedy caused by faulty hoist designs. In American battleships cylindrical lifts carried shells and powder for large-caliber guns from handling rooms deep in the ship directly to the turret above. A fire in the turret could easily spread via the hoist to the ammunition handling room and surrounding magazines. This was a critical shortcoming, particularly because it had been corrected in European designs. In contemporary European battleships, hoists worked in two stages, the charges being conveyed from the handling room to a platform under the turret, then transferred horizontally to a separate enclosed hoist that lifted them to the turret itself.

Public discussion of battleship faults prompted a search for those responsible for perpetuating them. Once again, *The Navy* led the attack, focusing on the bureaus. It claimed they had been "deaf to energetic protests of distinguished seagoing officers," and that the Navy Department built ships "with far too little reference to the requirements of the men who handle" them. The bureaus had had full access for several years to information regarding foreign advances in warship construction. The wisdom of separating turrets from handling rooms and of two-stage ammunition hoists had been known to the Bureaus of Ordnance and Construction and Repair for at least five years. *The Navy* concluded that the bureau system had been "twisted into a means of protecting 'conservatism' and perpetuating inexcusable defects in our warships," and recommended that Congress intervene.[20]

Clearly, the Navy Department was under heavy attack well before the fleet sailed from Hampton Roads. The chief of the Bureau of Construction and Repair, Washington L. Capps, devoted the bulk of his 1907 annual report to the secretary of the navy to defense against alleged defects. Capps claimed that in every instance since the Spanish-American War seagoing officers had had a role in designing the ships they were now criticizing, and that "the present battleship fleet of the United States Navy is fully equal in all respects to that of any equal number of vessels in any other navy designed during the same period."[21] Capps's explanation had no practical effect on the growing clamor for naval reform.

It was inevitable that the rising tide of criticism, corresponding as it did with preparations for the fleet cruise, would both affect and be affected by it. The connection between the cruise and naval reform was clear to S. S. McClure, the crusading magazine publisher. On 4 October Henry Reuterdahl informed Lieutenant Commander Sims that while he was discussing the fleet cruise with McClure, the condition of the fleet had been raised. Reuterdahl had told McClure about an article he had written in 1904, following exchanges of views with Sims, and McClure was enthusiastic about printing it.[22] The article summarized Sims's long-standing criticisms of the Navy. Originally, he had strongly advised against its publication, believing the necessary reforms could be achieved from within the service. But by October 1907 the situation was much altered. Although the reforms he sought had still not been implemented, Sims felt encouraged by *The Navy*'s articles.[23] The magazine's continuing campaign and Sims's lack of success in achieving reform from within the service undoubtedly influenced his attitude toward release of Reuterdahl's article. When Reuterdahl suggested that it "would be a campaign document for better things," Sims lent his support.[24]

The result was a piece entitled "The Needs of Our Navy," published in the January 1908 edition of *McClure's Magazine,* which appeared on newsstands on 21 December 1907.[25] Reuterdahl's list of battleship defects was not new, but *McClure's* had a mass circulation and Reuterdahl wrote in nontechnical language. An amazed public could easily understand that not one of the new battleships representing a public investment of 145 million dollars had, or had yet been planned to have, waterline armor reaching more than six inches above the water. Further, said Reuterdahl, freeboard was so low that it precluded effective use of the forward main battery in any seaway and limited the use of broadside guns on a ship's windward side.[26] He described at length the dangers of the open shaft leading to magazines and other deficiencies in design. Responsibility, he reported, lay squarely on the shoulders of the bureaus. In compelling detail he outlined the fifteen-year struggle for adoption of a safe ammunition hoist as proof that the bureaus resisted reform. Their programs required millions of dollars to implement. "It is clearly contrary to all reason to expect a board which instituted and developed such policies to do anything but defend them. Their reversal means confession, as in the case of the open turret, of fatal blunders, costing a tremendous sum to rectify," Reuterdahl wrote. He concluded by condemning the lack of external supervision of bureaus: "So long as any system exists which both originates the plans for the navy, and has the right to pass judgment on the criticisms of those plans, so long will the first interest of the men in charge of it be to crush all radical departure from the policies to which they stand committed."[27]

Reuterdahl's comments were not limited to ship design and the bureau system. Citing the advanced age of senior officers, he attacked the promotion system. In 1906 the chief of the Bureau of Navigation reported that the average age of American admirals was sixty-one, of captains fifty-eight, and that the age was increasing.[28] This situation was unique to the American navy; foreign navies selected officers for promotion and retired the rest at an earlier age, a process that cleared the way for more rapid promotion of promising officers. In the American navy, "the column of officers forms and passes on, Indian file, changed practically not at all but by death or retirement," Reuterdahl reported. He claimed that the late age of promotion meant senior officers had little training in higher command. Retirement age was sixty-two; just as officers reached the highest positions, they had to retire.[29]

The initial press response, which occurred as the battleship fleet approached its first port of call at Trinidad, was to adopt a neutral stance, reporting both Reuterdahl's and the Navy Department's side of the story. This studied impartiality almost immediately ended when an unrelated event highlighted problems within the bureaus.

Some months before the fleet's departure, Rear Admiral Willard H. Brownson, chief of the Bureau of Navigation, had been grappling with a nettlesome problem: the assignment of a commanding officer for the hospital ship *Relief,* scheduled for commissioning early in 1908 so that she could join the cruise. Under normal circumstances such an assignment would be a minor detail in the daily routine of his bureau. In this instance it was to become a *cause célèbre.* As a result of the influence of Surgeon General Presley M. Rixey, chief of the Bureau of Medicine and Surgery and the president's personal physician, President Roosevelt had in 1906 agreed that a medical officer should command the ship, with a civilian sailing master to tend to its actual navigation.

Brownson, like his predecessor, Rear Admiral George A. Converse, interpreted the current statutory regulations as excluding all but line officers from commanding navy ships. He therefore opposed the assignment of a medical officer to command the *Relief* but postponed the inevitable confrontation until after the fleet had sailed. On 22 December Brownson, Rixey, and Secretary Metcalf met with the president to resolve the issue. After Brownson and Rixey had stated their cases, Roosevelt decided in favor of Rixey. Two days later Brownson concluded that his position as chief of the Bureau of Navigation had been compromised by the president's veto of his objection, and resigned.[30]

News of Brownson's resignation was known within hours, and speculation as to the reason began immediately.[31] Disregarding navy regulations forbidding unau-

Trying on Her New Necklace
(*Literary Digest* 35:1908)

Au Revoir
(New York *Herald*, 16 December 1907)

Left: President Theodore Roosevelt bids farewell to Rear Admiral Robley D. Evans, 16 December 1907. Evans was permitted to retain command of the fleet even though the president and his cabinet had concluded he was in no condition for the job. Evans became bedridden shortly after the fleet's departure. He was reportedly often sedated with opium, but he retained command of the fleet throughout the South American portion of the cruise. (USNI)

Below: The Atlantic Battleship Fleet standing out of Hampton Roads, 16 December 1907. The *Connecticut* is in the foreground. The *Georgia,* flagship of Rear Admiral William H. Emory, commander, Second Division, is the fourth ship to the left. (USNI)

Top left: A battleship crew pauses to pose during coaling. (USNI)

Bottom left: Officers and men on liberty in Port of Spain, Trinidad, December 1907. The sailors seem intent on augmenting the shipboard menagerie by acquiring exotic tropical birds. One of the officers is carrying a Kodak box camera, which by 1907 was in general use. (USNI)

Right: Sailors being inducted into the Order of Neptune while crossing the equator en route to Rio de Janeiro, January 1908. The ceremony bears a striking resemblance to one in which the author participated fifty years later. (USNI)

Right: Rapt attention to the progress of this wheelbarrow race aboard the *Connecticut* attests to the popularity of shipboard entertainments in 1908. (Naval Historical Center)

Below: Punta Arenas with the Atlantic battleship fleet at anchor, February 1908.

Top left: Henry Reuterdahl (Naval Historical Center)

Bottom left: The fleet transitting the Strait of Magellan, viewed from the USS *Georgia.* Ships immediately astern are the *New Jersey, Rhode Island, Virginia,* and *Minnesota.* At the *Georgia*'s upper left is a training device for gunnery aiming.

Above: The Chilean training ship *General Baquedano* at anchor in Valparaiso. The ship is full dressed and has her yards manned to act as flagship for Chilean President Pedro Montt to review the American battleship fleet, February 1908.

PLAZA TOROS

LIMA BULL-RING

SEASON 1907-1908

GRAND GALA BULL FIGHT
IN HONOUR OF THE

NORTH-AMERICAN SQUADRON

to celebrate its happy arrival at the port of Callao

Twelfth bull-fight
MONDAY 24th OF FEBRUARY 1908

at three p. m.

Under the presidency of the commision of public spectacles of the Hon. Municipality

Six bulls will be played and killed; belonging to the famous stock of **"RINCONADA DE MALA"** the property of Dr. Don Jesús de Asín and the technical details of the programme directed by a competent judge of "sport".

THE PERSONNEL OF THE QUADRILLE IS AS FOLLOWS

CAPEADORES DE A CABALLO
Juan Francisco Céspedes — Emiliano Gallese

MATADORES
Francisco Bonal (Bonarillo)   Angel García Padilla
José Moreno (Lagartijillo chico)

SOBRESALIENTE DE ESPADAS
Emilio Gabarda (Gabardito)

BANDERILLEROS
José Balbastre (Pepín de Valencia) — Luis Estival (Africano)
Emilio Gabarda (Gabardito) — Manuel Marzal (Corrajillas de Valencia) — Tomás Ibáñez (Metralla)   Juan Siani (Rubio de Lima)

PUNTILLEROS
Africano y Corrajillas de Valencia

NAMES OF THE BULLS

1—The gallant **"ALFRED"** in honour of Admiral Evans.
2—The heroic **"RANGER"** in honour of Admiral Thomas.
3—The brave **TEDDY** in honour of Admiral Emory.
4—The **"SHU-FLY"** in honour of Admiral Sperry.
5—**"BANJO"** in honour of the Officers of the navy.
6—**"YANKEE DOODLE"** in honour of the Sailors.

N.B. The few disposable places on sale will be sold at calle Mercaderes Nº 148 until 12 m. of the day of the bull fight. —If any bull should be unrruled during the fight, the public will have no right to demand another. —Under pain of imprisonment it is absolutely forbidden to enter the ring or throw objects which may cause damage to the bull fighters, or ...

The special bullfight in honor of the fleet included bulls bearing the names Teddy, Shu-Fly, Banjo, and Yankee Doodle. A good many of the sailors left the Plaza de Toros when, after the first few kills, they became convinced the animals did not stand a fair chance.

A gunnery target shows the success of the *Vermont* during record target practice at Magdalena Bay, April 1908.

The *Ohio*'s crew members replace targets during the record target practice at Magdalena Bay.

Left: The combined Atlantic and Pacific fleets at anchor in San Francisco Bay, May 1908. To date this was the greatest display of naval strength on the Pacific coast. (USNI)

Right: Rear Admiral Charles Mitchell Thomas, commander, Second Squadron, U.S. Atlantic Fleet, and from 9 May to 15 May 1908, commander in chief. Thomas is boarding his flagship, the *Minnesota,* in San Francisco shortly before suffering a fatal heart attack.

Below: Men of the fleet, with the *Maine's* detachment in the foreground, parade through San Francisco, 7 May 1908. The city's Hall of Records is in the background, left.

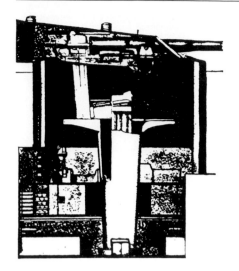

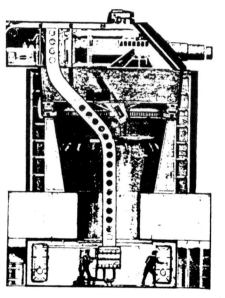

Left: The two-stage turret of foreign navies. This plan, taken from the Paris World's Fair catalogue of Vickers & Maxim in 1900, indicates the separation of the turret proper from the magazines below. The ammunition is hoisted through an enclosed trunk to a platform under the turret. From this trunk it is mechanically pushed into another closed passage and drawn by a second hoist up to the breech of the gun. At no time is the ammunition exposed. This turret was designed in 1898. (*McClure's Magazine* 30: 1908)

Right: The American navy's open turret. This drawing, based on a plan published in the *Scientific American,* shows the guns standing directly above the unprotected handling room and the magazine. The ammunition car, shown at the bottom of the plan, slides up on the steel guide extending above it to the gun. This car is entirely unprotected. The horizontal black line indicates the temporary partition between the turret proper and the handling room. (*McClure's Magazine* 30:1908)

A group of seamen, one holding the inevitable pet, poses beneath the after turret of the *Minnesota* while the fleet visits Seattle and a female visitor looks on. Sailors of the day devised as many ways to wear the white hat as sailors of later generations. (USNI)

Ensign Harold R. Stark (USNI)

Midshipman Raymond A. Spruance

Stark and Spruance, along with Halsey and Kimmel, paid their first visit to Pearl Harbor in 1908. All four became principal actors in the Pacific war thirty-three years later. (USNI)

Pigs, goats, monkeys, cats, dogs, exotic birds were numerous in the ships of the battleship fleet. At Seattle sixteen bear cubs were added to the fleet menagerie, to be followed later by kangaroos and a variety of other antipodean oddities. (Naval Historical Center)

Commander William Snowden Sims, USN
(USNI)

Chief Constructor Washington L. Capps, USN
(Naval Historical Center)

Following the Flag
(*Current Literature* 44:1908)

thorized public statements by officers, Rixey issued a lengthy typewritten statement to the press outlining his position regarding the *Relief.* In so doing, he inadvertently cast a spotlight on the interbureau conflicts about which Henry Reuterdahl had written. After summarizing the history of medical officers in command of army hospital ships, Rixey stated that the Bureau of Navigation had meddled too much with the Bureau of Medicine and Surgery.[32]

In the days that followed Admiral Brownson remained silent, asserting that navy regulations forbade him to make any public statements on the subject. The manifest inequity of a system permitting Rixey to air his views while Brownson remained stifled by navy regulations raised an outcry that the president publicly release all of the correspondence on the affair.[33]

The press immediately appreciated the significance of the affair. Who commanded the *Relief* was inconsequential; but the unbusinesslike nature of the organization that allowed internal struggles such as this was not. "The poor old navy hospital ship *Relief,*" one paper reported, "gives promise at last of affording real relief to the navy from the most serious ailment from which it has suffered in many years."[34]

President Roosevelt publicly rebuked Admiral Brownson, denouncing his resignation as "unseemly and improper." That and the criticism of battleship design, Roosevelt wrote, had "undoubtedly been prejudicial to the interest of the navy and may seriously impair the confidence in the navy which is essential to securing the legislation so sorely needed by [it]."[35] This intemperate intervention enlisted sympathy for the admiral and provoked severe criticism of the president, even by those journals that thought he was right on the subject of the *Relief.*[36]

Rear Admiral Thomas, who received full news of the incident while the fleet was in Rio de Janeiro, was "proud to death" of Brownson's stand and felt certain he would have navy backing. "Dear Old Willard has gained a great victory for the Navy and has wound up his Naval Career in a blaze of glory," he wrote.[37]

The tide of criticism that reached its high-water mark following publication of Henry Reuterdahl's article could not be ignored. Bureaucratic inefficiency and perpetuation of error threatened to jeopardize President Roosevelt's newly announced naval construction program, which included four new dreadnoughts.[38] Therefore, at the beginning of January 1908 when Senator Eugene Hale, chairman of the Senate Naval Affairs Committee, introduced a bill to increase navy and marine corps efficiency, he assured the committee that hearings would bring to the surface all the facts about "recent controversies between officers, charges made in magazine articles, and criminations and recriminations that have been flung back and forth."[39]

This promise of congressional investigation did little to slow the pace at which the subject was pursued by the press. *Scientific American* published a technical but biased defense of the Navy Department's design policies.[40] While it "proved conclusively" that the Navy Department's policy regarding the location of armor belts was sound, others were reflecting on the state of the battleship fleet when it left Hampton Roads.[41] *McClure's* renewed its attack in February, reporting that "except in one or two ships where [the armor belt] barely appeared, it was below water—in some cases nearly a foot. There was not, strictly speaking, a battle-ship in the fleet leaving Hampton Roads. It was, as far as its armor was concerned, a fleet of slow armored cruisers and was familiarly alluded to as such by one of its highest officers."[42] Remarkably, *McClure's* may have erred on the side of the conservatives with this comment. The battleships did have too much draft, and their armor belts were submerged. According to one naval officer, the commanding officer of the Boston Navy Yard said that when the battleship *New Jersey* left Boston for the fleet rendezvous at Hampton Roads, it was drawing twenty-eight feet four inches. "This put the top of the [armor] belt two feet underwater and the ship was dangerously overloaded. A collision in the harbor letting in water above the armor belt and she must have turned turtle."[43] On the same topic, however, *The Navy* was accused by *Scientific American* of "out-Heroding Herod" in claiming that when the *Connecticut* sailed for the Pacific, "her [armor] belt was submerged 'to the extent of a full foot'."[44]

The Navy Department, although stunned by the publicity from Reuterdahl's article, could not have been surprised by its contents. No less a personage than Admiral of the Navy Dewey had six months earlier summarized the armor belt problem for Secretary Metcalf, stating categorically that when "our battleships now in commission are loaded the waterline belt is awash or entirely submerged. In the *Connecticut* and *Louisiana* [the two newest types] the armor is about three inches below the waterline with full stores and not full ammunition." Dewey recommended that in future ships the armor belt be designed to afford maximum protection at full-load displacement, and that in earlier ships all unnecessary weights be removed and the belts raised as far as possible.[45]

Immediately after receiving this report Secretary Metcalf read another assessing the armor belt of the newly authorized dreadnought battleships *North Dakota* and *Delaware*. Lieutenant Commander Frank K. Hill, its author, concluded the belt would be only six inches above water at full-load displacement. These findings had been shown to Admiral Dewey, who requested they be submitted to Rear Admiral Converse, president of the Board on Construction. Hill reported that Converse agreed with his assessment but felt nothing could be done because Secretary Metcalf had ordered that no changes be made in those vessels.[46]

Admiral Dewey's comments elicited no reaction. However, the Navy Department's response to the submission from Hill, an officer lacking Dewey's seniority and influence, provides an illuminating example of the bureaucracy's attitude toward criticism from officers of the line. Referring to Hill's report, Admiral Converse reported that the Board on Construction was unanimous in its opinion that no change whatever should be made in the distribution of armor for the two dreadnoughts.[47] Five days later Converse addressed an arrogant letter to Secretary Metcalf about Hill, expressing regret that his board's time "should be unnecessarily taken up in giving serious consideration to . . . criticisms which have so little intrinsic merit."[48] As Hill's letter had been forwarded at the request of the Admiral of the Navy, Converse's response constituted an indirect attack on Dewey.

Another very senior officer, Rear Admiral Caspar F. Goodrich, commandant of the New York Navy Yard, shared the young officer's views. In August Goodrich, who would become the senior officer on active service upon Admiral Evans's retirement, reported to Metcalf "that planning the waterline armor so low in our original designs was a pardonable error; that retaining it so low in succeeding vessels was, to say the least, obstinate; that to retain it so low in future ships, if this does not border on the criminal, certainly involves a responsibility which none should care to accept."[49]

Reports such as this from within the system were acceptable because they could be quietly pigeonholed. When publication of the Reuterdahl article brought them out into the open, the Navy Department acted with unusual alacrity, albeit only to defend past practices. On 30 December 1907 it was announced that Rear Admiral Converse would prepare a response to Reuterdahl's criticisms.[50] The Converse Report, along with a similar document prepared by Chief Constructor of the Navy Washington L. Capps, presented apparently convincing, highly technical arguments in favor of current ship designs and the bureau system.[51] Nowhere in the official rebuttals was there any hint that Admiral Dewey and Rear Admiral Goodrich had found fault with the boards' end product, the American battleship.

Lieutenant Commander Sims, who had a brief opportunity to read the Converse Report, found it misleading in many respects and immediately communicated his views to President Roosevelt.[52] He illustrated the weakness of its defense of American ammunition hoists, then turned to the issue of draft. Converse, Sims pointed out, based all his arguments about displacement, armor belt placement, and height of gun batteries on "normal" displacement, omitting "all specific reference . . . to the well known actual height of the water-lines." He emphasized that substitution of normal displacement figures for actual figures conveyed a false impression of the actual height of armor belts, decks, and gun positions under normal operating conditions.

In concluding, Sims pointed out that Converse had ignored "the most serious and comprehensive of all criticisms that have been made of our Navy," namely, that all the defects were the "inevitable result" of the bureau system. This was an opinion Converse himself had expressed, Sims reported, when the admiral had been chief of the Bureau of Navigation in 1906.[53]

Senator Eugene Hale did not have the benefit of any critical assessment of the Converse/Capps reports. His comments, when he submitted them to the Senate on 19 February 1908, suggest he accepted their information at face value. "When our ships are built, armored, equipped and manned, and sent out to sail the seas," Hale said, "I believe they will compare favorably, ship for ship, with those of any navy on the globe. As for the bureau system of controlling the navy, I believe the system that has carried us through three successful wars is the best system we can devise."[54] In effect, the chairman of the Senate Naval Affairs Committee had announced his conclusions on the major issues to be investigated a week before the hearings began. Now all he had to do was ensure that only information supportive of his position was put before the committee. Elting E. Morison concluded of Hale that "he saw in such an investigation a weapon with which he could club into silence the reformers who had so long plagued him."[55]

Even as the Navy Department justified its past practices, it actively sought to identify the source of leaks to Reuterdahl. This was not too difficult, as many of Reuterdahl's points were strikingly similar to those previously submitted to and ignored by the Navy Department. Prior to the Senate hearings, Secretary Metcalf sent letters to a number of naval officers "containing categorical questions, the answers to which are expected to illumine the entire subject."[56] It was common knowledge that one of the recipients of these letters, which generated apprehension in navy circles, was Lieutenant Commander William S. Sims.[57]

Sims now faced a crisis. The secretary's letter required an immediate denial of any involvement in the affair, a denial Sims was unable to give. Fortunately, his position as naval aide to the president gave him a unique opportunity to maneuver. After acknowledging receipt of Metcalf's letter, Sims went to Roosevelt, admitting his own insubordination but managing to allude to a similar action by Roosevelt when he was assistant secretary of the navy in 1898. In response Roosevelt sent for Metcalf, reminded him that the Senate was investigating the matter, and directed him to stop further proceedings against Sims and the other witnesses.[58]

Thus the naval inquisition ended.[59] But before Roosevelt ordered the recall of Metcalf's letters, the secretary managed to stir up trouble in another quarter.[60] Overreacting to the pressure generated by Reuterdahl's claims, Metcalf wrote to Rear Admiral Goodrich demanding "a definite and explicit statement as to [his] exact meaning in stating that to retain the waterline armor belt so low in future ships, if this does not border on the criminal, certainly involves a responsibility which none should care to accept."[61] Goodrich's response was blunt and to the point: "I can only explain that I meant exactly what I said. The practice I condemned, I still consider to be fraught with danger to the fleet."[62]

The controversial Senate hearings convened on 25 February 1908—while the battleship fleet was peacefully visiting Callao. The record of those hearings as well as a reading of contemporary newspaper coverage confirms Elting E. Morison's conclusion that Senator Hale meant to use them to "club into silence the reformers." To do this, Hale needed to limit discussion to specific technical deficiencies cited by Reuterdahl and apparently refuted by Converse and Capps, without broadening the scope to include their ultimate causes.

The real issue, obvious to most, was not individual technical errors but the system of autonomous bureaus whose responsibility was compartmented and whose activities were specifically funded by Congress. The solution, equally apparent, was to subordinate bureau chiefs to a single senior naval officer who would coordinate their activities, and to provide general funds to the secretary, who would then allocate them to the bureaus. But this change was difficult to realize; if bureau functions were channelled through a single line officer, it would greatly reduce the ability of congressmen to pursue projects more beneficial to their constituencies than to the navy. Therefore the Senate Naval Affairs Committee, dominated by the senator from Maine, adopted a noticeably pro-establishment stance. Maintenance of the status quo in the Navy Department, with its implications for domestic political power, was more important than adopting a rational system of management.

When the hearings convened, the first witnesses were Admiral Converse and Chief Constructor Capps. In the opening session, Senator Hale made clear his intention to limit the scope of the investigation. He told Admiral Converse only to "bring out before the Committee the essential charges in the *McClure's Magazine* article, relating mainly to the position and extent of armor, the height of freeboard, the position of the guns, the turret and the turret hoists . . . ."[63]

On the issues of armor belt placement and ammunition hoist design, the establishment position was clear and had been convincingly presented in the Converse Report using the normal displacement line. With this figure as the point of comparison, it could be correctly concluded that American battleships had freeboard as great as or greater than their European counterparts, and that their armor belt offered the greatest possible protection. Concerning the open turrets, Converse and Capps held that accidents were not the result of design faults but rather of a failure to follow safety precautions in a desire to achieve speed of firing.[64]

The first four days were taken up with testimony in support of the Navy Department, led by Converse and Capps and followed by the chief of the Bureau of Ordnance and other officers involved in design and construction. This testimony was accepted uncritically, without allowing advocates of reform to crossexamine the witnesses.

On 29 February the first of Reuterdahl's supporters appeared before the committee. Lieutenant Commander Hill testified primarily on the location of armor belts. He reported that Admiral Converse's conclusions were based on the normal displacement line and that a check of ships' logs showed that with a "normal" coal load, American battleships drew "from one foot to two feet, one inch more than the so-called normal or trial draft where they were designed to be best protected." When the vessels were nearly filled with coal, the belt was at most two feet above the waterline, and on certain ships it was submerged.[65]

Hill was restrained both by his relatively junior rank and by the environment in which he testified. Rear Admiral Goodrich, writing to Secretary Metcalf on the same subject two days earlier, had shown no such restraint. Referring to the fleet flagship *Connecticut,* the admiral asked with no small measure of cynicism:

> Is the Department not aware that, when the actual vessel herself was tried last summer, her ammunition had to be taken out to lighten her and that at the end of the runs, with much of her coal expended, she still drew several inches more water than at her theoretical "normal displacement"? And does not the Department think that the adjective "normal" as applied to conditions which are in the highest degree abnormal is incorrect and certain to convey a wrong impression?

Goodrich concluded with an enlightening peroration on the difference between theory and practice in naval operations:

> Recurring to the flotation as of fact and not as of theory, would the Department approve the deliberate neglect by any captain to fill his magazines and storerooms and bunkers to overflowing, at every opportunity, merely that he may keep his vessel at, or nearly at, the hypothetical "normal displacement" for which the designs were made? If so, a general order is imperatively necessary to change the present practice of taking on board at all times just as much of these things as can be stored.

"This custom," pronounced Goodrich with a frankness doubtless ill-appreciated in Washington, "until prohibited by the Department, settles the question of how much water a ship will draw on leaving port, and it is at approximately this flotation that the armor belt should be placed to protect the waterline."[66]

Unknown to Goodrich or Hill, the condition of the fleet at the moment strongly supported their position. The battleships were taking on coal at Callao for the voyage to Magdalena Bay. On their departure, the day after Hill's testimony, all the *Connecticut*-class ships of the First Division had completely submerged armor belts. The worst was the *Vermont*—she drew twenty-nine feet eight inches aft, lay five feet two inches deeper than her designed normal displacement, and therefore had her armor belt submerged to a depth of over two feet.[67]

Lieutenant Carl T. Vogelgesang took the stand following Hill. Vogelgesang, member of a board that had examined all the turret ships on the Atlantic coast after the *Georgia* accident, limited his remarks to the subject on which he was specially qualified to comment. The general thrust of his testimony was that the interim measures adopted to make the open turret safer were cumbersome, and that accidents such as the one he had investigated could not happen on a foreign warship. This comment elicited an angry exchange between Vogelgesang and Chief Constructor Capps, who had been retained at the hearings and was permitted to crossexamine witnesses.

Seagoing line officers felt that greatest safety could be achieved through development of an automatic gas-ejection device for the guns and a two-stage hoist. Staff officers responsible for the design and construction of open turrets responded that a sure way to end such accidents was simply to slow down the rate of fire. The latter represented an ideal theoretical solution, but, as Vogelgesang pointed out, in battle men were not going to take such a precaution.

Next day Sims appeared before the committee. It had been his intention, rather then dealing with specific issues already covered by Hill and Vogelgesang, to discuss how opposition within the Navy Department had thwarted efforts to improve gunnery and from there to progress to a discussion of organization of the Navy Department.[68] Senator Tillman upset this strategy by instructing Sims to limit his testimony to "alleged faulty construction" and to say nothing of personnel or organization.[69]

Thus restricted, Sims could testify only in general terms on the technical topics already covered. Although this appeared to be a major setback to the young officers seeking reform, in fact, the manifest unfairness of his treatment by the committee gave rise to press claims of a whitewash; nothing the reformers said would have any influence on the Senate report.[70] As the hearings continued, many papers accused the Senate committee of attempting to hide rather than to discover the truth. The *New York Times* noted that "what really alarms the public is not reports that errors have been made . . . but the hint that those responsible for the errors think more of their own reputations for infallibility than of the safety of the bluejackets and of the country."[71]

On 11 March Commander Albert L. Key took the stand and, in testimony substantiated with impressive statistics, repudiated the Converse/Capps defense of armor belt placement and turret design. In exchanges during this testimony, Senators Tillman and Hale departed from strictly technical topics and in asides suggested that the success of critics, rather than improving the navy, might have the opposite effect. If, as Sims and his compatriots had argued, design blunders were to continue for several more years, Senator Tillman asked, "What reason has Congress to continue to order battleships?"[72] Key's solution was to establish a chief of naval staff responsible to the secretary of the navy for coordination of the bureaus. This was unwanted advice. Senator Hale concluded that Key's testimony proved only the folly of continuing programs for big ships before matters were straightened out.[73]

At this point, with the Navy Department's defense in disarray and with public sentiment growing in favor of the critics, the committee went into executive session and shortly thereafter adjourned. No report of the investigation was ever issued, no recommendations of any kind were ever presented. All that remains is a stenographic record of the hearings themselves.

Premature adjournment disappointed all parties. The work of bureaus in designing the battleship fleet had been discredited; the critics had made their revelations to no avail; and the committee members, rather than vindicating the bureau system they had sought to preserve, were now confronted with further proof of its inefficiency.[74]

While controversy raged in Washington, Reuterdahl enjoyed a friendly passage on board the *Minnesota*. Even though his authorship of "The Needs of Our Navy" was known before the fleet left Rio de Janeiro, officers' personal attitudes toward him remained generally favorable, and Rear Admiral Thomas found him to be better informed on the subject of the navy than almost anyone he had ever met. But the fleet's reaction to Reuterdahl, it would seem, was too unspectacular for the popular press. When a serious illness in his family forced him to leave the fleet at Callao, papers falsely claimed that he had been "expelled" for criticizing the navy.[75]

Facts such as Reuterdahl's intelligence gathering in Rio de Janeiro and his decorating the *Minnesota* there and in Punta Arenas indicate that he was well received by the fleet. But where officers stood in the bitter debate over the criticisms he had raised is difficult to ascertain. Thomas felt that what he had written in *McClure's* about battleship design defects and the inefficiency of the Navy Department was true, and that it hurt the "powers that be."[76] Sperry, occupied with his own maneuvers to ensure accession to command, never expressed a stand in writing other than to say he was glad he did not have to take one.[77] It would have been difficult, though, to remain uncommitted on an issue so central to the work of a seagoing officer. Sims, in forwarding a letter to the president from Captain Wainwright of the *Louisiana*, reported that Wainwright was not alone in supporting reform—that ten of sixteen battleship captains agreed with him, and it was probable the remaining ones did as well.[78]

If senior officers were reluctant to commit themselves, the same was not true of younger officers. Lieutenant Cone, commanding the fleet's destroyer flotilla, wrote to Sims from Magdalena Bay to say that officers of that flotilla were with him heart and soul. "In my last papers they were wasting time over the armor belt, etc., which of course is important, but not a fig compared to the big question of our left-handed organization, that chases responsibility around in a circle," Cone concluded.[79]

Of course there could be but one official view from the fleet, and that was expressed in the commander in chief's report of the voyage. In the summer of 1907 Evans had written that American battleships, in terms of protection, were hardly better than armored cruisers.[80] Later, in concurrence with a report from Naval Constructor R. H. Robinson, who had been assigned to the *Connecticut,* Evans altered his position. Although the officers of the fleet were far from unanimous on the issue, Evans concluded that even with "smooth seas, and practically no wind, the swell at times caused such rolling and pitching as to expose the lower portion of the armor belt even at heavy load, hence the lower limit of armor should not be raised."[81] Sims and his associates had emphasized the need for the *top* of the belt to be higher. Evans's conclusion, although not disputing the need for a higher top, seemed to suggest that the belt was properly placed. Key attempted to refute Evans in a closely argued submission to Secretary Metcalf.[82] His reason, he confessed to Sims, was that "of course those incompetents in power at the Navy Department will make all they can of it."[83] Key's concern was well-founded.

Lieutenant Commander Hill made one final attempt to convince the Naval Affairs Committee of the need for reform, forwarding his criticisms of the armor placement on the new battleships *Delaware* and *North Dakota.* Senator Hale asked Secretary Metcalf whether Hill's new comments should be included in the Senate's record of the hearings.[84] Metcalf sought Converse's opinion, and not surprisingly, the admiral discounted the validity of Hill's contentions. There was no need to change armor belt location on the new battleships, Converse assured the secretary. The president of the Board on Construction then quoted Admiral Evans's report and concluded that it was "definite, positive and conclusive," and that it sustained the board "in establishing the lower edge of the heavy armor as it now exists in vessels of the battleship fleet."[85]

So Converse, the accused, passed judgment on himself and found a verdict of innocence. Predictably, Metcalf, in answering Senator Hale's query, reported that "selective publication of correspondence" would be misleading and that it was not necessary or desirable to release Hill's letter.[86]

There the matter rested—for the time being. Written opposition views were excluded from the Senate record of the hearings under the pretext that "selective publication" might be misleading. This fear, of course, did not extend to the Converse/Capps submissions, which were included in the report and received wide publication in journals such as *Scientific American.* Although the establishment had prevailed through sheer bureaucratic strength, the younger, more progressive officers, the "insurgents," as Sims called them, were by no means defeated. Key perhaps best expressed their frustration in a private letter to Sims shortly after the hearings adjourned: "My cry is give the 'young' officers—the misguided youths under 55—a chance, and down with the senile incompetent old grafters on the retired list, or about to retire, who must devote the whole of their time to a hopeless defense of their errors of administration while on the active list."[87]

In the course of the hearings President Roosevelt seems to have become convinced of the validity of some of the criticism. "It seems to me," he wrote to Metcalf, "that the armor belt ought to be higher."[88] Evans's report had evidently made an impression on him, Key reported, for although the president wrote his former aide on 26 March to say he thought Sims, Key, and Winslow had performed "a real service by fearlessly calling attention to defects in our naval architecture," in the end he balked at full support of the rebel cause.

NINE

Please Extend a
Formal Invitation

$\mathbf{T}$he Reuterdahl article was published as a result of renewed interest in the navy generated by announcement of the cruise; the Senate hearings on Reuterdahl's charges commenced during the fleet's visit to Callao and its transit to Magdalena Bay. Another development propelled the navy to the front pages of the nation's newspapers while the battleships were at the Mexican port. It was announced that they would return to the Atlantic Coast via Australia, the Philippines, Suez, and the Mediterranean. Consequently, a spate of invitations was tendered by nations along the fleet's projected route.

The first invitation had come from the country farthest away. Little more than a week after the cruise was announced in July 1907, Dr. Richard Arthur, president of the Immigration League of Australia, wrote to Prime Minister Alfred Deakin to suggest that at least some of the battleships be invited to Australia. Deakin replied that his government would consider the matter.[1] Nothing more was heard of the proposal until Christmas Eve, 1907, when Deakin called on American Consul-General John P. Bray in Melbourne, leaving a letter containing a tentative invitation to the fleet. "No other Federation in the world possesses so many features [in common with] the United States as does the Commonwealth of Australia," Deakin wrote, "and I doubt whether any two peoples could be found who are likely to benefit more by any thing that tends to knit their relations more closely. . . . Australian ports and portals would be wide open to your ships and men. . . ."[2] The prime minister informed Bray that at a suitable time he would go through formal channels and send an official invitation to the president.

Deakin also contacted Whitelaw Reid, American ambassador to the Court of St. James. Deakin, who had struck up a friendship with Reid while attending the Imperial Conference in London in 1907, asked him to use his influence with the president so that the invitation would be accepted. This letter reached London, where its contents were immediately telegraphed to Washington, arriving three days before Consul-General Bray's letter from Melbourne.[3] In initial response to both letters, Root telegraphed that the invitation was appreciated but that it was too early to promise that any units of the fleet would visit.[4]

The Australian invitation was discussed at Roosevelt's cabinet meeting on 21 February. That day Secretary Root forwarded Deakin's letter to the president with a recommendation of acceptance. Root wrote, prophetically, "The time will surely come, although probably after our day, when it will be important for the United States to have all ports friendly and all causes of sympathy alive in the Pacific."[5] Roosevelt shared Root's vision. "Some day the question of the Pacific will be a dominant one," he told his naval aide, "and it will be necessary to know the sentiment of Australia and New Zealand."[6]

In his letter Root expressed reservations about the publication of Deakin's informal invitation.[7] These were overruled at the cabinet meeting, at the end of which Metcalf disclosed the Australian initiative and released all the related correspondence except Deakin's letter to Reid, which the American embassy in London had marked very confidential.[8]

At this point the British government's handling of Deakin's official invitation, which he had given to the governor-general on 24 January, had been overtaken by events. Colonial Office reaction to the Australian initiative had been "tepid to cool." The parliamentary undersecretary, Winston S. Churchill, opposed the visit. The Admiralty, unable to match the American demonstration of force, thought it "inconvenient," but left the decision to the Foreign Office. None had been reached by 21 February, when Metcalf made his announcement and left the Foreign Office with no option but to endorse the Australian invitation and forward it to Washington.[9]

The cabinet debate over Australia's invitation centered on the concern that if it were accepted, the United States could hardly decline others. But by mid-March, when a decision on the return route had to be made, Australia's invitation was the only one that had been received. It was accepted, and at the time of the announcement an itinerary was published to fend off the obligation of having to accept future invitations that might prove inconvenient.[10]

As if the Australian initiative were not enough, British Ambassador James Bryce was further embarrassed when acceptance of Deakin's invitation was published by the media before he had been informed.[11] Root immediately apologized for the premature release, then formally responded to the invitation.[12] This belated action virtually completed the circumvention of imperial channels that had begun with Deakin's first approach to Bray.

In Sydney the reaction to American acceptance was emotional. Alfred Deakin had been addressing citizens at Centenary Hall on the subject of national defense when a paper was handed to him. He rose, and in obvious excitement announced: "A cable message has just been received to the effect that the American fleet will visit Melbourne and Sydney. [Loud and prolonged cheering.] The least we can do is give three cheers for the United States. . . . I venture to say that a welcome such as no fleet has ever seen outside its own country will be given in Australia to the

American Fleet."[13] The following day Federal Minister of Defense Thomas Ewing told the press, "We feel that our future in the Pacific is bound with that of the United States."[14]

There was one issue in particular concerning which Australians felt bound to U.S. interests: Japanese immigration. Although President Roosevelt's tentative efforts to seek a convention of English-speaking nations that would bar Japanese from settling in their lands had come to nothing, anti-Japanese feeling remained strong in Australia and New Zealand.[15] The prospect of an American fleet visit to Australia was seen there as at least tacit American support for the "white Australia" policy.

The Melbourne *Herald* editorialized that "it would be impossible to over-rate the international significance of the new entente cordiale, pregnant with the greatest and most momentous possibilities, between the two peoples who stand in the Pacific for the dominance of the white race."[16]

The prime minister of New Zealand, Sir Joseph Ward, learned of the Australian invitation and decided to invite the fleet to his country through the American consul-general at Auckland. On 4 March Ward sent his invitation by telegram to Consul-General William Augustus Prickett.[17] Prickett, unaware that a decision in favor of the Australian visit was imminent, underestimated the importance of speed in this instance and sent Ward's message to Washington by mail.[18] Not until 15 March, after news had been received that the fleet was to circumnavigate the globe and call at Australia, did he cable the actual invitation to Washington.[19] This delay reduced the impact of the prime minister's circumvention of imperial channels; on the following day Ward addressed a formal invitation via the British governor, Lord Plunket.[20] Prickett's telegram, of course, reached Washington before the official invitation, but in this case there was no premature disclosure.[21] The Navy Department accepted the official invitation on 28 March, stating that a speedy return of the fleet to the Atlantic permitted a visit to Auckland only.[22]

For different reasons, Alfred Deakin, Sir Joseph Ward, and Theodore Roosevelt all wanted the American fleet to visit Australasia. Roosevelt had suggested that by this means American protection, Monroe Doctrine–style, could be extended to Australia and New Zealand. Roosevelt told Oscar King Davis of the *New York Times* that the fleet visit to New Zealand and Australia was intended "to show England—I cannot say a 'renegade mother country'—that those colonies are white man's country."[23]

Deakin attempted to clothe his actions in imperial rhetoric. The American fleet visit, he said, "had nothing to do with our national development but everything to do with our racial sympathies—if we can help to balance the pro-German and anti-British prejudices of the United States we shall have done good work for the Empire. . . ."[24] Imperial justifications notwithstanding, the invitation was a shrewd move to gain British acceptance of an independent Australian navy.[25] That Australians viewed the fleet visit as directly related to Australian naval aims seems clear. In a sermon given by the leader of Australia's Roman Catholic Church on the eve of the fleet's arrival, Patrick Francis Cardinal Moran told worshipers that the coming of the U.S. fleet should teach Australians "the comparative insignificance of the home fleet that pretended to guard their shores. The great lesson was that they needed a fleet of their own."[26]

In New Zealand, Sir Joseph Ward remained firmly dedicated to the concept of imperial defense. "I believe," he told his Parliament, "that if the necessity arises for the protection of New Zealand or any other portion of the Empire, [the Royal Navy's] last man and . . . last ship would be used for the purpose of maintaining the glory of that flag we are so proud to live under."[27] A substantial signal of continued support of the Royal Navy was given in July 1908—just a month before the U.S. fleet's arrival—when he announced an increase in New Zealand's annual contribution for imperial defense to £100,000.[28] Nevertheless, as G. P. Taylor has suggested, Ward regarded his invitation to the U.S. fleet as a method of seeking "dominion participation in imperial policy-making."[29]

Although it had been hoped that the announcement of a set itinerary for the fleet's return would preclude further invitations, this was not the case. On 18 March Baron Kogoro Takahira, Japanese ambassador to the United States, handed Secretary of State Root an invitation for the fleet to visit Japan. The Imperial Government, his note said, was firmly convinced that a visit would have a reassuring effect "upon the traditional relations of good understanding and mutual sympathy" between the two nations.[30] Next day it was discussed in a cabinet meeting during which the major issue raised was the possible effect of misconduct by American enlisted men in Japan.[31] President Roosevelt decided in favor of the visit, and the invitation was accepted with the proviso that, owing to the need for an early return to the Atlantic, the fleet could call at only one port.[32]

Public reaction was generally one of relief and satisfaction that, following months of often alarming rumors, common sense had prevailed. Interpretations of the event reflected various national perspectives on East Asia. The *Bristol Times & Mirror* found the invitation to be "a wise, as well as a clever, move on the part of [Britain's] Japanese allies."[33] Russian reporting highlighted the salutary effect of American naval strength and the forcefulness of U.S. foreign policy: "It is because they have shown . . . that they are not afraid of the Japanese of Tsushima that they are able to find again the Japan of peaceful chrysanthemums."[34] The Japanese newspaper *Jiji Shimpo* opined that the invitation would "furnish the world a conclusive proof that Japan's feelings toward America have not undergone any change whatever."[35] And *Mainichi Dempo* felt that Japan's welcome to the fleet should "open the eyes of the agitators. The idea of inviting to dinner a man who was supposed to have set out from his home for the purpose of tumbling one's house about one's ears is novel in the history of international diplomacy."[36]

The views of America's ambassador to Japan, Thomas J. O'Brien, had not been solicited in the process of considering the invitation. When O'Brien was informed of the decision, he suggested by mail that only part of the fleet should call at Japanese ports. It was his belief that this would reap the same political benefit, while reducing the burden of expense to the Japanese government.[37] Secretary Root discussed the idea with Ambassador Takahira, who after sounding out the views of Baron Sakatani said the Japanese people would be disappointed if the whole fleet did not show up.[38] It was decided not to alter the itinerary.[39]

Archives clearly show that the Australian, New Zealand, and Japanese invitations were accepted primarily for diplomatic reasons. Thus the purpose of the cruise had shifted. Whereas the Navy Department had originated plans for the first half and requested the State Department to obtain appropriate clearances, now the initiative lay with the State Department itself. Invitations were received from various governments; the secretary of state made recommendations to the president; decisions were made; then the Navy Department was informed. This arrangement worked well enough when the two departments agreed, as they did in the Australian case, but otherwise it caused considerable difficulty. The handling of China's invitation is a case in point.

On 23 March, three days after Japan's invitation had been accepted, Ambassador Wu Ting-fang delivered a telegram from the Chinese minister of foreign affairs inviting the U.S. fleet to China and stating that the imperial high commissioner for trade in the southern ports had been directed to make preparations.[40] Roosevelt's cabinet met the following day, decided to accept the invitation, and immediately informed Ambassador Wu.[41] As in the case of Japan's invitation, a decision was reached at the cabinet level without the consultation of specialists in either the State or the Navy Department. But whereas no difficulties arose with the earlier invitation, with China's the situation was different. Problems that would have surfaced in the State Department's Division of Far Eastern Affairs and the Bureau of Navigation before a decision had been reached now surfaced after acceptance had been communicated to the Chinese government and the press.

One day after publication of the news, the State Department officially forwarded China's invitation to the Navy Department.[42] From Magdalena Bay Admiral Sperry, who had been directed to submit an itinerary for the return trip, strongly advised against a fleet visit to Shanghai, the major port within the viceroyalty of Nanking.[43] As he explained in a private letter, the battleships would have to lie fifteen miles below the city in a dangerous river, and two thousand men would have to be transported back and forth every day, inviting certain death by drowning to many.[44] After receiving the admiral's comments, the Navy Department concluded that no other ports in the viceroyalty of Nanking were suitable either.[45] That day the department cabled to Sperry its approval of his proposed itinerary, which did not include a Chinese visit.[46]

Attempting to retrieve the situation, Secretary Root discussed ports with Ambassador Wu. In response to Root's inquiries the Chinese Foreign Office cabled that the northern port city of Chefoo (Zhifu) was best suited for the visit.[47] When this city was proposed to the Navy Department, further problems surfaced: a visit there would require an additional two thousand miles of steaming and eight thousand tons of coal, and would further delay autumn target practice at Manila. Realizing now the inevitability of a visit to China, the Navy Department suggested to the State Department that only one squadron visit Chefoo, while the other squadron proceed directly to Manila for target practice.[48]

Two weeks later Secretary Root had further reason to regret the precipitate acceptance of China's invitation. On 18 April William W. Rockhill, American minister to China and one of Theodore Roosevelt's trusted advisors, cabled to express his fear that the Chinese might interpret a visit as an indication that the United States would help China recover those sovereign rights it had surrendered to the European powers and Japan in the "unequal treaties" signed in the nineteenth century. Rockhill urged caution and added a practical reservation: if the fleet was to reach Japan in autumn, it would not be safe to visit Chefoo, which was an open roadstead.[49]

The State Department reviewed the situation, and the Navy Department was directed to draw up two itineraries for the president's consideration: one with the First Squadron calling at Chefoo, another with the Second Squadron calling at Amoy. The latter plan, which involved no significant increase in fuel requirements, was approved by Roosevelt on 27 April. Thus the itinerary had been fixed up to the fleet's arrival at Manila, following visits to Japan and China.[50]

Amoy, from a purely naval viewpoint, was the ideal alternative to Shanghai. It was a protected harbor, and two thousand miles closer than Chefoo. Given Rockhill's objections, it seems likely that the State Department and the president were well disposed to agree upon Amoy: the port was acceptable to the navy yet sufficiently distant from main population centers to limit the possibility of misinterpretation by the Chinese.

When the president's decision had been made, Root directed Rockhill to inform the Chinese Foreign Office of the altered itinerary. In a separate, confidential section of the cabled message, the secretary of state acknowledged Rockhill's apprehensions and said that any misinterpretation of the implications of a fleet visit would have to be corrected. He further expressed the hope that "the Chinese Government clearly realizes that . . . we favor their legitimate aims, but that we see grave danger in any unduly captious attitude which could give just cause for serious offense in any quarter."[51] In plain words, while the Roosevelt administration was prepared to champion Chinese rights recovery in theory, it was unwilling to encourage any development that might endanger efforts toward a rapprochement with Japan, a foreign policy objective of the highest priority.

The final itinerary for the middle portion of the cruise had been approved by President Roosevelt on 27 April. To keep it within reasonable limits a number of invitations had to be declined, including one from the government of Fiji.[52] In declining, Secretary of the Navy Metcalf mentioned that some of the fleet's auxiliaries would visit that island to use its cable communications.[53] The information became distorted in the process of transmission through British channels. Although the Admiralty told Vice Admiral Sir Richard Poore, commander in chief of the Royal Navy's Australian station, that the fleet would not call at Suva, the colonial government of Fiji was not notified.[54] Not until the American vice consul reported in May that the governor of Fiji had informed him of the fleet's coming was the situation resolved.[55]

The British colony of Hong Kong also tendered an invitation, which was promptly declined.[56] Unfortunately, once again the American response failed to reach its intended recipient. Colonial authorities incorrectly assumed that with the acceptance of the Chinese invitation Hong Kong would also be visited. Only when the American consul-general at Hong Kong queried the State Department was the failure of the British imperial government to notify Hong Kong discovered.[57]

An invitation to Great Britain was declined because it could not be fit into the fleet's schedule. However, the British government's generous offer to have the authorities in Malta, Gibraltar, or any other port within the British empire make available to the fleet all facilities was much appreciated.[58] Invitations to Fremantle, Adelaide, Hobart, and Moreton Bay in Australia were declined, the fleet's visits to that nation being limited to Sydney, Melbourne, and Albany.[59]

The American consul at Vancouver, British Columbia, forwarded a local resolution inviting the fleet to visit; it too was declined.[60] A formal invitation subsequently presented by the British ambassador on 1 May elicited a similar response.[61] Other invitations to the German-controlled port of Kiao-chow (Jiaozhou), to Natal, in the Orange Free State, and to Tandjong Priok, in Java, arrived much later and were also turned down.[62]

As we have seen, when the long-overdue decision to relieve Admiral Evans as commander in chief was finally taken, the choice for command was Rear Admiral Charles Stillman Sperry. But first Rear Admiral Charles M. Thomas, Sperry's senior, was given a short turn at the helm. Thomas's mandatory retirement date, October 1908, was too close at hand to allow him to retain command for the remainder of the voyage. Rear Admiral William H. Emory, the Second Division commander, would also retire before the end of the cruise. Thus, of the four admirals who had set out from Hampton Roads with the battleship fleet, only Sperry had sufficient active service time remaining before retirement to complete the voyage.

This consideration indicates the purely mechanical nature of officer promotion at that time. Little in Sperry's long career was remarkable; he had no unique talent qualifying him for command of the greatest fleet the navy had ever sent from home. His main strength, as the *New York Times* pointed out, was the result of events that had occurred forty-six years earlier. Sperry, the youngest of the Naval Academy cadets that commenced training in 1862, had graduated near the top of his class in 1866. His high academic standing on graduation established his relative seniority among peers, while his youth meant that he could spend more time in the promotion line.[63]

His most recent duties had included three years as president of the Naval War College at Newport, with ex officio membership on the navy's General Board, followed by service as U.S. naval representative at the Hague Conference in 1907. He had a "bespectacled, wrinkled, sallow, and severe countenance," showed little outward humor, and had earned the service sobriquet Coffin Face.[64] Nevertheless, he was a man with more than average academic interest who had twice served as instructor of mathematics at the Naval Academy before his appointment to the presidency of the Naval War College. He had a reputation as one of the navy's better tacticians, and also as a "stickler for the best form" in naval affairs.[65]

The retirement of the two senior admirals and the elevation of Sperry to fleet command brought Emory to command of the Second Squadron and created two flag officer vacancies. These were filled by Captain Seaton Schroeder, skipper of the *Virginia* and senior captain of the fleet, and Schroeder's brother-in-law, Captain Richard Wainwright of the *Louisiana,* both being promoted to the rank of acting rear admiral. Each man was given a division command.

These promotions resulted in the assignment of Captain Kossuth Niles to the *Louisiana* and Captain Alexander Sharp to the *Virginia.*[66] Captain Henry McCrea, who was seriously ill, was relieved of command of the *Georgia* by Captain E. F. Qualtrough. McCrea died of Bright's disease two months later, while Qualtrough went on to achieve notoriety when the fleet was in the Mediterranean.[67]

A few days before the fleet left San Francisco for Hawaii, the officers and men of the fleet were shocked and saddened to learn of the sudden death of Rear Admiral Thomas. Although it was not widely publicized, he had suffered from a chronic heart condition, and the strain of de facto command had proved too much.[68] But the danger of his situation had not been apparent; he wrote that he had never felt better, and had assured his wife in February that he had the "constitution of an Ox."[69] After Sperry's assumption of fleet command, Thomas had gone south to Monterey and there, at the Del Monte Hotel, where the officers of the fleet had enjoyed Monterey's welcome ten weeks earlier, he died suddenly while dining with his family.[70] His death was attributed to heart disease.[71]

Two battleships already on the West Coast, the newly completed *Nebraska* and recently overhauled *Wisconsin,* were scheduled to join the fleet at San Francisco. They were originally meant to augment the fleet for the remainder of the voyage; however, the poor engineering performance of the *Maine* and *Alabama* led to a decision to substitute for them the *Nebraska* and *Wisconsin.* The *Maine* was notorious for her coal consumption; the *Alabama* had had difficulties with her engineering plant since September 1907, when it had developed a cracked cylinder head.[72] Her commanding officer had expressed continuing concern to his division commander, Rear Admiral Sperry, during the transit around South America. When Sperry was designated commander in chief, he took the opportunity of the assignment of the two new battleships to rid himself of the two that had become headaches.

This was first aired publicly on 1 April 1908, and was subsequently included in fleet circular letters outlining plans for the ships after their arrival in San Francisco.[73] When the fleet left San Francisco on 18 May to visit Puget Sound, the *Maine* and *Alabama* were detached to form a special service squadron under the command of Captain Giles B. Harber of the *Maine.*[74] At the end of May the Bureau of Navigation circulated an itinerary for the return voyage of the squadron via Honolulu, Manila, Singapore, Colombo, Suez, Naples, and Gibraltar.[75] The schedule was strictly adhered to, and the progress of the two battleships received fairly regular reporting, even though their activities were consistently overshadowed by those of the battleship fleet.[76]

It is obvious that in scheduling the Special Service Squadron's return to the Atlantic no effort was made to keep the two battleships in the Pacific until after the fleet visited Japan. In fact, the two ships entered the Mediterranean before Sperry's fleet reached Albany, in Western Australia. Maintenance of this additional naval strength in the western Pacific could have been easily and discreetly arranged by delaying the squadron's departure from San Francisco; this certainly would have been done had any serious concern existed about Japanese intentions.

One other noteworthy naval deployment was planned while the Atlantic battleship fleet was on the West Coast. On 19 May the Navy Department approved a plan for the First Squadron of the Pacific Fleet to cruise to Samoa under the command of Rear Admiral W. T. Swinburne.[77] The cruise would be short—two months—with the estimated date of return almost coinciding with the battleship fleet's arrival date at Yokohama.[78]

A unique feature of this cruise was that each of the squadron's armored cruisers was to tow a torpedo boat destroyer. The experiment, undertaken to test this method of deploying the short-range destroyers anywhere in the Pacific in company with the fleet's main battle formation, reflects U.S. efforts to resolve another facet of the Pacific defense problem: how to protect against torpedo boat attack in the vast expanse of that ocean.

The itinerary for the Pacific Fleet squadron was a straightforward one, involving a coaling stop at Honolulu and then a direct transit to Samoa. From Samoa, two cruisers and two destroyers would briefly visit Apia, the major settlement in the German-controlled portion of the islands. Roosevelt had promised this visit to German Ambassador Speck von Sternberg, and it had been formalized following receipt of an official invitation from the German chargé d'affaires, Count Hermann von Hatzfeldt-Wildenburg.[79]

The timing of the cruise led to some speculation about its relationship to the battleship fleet's visit to Japan. "We had the idea in the fleet at that time," Bradley Fiske later wrote, "that the real purpose of the trip was to get a considerable fighting force into the neighborhood of Japan."[80] But official correspondence suggests this was a misconception. Secretary of the Navy Metcalf, in letters to the Pacific Fleet commander and to the commanding officer of the destroyer tender *Solace,* ordered the ships to "sail from San Francisco for Honolulu, Samoa, and Magdalena Bay, arriving at the last-named place for target practice about November 1, 1908."[81] The itinerary ultimately approved by the secretary envisaged the ships' return to Honolulu on 7 October, a fortnight before the battleship fleet was scheduled to reach Yokohama.[82]

Further, the suggestion that the ships had been sent to Samoa in anticipation of possible complications with Japan failed to take into account logistic and communications difficulties created by such a deployment. No coal was available in Samoa, and like the battleships, the armored cruisers were dependent on foreign-flag colliers. The unreliability of this arrangement was graphically illustrated when two chartered British colliers, the *Strathlyre* and *Strathlaven,* were late in arriving at Samoa.[83] Additionally, American Samoa possessed no communications link with the outside world. Commenting on the concern caused by the delay of these colliers, Captain Fiske wrote that in the "days of anxiety which ensued there were many people who deplored the fact that there was not on the island of Pango Pango [*sic*] any wireless telegraph."[84]

Another important clue to understanding the Pacific Fleet's mission is the fact that no special effort was made to increase its battle readiness before departure. The Pacific Fleet gunnery officer recorded that not a single ship had a complete fire control installation, a deficiency that could have been corrected by an additional two weeks in port. Furthermore, according to the officer, the destroyers scheduled to accompany the fleet were not in good condition for active service.[85]

It is difficult to imagine any rational person organizing a contingency plan for reinforcement of the battle fleet in the event of war by dispatching an important but insufficiently battle ready fighting force to a remote island that possessed neither fuel supplies nor communications with the outside world.

At Magdalena Bay, while Admiral Sperry and his Fourth Division staff were planning the Australian and Oriental visits, Admiral Evans's staff developed and published the general outline of activities from the fleet's arrival at San Francisco until its departure for Hawaii two months later.[86]

When the plan to have the fleet visit Puget Sound became known, Secretary Metcalf and Admiral Sperry were inundated with invitations from coastal communities and influential senators.[87] It was obvious that not all requests could be honored. The problem was resolved on 1 May when Acting Secretary of the Navy Newberry directed Sperry to time the movements of the fleet so that it would pass the mouth of the Columbia River, as close to shore as possible, in daylight.[88] Sperry set an arrival time of noon, 20 May 1908, calculated estimated arrival times off other localities, and informed the various communities whether they would have an opportunity to glimpse the great war fleet.[89]

The battleships departed San Francisco at 11:00 A.M. on 18 May. They encountered stormy weather after leaving the Golden Gate, but within a few hours it moderated. As the fleet steamed north, the ships conducted a speed trial at thirteen knots while remaining close to the shore so large crowds from each successive population center had a view.[90] On 21 May the fleet encountered a typical Puget Sound morning of rain and mist as it approached the Strait of Juan de Fuca.[91]

After a two-day visit to Puget Sound ports, the fleet (without two of its battleships, which went directly to the Puget Sound Navy Yard for docking) got under way and steamed into Seattle, the focal point of this visit.[92] On their approach the battleships were greeted by the now-standard flotilla of small craft.

The program of entertainment was as full as it had been in San Francisco and Los Angeles. The official visit culminated with a "monster parade" on the final day. Some 400,000 people from Washington, Oregon, Idaho, Montana, and British Columbia—an unprecedented crowd for this remote region of the nation—watched.[93] Next morning the fleet left Seattle, then divided and headed for various destinations. The First and Third Divisions returned to San Francisco, where they were scheduled to be docked at Hunters Point, with the First Division making a brief overnight stop at Tacoma en route. The Fourth Division proceeded directly to Bremerton and completed docking, while the Second Division made a three-day visit to Tacoma before going to Bremerton.

Each battleship now carried a new recruit: the fleet had been presented sixteen bear cubs to act as ships' mascots. They became part of a large menagerie that included cats, dogs, pigs, goats, monkeys, parrots—and had included a fully grown tiger, until it jumped into the Strait of Magellan. Kangaroos, dingoes, and other antipodean oddities would soon swell the ships' companies. All these animals roamed the decks freely, creating, it would seem, a number of health hazards.

TEN

Union Jack and Stars and Stripes

Fourth of July 1908 found the Atlantic Fleet at anchor in San Francisco Bay, taking on supplies of coal and provisions and making final preparations for continuing the voyage. Each battleship also received a draft of midshipmen recently graduated from the Naval Academy's class of 1908. Midshipman Caswell Saufley, one of those graduates, reported on board the *Kansas*.[1] For Saufley and his fellow midshipmen a personal adventure was about to begin. For many others, already separated from home and family for six months, the prospect of additional months at sea and the possibility that the voyage might be extended seemed daunting: Surgeon Stone was "overwhelmed with . . . depression."[2]

The fleet's departure had been scheduled for 2:00 P.M., 7 July, and on that day the ships got under way promptly. No official ceremonies had been organized, but thousands of people turned out to cheer. President Roosevelt sent a bon voyage message to Admiral Sperry and the men of the fleet expressing his pride in the country and in the navy. As individual battleships gathered way, they quickly formed into divisions and squadrons in accordance with assignments made after the detachment of the *Maine* and *Alabama*. The fleet numbered only fifteen battleships. The *Nebraska* had been hit by scarlet fever before sailing and placed in quarantine at Angel's Island in San Francisco Bay.[3] She would catch up with the fleet after clearance by health authorities.

Once the ships were clear of land the new commander in chief lost little time establishing a routine considerably more energetic than the one followed during the first half of the voyage. There were maneuvers morning and afternoon, and the fleet continued the competition for coal conservation that had begun at Rio de Janeiro.[4]

The developing professionalism reflected in record gunnery practice at Magdalena Bay and the continuing attention to drill and engineering efficiency undoubtedly promoted the crews' satisfaction with and pride in their navy, homesickness aside. When the fleet sailed from San Francisco it left behind just 129 men—less than one percent of the personnel. "The record is gratifying," the *New York Times* editorialized, "at a time when desertions from the Army are numerous enough to cripple whole companies and regiments." The paper suggested another reason for the low desertion rate: the navy's greater popularity, which must lie "in the 'lure of the sea,' in the anticipation of visiting many lands, peoples and climes, and in the rivalry of the ships and the superior training of the men."[5]

The *Nebraska,* which had been detained in San Francisco for fumigation, sailed two days late and overtook the fleet on 14 July.[6] Now reunited, the ships reduced speed to nine knots, eight knots the next day, in order to maintain their schedule.

In Honolulu the fleet's arrival date was to be a holiday, and a correspondent reported that the city had been decorated as never before. The morning of 16 July thousands of people from throughout the islands assembled at Diamond Head and other points of vantage to see the ships.[7] As the crowds waited, the fleet detoured from its course to steam by the leper colony on Molokai, giving the sufferers there a view. After passing the island the Third Division departed for Lahaina to coal, a measure made necessary by the shortage of facilities at Honolulu.[8] The Third Division would go to Honolulu on 19 July.

The remainder of the fleet approached Diamond Head, being met by "quite a number of decorated steamers, crowded with people."[9] The naval station at Honolulu saluted Sperry's flag as the *Connecticut* entered port, but no national salutes were fired because Hawaii was an American territory. Limited space within the sheltered harbor permitted the entry of only the *Connecticut* and one division of ships; the others anchored outside the breakwater and entered the harbor one by one for coaling.[10]

At Honolulu Sperry performed official duties ashore at an energetic pace that he would maintain for the remainder of the cruise. Immediately he paid a call to Governor Frear, which was returned with appropriate honors.[11] In this respect, the difference between Sperry's performance and that of Evans, particularly at Callao, was striking.

Although not originally scheduled, a parade was held on Friday, 17 July. A committee of Hawaiian women placed leis around the marchers' necks beforehand, and the route was strewn with flowers. *Les filles de société,* bedecked with carnations and roses, threw basket after basket of wreaths at the sailors so that Midshipman Saufley's cap was almost knocked off. More than once, by tilting his sword, he caught garlands on his hilt.[12]

To Americans of 1908 Hawaii remained a little-known community in the distant Pacific. The fleet visit did much to change that. "Many Americans were looking up the Sandwich Islands yesterday who had never greatly cared to know about them before," commented the *New York Times* editorial the day after the fleet's arrival. "The visit of so large a part of our navy to the remote Pacific colony seems to bring Honolulu and Hawaii closer to us."[13] Newspaper readers and recipients of letters from crew members learned about the pleasant climate in Hawaii and about various aspects of its culture. Native Hawaiians were the objects of considerable interest. Louis Maxfield found them "rather good looking; the men better than the women, because the latter . . . are fat and ugly."[14] In their descriptions some of the officers echoed the racial prejudices all too common in the United States at the time. Caswell Saufley, a proud Southerner, met a few young Hawaiian women who were "in education and wealth the equal of any English woman" he knew, and yet, "despite their straight black hair, the resemblance to the brown skin nigger" was so great that he could not induce himself to dance with them.[15]

But if the American attitude toward native Hawaiians wavered between patronizing superiority and unregenerate racial prejudice, the attitude of at least one Hawaiian was equally uncompromising. Queen Liliuokalani, the last reigning Hawaiian monarch, who had been deposed in 1893 by a group of American plantation owners with at least tacit support from naval officers and diplomatic representatives on the scene, refused to participate in the fleet reception.[16]

Her Majesty received little publicity compared with lei-bedecked officers and men who participated in luaus, toured Waikiki, viewed pineapple plantations, and reported on the fabulous view from the Pali. In fact, the fifteen thousand men might be seen as the first great tourist group to visit the islands, the attention they received the first Hawaiian publicity drive.

One aspect of the 1908 naval appropriations bill that had excited little debate was a request for funds to develop Pearl Harbor, just outside Honolulu, as the navy's main Pacific base. The request had been approved by Congress, which had appropriated an initial one million dollars. The Navy Department therefore took the opportunity of the fleet visit to have a special board headed by Rear Admiral Seaton Schroeder investigate the proposed site.[17] During one of their numerous trips to Pearl Harbor board members encountered an unanticipated snag: the naval tug *Cherokee* ran aground, and they had to go ashore and walk several miles to a train station.[18] Tours were arranged for all officers to see the site. Ensigns Harold R. Stark and Husband E. Kimmel did not record their impressions, though Pearl Harbor would figure significantly in their later careers. Kimmel, as commander in chief of the U.S. fleet thirty-three years later, would watch his battleships being attacked by the Japanese; Stark, as chief of naval operations, would share with Kimmel the burden of responsibility for the navy's lack of preparedness. Neither is there record of the impressions of either Ensign William Halsey or Midshipman Raymond Spruance, who three decades later would emerge as America's great fleet commanders in the Pacific war.

In 1908 Pearl Harbor was undeveloped, so the fleet had to rely on the limited facilities of Honolulu's naval station for coaling. This situation had been anticipated by the General Board in its war planning, and Lahaina Roads had been nominated as the most suitable anchorage for the overflow of ships from Honolulu.[19] Some assistance had been anticipated from the British collier *Craigvar,* which had been contracted to deliver coal to the fleet at Honolulu, but she did not arrive until a few hours before the fleet sailed and the navy's stockpile had to be used.[20] A more serious shortage would develop in New Zealand and Australia.

Only one significant engineering accident occurred during the cruise, and that was at Honolulu. On 18 July a steampipe in the *Kearsarge* burst, injuring five enlisted men. The ship's fires were extinguished, and the steam plant was disabled for nine hours.[21] This did not alter the scheduled departure date. At 6:00 P.M. on 22 July, after a farewell message had been delivered from Admiral Sperry to the people of Hawaii, the fleet got under way for Auckland, New Zealand.[22] The *Minnesota* remained behind to collect mail expected to arrive shortly on the steamer *Virginian.*

Surgeon Stone, who lingered on deck watching the islands disappear, recorded: "Honolulu never looked prettier than it did in the evening light, as we sailed away from it. We saw the lights of the town for several hours after we sailed, and as soon as it was a little dark a good many fireworks were sent up. . . ."[23]

The voyage from Honolulu to Auckland was the longest uninterrupted run of the cruise. The 3,850-mile trip was easy for the newer *Connecticut-* and *Virginia-*class ships of the First Squadron, with their greater bunker capacity. But for the ships of the Second Squadron, particularly the *Illinois* and *Wisconsin* in the Fourth Division, the distance represented extreme steaming range. Watch officers in the *Illinois* enforced tight control over coal to conserve precious supplies. The bunkers were locked, and every hour the watch officer entered the firerooms, unlocked the bunkers, and counted out eleven buckets of coal for each boiler. Despite this stringent measure, there was still the possibility that fuel would run out. Midshipman Maxfield recorded that it would be "a disgrace" if the *Illinois* had to be towed into Auckland by one of the bigger battleships.[24] But the continued effort to save coal ultimately paid off. All sixteen battleships arrived in Auckland under their own steam, the smaller ships just making it.

Noteworthy in the accounts of this long leg is the absence of engineering casualties. The interruptions so common during the voyage around South America belonged to the past. Engineering staffs had developed skill, efficiency, and confidence in operating their plants, significantly improving the navy's capabilities.

The *Minnesota* rejoined the fleet on 28 July, and the ships stopped in midocean long enough to collect her much-anticipated cargo of mail. That day the fleet crossed the equator once again, and the traditional ceremonies were again carried out, with fewer novices this time.

On 1 August the battleships approached Tutuila, in American Samoa. At 8:00 A.M. they swung in a long column around the eastern tip of the island and then turned west, steaming along the south side.[25] The governor, a U.S. naval officer, had learned of their approach only when a fleet auxiliary called to coal and establish a communications link. Responding to this rare interruption of the routine of his remote domain, he boarded the station ship USS *Annapolis* and, as she lay to off Tutuila's main port, Pago Pago, rendered a gun salute to the passing fleet. Without stopping, it continued toward New Zealand.[26] Samoa had missed out on a visit from the Atlantic fleet, but it would soon be visited by the armored cruisers and destroyers of the Pacific Fleet.

A week later the battleships approached New Zealand in stormy seas. The weather put them behind schedule; however, when conditions improved on 8

August, Admiral Sperry ordered twelve knots and the fleet had no difficulty arriving at the appointed time.

There is little reason to question Thomas A. Bailey's conclusion that "the alleged Oriental peril bore an important relation to the extravagance of the welcome [in New Zealand and Australia]."[27] In both countries there existed a current of popular concern, sometimes approaching hysteria, over the intentions of the Japanese.

Even before Russia had suffered any of the crushing defeats that ultimately befell her in the Russo-Japanese War, the press had begun considering the results of a Japanese victory and concluded that it would unleash an expansionist drive by millions of Japanese toward the sparsely populated and ill-defended English-speaking colonies of the antipodes. The cover of New Zealand's *Weekly Graphic,* for example, presented a full-page map of the western Pacific in which maritime Russia, Korea, Manchuria, and China had been painted brown by a Japanese military man, who was facing south toward Australia and New Zealand. The caption said, "Painting the World Brown. Will Our Turn Come?"[28]

The expression of such sentiments assumed new stridence at the beginning of 1908. The renewal of the Anglo-Japanese Alliance in 1905 elicited little or no discussion in the Australasian colonies because its most significant implication, the withdrawal of the Royal Navy's battle fleet from the Pacific, was at the time unknown.[29] The fleet's redeployment to Europe was carried out quietly and without publicity. It was not until Captain Alfred Thayer Mahan's article in the December 1907 issue of *Scientific American* that the public became aware of the changed naval dispositions.[30] That these had been effected without notice was confirmed by the personal correspondence of Admiral Fisher. In a handwritten note Fisher recorded a conversation with King Edward in which the latter had agreed that war with Germany was inevitable. Fisher wanted to launch a preemptive strike against that country but couldn't get approval: "So all that could be done was to concentrate the whole British naval strength in northern waters, which was done, and *done without exciting observation* until Admiral Mahan unfortunately wrote an article to say that 88 [86] percent of England's guns were pointed at Germany."[31]

Thus the debate over the defense of Australia and New Zealand was renewed. Their lack of military preparedness and the apparent conflicting commitment of Britain's alliance with the perceived enemy heightened concerns about Japanese intentions. Australians' fears surfaced in a war novel published at the beginning of 1908, *The World's Awakening,* which describes a hypothetical world war sparked in 1920 when Japanese sailors in Sydney riot and Japanese cruisers shell the white crowds. Britain seeks to negotiate, but Japan's chief demand is unrestricted Japanese immigration to Australia, which is refused. Japan destroys the British fleet in Asian waters along with the British prime minister's "pathetic belief in arbitration as a panacea for all ills," and Germany, in "unholy alliance" with Japan, invades England.[32] In the same vein, the Sydney *Bulletin* published a lengthy article using incidents reported in the Japanese assumption of control over Korea to draw a parallel fictional scenario for Japanese takeover of Australia. It concluded with the assertion that "the Japanization of Australia—the Japanization, also, of our wives and daughters—is only a question of time."[33]

These emotionally charged, racist works reflected popular concern about the military and naval weakness of Australia. At thirteen knots Sydney was thirty-nine days from Portsmouth, only fifteen from Yokohama. The British fleet had gone, and, according to the military correspondent of the London *Times,* it might never return to Asia.[34]

Similar fears were felt in New Zealand. The Wellington *Evening Post* commented that New Zealanders could not "expect Britain, at half a world away, to realize Australasian thought and feeling in regard to wakening Asia—no matter how definitely, how eloquently, the thought or feeling may be uttered." The suggestion in the British press that the alliance with Japan had enabled Britain to withdraw its battleships from the Pacific begged the question of "whether Japan's progress involves a threat to Australasia. And if there is such an involvement, then plainly Australasia would be safer if the battleships remained in the Far East, instead of being supplanted by a treaty."[35] Quite apart from the influence of the American fleet's cruise, by 1908 a considerable gap had appeared between British imperial and Australasian perceptions of defense requirements in the Pacific.

This gap may to some extent be attributed to too rigid an adherence to strategic orthodoxy by British naval planners—particularly the First Sea Lord, Admiral Sir John Fisher. The logic of the Admiralty's position that concentration of the fleet in home waters provided the best disposition for defense of the empire against all conceivable threats was indeed sound. Unfortunately, steadfast implementation of this strategy represented a simplistic solution to the complex problem of imperial defense. The peacetime disposition of the imperial fleet carried with it important political connotations. Withdrawal of the battle fleet from Pacific waters and manning of the Australian station with militarily insignificant ships signaled to the Australian people an apparent lack of interest in or understanding of their concerns regarding Japan.

The growing disparity between Australasian and British positions was matched by an apparent confluence of American and Australasian interests. Of importance in the Australasian view was not only American concern but also the rapidly expanding naval strength that backed it: ten first-class battleships had been completed in 1906–7. The decision to deploy the battleship fleet to the Pacific— America's effort to resolve her own Pacific defense problem—comforted Australians and New Zealanders; here was a potential source of aid against the mother country's ally. As one New Zealand "poet" put it:

> The grey fleet falters and plays with Time,
> While the Yellow ships presume,
> But the ships that are as white as frosted rime
> Are making the East give room.[36]

Rear Admiral Sperry held views considerably less extreme on the subject of the Japanese threat. Early in 1907, in a letter to the secretary of commerce that found its way to President Roosevelt in much the same manner as the letter he wrote while circumnavigating South America, Sperry maintained that while the Anglo-Japanese Alliance assured Japan control of the western Pacific, America's interests would be best served if Great Britain, Japan, and the United States remained in accord. Differences between the United States and Japan he dismissed as "incidentals." Furthermore, Japanese conquest of Korea had relieved the population pressure that had dictated an expansionist policy. "Apart from any sentiment of traditional friendships," Sperry concluded, it seemed "impossible that any responsible Japanese statesman should contemplate a rupture with this country, for which there is not adequate motive, and which would entail great expense."[37]

With this more practical assessment of the situation in the Pacific, Sperry was loath to contribute to an atmosphere of "yellow peril" in Australasia and reluctant to give the speeches his hosts hoped for, speeches making common cause with Australasia against Japan. He emphasized the "community of *commercial* interests in the development of the islands we both possess in the Pacific," but was careful to go no further.[38] This cautious approach also reflected appreciation of British sensitivity regarding the projection of American strength into Australasia. At the end of the Melbourne visit he recorded that the "general aspect of goodwill" was undeniable, though he did not think the "Imperial English" enjoyed it, even if they knew it was for the "common good."[39] He used every speaking opportunity during the Australasian visits to preach the gospel of Anglo-American cooperation and mutual interests in the Pacific. As Richard D. Challener has pointed out, Sperry, like Root and Roosevelt, "felt that Anglo-American friendship was a vital key to America's future position in the Orient."[40]

The scene in Auckland as the fleet approached was one of intense activity. The evening before the arrival the first train of the new North Island Main Trunk Railway set out from Wellington to Auckland with Prime Minister Ward, his cabinet, and many members of Parliament, which had adjourned for the duration of the fleet's visit.[41] Finishing touches were being put on extensive decorations throughout the city and thousands of visitors, arriving by steamer, rail, and road, swelled the city's population.

With the unconsciousness of world travellers, the American fleet had the temerity to approach New Zealand's shores early on a Sunday morning. At 7:10 A.M. on 9 August, as a mist began to lift from the calm surface of Hauraki Gulf, the maritime training ship NZS *Amokura* broke the early morning silence with a thirteen-gun salute to the commander in chief of the approaching ships. Despite the day, the early hour, and some local confusion concerning the fleet's arrival time, it was estimated that approximately 100,000 people—ten percent of New Zealand's population—lined the shores of the Waitemata Harbor and Rangitoto Channel to watch as the mist cleared, revealing sixteen gleaming white- and buff-colored battleships led by the *Connecticut*.[42]

They conducted an intricate S-patterned maneuver in the outer harbor of Rangitoto Channel and then, escorted by a flotilla of local craft dangerously overloaded with cheering passengers, rounded North Head and swept up the channel to anchor in modified line of squadrons in the Waitemata Harbor.[43] A plan for the ships of each division to anchor simultaneously went well except when the *Rhode Island* found insufficient room in her assigned anchorage and nearly rammed the British flagship *Powerful*. After much backing and filling, the unfortunate ship was assigned an alternate anchorage and guided there by the harbor master.[44]

Official calls were exchanged on Sunday, but the program of entertainment began the following day when Admiral Sperry went ashore.[45] For the landing ceremonies some twenty thousand people jammed into the short section of Auckland's main thoroughfare, Queen Street, nearest the wharf. Following these ceremonies, which included the first three of many speeches focusing on the common language, common ancestry, and common interests of the United States and its host—themes that were to be repeated endlessly throughout the visit and again in Sydney and Melbourne—the official party proceeded to a civic reception.[46] The morning's ceremony was completed with the planting of sixteen commemorative oaks in Albert Park, each bearing the name of a battleship.[47] Monday afternoon was marked by a military review of over three thousand men under arms from various military units of the Dominion. As many as fifty thousand people watched.[48] That night more than seven hundred invited guests showed up for a state banquet, the first ever given in Auckland.[49] Enlisted men of both navies and citizens celebrated in the streets of Auckland, which took on a decided holiday atmosphere during the visit.[50]

The official program ground on with a tedious round of receptions throughout the week: for enlisted men, chaplains, doctors of the fleet, newspaper correspondents, members of the temperance movement, Good Templars, Hibernians, and so forth. Activities were held nightly at the YMCA and Sailors' Home. One thousand enlisted men were taken on tram car tours of the city and suburbs and entertained afterward.[51]

Thus the people of New Zealand had ample opportunity to observe officers and men of the fleet, even as the Americans were observing and commenting on them. As Professor Peter Coleman has pointed out, the pioneering social legislation of New Zealand had excited considerable interest in the United States at this time, when Progressives were seeking new solutions to the social dislocations and inequalities that had been brought about by industrialization in America.[52] That officers of the fleet had access to some information suggesting the value of the New Zealand model as a possible remedy to these problems was apparent when Admiral Sperry, in response to Prime Minister Ward's address to President Roosevelt, noted that the government there was "securing all the benefits of nature for the people, in order that when they grow old they will not have to face poverty and distress. . . ."[53] The New Zealand achievement was unique; another quarter century would pass before Americans enjoyed the security of a government-sponsored old-age pension.

Carrying more impact in America than Admiral Sperry's speeches were Franklin Matthews's reports. Through his nationally syndicated column, estimated to have reached some thirty million readers, Matthews observed "that a government [had] been established . . . where millionaires as Americans know them do not exist, but where the wealth of the people reaches the tremendous total of nearly

$1,500 a head, the highest in the world; where there is no poverty; where, as nowhere else in the world, the good old democratic doctrine of the 'greatest good for the greatest number' [was] exemplified. . . . If healthier, happier, more prosperous human beings than the residents of New Zealand exist anywhere in the world," he did not know where to find them.[54]

The native Maori people also attracted interest. They were considered handsome, a cut above the average indigenous race. "Now these Maoris," Louis Maxfield wrote admiringly, "are not like our niggers or Indians. They are highly intelligent [and] go to school where they are brighter than the whites."[55] Caswell Saufley, whose unfavorable impressions of Hawaiians have already been presented, found the Maoris to be exceptional: "While in language and appearance they are similar to other South Sea Islanders, they are in character and temperament far different." Reflecting the current ideas of Social Darwinism, Saufley speculated that the difference between the Maori and Fijian could be attributed to evolution and climate: "Tropical environment causes retrogression while that of the cooler regions causes progress."[56]

Wednesday's official program drew officers to Ellerslie Race Track south of Auckland for a special "fleet race meeting."[57] After the races two hundred officers and a large parliamentary party boarded a special train for Rotorua, a thermal resort in central North Island, where Prime Minister Ward opened a new government bathhouse and the Maoris offered an official welcome to the Americans.[58]

While the Rotorua party enjoyed the splendors of the resort, the remainder of the fleet continued normal shore leave at Auckland. American sailors displayed "an evident desire to exchange their . . . capital for Auckland commodity," and local shopkeepers responded happily, experiencing the equivalent of a Christmas week in mid-August. There was a heavy run on native products and toys of all descriptions. Over forty thousand picture postcards were mailed from a special Queen Street post office open only to sailors, and this figure represented only a portion of their total mailings because they were free to use any post office.[59] The American propensity to send postcards was duly noted by Australian journalists— they called it the postcard craze and said it was yet another manifestation of "the advertisement of New Zealand."[60]

The visit drew to a close with the now-standard reception in the *Louisiana*.[61] Midshipman Saufley captured the atmosphere of the visit:

Union Jack and Stars and Stripes were intertwined upon everything. Toasts, songs, poems on this theme were written expressly for the occasion, in the commemoration of which I did and said things which I had, a few years back, as little dreamed of, as any of the Pharaoh's bricklayers did of Solomon's Temple. I had never before thought of drinking a toast to His Majesty, or of singing "God Save the King." These things I have done with as much zest as the veriest red coat in British service.[62]

This spirit of friendship was amply displayed in the streets of Auckland in the hours before the expiration of liberty at midnight on Friday, the final night of the visit.[63] As liberty launches gathered at the fleet landing to convey the last sailors back to their ships, a crowd of New Zealanders gathered at the wharves and together with the departing sailors lamented the visit's end. The launches left, and people on the shore sang strains of the popular music hall song, "We Parted on the Shore":

> We parted on the shore, yes, we
> Parted on the shore,
> I said good-bye my love, I'm
> Off to Baltimore . . .[64]

Next morning the fleet departed. The flagship *Connecticut* steamed between the lines of battleships, which weighed anchor in succession and followed her to sea.[65] Prime Minister Ward, on a government steamer, led a somewhat more subdued flotilla of local craft than the one that had met them at the beginning of the week. As the battleships passed him they rendered a final salute and their bands played the two national anthems. When the last ship, the *Kentucky,* passed by, Ward personally led his party in three rousing cheers for the United States.[66]

Though thousands of sailors had gone ashore daily, very few had failed to return to their ships at the appointed hour. Only fourteen men were unaccounted for at the expiration of liberty on the final night in Auckland. Of these, all but three were back on board before the fleet sailed next morning.[67] The recruitment of two men in Auckland reduced the net manpower loss to a single man.[68]

So ended New Zealand's only significant prewar contact with the American navy. All that remained for those who had earlier sung "We Parted on the Shore" was to weigh up the results of the visit. The *New Zealand Herald* editorialized that the American fleet was not bound to the British empire "by treaties which may be broken [that is, the Anglo-Japanese Alliance] or by conventions which may be thrust aside," but rather by "ties of blood, of religion, of origin, of ideals, of aspirations." If further ties were needed, they could be found in the "quickening sense of a common danger and in the rousing necessity for making good our English-speaking hold upon the Pacific."[69]

The implications of New Zealand's warm hospitality became the subject of English editorial comment. The *Daily Telegraph* felt that nothing but good could come from the close alignment of America's and New Zealand's interests. The cruise was an "epoch-making event . . . pregnant with mighty consequences," marking "in a most decisive fashion the emergence of the United States as no longer a Western, but a Cosmic power."[70] The London *Daily Chronicle* commented that the reception was "primarily and sincerely a demonstration of friendship for the United States," also a demonstration "against Oriental immigration into the White Man's Lands."[71]

English reporting of the deeper issues was somewhat muted. New Zealand, after all, was the most loyal of the empire's dominions, firmly committed to support of the Royal Navy as the best means of defense against aggression, and had clothed the visit to a large extent in the rhetoric of imperial objectives. As the fleet rounded New Zealand's North Cape and crossed the Tasman Sea en route to Sydney, the mother country was about to be confronted with an unprecedented celebration in the course of which Australians would show much less reluctance than New Zealanders to condemn the British alliance with Japan.

ELEVEN

Gorge, Guzzle, and Gush

The fleet's Tasman transit proved a typically tempestuous one, with stormy weather on 18 and 19 August causing fleetwide discomfort.[1] Conditions improved overnight as the ships approached Sydney. So intense was Australia's interest in the visit that half the population of that city "remained awake the entire night and thousands upon thousands of them long before night was over were on their way to the hill tops outside the city limits, where they massed seemingly in unbroken lines" to view the spectacle.[2] Estimates of the number of spectators vary from 500,000 to 650,000; the crowds were generally agreed to have been larger than those that gathered to celebrate the founding of the Commonwealth.[3] From Manly to North Head and Botany Bay to South Head, there was a "vast bivouac stretching over fourteen miles. Men, women and children, undismayed by the cold, . . . wrapped themselves up in blankets and waited for the dawn and the coming of the fleet."[4]

The spectators' vigil was rewarded when at 5:00 A.M., well before dawn, the signalmen at South Head detected the masthead lights of the approaching fleet. It grew more distinct as it gradually closed with the coast and shifted from line of squadrons to single column formation. By 9:00 A.M. the fleet was off Botany Bay, with commercial craft of all sizes trailing it. An hour later the ships stopped opposite Bondi to take on pilots, at which time Sperry was requested not to enter harbor until after 11:00. Thus the half million spectators enjoyed an unanticipated show as the fleet headed once more to sea, inscribed a huge square, and returned to the harbor entrance. A little after 11:30 A.M. the *Connecticut* passed North Head and entered Sydney Harbor, firing a twenty-one-gun national salute that was returned by Fort Denison. Then the fleet's four divisions moved to individual anchorages within the harbor.[5]

The governments of Australia, New South Wales, and Sydney had cooperated in putting together a comprehensive entertainment program, which included the usual range of banquets, balls, teas, luncheons, and tours, plus typically Australian activities such as boomerang throwing, buck jumping, sheepshearing, wood chopping, and sheep dog trials. Sydney was elaborately decorated, with streamers of bunting forming a triumphal arch for troops to march through.[6]

Enthusiastic welcome notwithstanding, in the course of official visits an embarrassing problem arose. Imperial regulations forbade the landing of armed men in Australia, but the official program, developed by Australian authorities, included the participation of the U.S. naval brigade in two parades and a military review. When informed of the regulation, Sperry told the Australians he would not permit his men to parade unarmed. A conference between Sperry and the commonwealth government followed in which an adequate compromise was reached: the Americans would land with arms but without ammunition.[7]

With this difficulty resolved, the program went forward with the naval brigade landing next morning at Farm Cove and Woolloomooloo Bay. The brigade assembled and marched up through the city. A section of Pitt Street, one of the main thoroughfares of Sydney, had been renamed American Avenue. Down it the bluejackets proceeded, smiling at the compliment paid them. With "cheer upon cheer . . . arising on either side" they made their way through the city and came to a stop in the Domain.[8] After a short ceremony there, they marched back through the city to Mrs. Macquarie's Point, where a luncheon was provided.

The noteworthy feature of the next day's agenda was a series of railway excursions hosted by the New South Wales government. Louis Maxfield went to Newcastle. He and his companions thought they were merely on an excursion to see coal mines and local sights, but they were mistaken, for every town along the train's route had been decorated in their honor and entire populations hailed them as they passed. At the Newcastle station they were received by the lord mayor and clerk dressed in robes, the city council, two brass bands, an honor guard, and 200,000 people.[9]

Sunday, 22 August, was given over mainly to religious services. The Roman Catholic church party, which included 90 officers and 1,500 men, attended a high mass celebrated by Navy Chaplain Matthew C. Gleeson at St. Mary's Cathedral. After the service, Archbishop of Sydney Patrick Francis Cardinal Moran, a colorful figure in Australian history, hosted an elaborate banquet at the town hall.[10] There, under the prominently displayed Irish and Vatican flags, Cardinal Moran chose to deliver a provocative address in which he suggested that the moral influence of the United States had been greatly responsible for the liberation of Catholics "from the fetters of oppression of those penal laws that were an indelible blot in the statute books of England." He concluded with the wish that the "same beneficent influence" might also bear fruit in achieving the "contentment, prosperity, and peace, associated with the triumph of Home Rule for Ireland."[11] In responding, Chaplain Gleeson skillfully avoided any implication that the United States might influence the issue of Irish home rule. He was "proud to be able to say that in the United States they had no religious problems. . . . In America, in every movement for the progress and well being of the human race, Catholics and Protestants worked shoulder to shoulder."[12]

But Gleeson's discretion could not quell the suspicion of Australia's Anglican majority. During the procession to the Domain, "stout-hearted Protestants in the vicinity nearly dropped dead at the spectacle of Sperry uphoisting himself, as his carriage passed the Cathedral dais, to salute the Cardinal," reported the Sydney *Bulletin*. American admirals, it claimed, were ever sensitive to the Irish question, and news that they had "been junketing in large numbers with Australian-Irish" would give more "genuine gratification to the numerous and politically influential American-Irish . . . than any other social item could."[13]

This tendency to attach political significance to American attitudes toward Australian Catholics credited the U.S. naval officer corps with a higher level of political awareness and involvement than had ever existed. More accurately, such interpretations reflected religious division in Australian society. There was no conscious effort on the part of American officers to court the favor of the Australian-Irish community. Sperry's salute to the cardinal amounted to nothing more than a courteous gesture; had the naval brigade paraded in a city of the United States, such an act would have passed without comment.

On Monday nearly a quarter million Australians mobbed Centennial Park to watch the viceregal review of the combined Royal Navy, American navy, and commonwealth naval and military forces of New South Wales. The twelve thousand men under arms constituted the largest military review held in Australia to date. All along the line of review American bluejackets were cheered as they marched to the beat of "Annie Laurie," played by navy bandsmen wearing red tunics.[14]

By Tuesday even the most ardent spirits were flagging from the furious pace, and stormy winter weather set in. Australia continued to show off for the Americans, "but the visitor was overtired; and the shows were overlong; and the skies overcast; and the winds overcold. There was plenty to look at, and not many to look. . . ."[15]

The last full day in Sydney was highlighted by a massed demonstration by nine thousand school children at the Sydney Cricket Grounds, a tour to Parramatta, a rifle match, baseball games, a viceregal garden party, and in the evening, a dinner party in the *Connecticut*.[16] Thus the final hours of liberty passed, while ships' launches carried contingents of men back from shore. Ninety-one men failed to report. Of this total, about a dozen were found next morning asleep in the Domain. These men and a few others were returned to their ships before the fleet's departure. Before the day was out an additional sixty men had been returned to the *Yankton*, leaving about seventeen—a remarkably low number, about one-tenth of one percent of the fleet—unaccounted for.[17]

The presence of stragglers proved useful when the members of Sydney's Coal Lumpers Union refused to coal the hospital ship *Relief* because nonunion labor— American bluejackets—had been used to load the battleships.[18] The collier *Tamar* and a hulk were brought alongside the *Relief*, and the stragglers as well as crew members from the *Yankton* loaded 350 tons of coal into the hospital ship, preparing her for a direct transit to Manila.[19]

At 8:00 A.M. on Thursday, 27 August, the *Connecticut* departed from Sydney, followed in sequence by the battleships of the fleet. Under a cloudless sky thousands of Australians once again lined the shore to bid the fleet farewell.

The run to Melbourne was only six hundred miles and therefore offered the officers and men only two nights to recover from Sydney's overwhelming hospitality. Louis Maxfield, whose examination for promotion to ensign would begin while the fleet was at Albany, expressed the wish that he could have an additional fourteen days at sea "so that festivities would not interfere" with his studying. "We have at last escaped from the hospitalities of Sydney," H. Kent Hewitt wrote, doubtless reflecting the feelings of many on board the battleships, "only to be swallowed up in those of Melbourne."[20]

As the fleet approached, Melbourne was "in the midst of its last . . . bustle in preparation for . . . jollifications," the *Sydney Morning Herald* reported. The paper likened the American visit to Australasia to a three-act play in which the crisis was reached during the second act, in Sydney. It would take "something like genius in stage management to prevent the third act proving a mere anti-climax."[21]

The Melbourne reception committee had taken note of the American bluejackets' reluctance to attend prearranged activities and reportedly had made special efforts to leave the sailors as much free time as possible to "partake of private hospitality, or to follow unhindered their own particular bent."[22] The schedule of formal events was nevertheless daunting.[23]

Shortly after 11:00 A.M. on Saturday, 29 August, the fleet rounded Port Philip Heads and started the thirty-mile trip north to the anchorage in Hobson's Bay. The magnificence of Melbourne's aquatic welcome, however, failed to impress the jaded travelers. Louis Maxfield duly reported the throng of steamers and yachts which greeted the fleet, noting that it was an "old story now" and the men hardly noticed.[24]

One peculiar difficulty during this visit was reaching Melbourne, which was a long way from the fleet landing. It took thirty minutes in a steamer to get to the landing in Williamstown, then the men had to walk a mile or so to the railroad station and take a forty-five-minute train ride to the city.[25] "I might remark," Chaplain Gleeson said in a speech at the Pressmen's Banquet, that "it's almost as easy to get to Heaven as to come to Melbourne . . ."[26]

The fleet anchored in Hobson's Bay at 3:00 P.M. on Saturday, and thus the calendar allowed the men a short reprieve. Functions that day were limited to official calls and social events for senior officers, and Sunday, with the exception of an optional church parade, was free. Twenty-five hundred men were granted liberty on Sunday, of which one thousand marched along Collins Street to Saint Patrick's Cathedral for a pontifical mass. The bluejackets were led by two thousand Australian cadets and bands playing marching music. The streets along the route were thronged with eager spectators.[27] Whether this was a spontaneous outpouring of religious fervor on the part of the Americans or whether it had been discovered that a trip to the cathedral was a good way to make personal contacts with the people—particularly young ladies—is impossible to say.

Monday's festivities commenced with the fleet's formal entry into the city of Melbourne. The naval brigade landed as scheduled and set out on a lengthy march from Port Melbourne with a "boisterous north wind . . . pelting dust through the streets," directly into the faces of the marching bluejackets. When they reached Melbourne the dust-covered men received a rousing welcome, "while from every packed window on either side there broke forth in feminine greeting a snow-white cloud of fluttering kerchiefs. . . ."[28] The *Sydney Morning Herald* reported that the bluejackets "certainly paid for their portion of the Melbourne holiday," the length of their march being "unconscionable."[29] Afterwards the commonwealth government gave an elaborate luncheon for the men.

That evening there was a banquet for the officers, free theater performances, and a torchlight procession through the city.[30] Tuesday was filled with more formal engagements, and Wednesday was a repeat of Tuesday.[31] Though none of the Americans denied the sincerity of the Melbourne welcome, they would have preferred time to pursue personal interests.

The official program reached its climax with a military review on Thursday, which had been declared a full holiday. In bright sunshine crowds gathered early.[32] After an unusually long wait in parade formation for noteworthies to take their positions in the reviewing stand, the event finally got under way. The Americans were well received, but the heartiest welcome was extended to a squad of naval cadets from Ballarat who had captured the imagination of Australia when, refused public transportation by the Ministry of Defense, they marched five days to participate in the festivities.[33]

That night dinner for three thousand men was prepared at the Exhibition Building. At 7:00 P.M., when it was ready to be served, a grand total of one American sailor had arrived. Dinner was postponed until 9:00 P.M., by which time the number of diners had risen to seven. The *Morning Herald* explained the fiasco of "The Uneaten Dinner": "When every tar . . . has a girl on his arm it is easily understood that he does not want to leave the lights and the crowd to pass the time in company of men with whom he has to live on board ship."[34] This embarrassing incident might suggest American ingratitude for Australian hospitality, but in fact the dinner's failure measured Melbourne's success. It was universally acclaimed as the best port of call of the entire cruise.

Fleet Week ended with a fireworks display in Albert Park. Among the thousands of Australian spectators American bluejackets seemed few and far between. "But they were *there,* very much so! Every rocket revealed tender scenes. Only here and there a girl had secured the attention of a sailor boy all to herself. Most of them walked with two girls—an arm around each!" Given such friendly relations, it is not difficult to understand the "epidemic" of liberty violation that broke out in Melbourne.[35]

Liberty ended at 11:00 P.M. on Friday, 4 September. By that time many enlisted men were still making their way through dense crowds to the railway station in Melbourne. "The last quarter-mile of their track to the station lay through packed crowds where girls hugged and kissed them—and snared the buttons from their tunics—till at last they were hoisted shoulder-high, and tumbled jumpily over the crowd, 'mid applause and kisses, till the platform received them."[36] It is little wonder that some of the men chose to take permanent leave of the American navy in Melbourne. At first count it was estimated that some 85 men failed to make the Saturday morning muster, but that figure was rapidly revised to 221.[37] Thus, while "crowds of Fleet-bitten girls got up on Saturday morning . . . and went to the edges of our Bay to wave a heart-broken umbrella to the departing Armada," many others must have gotten up that morning with the objects of their affection still with them.[38]

Preparations for departure were marred by an accident. The naval collier *Ajax,* getting under way one day before the rest of the fleet and with a pilot on board, collided with the steamer *Leura,* heavily laden with passengers returning from an excursion around the fleet. She struck the *Leura*'s starboard quarter, and both ships were badly damaged.[39] The *Ajax* had to be dry-docked in Williamstown and would not rejoin the fleet until the battleships reached Colombo.[40]

The following morning, blanketed by a fog, fifteen of the battleships departed. The *Connecticut* led them slowly down the bay and only at intervals, when the fog thinned slightly, could people ashore catch a glimpse of their masts.[41] The battleship *Kansas* was left behind in Melbourne to conduct, as the Navy Department much later claimed, an inquiry into the *Ajax-Leura* collision.[42] The local press reported that the ship's mission was to pick up mail and take on stragglers.[43] The *Bulletin* whimsically reported that "there was no 'Murkan mail due, but there were a lot of males very much overdue."[44] In fact, the *Kansas* stayed behind for all three reasons. American mail was expected, and officers of the *Kansas* did make a concerted effort to recover as many deserters as possible.

When the *Kansas* finally left Melbourne on 10 September she carried 458 bags of mail for the fleet and well over a hundred stragglers.[45] The number of men still unaccounted for ranged from 100 to 115.[46] With the additional fifteen that had stayed behind in Sydney, the total manpower loss in Australia was 115 to 130 men.[47] One suspects that many men who returned to the fleet secretly envied the successful deserters. Midshipman Saufley wrote his parents, "If I were not in the Navy I would settle here myself. For a young man of energy there is a fortune waiting."[48] Indeed, it is not difficult to discern a tone of wistfulness in the more formal words of Admiral Sperry in his farewell message to Australia. Acknowledging that some men were apparently determined to be adopted by Australia, he confessed that the feeling was understandable because everyone from the prime minister down had treated them in a way that could "engender but one desire" in their hearts: to remain in Australia "for the rest of their days."[49]

From Melbourne the fleet headed west on the 1,300-mile voyage to Albany, in Western Australia. The men had been fully briefed to anticipate heavy seas in the Great Australian Bight, where, unimpeded by land for thousands of miles, the Southern Ocean normally develops swells of monumental proportions. The battleships experienced generally fair seas for the first four days of the voyage. On 9 September they encountered swells, but with the exception of heavy seas during the last two days of the voyage the trip passed rather uneventfully.[50]

Ashore, in the small community of Albany, there was uncertainty about the fleet's arrival time. When the Reuter's correspondent there finally managed to establish contact with the *Connecticut,* at 1:00 A.M. on 11 September, he learned that the ships were only seventy miles away and scheduled to arrive at 7:00 A.M. Unfortunately it was too late to pass this information to the townspeople, who expected them later. The premier of Western Australia embarked in the government launch *Penguin* to greet them, but only a "handful of rainbeaten, shivering spectators" stood on the slopes of the harbor.[51]

The fleet entered the outer harbor of Albany at about 7:00 A.M. and came to anchor in line of divisions. Shortly afterward the *Connecticut* fired a twenty-one-gun salute to which the local fort responded. The British cruiser *Gibraltar* and the Chilean training ship *General Baquedano* fired thirteen-gun salutes to Admiral Sperry's flag.

Though Albany was the smallest city the fleet had been to, the townspeople went all out to receive it. A series of entertainments had been arranged and an ornate "souvenir and official program" published.[52] Social activities, however, were secondary; the main reason for the fleet's presence in Albany was to coal and prepare for the next long leg of the trip, the 3,500-mile voyage to Manila. Coal, by the time the fleet reached Albany, had become a burning issue.

The problem of coal had first grown serious at Auckland. The U.S. consul-general there had advised the State Department of local companies' interest in supplying the fleet and of the fact that, as only limited stocks were normally available, advance notification was required if a large supply was desired.[53] This information was forwarded to the Navy Department, which replied that no coal would be needed because contracts had been let for the delivery of 30,000 tons of American coal.[54]

When the fleet anchored at Auckland, senior officers made the unpleasant discovery that only half the contracted collier force, three ships with a total cargo of 17,538 tons, had arrived, and some concern was being expressed for the safety of the three remaining ships. Local suppliers, earlier told that no coal would be required, had not brought in additional stocks to cover this unanticipated situation. The fleet was able to purchase only 353 tons, which was used to resupply the hospital ship *Relief.* With the fleet short 16,000 tons, Lieutenant Commander Fullinwider, Sperry's flag secretary, attempted to minimize the problem, suggesting that there was plenty of coal to proceed to Sydney, and if the colliers didn't turn up there the fleet could buy enough to take it to a port where supplies would be waiting. But Admiral Sperry painted a completely different picture in his official correspondence. The failure at Auckland, he reported to the chief of the Bureau of Navigation, was the result of Navy Department negligence. It had "caused great embarrassment," "entailed coaling day and night in Auckland" to distribute limited amounts of coal throughout the fleet, and meant that coaling would have to be conducted in Sydney and Melbourne.[55]

Sydney suppliers had also been informed that the fleet would need no coal, and being situated so near the mines, the city seldom had on hand any great amount.[56] Immediately upon arrival in Sydney, Sperry's chief of staff, Commander Albert Weston Grant, ordered 5,000 tons from local stock. This was followed by an additional order of 8,000 for delivery in Melbourne.[57] Confronted with these large orders, placed on a Saturday, local colliery owners were unable to meet the demand immediately.[58] They did manage to have 3,000 tons transferred to the battleships from the coastal collier *Palmerston* and the hulks *Lassie, Tamar,* and *Argo* on

Saturday and Sunday, and an additional 2,000 from the colliers *Malachite, Wallsend, Illaroo,* and *Wallarah.* The steam colliers *Herga, Palmerston,* and *Currajong* were dispatched to Wollongong and loaded; they returned later in the week with 1,200 tons. Thus a total of 6,200 tons was delivered at Sydney.[59]

The American request for coal at Melbourne was met by diverting the collier *Kooringa,* already en route to Breaksea, near Albany, to Melbourne with 5,000 tons, and by buying 2,000 tons already in stock at Melbourne.[60] These makeshift arrangements required the consul-general's "entire reserve supply of ingenuity and resourcefulness," involving ten straight hours of negotiations with coal company heads and local labor unions while messages were diverting ships at sea.[61]

By such means the fleet acquired sufficient fuel to carry on. Meanwhile the *Usher,* one of the colliers originally scheduled to supply the fleet in New Zealand, had arrived at Auckland on 22 August and received orders from Sperry to proceed without delay to Cavite.[62] Her master balked at these orders and cabled the owners, who directed him to proceed to Melbourne and exercise one of the follow-up options contained in their contract, which permitted a Melbourne delivery if made by 29 August. There she met the fleet on 1 September—late again, at least according to the terms of the contract.[63] Sperry informed Washington that she had arrived in Melbourne contrary to his instructions and that the fleet could not coal from her without delaying its departure.[64] It seems possible that the reason the *Usher* was not unloaded was not her late arrival but that Sperry had already managed to obtain enough coal from local sources to carry the fleet to Albany, where six colliers were expected. It would have been reasonable, though, to anticipate that those ships, transiting the Southern Ocean at approximately the same time as the tardy Auckland trio, would encounter the same heavy weather and experience the same delays. When the fleet reached Albany, only three of the six contracted colliers were there, and the fleet was again strapped for coal.[65]

In the wake of previous difficulties, a shortage of colliers in this isolated location understandably caused concern. After loading from the three colliers, each battleship was about 500 tons short of coal. To complicate matters, the Australian coal taken on board was not suited to the battleships' grate bars.[66]

Admiral Emory recorded that the fleet was looking for the three additional colliers "as eagerly as Sister Anne's lookout for the three horsemen in Blue Beard."[67] On 15 September the colliers *Tarus* and *Epsom,* with 13,606 tons of cargo coal, entered King George's Sound.[68] The sixth collier, the *King Robert,* had only cleared Natal on 6 September and on 15 September was still more than two weeks away.

Sperry had already devised an alternate plan to coal the fleet from two naval colliers at Zamboanga, in the southern Philippines.[69] With the arrival of the *Tarus* and *Epsom,* this plan was abandoned and it was decided to delay sailing until the evening of 18 September, so that each battleship could take on additional fuel.[70] On 17 September, however, the *New York Times* reported from Albany that the collier *Epsom* had not discharged there, that she would carry her cargo to Cavite.[71] It is possible there was simply not time to offload the cargo of both colliers, even with the fleet's delayed sailing, and that the *Epsom* consolidated the remainder of both cargoes for transportation to Cavite. Because of the range of the tide, Vice

Admiral Sir Richard Poore, RN, had earlier counseled Sperry, "it [was] seldom practicable for two vessels to make fast alongside each other in King George Sound."[72] Therefore the battleships had had to enter the small inner harbor one by one and coal there—a time-consuming procedure. That time was the factor limiting coaling operations at Albany is confirmed by the delay of the *Missouri* and *Connecticut*, which remained behind to complete coaling after the fleet departed at 5:00 P.M. on 18 September.[73]

The unreliability of the foreign colliers, which had caused embarrassment and delay, also had serious implications for America's defense.[74] But the suggestion in a modern treatment of the cruise that the failure could be traced to the British government's desire to deny coal to the fleet is not supported by fact.[75] Though most of the colliers were British, they were under contract to American firms and they loaded their cargoes of American coal at American ports. Rather, the late arrivals at Auckland can be explained by the timing of the collier's contracts. The final contract for the three punctual colliers had been let on 29 April 1908; that for the three latecomers had not been let until 23 May. The Bureau of Equipment knew it had left little margin for delay in this instance, and therefore the later contracts had included provisions for delivery at Sydney and/or Cavite.[76] Unusually heavy weather encountered by the *British Monarch* and *Baron Minto* further taxed their ability to arrive on time.[77] Of the Auckland failure, Sperry concluded that it would have been impossible for the other three colliers to steam fast enough to reach Auckland in time. The Bureau of Equipment, he felt, had been dangerously negligent.[78] The culprit in the coaling performance was clear to Sperry. "Admiral Cowles, the President's brother-in-law [and chief of the Bureau of Equipment], was responsible for this bungling," he confided to his son, "and if Teddy's fleet had been hung up for a laughing stock it would have been a warm day for Cowles."[79]

In reality, Cowles had worked under serious restraints: late announcement of the cruise—a political consideration–and the need to accept competitive bids before granting contracts—a statutory limitation. These resulted in unacceptably short periods for successful bidders to get empty bottoms to Virginian ports to pick up cargo. A late start with no margin for delay in shipping more than a dozen cargoes over a route notorious for heavy winter weather was nothing less than a recipe for disaster. The results were predictable. Had the American navy had an adequate force of dedicated naval colliers, it would have been possible to load and deploy them to the area of most likely need without such restraints.

A more important lesson that might have been learned from the failure of foreign-flag colliers was that an adequate naval collier force would give the fleet independence of movement, enabling it to deploy anywhere in the world without political and military restraints. There is no evidence to suggest the British government obstructed or delayed the fleet's coal supply, but the awareness that it might do so in the event of war with Japan remained an unsettling consideration throughout the cruise.

As the evening of 18 September approached, the fleet once again made preparations to get under way. Having largely missed the arrival, townspeople of Albany now had ample opportunity to see the departure. At 5:00 P.M. a large crowd that had gathered on the hills surrounding the harbor was rewarded with a series of precision maneuvers as the battleships took their leave.[80] The division flagships were anchored nearest the shore, and to resume their places at the head of the formation they, followed in turn by each ship in its respective division, counter-marched from the anchorage; it was a spectacular, if functional, maneuver.[81]

A final round of farewell messages repeated all the sentiments so often expressed during the Australian visit.[82] But not even this departure was final: the *Missouri* remained a few hours longer and the *Connecticut* stayed until 6:30 the next morning to complete coaling.[83] That day the people of Fremantle and Perth had a brief opportunity to greet the battleships. As they passed Rocknest Island, with the mainland indistinct in the background, a number of small steamers appeared, their decks crowded with cheering, flag-waving citizens.[84] With this final goodbye, exactly one month after its first contact with Sydney, the fleet's visit to Australia drew to a close.

TWELVE

Trial, Tempest, and Triumph

While the battleship fleet had been completing preparations for departure from San Francisco, a book was published in Berlin that attempted to rekindle anti-Japanese feelings in the United States. *Banzai!* described in lurid detail a hypothetical Japanese invasion of America.[1] A similar work, *Der Krieg von 1908* (*The War of 1908*), suggested that the U.S. government had deliberately caused the 1907 financial panic in order to draw gold to the United States and prevent Japan from raising a war loan in Europe.[2] Works of this genre did nothing to calm the fears of Americans on the Pacific Coast. In essence, they described situations that would best suit the goals of German *Weltpolitik*. Virtually any development that disturbed the fragile equilibrium of British defense arrangements seemed certain to strengthen Germany's strategic position.

While the fleet was crossing the Tasman Sea to Australia the normally conservative *New York Times* published a lengthy article reporting widespread American distrust of Japan's motives in China and suggesting that Japan's ally, England, could not be included in any plan to curb Japanese ambitions there. "It is known here," the paper said, "that the reception accorded the fleet by the British colonists has caused the greatest uneasiness in London." France and Russia were ruled out as possible partners in curbing further Japanese encroachment. "What Power remains . . . with which the United States might strike hands for the defense of China's sovereign existence and the equal rights of white men within her borders?" The answer was clear: Germany, the nation that had shown a "keener realization of the antagonism between the yellow race and the white than had any other Power except America." Further, it was suggested that Germany, isolated on the continent, might "look with favor on the idea of an alliance with the United States."[3] This speculation was a gross understatement, for the achievement of an alliance between the United States, China, and Germany had been a goal of Kaiser Wilhelm's for more than a year.[4] He had, as early as January 1907, thought of enlisting

American support against the "machinations of King Edward." "In connection with this," Wilhelm had written to his chancellor, Prince von Bülow, "my insurance treaty with Theodore Roosevelt, who is afraid of the Japanese, would be appropriate and worthy of consideration."[5] He completely misread Roosevelt's sentiment toward the Japanese, his concern for Chinese sovereignty over Manchuria, and his readiness to ally the United States with Germany—in short, the overall direction of American foreign policy. This misreading colored all subsequent German calculations.

In July 1907 the German minister in Peking, Count von Rex, suggested the possibility of an agreement with the United States that would protect German industrial interests in China. In response, Foreign Minister von Tschirschky directed the German ambassador in Washington, Baron Speck von Sternburg, to consider the possibility of an arrangement to "offset the ententes of the other powers."[6] Capitalizing on the strength of his intimate personal relationship with Roosevelt, von Sternburg pressed the kaiser's scheme in Washington. In November 1907 he reported to von Bülow that he had urged Roosevelt to enter into an alliance supporting the Open Door in China. The president, according to von Sternburg, had replied that an alliance was not conceivable until the battleship fleet arrived in the Pacific, at which time it might be appropriate to announce one.[7] Most likely, as Raymond Esthus has suggested, von Sternburg's report was inaccurate: "Sternburg and the Kaiser deluded themselves into believing that the President would enter a genuine entente or alliance which would align the United States against the British-Japanese-French-Russian combination" in the Far East.[8]

As the fleet set out on its world cruise, the prospect of a German-American-Chinese alliance seemed good to Germany. An entente might be precipitated by heightening Japanese-American tensions, and this was attempted through various means, including the kaiser's "intelligence" reports of Japanese army formations in Mexico, of plots to destroy the fleet, and so forth.[9] These, and his contention that Japan planned to start a war with the United States, were balanced by a more realistic appraisal from the German military attaché in Peking, forwarded to Roosevelt by von Sternburg. The attaché "was convinced that Japan did not at this time meditate war on the United States, but, on the contrary, its preparations were for trouble with or in China."[10]

That the Japanese were also aware of German efforts to disrupt their relations with America was strongly suggested when, on 16 March 1908, British Ambassador Bryce asked Japanese Ambassador Baron Takahira to what cause he attributed the constantly renewed press reports of a rift between Japan and the United States. According to Bryce, Takahira responded that "perhaps there might be persons or Governments whose aim it was to weaken the alliance between Great Britain and Japan by endeavouring to create a position in which Great Britain might seem put to the alternative of choosing the friendship of one or the other. . . ."[11]

Baron Takahira need not have worried. The United States was unprepared to create a situation that would involve it in a Sino-Japanese conflict. Pursuit of the Open Door remained an important aspect of the rhetoric of American foreign policy; however, rapprochement with Japan, regardless of its policies in Manchuria and Korea, had become the reality of that policy. Roosevelt was convinced that Germany's aspirations presented the greatest threat to world peace, while Japan's centered only on Manchuria and East Asia. By acquiescing in Japanese policy toward Manchuria, the United States would be free to continue concentrating its naval forces in the Atlantic—the area still seen as most threatened.

Reduction by one half of the fleet battleships visiting China, the shift of port to remote Amoy, and continued progress in efforts to reach agreement on a range of issues that had strained Japanese-American relations should have clearly signaled the poor prospect for a German-American-Chinese alliance. These developments, however, seem to have escaped the attention of Kaiser Wilhelm. Shortly after the fleet left San Francisco, he granted an interview to *New York Times* correspondent William Bayard Hale in which, in an uninterrupted string of indiscretions, he claimed that there would be a revolt in India in the winter of 1908–9, that Germany would soon have to go to war with England, and that Japan and the United States would also fight a war. He had planned with the United States, he said, to "back up China against Japan and thereby keep the equilibrium in the East," an arrangement a Chinese statesman was on his way to Washington to work out.[12]

Hale took the contents of this interview to the American ambassador in Berlin, who recommended its suppression, and to the German foreign minister, who "had apoplexy" when he read it. It was then sent to the head office of the *New York Times*, where Oscar King Davis took the document to Roosevelt. The president reacted by saying that he had "not the slightest hesitation in believing that it was absolutely accurate." He urged suppression of the interview because publication would jeopardize world peace.[13] It was not made public until the 1930s.[14]

While the kaiser may have believed that the interview would advance his Far Eastern strategy, in fact it achieved a result opposite to that intended: it set Roosevelt even more on his guard toward the German ruler. Just before a similar intimidating outburst from Kaiser Wilhelm, the publication of which led to an almost unanimous demand for more British battleships and thus stirred Britain's Dreadnought Scare, Roosevelt discussed the Hale interview in a letter to one of his British correspondents, Arthur H. Lee.[15] He warned Lee not to disclose the contents of his letter to anyone but Balfour and Grey, then pointed out that if the kaiser had been "indiscreet enough to talk to a strange newspaperman [Hale] in such fashion it would be . . . possible that sometime he would be indiscreet enough to act on impulse in a way that would jeopardize the peace."[16]

The Hale interview reached Roosevelt while the Newport Conference to discuss battleship design defects was in progress, and two days before Sims submitted a proposal suggesting the president appoint a commission to investigate reorganization of the Navy Department. Although Roosevelt enthusiastically endorsed the concept of Sims's plan, it seems reasonable to assume that, having reached the conclusion about Kaiser Wilhelm's willingness to jeopardize the peace, he was reluctant to arouse congressional opposition to his battleship construction program by actively pursuing a reorganization plan. As a result of the kaiser's actions—that is, the emergence of the German threat—and the increased pace of dreadnought construction in Europe, he chose to concentrate his efforts on getting congressional approval for more dreadnoughts. Gaining authorization for as many as four dreadnoughts in 1909 therefore assumed the highest priority in his naval policy.

But this battle would not be fought for a few more months. The suppression of the kaiser's interview was followed eight days later, as the fleet steamed toward Sydney and Japan prepared to receive its guests, by a *New York Times* article, "Firm Policy in the Far East." The piece was widely reported in Japan, where it was concluded that the idea of an alliance with China lacked support in the United States. Concerning American distrust, Japanese papers asserted that it was unfounded, and that the battleship fleet's visit to Yokohama would ease relations between the two countries.[17]

Most Americans also discounted talk of an alliance with China. A. Maurice Low, writing in the *Forum,* observed that the idea could not be taken seriously. The real source of difficulty, he correctly pointed out, was European maneuvering. If it was true that Germany was awaiting an opportunity to pounce on England, then obviously it would want to encourage friction between the United States and Japan. Were hostilities to break out, Japan might have to ask its ally for assistance; this could put England in an awkward position. Low could hardly conceive the possibility of England fighting against the United States but suggested that the terms of its alliance with Japan might force such a development. That would be a "triumph of German diplomacy worthy of the best traditions of the Bismarckian Era," because any assistance England might give Japan would weaken the Royal Navy in home waters and tempt Germany to invade England.[18] And so the cruise of the American fleet to the Orient assumed importance in relation not just to Japan and the United States but also to the strategic calculations of the European powers whose array of alliances and ententes had already become so threatening to the peace of Europe that references to a "coming Armageddon" had grown commonplace in the press.

Thus the European balance of power, the wide publicity given to Australasian proclamations of the battleship fleet as their protection against the yellow peril, reports circulating about American distrust of Japanese, and speculation concerning an alliance with China all raised the level of tension connected with the anticipated fleet visit to Yokohama.

The only difficulty encountered in the long trip from Albany to Manila involved coal. The high consumption rate of two ships in the Fourth Division caused concern a few days after the fleet set out. Sperry therefore ordered the division to reduce speed to a more economical nine knots.[19] With a speed difference of two knots, the remainder of the fleet gradually drew ahead and disappeared over the northern horizon.[20]

On 26 September the main body of the fleet reached Lombok Strait, off the eastern extremity of Java, after its smoothest run since leaving San Francisco.[21] Early morning haze forced the ships to lay to off the strait until about 8:00 A.M., when it cleared enough to permit safe navigation of the passage.[22]

With calm weather and the introduction of measures for fuel economy the

Fourth Division had gradually increased speed so that by the time it reached the strait it was less than thirty miles astern of the fleet.[23] As the other ships crossed the Java Sea en route to Macassar Strait, the Fourth Division slowly closed the gap, and next night the two groups were able to communicate with each other by searchlight.[24] The following day the Fourth Division steamed northward, with the western shore of Celebes (Sulawesi) on the starboard beam and the rest of the fleet on the port bow.[25] Because all the ships of the fleet were steaming at a signaled speed of eleven knots, the Fourth Division closed with the main formation at a painfully slow pace. The fleet was reunited again on the morning of 30 September when it formed single column to transit Basilan Strait.[26]

The battleships steamed close inshore as they passed Zamboanga, the largest city on the southern island of Mindanao, and rendered a gun salute to the commander of the Mindanao Department, General Tasker Bliss. Water craft from the island came out to hail the fleet, including two brightly painted Moro war canoes, one carrying an elaborately dressed chieftain.[27]

On the afternoon of 2 October the fleet steamed past Corregidor Island and entered Manila Bay, coming to anchor two miles off Manila in two columns, the First Squadron closer to shore.[28]

While the fleet had been steaming north, the health situation in Manila became a source of considerable concern. Cholera, which had swept the island in 1902 and killed over sixty-five thousand people, reappeared. Starting with a few cases in northern Luzon, the disease had spread so quickly that by 20 September an average of fifty new cases were being reported daily in Manila alone. At this point Secretary of the Navy Metcalf announced that the situation would not keep the fleet from calling at Manila, although if the epidemic continued, shore leave would be forbidden.[29] He cabled Sperry authorizing him to restrict contact with the shore to official business, or to prohibit it completely, if the disease became epidemic, until after the fleet's return from Japan.[30]

These precautions doubtless would have been applauded by families of crew members, for fear of a cholera epidemic such as that currently claiming thousands of lives in Russia was great. The mother of one future four-star admiral, H. Kent Hewitt, "ill with anxiety and dread," wrote directly to Secretary Metcalf, begging that he countermand the order for the fleet to visit Manila.[31] But no such action was necessary. A few days before the ships reached Manila, the committee in charge of fleet reception met with Governor-General James A. Smith and a group of prominent businessmen and, bowing to the inevitable, canceled all preparations for the celebrations until after the return from Japan.[32]

All these announcements and decisions had been made without communications from the fleet; atmospheric conditions had prevented the battleships from contacting the wireless station at Macassar and from communicating via Jolo and Zamboanga.[33] Not until the day before its arrival did the fleet establish radio contact through Zamboanga. Then, confronted with news of the epidemic and Governor-General Smith's decision, Sperry concluded that the safest course of action would be to curtail liberty.[34] This decision was completely logical given the circumstances, but it left the people of Manila disgruntled. They had raised $120,000 to entertain the fleet and already procured supplies, many perishable.[35]

With liberty canceled, the fleet's main activity at Manila was the unpleasant one of coaling, made worse by the Philippine heat. Toward the end men grew exhausted and the last tons of coal were loaded very slowly.[36] The plan for the cruise north to Yokohama did not include any provision for coaling. Therefore at Manila the ships took on additional supplies, which were either stowed in sacks on deck or in loose piles with filled gunny sacks around them.[37]

The fleet's in-port routine was disrupted when a typhoon passed over the anchorage area on 4 October. One hundred mile per hour winds forced the battleships to get up steam, the six nearest the breakwater to get under way.[38] Last day in port, word arrived that another typhoon was expected and the fleet's sailing was postponed until the following day, 10 October.[39] Although the revised departure time had been publicly announced as 8:00 A.M., the fleet actually departed at 6:00 A.M. Thus the local people, who had missed out on their celebrations, also missed the opportunity to see the ships depart.[40]

Manila authorities started a new campaign to eradicate cholera in anticipation of the fleet's return. Police conducted daily house-to-house checks; the disinfecting force was augmented. Every effort was being made to ensure that Manila would receive a clean bill of health before the Americans got back from Yokohama.[41]

Though the typhoon had not materialized as predicted, when the battleships steamed north off the west coast of Luzon they experienced calm, sultry weather of the sort that makes seasoned mariners uneasy.[42] This foreboding was borne out when the barometer began dropping rapidly and storm conditions developed.[43] By the morning of 12 October the fleet was heading into the teeth of a typhoon.[44] The bigger ships of the First Division "practically hove to for a day and wallowed like a herd of swine."[45] But mountainous seas most affected the low-freeboard ships of the Fourth Division, which once again dropped astern of the fleet's main body, reducing signaled speed to seven, then to six knots. The storm continued through 13 October. The *Missouri* took huge seas over her forecastle, her upper top was drenched, and bridge watchstanders were continually inundated by cold spray.[46] The foretopmast and wireless antenna of the *Kearsarge* were carried away, and a number of ships lost their lifeboats.[47] Three men were washed overboard. Two were rescued, but the third, a gunner's mate, had the misfortune of falling from the *Rhode Island,* at the end of the formation. She could not come about, her boats could not be launched, and there were no ships astern to pick him up. His shipmates last saw the poor fellow "standing up in the water looking after the ship."[48]

The storm moderated late on the thirteenth and by the next day it was over, giving the battleships a chance to repair damage and prepare for the journey to Yokohama. The storm had caused considerable delay, and as the scattered units slowly drew together, the arrival was postponed twenty-four hours. This information was signaled to the Japanese authorities at the earliest possible opportunity; on 16 October they officially announced it.[49]

TRIAL, TEMPEST, AND TRIUMPH

One account of the cruise suggests that throughout the storm Sperry had been dwelling on larger problems. The admiral knew that the "entire Imperial Navy was at sea, ready for battle," presumably with the American battleship fleet.[50] But during the storm the main fleet units of the Japanese navy had been secure in Kure Naval Base. Subsequently they moved to Yokohama, where they anchored on 14 and 15 October while the American fleet, far to the south, was just starting to straighten itself out after the big blow.[51] The Japanese navy's autumn naval maneuvers, which it has been supposed caused Sperry such great worry, were not actually scheduled to commence until after the visit of the American fleet. Rather than being cloaked in mystery, the maneuvers had been publicly announced more than six months earlier.[52] Japan had published a full order of battle prior to the American fleet's departure from San Francisco, and the mid-November commencement had been confirmed by the U.S. naval attaché in Tokyo before the fleet reached Auckland.[53]

The battleships approached Yokohama in fog, obscuring the men's view of Tokyo Bay and Fujiyama. The spirit of the assembled crowd, however, was not dampened.[54] The official reception, which had begun with a shower of telegraphed greetings from Japan's political and naval noteworthies, now took solid shape with the appearance of an escort squadron.[55] This was followed by a flotilla of six oceangoing merchant steamers with WELCOME painted in large white letters on their black hulls, their decks crowded with soldiers, women, and children, all cheering and singing American patriotic songs in English.[56] The battleships, preceded by their Japanese escorts, continued up Tokyo Bay to their anchorage.[57] As they anchored and commenced exchanging gun salutes, the mist cleared, revealing the contrasting colors of white American warships and their gray Japanese counterparts already at anchor.[58]

The fleet's safe arrival triggered the most intense round of social engagements during the entire cruise. The people of Tokyo and Yokohama had been preparing for months and had gone to great lengths to ensure that absolutely nothing was overlooked. In addition to the more or less standard decorations put up in other cities along the route, citizens of Yokohama had been directed to hang their houses with Japanese and American flags, lanterns, and so forth, and the mayor had ordered various public bodies to organize lantern processions and fireworks displays.[59] The monument at Kurihama commemorating the visit of Commodore Matthew C. Perry half a century earlier had been spruced up, given new railings, and included in guided tours conducted by the America's Friends Association.[60]

The Foreign Office and superintendents of police did everything possible to avoid misunderstanding by Americans unfamiliar with Japanese customs. Thousands of school children had been taught to sing the "Star-Spangled Banner," "Hail Columbia," and other patriotic American songs, and a corps of student volunteers had been organized as interpreters for the men of the fleet.[61] Finally, the U.S. naval attaché, Commander John A. Dougherty, had been invited to meetings of the Japanese navy's fleet reception committee; he had forwarded advance information about the visit to Washington.[62]

Admiral Sperry had made whatever preparations he could. His first step was to write a lengthy letter to Henry Willard Denison, an American citizen who had been in Japan since 1874—initially as a consular official, but since 1880 as legal advisor to the Japanese Foreign Office.[63] Sperry had met him at The Hague, where Denison had served as technical representative for the Japanese government. The admiral, well aware of Denison's influential position, took pains to describe the arrangements necessary to accommodate the fleet. He explained the "character of our men, their desire for sightseeing, temperance, the necessity of rest places for them on shore, ample landing places to permit handling as many as 3,000 men twice a day quickly, guides, etc."[64] As anticipated, Denison showed Sperry's letter to officers of the Japanese naval staff who undoubtedly appreciated the guidance it offered. This indirect consultation helped complete arrangements which, Sperry reported to President Roosevelt, were perfect.[65]

Roosevelt's main concern when he accepted the Japanese invitation had been misbehavior on the part of enlisted men ashore, and he was inclined to order that no enlisted liberty be given in Yokohama.[66] Sperry strongly advised Roosevelt against any "obvious departure" from normal practice.[67] Nevertheless, to reduce the possibility of mishap the admiral limited liberty to special first-class libertymen who were fully briefed on their responsibilities before being permitted ashore. Arrangements for 2,400 enlisted men to attend a garden party at Hibaya Park, Tokyo, illustrates the extent to which discipline was taken. The men were organized into companies of fifty, each under the command of an officer, and told that although the party was an entertainment, it was also "a matter of military duty." They were kept "under military discipline while in ranks . . . as if they were under arms and the same degree of military precision [was] exacted."[68] With such measures it was made clear from the beginning of the visit that order would prevail. Drunkenness on the part of enlisted men was actively discouraged; should any officer do something to attract official attention, it would result in a general court-martial. Despite the strict discipline, there was still plenty of scope for enjoyment.

The fleet's late arrival did little to disrupt the formal program. Only two functions had been scheduled for 17 October, and these were rescheduled for later in the week. Official calls were promptly made and returned and all other customary courtesies taken care of before the first scheduled event. At 2:00 P.M. on Sunday, 18 October, Sperry attended the garden party given by the municipality of Yokohama. On his way there he passed along a road decorated with red and white banners, a custom from former days when shoguns traveled through a district.[69] The entire route was lined with rows of "cheering and singing children" waving bouquets and small American and Japanese flags.[70]

The evening's entertainment was an elaborate reception given by Baron Kohei Sufu, governor of Kanagawa, the prefecture in which Yokohama was located. Riding there in rickshaws, naval officers made their way through crowded streets, their progress marked by shouts of *banzai!* from the townspeople.[71] Like all the other Japanese affairs, this was a masterpiece of organization. So complete was the attention to detail that a bust of Commodore Perry, displayed prominently in the main reception room, was illuminated from behind in red, white, and blue when the "Star-Spangled Banner" was played.[72]

On Monday, 19 October, which had been declared American Day in Tokyo, all flag and commanding officers and their aides moved to the capital. Flag officers and their aides took up residence at the Shiba Detached Palace, the others at the Imperial Hotel, where they remained as guests of the emperor until Friday, 23 October. The center of social activity shifted to Tokyo as well. The stay there reached its height when the emperor granted an audience on Tuesday, 20 October.

Arranging to host the distinguished visitors at this affair had presented difficulties for Japanese protocol. The Meiji Emperor had prepared an address to President Roosevelt that would be read in front of the guests, an initiative for which his advisors could find no precedent.[73] Fortunately, the address was put aside shortly after the fleet arrived. Without informing Ambassador O'Brien, President Roosevelt sent Sperry a message of greeting to deliver to the emperor.[74] Sperry had the presence of mind to send a copy immediately to O'Brien for delivery to Japan's Foreign Office.[75] Receipt of advance copies of the president's message resolved the protocol problem; the emperor's message of welcome was abandoned in favor of a more traditional response.[76] Concerning this episode, Sperry later wrote that there had been an "almost distressing nervous tension in Japanese government circles" that dissipated immediately and made way for a happy conclusion.[77]

With this touchy issue deflected, the audience was conducted without incident, and the party proceeded to a state luncheon. Not until the officers stood behind their chairs at the banquet table did they learn that the emperor himself would attend. The normally taciturn man entered the hall and chatted amiably throughout the affair. His relaxed attitude, Sperry concluded, was undoubtedly a reaction to the resolution of the protocol issue.[78]

Although the American navy maintained a small coal depot in Yokohama, it was located on a shallow creek and therefore presented difficulties. Because of this and the heavy entertainment schedule, Admiral Sperry's original plan had not included coaling at Yokohama. The battleships had taken on a particularly large supply just before leaving Manila. But heavy weather en route to Yokohama had increased coal consumption, a major consideration in the decision to postpone the fleet's arrival. Sperry could have brought the first three divisions into Yokohama on schedule, but the necessary speed increase would have consumed more coal and the admiral was cautious after his Australian experience.[79] Despite the delayed arrival, the ships still needed to take on some coal in Yokohama. Sperry explained to Denison Secretary Metcalf's continuing concern over the anarchist threat to the coal supply and called upon him to keep the American supply at Yokohama free of explosives.[80] With security arrangements in place, about 3,500 tons of coal were slowly loaded into barges and, as the fleet enjoyed Japanese hospitality, were conveyed to the ships and stowed in their bunkers.[81]

The afternoon of Friday, 23 October, Tokyo's official reception ended with a luncheon at the Shiba Detached Palace, given at the emperor's command by the chamberlain of the imperial household. Admirals and captains then returned to their ships to begin a round of farewells at Yokohama that included an elaborate dinner in the battleship *Fuji,* followed by a reception in the battleship *Mikasa* at which champagne and rare wines flowed freely. In a spirit of intimate camaraderie junior Japanese admirals and captains hoisted up the American admirals and Ambassador O'Brien and paraded them about the decks of the *Mikasa*.[82]

Saturday, the final day in port, was given over to American hospitality. In view of Japan's lavish reception, much was expected of the affair in the *Connecticut*. But that unfortunate ship was the site of a grand faux pas, the only one of the entire week. Some 3,300 guests had been invited; it was reported that many hundreds more actually managed to make their way on board. They began arriving early, and by the time the reception was officially scheduled to commence, the food had run out.[83] "It was as sad as the affair on the *Mikasa* was beautiful," Louis Maxfield lamented. "Oh My, Oh My, Americans have a great deal to learn in polite manners."[84]

The flagship had hired caterers from the Grand Hotel in Yokohama, and it was generally supposed that the fiasco was their fault.[85] In fact, it was the result of an exhausted entertainment fund. A paltry sum of $1,300 had been made available for food and drink, cigars and cigarettes, and decorations to return the Japanese hospitality.[86] With characteristic courtesy, the press refrained from commenting on the shabby American reception; however, it is certain that the unfavorable contrast between Japanese lavishness and American meanness was duly noted.

Next morning the visit came to a close. Watched by the usual crowds on shore and afloat, a farewell party of Japanese led by the vice minister of foreign affairs was received with full honors on the *Connecticut*. Salutes and farewells completed, the flagship got under way and led the First Squadron toward the small inner harbor, where each ship executed an impressive turn and then proceeded to sea, followed by the Second Squadron and escorted by the Japanese cruisers *Kashima*, *Katori*, *Tsukuba*, and *Ikoma*.[87] The remaining Japanese warships cheered the Americans as they departed; the Americans, in turn, played Japan's stirring anthem.

So ended the visit to Japan. Admiral Sperry reported to President Roosevelt that it had been "profoundly successful [and] beneficent in effect."[88] These observations seem to sum up the general reaction. The Japanese were unanimously applauded as the perfect hosts whose generous treatment of the men went a long way to dispel much of the suspicion generated in the preceding two years. The visit, a success for Japanese diplomacy, would be followed by negotiation of an entente with the United States.

In Washington, President Roosevelt was delighted. The receptions in Australia and New Zealand had been so "extraordinary" that he had not thought it possible to surpass them, he wrote to Sperry, "but Japan has done at least as well."[89] He interpreted the success as an indication of the efficacy of brandishing the big stick while making every effort at politeness and friendship.[90] "My policy of constant friendliness and courtesy toward Japan," he wrote to Arthur H. Lee, "*coupled with sending the fleet around the world,* has borne good results."[91]

On the surface these sentiments seemed well-founded, for on 26 October, two days after the fleet left Yokohama, Japan's ambassador in Washington proposed an exchange of notes concerning issues of mutual interest in the Far East.[92] Negotiations over the final form the note would take were concluded and the document signed by Ambassador Takahira and Secretary Root on the last day of November, 1908.[93] One searches in vain for information to support the belief of the German minister at Peking, Count von Rex, that Roosevelt "had realized too late that the sixteen battleships were inferior to the waiting fleets of Japan. Frightened, he had submitted to the [Root-Takahira] Agreement as a face-saving means of getting out of the trap. . . ."[94] It seems reasonable to conclude that this interpretation was little more than a reflection of German frustration over failure to achieve the German-American-Chinese alliance, which Count von Rex himself had initiated. In fact, as Raymond A. Esthus has asserted, the United States made no significant concessions to the Japanese in the Root-Takahira Agreement; certainly none sufficiently important to deter Japan from attacking the battleship fleet, had that been its intention.[95]

On the other hand, Admiral Sperry's interpretation of the relationship between the fleet visit and the Root-Takahira Agreement seems equally unbalanced. In private letters to his family, he confided that in his opinion the president had received bad advice from the General Board concerning the possibility of war with Japan.[96] When Rear Admiral Richard Wainwright was a member of that board, he had been "stubbornly confident that a row with Japan was imminent," Sperry wrote.[97] "Evans was another war fiend," because staff officers Sperry retained after Evans's retirement did "not believe the fleet would go home." Sperry had little patience for such fears.[98] The visit, he wrote, had "knocked the stuffing out of" the war scare "bug-a-boo," and it seemed to him that the recently signed agreement with Japan was the "immediate fruit."[99]

Clearly the trip to Japan coincided with the end of war talk between that country and the United States, and conclusion of the Root-Takahira Agreement put bilateral relations on a firmer footing. But to suggest that the former was the immediate fruit of the latter is to ignore the general development of those relations. In fact, it seems probable that the Root-Takahira Agreement—or a similar pact—would have been negotiated regardless of the fleet visit. Its successful completion merely provided a suitable opening to initiate negotiations upon which Japan had decided to embark before the ships arrived.

Following the Russo-Japanese War, Japan had undertaken an ambitious military and naval expansion program. The burden of heavy military expenditures contained in the 1906 budget was justifiable immediately after the war. The 1907 budget, however, included the initial ¥11,000,000 appropriation of a ¥32,000,000 program for the establishment of four new army divisions, and the first ¥25,000,000 of a seven-year, ¥175,000,000 shipbuilding program; it was severely criticized by all.[100] In 1907 these expenditures were covered by compensation for support of Russian prisoners of war, and funds raised through a bond issue. But in 1908 the continuing army and navy expansion programs created a budget deficit of ¥4,910,000 which the government planned partially to recoup through a series of new and onerous taxes on alcohol, sugar, and tobacco.[101] The *genro* (former prime ministers whose advice was sought on major issues) became alarmed over the deficit; the United Chambers of Commerce condemned the new taxes and passed a resolution that government spending be either postponed or reduced.[102]

As a result, the 1908 budget was trimmed and resignation of the cabinet avoided, but defense expenditures remained an important political issue. When the U.S. battleship debate of 1908 resulted in congressional authorization of only half the number of dreadnoughts demanded by the president, the *Japan Daily Mail* addressed Japan's own need to reduce expenditures and concluded that she was "paralyzing her financial hand in order to strengthen her military one."[103]

The elections of May 1908 returned the ruling *Seiyukai* (Association of Political Friends) Party to power, but continuing pressure on the government to rein in expenditures led to the resignation of Prime Minister Saionji Kimmochi and his cabinet in July 1908. The new prime minister, Katsura Taro, would have to carry out a policy of financial retrenchment.

As Japan struggled with its financial crisis, one aspect of foreign policy— entente with the United States—assumed increased importance. Arbitration and trademark treaties had been concluded in May 1908, while the next month a longstanding mining dispute was resolved.[104] Further, the new Katsura ministry assured the United States that immigration would be strictly limited.[105]

Rumors of an American-German-Chinese alliance did not interrupt the rapprochement between Japan and the United States. Takahira had been told by President Roosevelt that he had no intention of being party to such an arrangement. Potential misunderstanding was further diffused when the Japanese ambassador received and cabled to Tokyo a copy of the Hale interview with Kaiser Wilhelm. Nevertheless, the fleet's approaching visit and a rumor that Chinese Envoy Tang Shao-yi would soon go to the United States fueled Japanese desire to formalize the relationship with America through an official agreement. Doubtless Roosevelt's growing appreciation of the German threat—the impression created by Hale's interview had been reinforced by a similarly unsettling and sensational interview published in the *London Daily Telegraph* two days after Takahira's initiative— increased his desire for a modus vivendi with Japan that would allow the U.S. battleship fleet to remain concentrated in the Atlantic.

Apparent resolution of one final irritant in bilateral relations—the continuing flow of Japanese laborers to the U.S. Pacific Coast—occurred most fortuitously as the fleet was en route to Japan. On 3 October Secretary of Labor and Commerce Oscar Strauss told Root that the latest immigration figures, those for July 1908, suggested the new Japanese restrictions were being enforced.[106] A similarly positive assessment came nine days later, when the fleet visit started. Root directed Ambassador O'Brien to inform the Japanese government that he regarded the statistics as a "fair promise for the future . . . indicating that economic questions growing out of emigration and immigration may be successfully solved by cooperation on the part of the two Governments."[107]

Resolution of the immigration issue, a successful fleet visit, and conclusion of the Root-Takahira Agreement solidified bilateral relations. As Robert Neu has concluded, "Immigration and racial tension, not Japanese expansionism, endangered Japanese-American friendship and Roosevelt subordinated the vague American stake in China to the control of those explosive issues."[108] It might also be added that he subordinated that stake to the need for continued naval preparedness in the Atlantic.

Despite these developments, the general strategic situation in Asia remained unaltered. The American naval staff continued to plan with Japan as an anticipated enemy, and, noted Admiral Fukudome Shigeru, "in 1907, the Imperial Navy made the United States its sole strategic enemy."[109] In the case of America, the cruise itself was an exercise of plans for implementation in the event of hostilities with Japan, even though Germany remained the main threat. Japanese plans also had to be tested, and this obviously was the purpose of the 1908 autumn maneuvers. To prepare for them, Admiral Togo and other high-ranking officers moved south to Hiroshima once the U.S. fleet had departed from Yokohama.[110] The main exercise commenced on 6 November when the defending squadron sailed south from Sasebo in search of the raiding force, which it expected to encounter in the vicinity of the Ryukyu islands.[111]

The Japanese navy's strategic task, James Crowley has written, was to establish naval hegemony over the United States in the Philippines.[112] Indeed, from the few details given above, gleaned from the Japanese press of the day, it can be seen that the navy was exercising plans for operations against a naval force moving north from the Philippines. The Japanese had already ruled out a clash with the Royal Navy because of the Anglo-Japanese Alliance, and as the American navy was the only other force of consequence in the Pacific, it was inevitably the one against which Japan had chosen to maneuver.

Even while words of friendship and good will swirled in the wake of the American visit to Japan, naval strategists of each country were actively considering plans for a Pacific conflict with the other as antagonist. It is remarkable that even at this early date the essential elements of America's plan for resistance against Japanese aggression—the fortification of Corregidor as a defensive bastion for the army in the Philippines and the development of a base at Pearl Harbor to act as a springboard from which to conduct operations to relieve the Philippines—had already been decided, although many years would pass before the necessary infrastructure was in place. Therefore, while in the diplomatic sphere the fleet visit helped assuage surface tensions between Japan and the United States, in the naval sphere, though officers were suffused with warm new feelings toward their counterparts, it failed to convince them to alter their basic conclusion about who posed the main threat in the Pacific.

At 8:00 A.M. the day after the fleet's departure from Yokohama, the Second Squadron parted company with the First and headed southwest toward Amoy. Official Chinese reaction to the upcoming visit bore out Minister Rockhill's assessment: the Chinese had read too much into it and, possibly with the encouragement of the German minister, had come to believe that it was the precursor of American acceptance of an alliance with Germany and China. Laboring under this illusion, the government commenced arrangements for an elaborate reception for the fleet. But when the response—that initially wholehearted but ill-considered cabinet response—encountered opposition from the Navy Department and Rockhill and was altered, Chinese enthusiasm waned. When distant Amoy was finally chosen and the guests limited to the Second Squadron, the hosts were not at all pleased.[113] They dutifully appropriated 400,000 *taels* for entertainment and an additional 400,000 to cover expenses incurred on account of the "isolation and comparative inaccessibility" of Amoy. Such largess could not hide their considerable embarrassment at receiving only half the fleet just after Japan had hosted it in its entirety. When local authorities at Amoy displayed apathy in preparing for the visitors, Peking had to send a special commissioner for preparations who "left no doubt" that he intended making the reception an unqualified success.[114]

The task of that commissioner, Dr. George Mark, a European in the Chinese government's service, was monumental. Amoy's resources offered virtually nothing suitable for a reception. so everything had to be brought in from the outside, at great cost. Work started with the installation of an electric power plant. Meanwhile hundreds of coolies were kept busy day and night building an entertainment ground where most of the activity would take place. Unfortunately, preparations met with setbacks. Unlike citizens of other host countries, the local Chinese were not enthusiastic, and soon after the visit was announced a rumor spread that the United States planned to seize Amoy and use it as a base in a war against Japan. Some locals began leaving for safer regions. Amoy's governor issued a "Proclamation to Dispel False Rumors," but this failed to stem the flow. Not until several fleeing souls were arrested and severely punished did the exodus stop.[115]

Nature also dealt a heavy blow when the same typhoon the fleet encountered en route to Japan came ashore near Amoy, killing about three thousand people and inflicting extensive damage on the entertainment park.[116] Special Commissioner Mark immediately sent to Canton for an additional shipload of workers and material. In ten days of round-the-clock effort they managed to make good the storm damage and complete an elaborate assembly of halls in the entertainment center.[117]

As the pavilions neared completion, another complication arose. Authorities uncovered a plot to assassinate an unidentified high Chinese official during the fleet reception. Allegedly originating among Chinese revolutionaries in Singapore, it resulted in extraordinary security measures.[118] Guards were placed every ten feet along the route from the fleet landing to the entertainment ground, where an additional one hundred armed men guarded each entrance, and no Chinese were admitted without passes.[119]

Further complicating the government's efforts was the antagonistic attitude of the American legation in Peking to the fleet visit, a result of intradepartmental wrangling in the U.S. State Department. In Amoy Consul Arnold received a sharp rebuke from Minister Rockhill when he assisted Dr. Mark in getting the storm-damaged reception facilities repaired.[120] Rockhill made clear his personal disapproval by declining to attend the reception and appointing the military attaché, an army captain one rank below the naval attaché, to represent the legation at Amoy.[121] The hapless Chinese, caught in the middle of the skirmish, had no one to confer with about coordinating plans for the visit.[122] No wonder their welcome was not wholehearted.

Local apathy, revolutionists' plots, typhoon damage, the legation's attitude—all complicated Chinese efforts in preparation for the fleet. When Germany tried to assume a role in the festivities, the diplomatic web grew even more tangled.

The first indication that the Germans sought to influence events came when the German gunboat *Niobe* called at Amoy a fortnight before the American battleship squadron. Germany's consul maintained she would be staying only long enough to coal. However, when the principal imperial commissioner, Prince Yu Lang, arrived at Amoy nearly two weeks later, she was still in port.

As senior diplomat at Amoy, the German consul led the diplomatic community in matters of protocol. Foreign consuls were organized to call on the prince in a body, and Consul Arnold inquired of the German consul whether it would be out of place to bring the U.S. military attaché from Peking, who was representing the American legation. Yes, the German consul replied, it would. So the American army officer did not attend. When the consuls made their call they had only been with the prince a few minutes before officers of the *Niobe* arrived. The German consul spent a longer time introducing them to the prince than he had the entire consular body. As if this were not imperious enough, the German consul impressed upon the prince his obligation to return the German naval officers' call.

Prince Yu Lang must have wondered whether it was a German or an American fleet he had been sent to welcome. At any rate, he honored the German consul's wishes and visited the *Niobe*. Her departure following the prince's visit was anticipated, as the consul had two weeks earlier implied. But she remained in port and took part in all the festivities connected with the fleet reception, thereby, according to Arnold, creating "unpleasant feelings . . . in the minds of our hosts."[123]

The Second Squadron arrived off Amoy on the morning of 30 October and came to anchor in line of divisions. Owing to unhealthy conditions in the village—and, one suspects, Chinese concerns about security—enlisted men on liberty were confined to the entertainment ground, some distance from the town. Officers were permitted additional freedom of movement: they could visit the adjacent island of Kulangsu, where the foreign settlement of Amoy was located.[124]

The first day officers and men traveled by launch to a specially built landing, where they were met by rickshaws and carriages and conveyed to the entertainment ground along a road lined with Chinese soldiers and imported exotic plants. At the gate to the grounds the men passed under a huge welcome arch and through the massed Chinese soldiers, which gave the place a feeling of being under siege. But once inside, they found an uninterrupted succession of entertainments, meals, and beverages laid out for them.

There was an air of unreality about the reception, so removed from the populace of Amoy and lacking the spontaneity that had marked the Japanese visit. Peking remained uncertain about how to react to the perceived humiliation of the reduced number of visitors. Two days after their arrival, events in Amoy were virtually unknown in Peking. Chinese newspapers remained silent on the topic, and no official statements were forthcoming.[125] Only the Japanese-controlled papers in Peking reported details, and one can almost imagine the pleasure with which they covered the event, which compared so poorly with the Japanese reception.

Undisturbed by this lack of official recognition, the American squadron honored the dowager empress on her birthday (her last, for both she and the emperor would be dead within a fortnight). Adhering to the normal procedure for such events, battleships were full dressed with China's ensign at the main. At noon they all fired a twenty-one-gun national salute. After dark the ensign was kept at the main, illuminated by searchlights.[126]

The visit came to a close on 5 November. That morning seven battleships shaped a course for the Philippines. Shortly after leaving Amoy, the flagship *Louisiana* detached from the formation and stopped briefly at Hong Kong to disembark Rear Admiral Emory. Emory, who had reached mandatory retirement age, would now proceed home in a civilian steamer. Captain W. P. Potter of the *Vermont* was promoted to rear admiral and given command of the Fourth Division, while Rear Admiral Schroeder moved from command of that division to fill Emory's position as commander of the Second Squadron.

After the fleet had been reunited in the Philippines a Chinese paper, described as "official" and "controlled by Grand Councillor Yüan Shih Kai," offered a disingenuous explanation of why only part of the American fleet had visited China: it had been "dispersed by a storm on its way to the Chinese coast. The fate of the other eight vessels is unknown; only half of the fleet reached Amoy."[127]

THIRTEEN

The Battle Joined

While the fleet had been visiting Californian ports, the Roosevelt administration had done battle with Congress to gain authorization for more dreadnoughts. After the fleet's departure from San Francisco criticism of the new dreadnought designs resurfaced. And as the fleet completed the last stages of its voyage, President Roosevelt, in his final weeks in office, made an eleventh-hour effort to reform the administration of the Navy Department.

Following his concerted and successful efforts to obtain battleships in the first years of his presidency, Roosevelt had decided in 1905 that the authorized strength was sufficient to meet American defense requirements. Therefore in his annual address to Congress in 1905 he announced that henceforth he would seek only one battleship a year to replace outworn ships. The launching of HMS *Dreadnought* and the rush by other naval powers to build dreadnoughts radically altered the naval scene. Failure at the second Hague Conference to reach agreement on the limitation of size and number of battleships meant that the dreadnought building boom was likely to continue unabated.

These European developments had direct implications for the American navy. If it was to retain its position as the world's second naval power, the United States had to embark upon a more active dreadnought construction program. That the Roosevelt administration was moving in this direction was suggested as early as August 1907, when a member of the House Naval Affairs Committee stated that "four battleships of the most powerful type" would be recommended for the 1908 naval program.[1]

Roosevelt received and apparently accepted the General Board's shipbuilding recommendations at the end of September. In a speech in St. Louis a few days later he made his first public plea for significant enlargement of the navy. Using classic Roosevelt rhetoric, he emphasized the importance of naval strength to the nation's foreign policy:

We have definitely taken our place among the great world powers, and it would be a sign of ignoble weakness, having taken such a place, to shirk its responsibilities. Therefore, unless we are willing to abandon this place, to abandon our insistence upon the Monroe Doctrine, to give up the Panama Canal, and to be content to acknowledge ourselves a weak and timid nation, we must steadily build up and maintain a great fighting navy.[2]

This shift in policy put reporters on the trail of Secretary Metcalf, who next day suggested Congress should authorize four battleships, several scout cruisers and large fast colliers, and at least one new dry dock on the West Coast. Thus the campaign to drop the old program of one battleship a year started in October, over two months before the president's annual address to Congress. The *New York Times* noted that the battleship debate in Congress would occur when the Maine coast—Senator Hale's constituency—was denuded of battleships; it suggested that "that circumstance was not overlooked" by Roosevelt at the time he decided to send the battleship fleet to the Pacific.[3]

Details of the administration's naval construction program were made public on 1 December when Metcalf's recommendations were published in his annual report.[4] It came as little surprise, therefore, when a few days later President Roosevelt in his annual address decried the failure of the second Hague Conference and warned Congress that it would be "folly for this nation to base any hope of securing peace on any international agreement" limiting armaments. It would be unwise to stop "upbuilding" the navy, he asserted, going on to recommend construction of four battleships in 1908.[5] This request touched off one of the most bitter congressional struggles in America's naval history.[6]

The months that elapsed between delivery of Roosevelt's message and debate over his naval program witnessed events that would influence congressional and public perceptions of the navy and its needs: the departure of the battleship fleet on its much-heralded cruise; Henry Reuterdahl's article and the rancorous exchanges it sparked; the resignation of Admiral Brownson and Roosevelt's role in it; and the triumphant procession of the fleet around South America. Coloring these events was the longstanding antagonism between Senator Hale and Roosevelt and the latter's manhandling of the Senate in regard to coal appropriations for the fleet's return.

The House Naval Affairs Committee took up the naval appropriations bill in early February—before the Senate hearings on Reuterdahl's criticism—and severely trimmed the administration's request, recommending construction of two battleships, four submarines, and ten destroyers. Furthermore, the chairman of the House Appropriations Committee, Congressman James A. Tawney, warned that his committee would oppose any appropriations for newly authorized battleships.[7]

The Senate Naval Affairs Committee had begun to consider the administration's 1908 program in early February. That that body was moving in the same direction is suggested by the position adopted by Senator George C. Perkins. He observed that the United States had become the second sea power in the world, surpassing France by a small margin and Germany, Russia, and Japan by a large one. "By authorizing only two more battleships of the big-gun type this year we shall still lead France by 40,000 tons in sea-fighting force," he said.[8]

President Roosevelt attempted to overcome congressional apathy for his naval program by meeting with Senator Hale, Speaker of the House Joseph C. ("Uncle Joe") Cannon, and other congressional leaders, but he failed to impress on them the reasons for his urgent request.[9]

At this point the Senate hearings intruded into the legislative process. As noted earlier, they were intended to put an end to criticism and affirm the efficiency of the Navy Department, but they achieved neither goal, instead stirring popular resentment over the treatment meted out to reformers by the Senate Naval Affairs Committee. On 14 April, the hearings over, Roosevelt sent a special message to Congress again urging authorization of four battleships. The United States could "hope for a permanent career of peace on only one condition, and that is . . . building and maintaining a first-class navy."[10]

Following a spectacular debate on 15 April in which the opponents and proponents of naval expansion once again aired their arguments, the House of Representatives voted on amendments to the bill, finally authorizing two battleships.

Viewing the unfolding debate from London, the *Spectator* commented that Roosevelt, a diplomat trying to extract the best possible bargain for his cause, made a much higher demand than he knew would be granted in order to obtain at least two battleships.[11] The article spoke almost as though the House of Representatives' decision on the matter was final. But American appropriations are secured in a circuitous manner, and the issue was still very much alive. The Senate still had to deal with the bill; should that body approve a substantially different program, a final compromise bill could possibly yield more than two battleships.

Like the House Naval Affairs Committee, Senator Hale's committee cut the president's request to two battleships and failed to provide funding for them. The Senate position was adopted, it has been suggested, because this committee wanted, in some tangible way, to express its displeasure over not being consulted on the matter of the cruise.[12] The administration went on the offensive: Senator Albert Beveridge served notice that on 22 April an amendment would be introduced authorizing four battleships.[13] This was an attack on the chairman of the Naval Affairs Committee, who had erred so egregiously in his handling of the recent hearings. By introducing the amendment against Hale's wishes, Senator Beveridge was also attacking the clique of politicians, popularly known as the Senate Oligarchy, who had long used their seniority to control important Senate committees. Beveridge's goal was to unseat the oligarchy; the battleship authorization was merely a tactical move. Nevertheless, his efforts would benefit the navy.

Upon learning that the proposed bill did not include funding for battleships, President Roosevelt called Senate leaders to the White House and warned them that should the Senate fail to appropriate funds, he would veto the measure. Roosevelt called the House bill a "paper" provision; it was, he said, a "travesty" of effectiveness and bore "all the earmarks of Legislative legerdemain. . . ."[14]

The most intense lobbying of the session occurred before the Senate battleship debate. A line was clearly drawn between Senator Beveridge, Piles, and a small group of their reform-minded colleagues and Senator Aldrich and his more conservative supporters, who were "raising the cry, 'Stand by the Committee.' "[15] Debate on the naval appropriations bill opened on 24 April with a statement by Senator Hale to the effect that the United States already had strength "sufficient to equip two fleets, one in the Atlantic and the other in the Pacific Ocean." A debate then developed over the president's right to send the fleet on a world cruise, which again highlighted the connection Americans made between the battleship cruise and developments on the naval scene at home.[16] Next Senator Piles introduced his amendment authorizing four instead of two battleships. The Senate "organization" forced a postponement of the vote on this amendment until the following day, and after a day of "bitter wrangling, personal recriminations, and parliamentary jockeying," consideration of the naval appropriations bill was postponed yet again until Monday, 27 April.[17]

The debate resumed then, after a Sunday of intense lobbying. At the end of Monday the Senate voted down the Piles amendment, but, largely as a result of unexpected support for the administration's program, it approved a compromise proposal: a fixed program of authorizing and appropriating funds for two battleships per year.[18] The strength of support shown Beveridge and Piles by younger senators came as a rude shock to the Senate Oligarchy, and although they failed to obtain four battleships, the insurgents managed to deliver a serious setback to the enemy. Wrote Beveridge a day after the debate: "It was a glorious victory after all. It was the last victory of the old gang."[19]

The immediate significance for the navy was that, despite an increasingly hostile Congress, Roosevelt was able to obtain two dreadnoughts in 1908 and the promise of another two in 1909. In the longer term, the assertion of influence by younger senators contributed, along with growing Democratic strength in Maine, to Senator Hale's decision not to seek reelection in 1910.[20] Thus the Beveridge insurgency helped end Hale's chairmanship of the Senate Naval Affairs Committee and the influence he had exerted for so long to hinder development of the navy.

In many respects that insurgency bears a striking resemblance to Sims's efforts within the Navy Department. Both Beveridge and Sims had sought, through unconventional means, to alter the establishment to which they belonged; both were articulate, accomplished in their fields, and widely respected; both were of the younger generation and interested in reform; both would engage in further skirmishes with their respective establishments before their reform objectives would be realized.

In essence, Beveridge had used the naval debate to challenge the rule of the oligarchy. His battle was not so much for naval expansion as against the Senate establishment. But the navy would reap the reward.

The inconclusiveness of the Senate hearings on Reuterdahl's criticism had left the insurgents frustrated but by no means defeated. A new issue with which to renew their assault on the bureaucracy soon surfaced with the USS *North Dakota*. The *Delaware* and her sister ship *North Dakota* had been authorized by acts of

Congress on 29 June 1906 and 2 March 1907, respectively. The *Delaware* had been defined as a first-class battleship carrying armor as heavy as and armament as powerful as that of any known vessel of its class. The *North Dakota* was to be "similar in all essential characteristics" to the *Delaware*.[21] Displacing twenty thousand tons and mounting ten twelve-inch rifles in five turrets, the sister ships were designed as America's first true dreadnoughts.

The Navy Department's dreadnought design was not faultless. Belt armor had been subjected to early and severe criticism by Lieutenant Commander Frank K. Hill.[22] However, the Board on Construction had unanimously rejected the junior officer's criticisms and advised Secretary Metcalf that no change should be made in the distribution of armor.[23] The board's plans went forward unaltered, and in due course the contract for construction of the *North Dakota* was let to the Fore River Shipbuilding Company of Quincy, Massachusetts. The first keel plate was timed to be laid when the battleship fleet departed from Hampton Roads on its cruise to the Pacific.[24] Also building at the Fore River yard, and in an advanced state of construction, was the fast scout cruiser *Salem*.

After the adjournment of the Senate hearings, Commander Albert L. Key, one of the principal insurgents, was ordered to Fore River to assume command of the *Salem* upon her commissioning. While there Key had frequent opportunities to inspect plans for the *North Dakota* in detail. By early June he had discerned a number of critical defects in the battleship's design and informed Sims that he was forwarding his criticism to "Old Muttonhead," Secretary Metcalf.[25] Key's letter to Metcalf elicited no response from the Navy Department, and Sims concluded that it had been pigeonholed in one of the bureaus. Therefore he wrote a "pretty drastic" letter to the president that he felt would be "something of a shock," and forwarded a copy of Key's letter with his correspondence.[26] Key's criticisms, Sims told Roosevelt, "show that our most recent designs embody many of the defects of our earlier vessels—defects which have long since been corrected in advanced foreign navies."[27]

The major complaints dealt with the location of the torpedo defense guns, the number-three turret, and the belt armor; the armor protection of torpedo defenses, funnels, and uptakes; and the strength of the main battery armament. Key reported that the five-inch torpedo defense guns were placed too low for use even in normal trade wind conditions. He condemned the five-inch main deck citadel armor enclosing and protecting these guns, claiming it was so thin that twelve-inch shells would explode and inflict great damage. He recommended complete removal of the five-inch citadel armor, which would save weight that could be better used to provide turrets for the torpedo defense battery and armor for the funnels.

According to Key, the location of the number-three twelve-inch turret between the engine and boiler rooms was the feature of the *North Dakota*'s design most generally criticized. The turret's magazine, enveloped by steam pipes and subjected to extremes of heat, would cause deterioration of the ballistic qualities of the powder.

Key also attacked the decision to arm the *North Dakota* with twelve-inch forty-five-caliber rifles, which had been installed in earlier battleships and were less powerful than their English, French, and Japanese counterparts. He concluded that the Navy Department was wrong to depart from the long-established policy of equipping battleships with ordnance as powerful as that of possible enemies.

Finally, turning to the armor belt, Key reported that virtually everyone in the Navy Department had officially agreed with the findings of the Walker Board of 1898 regarding its placement. Yet those findings had been "consistently and deliberately ignored, with the result that the vessels of the Atlantic Fleet are over draft." This assertion he supported with statistics for each class of battleships. The problem was being perpetuated in the *North Dakota*.[28]

Key's letter was a model of professional criticism of technical problems. In his own letter to the president Sims did not limit comment to technical detail. Giving vent to some of the personal bitterness the controversy had generated, he wrote that Rear Admiral Converse had "lost the confidence, not to say the respect, of the service. . . . Similarly, Chief Constructor Capps is unable to withdraw from his former position without acknowledging that both he and his predecessors have made serious errors. New men in these positions, or else an entire change in the methods of developing designs, seems to be inevitable if we are to make adequate progress."[29]

Roosevelt responded to these new criticisms by proposing that Key's letter be sent either to Evans or to the General Board for their views. Sims particularly objected to having Evans comment—he held a low opinion of the admiral as commander in chief—and therefore advised Roosevelt to have Secretary Metcalf submit Key's letter to the General Board and the Naval War College, which would meet jointly to consider the criticisms and recommend improvements in future ships.[30] The president accepted this advice and ordered a formal conference along those lines.[31]

The bureaucracy reacted swiftly to the threat of a new investigation. Sims "learned that the bureau gang intend to pack the 'Conference' in favor of the Board on Construction."[32] Acting immediately, he wrote Roosevelt to suggest that officers of all grades, "including a considerable number of commanders, lieutenant commanders and lieutenants selected for their special knowledge of the practical problems of long-range gun fire and fire control," be ordered to attend the conference.[33] Thus even before it convened the lines of confrontation were drawn, and in a pattern repeated at strategic points later, Sims would without hesitation use his special relationship with Roosevelt to strengthen the insurgents' position.

The conference convened at Newport on 22 July with a flurry of nationwide publicity. At his aide's suggestion, Roosevelt traveled from Oyster Bay in the *Mayflower* to open the affair. As he walked from the landing at Newport accompanied by Sims and Rear Admiral John P. Merrell, president of the Naval War College, the latter tried to persuade him to send away all the extra officers ordered to attend, leaving the report to the General Board and the college. Sims "strenuously opposed" this, and when Admiral Merrell was momentarily distracted, he explained why to the president. Roosevelt agreed to have all officers remain. Sims then requested that votes be recorded by name, to which the president also agreed.[34]

Flanked by antagonists, each jockeying for a position of advantage, Roosevelt arrived at the Naval War College. At the conference's first session, which was open to the public, he delivered a typically energetic address to the nation dealing with immigration and the need for a strong navy if the United States was to claim the right to exclude immigrants.[35] At the closed session that afternoon, following Sims's advice, he directed that all officers remain for the conference and that all votes be recorded by name and reported to the Navy Department.[36] Sims hailed this as a particular victory: senior officers with bureau connections had failed to have the independent officers removed, and the requirement to record votes would make it difficult for conservative officers to oppose motions concerning obvious defects.[37]

Despite these initial successes, the mere necessity of such measures must have suggested that the atmosphere was not yet receptive to extensive reform. The conference that ensued was, as Elting E. Morison has stated, "a very complicated tangle of men, methods, and issues."[38] Memories of the acrimonious Senate hearings earlier in the year were still fresh in the minds of all, and, particularly to officers with bureau connections, participation in the Newport Conference must have been viewed as a continuation of the earlier defense of the bureaus' performance record. Given the bitterness and divisions left unresolved by the Senate hearings, it was perhaps inevitable that this conference would become yet "another test of strength," and officers in some way connected with the design of the ships in question constituted the working majority.[39]

The tangled web of personalities and groups notwithstanding, Commander Key's design criticisms were fairly clear-cut. In two weeks of often heated discussion the conference found five major defects in the *Delaware* and *North Dakota:* location of the twelve-inch powder magazine between the engine room and fireroom and surrounded by steam pipes; placement of the fourteen five-inch guns "so low that they cannot be used efficiently in ordinary trade wind weather"; placement of the two after turrets close together and at the same height, so that if one were disabled it would limit the train of the other; inadequate armor protection for the supply ventilator pipes and uptakes within the citadel; and main battery guns, which were inferior to those of certain foreign ships of the same date of completion.[40]

What Sims called "the great question of the waterline armor belt" was somewhat more complex. The insurgents gained an early victory when they successfully pressed for clarification of the displacement figure on which calculations for belt location should be based. The conservatives insisted that placement should be determined according to a "light-fighting line" arrived at by calculating displacement when the ship had a third of its normal supply of coal, ammunition, and other expendable supplies. The insurgents held out for calculations derived from displacement with all ammunition and two-thirds of all other weights; after a full day's debate a resolution to that effect was successfully passed.[41] Using this reference line and the Board on Construction's own established practice of locating the bottom of the belt five feet below the "normal" waterline, the insurgents concluded that the *North Dakota*'s belt was approximately sixteen inches too low.[42]

Sims was unable to convert this initial success into a practical result, for the conservatives—referred to more frequently as the enemy in his personal correspondence—succeeded in passing a resolution that the bottom of the belt be placed six feet below the "fighting draft." By thus altering the established standard to compensate for specific design shortcomings, the ship, which in accordance with the Board on Construction's original standard would have been considered overdraft, was made acceptable. This exercise in legerdemain left the *North Dakota* now only four inches overdraft, and therefore the conference resolved that there was no need to take corrective action. The Board on Construction later cited this failure to recommend changes as confirmation of the validity of the *North Dakota*'s design.

Although this was a defeat for Sims, changes in armor placement above the belt limited its impact on the ship's safety. Earlier battleship designs had incorporated ten- to thirteen-inch belt armor, above which had been placed six-inch armor; in these ships, proper flotation of the belt armor was critical. The *North Dakota,* however, incorporated an eleven-inch belt with ten-inch armor above—protection not significantly less than that offered by the belt itself. In view of this, acceptance of the change in the bottom of the *North Dakota*'s belt was a tactical concession necessary to ensure a strategic victory: future ships would be designed with belts giving protection at fighting draft rather than at an arbitrarily determined normal draft.

The importance of heavier above-belt armor in the *North Dakota* became apparent when, in reviewing the resolution passed on belt location, Sims and his friends determined that it could be interpreted as applying the six-foot lower limit to all earlier battleships. Therefore the insurgents introduced a new resolution stating that the six-foot bottom line was limited to the *North Dakota* type. When the resolution was introduced, Sims recorded, "The enemy was up in arms at once. They attempted to rule the resolution out of order but the conference would not have it," and after some debate the measure was passed unanimously.[43]

Although the insurgents succeeded in eliciting admission of some defects in the design of the *North Dakota,* discussions did not deal with practical remedies. "Let us not commit the folly of approving poor work," Rear Admiral Caspar F. Goodrich, by then senior active line officer of the navy, admonished the conference, "because the workmen are good fellows whom we all like."[44] But that is precisely what happened. Having admitted the existence of certain defects, the majority of participants proved remarkably reluctant to take decisive action. The enemy's strategy was clear to Sims: although defects could not be denied, they could be described as minor and then discounted.

In the case of the *North Dakota* and *Delaware,* conservatives successfully argued that their advanced state of construction allowed only two improvements, half-inch splinterproof armor protection to uptakes and ventilator supply systems and air conditioning for the number-three magazine.[45] However, contracts had not yet been let for the *Utah* and *Florida,* and the insurgents held out in the hope that all noted defects could be corrected in them. But the conservatives used their majority to establish a principle ruling out changes that would delay bidding. To counter this move Sims asked Roosevelt to order the conference to submit two alternative sets of recommendations: one that would involve no delay and a second that would remove all defects regardless of delay and any plans or arrangements already made.[46] This Roosevelt did, concluding, in his telegram directive to the conference, that he wanted all sides of the issue put before him for his judgment.[47]

The principle feature of the *Utah* and *Florida* on which the parties differed was main armament. Ordnance officers claimed that the fourteen-inch guns the insurgents sought could not be built before the ships were ready. Sims, however, received assurances from Bethlehem Steel Company that the guns could be delivered within twenty-four months. The *Utah* and *Florida,* Sims told Roosevelt, should "be provided with 14-inch guns . . . capable of smashing a British *Dreadnought* or a *North Dakota* in short order, and also with the heaviest armor that can be carried. . . ." He also suggested that the conservatives wanted to limit recommendations to designs "that are practically *North Dakotas,* thus tacitly approving the design of the latter—vessels which could not resist the fire of their own guns."[48]

Even Roosevelt's active intervention in this issue failed to sway the conservative majority. On 22 August the conference came to a final vote on the two designs for the *Utah* and *Florida.* The progressives had advocated 21,500-ton ships mounting eight fourteen-inch guns in four turrets, with armor twelve percent thicker than the *North Dakota*'s. The conservatives recommended ships in most respects similar to the *North Dakota,* but with some rearrangement of turrets three and four. Their plan won, and furthermore, despite the information provided by Bethlehem Steel, they passed a resolution stating that adoption of the fourteen-inch gun would cause a delay of fifteen months.[49]

In researching the subject of the bureaus' resistance to change, one is tempted because of Sims's strong and outspoken position to temper his criticism of the bureaucrats' mentality and arguments, regardless of their validity. Particularly instructive, therefore, is a confidential Bureau of Ordnance memorandum written by Professor Philip R. Alger at the time of the conference's public debate in November. In it Alger concluded that forty-five calibers was the longest a gun as large as the twelve-inch could be. A larger gun should not be adopted because the bureau had earlier abandoned the thirteen-inch gun as "unnecessarily powerful." As there had been no significant improvement in armor since that decision, to go to a larger caliber now would therefore "acknowledge that our former action was in error."[50] That such reasoning could be used by a responsible bureau official as justification for an important policy greatly strengthens the credibility of Sims's criticism.

Although Sims held out hope that Roosevelt would adopt the minority proposal for a fourteen-inch gun, in his response the president "reluctantly" concluded that he had to support the majority finding.[51] In accepting the conservative proposal, however, he administered a sharp rebuke to the Navy Department, stating that had officials there been more receptive, the *Utah* and *Florida* would be "much more formidable vessels. . . . But the officials responsible for these ships seem to have limited themselves to the desire not to lag far behind other nations instead of doing what they of course ought to have done; that is, tried to lead other nations." That, the president wrote, was not "to their credit."[52]

Almost hidden in the welter of resolutions with which the conference ended was one passed on the penultimate day signaling a major change in the design process for future battleships: "Several designs representing different schools of thought" would be prepared and submitted to a specially convened board of seagoing officers. This board would be responsible for recommending to the Navy Department the design best suited to the needs of the navy.[53]

In essence, although conservative opposition prevented the production of a more effective *Utah* and *Florida,* the compromise resolution put in place the machinery to ensure that future battleship designs would be reviewed, revised, and finally approved by experienced seagoing officers.

A complete victory by the conservatives would have perpetuated the inadequate design procedures of the past. Conversely, had the insurgents held the day, it is possible that future designs might not have sufficiently emphasized highly technical design functions performed by the Board on Construction and various bureaus of the Navy Department. The main achievement of the conference was to establish a functional balance between technical and practical, or tactical, inputs into the design process. Although the contending parties left Newport dissatisfied with the conference's results, the navy was well served by them.

One of the remarkable aspects to emerge from the months of debate, of which the Newport Conference was but a noteworthy peak, was the lack of official contribution from the battleship fleet. Great issues shaping the future battleship fleet had been debated and decided by a small group of officers almost without reference to the experience and opinions of officers of the fleet in being. This is not to say that officers actively debating the issues were not informally aware of attitudes prevalent in the fleet. Sims had privately sent copies of Key's letter concerning the *North Dakota* to "progressive" line officers for their impressions.

One Pacific Fleet staff officer reproduced and circulated Key's letter. A copy fell into the hands of Chief Constructor Capps while he was inspecting Mare Island Navy Yard in early August and stirred up some excitement in the Construction Corps. Capps had Naval Constructor Holden Evans present a reply to the Pacific Fleet, but officers there, lacking even a drawing of the *North Dakota,* could offer no effective riposte. Inevitably the discussion reflected the acrimony of the ongoing staff-line struggle: a Pacific Fleet officer informed Sims that most of Evans's presentation "was taken up in criticizing those who are responsible for the present investigation of the construction system, and time and again he [Evans] became quite sarcastic."[54]

In the Atlantic battleship fleet, then on the Pacific Coast, unofficial copies of Key's letter were circulating by 1 July, but no official request for comment reached the fleet until the *Minnesota*'s midocean mail delivery after the fleet had left Honolulu.[55] Rear Admirals Seaton Schroeder and Richard Wainwright, the two leading contenders to succeed Sperry as commander in chief, both responded strongly in support of Key's criticisms. Schroeder referred to the "suicidal effect of 5″ shell-bursting armor." If a twelve-inch magazine were placed between the engine and boiler rooms, he maintained, the powder would deteriorate and perform erratically, inviting disaster.[56] Both officers severely attacked the problem of over-draft in the existing battleship fleet.

Schroeder, who succeeded Sperry as the fleet's commander in chief in 1909, presented detailed figures illustrating the actual condition of the *Virginia,* the ship he had commanded during the cruise around South America. Then, in a convincing condemnation of past design practices, he argued that "if the *Virginia* is not over draft, then 7 feet is the proper immersion for the lower edge of an armor belt 8 feet wide; if 5 feet is the proper immersion [the Board on Construction's long-held policy], the corresponding draft is produced by . . . carrying about 300 tons of coal and water and no ammunition." That the *Virginia*'s present condition was not what the naval constructors had planned seemed apparent to Schroeder. Everything tended to show that she "had been designed to float lighter—the slope of the gangway accommodation ladders, position of propeller booms, outlets of lavatories, etc."—and that weights had subsequently been added by the various bureaus.[57]

Admiral Sperry's response, if indeed he did respond, has not been located. However, the commander in chief sent a letter on 29 August 1908 recapitulating the actual overdraft condition of the sixteen battleships under his command. At her lightest load during the voyage, with only 869 tons of coal, his flagship *Connecticut* "displaced 1009 tons more and drew 16 inches (mean draft) more than her designed normal load, though at this time she had just finished a 3900-mile voyage." Moreover, at her "observed heaviest load on the voyage" she "displaced 858 tons more and drew 14½ inches more than at her designed full load." At this "observed load it would still have been practicable to carry additional coal and supplies which would make her real full load displacement 1543 tons more, and her draft 24.4 inches more than her designed full load displacement."[58] Perhaps Sperry assumed that the conclusions to be drawn from this and other detailed data he presented were too apparent to warrant further elaboration. The *Connecticut* and all other battleships were in fact seriously overdraft. Under full-load conditions their armor belts were submerged. Given the armor design of the ships, it was a grave defect.

Had it been available, this feedback from the commanders of the fleet might have significantly affected the conference's outcome. Unfortunately, it was not received until long after adjournment. Although one can but speculate, it seems reasonable to assume that the absence of most battleship line officers greatly strengthened the position of the conservatives at Newport. Concerted opposition mounted by two or three actual battleship division or squadron commanders almost certainly would have yielded a more constructive outcome with regard to the *Utah* and *Florida* and probably also the *North Dakota* and *Delaware.*

The decision to restrict public discussion of the Newport Conference may well have reflected a justifiable desire not to publicize the weaknesses of America's new dreadnoughts. However, it failed to take into account the animosity that fueled the staff-line struggle. Hardly had the conference ended and the participants returned to their normal duties than Sims complained to President Roosevelt about inaccurate reporting of the conference. Belt armor placement was a complicated, technical issue. The significance of the decision to use "most probable fighting waterline" instead of "normal waterline" was initially misreported or misunderstood by the press, and the failure to take corrective action on belt location was hailed as a vindication of the Board on Construction.[59]

A fairly accurate account of the conference finally appeared in the *New York Times* in October, leading that paper to observe editorially that "it is clear that the bureaus of the Navy Department are, if not hopelessly inefficient, yet ineffective and badly organized." Of the conference itself the paper reported that it "generally voted to uphold the bureaus, on the ground that delay of the work on the ships would make Congress inquisitive and compel the department to admit that the plan was defective." In consequence, the nation was likely "to have four new and very expensive battleships that are not up-to-date, in some respects, and inferior to the newer ships of other nations."[60]

When further detail on the conference was released in early November, the *New York Times* retained its healthy skepticism, reporting "that while the decision of the assembled experts is strong in assertion and denial, it is a bit weak in facts and arguments, and . . . it was reached by a vote that came far from being unanimous. . . . [T]he navy will seem to have investigated itself, with the result that those who made it what it is declare that it is all right—a not surprising, but somewhat inconclusive, verdict."[61] This interpretation was contested by journals supportive of the bureaus or representing the views of marine architects and engineers. *Scientific American* first reported "that the broad principles of construction upon which the modern ships of our navy had been built received the endorsement of a very strong majority of the officers present."[62] Following release of the official report of the conference on 22 November, this magazine claimed that it was the most complete refutation of recent criticisms of the navy.[63]

On 30 October the Navy Department had issued an order permitting officers to discuss the work of the Newport Conference. The most noteworthy result was a speech by Chief Constructor Capps to the Naval Academy alumni in Chicago on 23 November. He declared that "the vessels of this country were fully abreast of the times," then read letters from Admiral of the Navy Dewey and retired Rear Admirals W. S. Schley and R. D. Evans supporting his position. Evans had concluded with a ringing condemnation of the critics: "I have no words with which to tell you how unjust, misleading, and silly [the recent criticisms of battleship design] are," he wrote.[64] The same edition of the *New York Times* that reported Capps's speech, however, also reported that "many of the officers of the battleship fleet are not satisfied that the *North Dakota* design is a good one to follow." The opinions of the fleet on the subjects discussed at the Newport Conference were only now reaching Washington, but the Navy Department announced that no steps would be taken "toward making public the correspondence with the fleet commanders."[65]

A few days after release of the official report, the secrecy order was reimposed on naval officers: "The President has now concluded that public discussion of alleged defects of battleships will not serve any good purpose."[66] Rear Admirals Wainwright and Schroeder's criticisms, which certainly would have rekindled the entire debate, were not published. Renewed restrictions, perhaps inadvertently, left the condemnation of Capps, Dewey, Schley, and Evans as the last public pronouncement on the subject. The insurgents were denied an opportunity to respond.

The specter of yet another administrative reform effort had cast its shadow over the Newport Conference and affected every aspect of its deliberations. At the opening of the conference Roosevelt had asked Sims whether he should have the conference develop a plan for reorganization of the Navy Department. Sims advised against this, saying he had another plan to propose and that it would be better not to complicate issues at the conference.[67]

Sims consulted with the venerable Rear Admiral Stephen B. Luce, Rear Admiral Goodrich, and other officers. From Goodrich he received particularly sound advice: "Most of the [reorganization] schemes I have heard want to capsize every blessed thing and raze the whole edifice to the ground," wrote Goodrich. "The real want is a *naval* power to *control* the bureaus leaving the latter the *business* agents of the Secretary. You want level-headed and—conservative men." Sims followed this advice and proposed the establishment of a mixed commission composed of senior officers and civilians of "high character, national reputation and large experience in public affairs" to investigate and make recommendations on reorganization.[68] This idea received initial enthusiastic support from Roosevelt.[69] But as the weeks passed without any action, reformers became increasingly concerned. One week after the presidential election of 1908 Key wrote Sims that now was the time for Roosevelt to act if he was to reorganize the Navy Department during his incumbency.[70]

The reformers' plans were further delayed by the resignation of Secretary Metcalf. Assistant Secretary of the Navy Truman H. Newberry replaced him on 1 December. The new secretary, who had approved original plans for the *North Dakota* and been particularly stung by Sims's complaints that the Newport Conference had been "stacked" in favor of the establishment, adopted a cautious approach to administrative reform.[71]

Newberry proposed a reorganization plan that amounted to amalgamation of two bureaus, Construction and Repair and Steam Engineering, and enlargement of the General Board membership to include bureau chiefs. This did little to meet the goals of the insurgents, who remained inflexible in their insistence that any reorganization of the Navy Department within the framework of the existing law would be ineffective.[72] Admiral Luce roundly condemned Newberry's arrangement, asserting that those responsible for it "are ignorant of the most elementary principles of naval administration. The General Board is a military and executive body. *Its functions are not administrative.* It is an office for line officers exclusively—for *Militant Seamen.*"[73] Nevertheless, Roosevelt approved the plan—perhaps because it could be implemented without congressional approval—and included it in his final annual message to Congress.

As the Roosevelt administration drew to a close, the reformers' efforts to achieve reorganization took on an air of desperation. Sims wrote to the president arguing that the enlarged General Board would still have no control over the bureaus and that the increased presence of bureau representatives might permit the bureaus to further dominate the navy.[74] In the final days of 1908 he addressed an emotional appeal to Roosevelt, attributing the great improvement in the navy of recent years to the fact that his "powerful influence [had] largely suspended the evils of the bureau system." But if Roosevelt should leave the navy with an unsound organization, it would revert to its "former condition." In that case, Sims argued, the failure to reorganize would be remembered "long after our minor improvements had been forgotten."[75]

Sims's points seemed to be confirmed by the actions of Chief Constructor Capps. In the Bureau of Construction and Repair's annual report, Capps included a savage attack on the officer, Commander Key, who had originated criticism of the *North Dakota,* and noted that the Newport Conference had only recommended changes of "comparatively minor character."[76] Capps, who may have misjudged the strength of his position—he had been appointed to assume the collateral duties of chief of the Bureau of Steam Engineering in Secretary Newberry's first step toward amalgamation of that bureau with Construction and Repair—concluded his annual report by completely exonerating his bureau and characterizing the criticisms as "ill-mannered" and "adverse."[77]

Commander Key, furious with what amounted to an official attack on his integrity, appealed to Roosevelt, who demanded an explanation.[78] The chief constructor's justification proved unacceptable, and to show his disapproval Roosevelt revoked the order conferring the duties of chief engineer on him.[79] Two days later, after further thought about "the Capps matter," Roosevelt told Newberry he was not satisfied with the reorganization scheme and was going to convene a commission to ask for its advice. He then empowered a distinguished panel of former secretaries of the navy and retired admirals to commence their investigations.

Thus, in the final months of Roosevelt's tenure long-sought administrative reforms promised finally to receive an unbiased hearing. But events on the West Coast once again caused a reordering of his priorities. A recrudescence of anti-Japanese feeling and a series of discriminatory legislative measures introduced into the California state legislature in early January 1909 led Roosevelt reluctantly to conclude that for the general welfare of the nation, Japanese immigration to the United States should be stopped. Having reached this conclusion, he wrote that his policy was threefold: "to keep out the Japanese; to do it with a minimum of friction and the maximum of courtesy; and to build up the navy."[80]

This desire to strengthen the navy—heightened by new anti-Japanese feeling and, undoubtedly, his conviction that Germany represented the greatest threat to world peace—further delayed the work of the commission investigating naval organization. In a complex maneuver designed to neutralize the naval reform issue during the congressional debate over naval appropriations for 1909, Roosevelt ordered the commission to meet the day the House debate began, 16 January 1909, to consider Secretary Newberry's original reorganization plan. The commission's presence in Washington during the congressional debate, Elting E. Morison has concluded, was "a master stroke" because the reform issue was actively being investigated and did not therefore enter into debate over the navy bill. This session of the commission actually produced little outside an endorsement in general terms of the secretary's plans.

The navy bill for 1909 left the House Naval Affairs Committee on 16 January, and on 22 January the House of Representatives, where opposition to naval expansion was greatest, passed it by a surprising 150 to 60 vote, thereby assuring Roosevelt of his two dreadnoughts.[81]

Not until the authorization was secured was the president prepared to proceed with the real and predictably contentious work of effective naval reform. Therefore it was not until 27 January that he directed former commission members—ex-Secretaries Moody and Morton, former Chairman of the House Naval Affairs Committee Alston G. Dayton, and retired Rear Admirals Mahan, Luce, Folger, Cowles, and Evans—to form a commission to consider "certain needs" of the navy.[82]

The Moody Commission met and produced two preliminary reports: one dealing with the general principles of naval organization, a second that offered specific proposals.[83] The commission recommended reorganization of the Navy Department into five "grand divisions," of which three—naval operations, personnel, and inspection—would be purely military and headed by line officers. The two remaining divisions were materiel, which might be headed by a line officer, a naval constructor, or a civilian, and which encompassed the navy's technical bureaus, and the assistant secretary's division, which included the Bureaus of Yards and Docks, Supplies, and Medicine and Surgery. Additionally, the commission recommended establishment of two councils: the secretary's general council, composed of the chiefs of the five grand divisions, and his military council, composed of the chief of naval operations and the chiefs of the Bureaus of Personnel and Inspection. But of these, the commission recommended, the chief of naval operations would be the "sole responsible advisor."[84]

This plan of organization would have given the navy significant centralization of control. But the Moody Commission's findings were submitted to Congress less than a week before Roosevelt left office, and no action was taken. Elting E. Morison has concluded that apparently "the President was anxious before leaving office to place on record a document which not only clearly demonstrated the need to eliminate the defects in the independent bureau system but also set forth a plan for making the necessary changes."[85] Within Roosevelt's rapidly expanding navy the need for reorganization, like the need for naval colliers, was clearly recognized; but against the competing demands for more and larger battleships, championed by the president, and continuation of the inefficient, expensive system of congressional political patronage, effective reorganization had been sacrificed.

FOURTEEN

Homeward Bound

Although the fleet's progress through Pacific waters has been interpreted primarily in terms of the cruise's impact on the foreign policy objectives of the Roosevelt administration, senior naval officers steadfastly kept in sight their immediate professional goal: success at the annual battle practice to be held in Manila Bay in November. Admiral Sperry's desire to limit diplomatic duties in preparation for battle practice had contributed to the decision to cut in half the number of ships visiting China.

While the Second Squadron was being entertained at Amoy, the First Squadron had retraced the fleet's northward route to Japan and arrived at Subic Bay on the morning of 31 October to conduct range-finder calibration exercises.[1] Upon completion of this work, it proceeded to Manila Bay to commence final preparations for battle practice. The ships of the Second Squadron continued directly to Subic Bay from Amoy, where they in turn conducted their own calibration exercises. The Second Squadron then rejoined the First in Manila Bay, where annual battle practice took place from 14 to 25 November.

The progress of battle practice was of great importance to the fleet, but to the people of Manila interest focused once again on the pending reception. Therefore when Sperry informed Governor-General Smith on 21 November that the fleet's medical officers as well as his "own strong convictions" had convinced him not to grant liberty in Manila, there was considerable discontent in the city.[2] The admiral's decision was "pronounced unjust, unnecessary, and unduly timid."[3] Governor-General Smith complained to Secretary of War William Taft, the result being a "haughty cable" from Secretary of the Navy Newberry on 22 November directing Sperry to reconsider his decision and appoint a board of medical officers to review the situation.[4] While it was meeting the next day, Sperry received another "rude telegram" from Secretary Newberry containing an order from the president:

Sperry was to confer with Smith and read his, Smith's, confidential report to Secretary Taft, the gist of which was that the admiral's refusal to grant liberty was unjustified.[5]

The following day Sperry doubtless took some perverse pleasure in reporting that the board of medical officers convened in accordance with the secretary's orders had advised against liberty in Manila. However, in compliance with orders from the Navy Department, leave would be granted. In Sperry's view, handling of the issue had been "too stupid all around."[6]

When liberty finally commenced, the men received specific warnings about food and drink. Anyone who returned on board "not clean and sober, with uniform soiled by mud and filth from the streets," would be disinfected and placed in isolation for five days.[7]

With the ships lying at anchor off Cavite, actually getting ashore to enjoy the reluctantly granted liberty proved tedious because of the long boat ride to Manila.[8] Despite inconveniences, liberty parties made their way there each day, saw the sights, and enjoyed tours of the city's cigar factories, while the fleet took on final stores of coal and did maintenance work on engineering plants in preparation for the voyage home.[9]

The governor-general's reception for the officers of the fleet took place despite the threat of an approaching typhoon. Admiral Sperry declined an invitation. Although this action has been interpreted as indicating strained relations between Sperry and Smith, the admiral actually felt he should remain in his flagship to assume responsibility if the storm worsened at a time when he had permitted the battleship captains to bank their fires. To encourage more active participation by junior officers, he offered overnight liberty to any who would attend the reception.[10]

Seven months earlier, when the battleships were at Magdalena Bay, a ship that enjoyed publicity out of all proportion to its importance had arrived at the fleet anchorage. "With its magazine stored with pills, and high explosive seidlitz powders in its handling room within easy reach of the ammunition hoists," the hospital ship *Relief* had steamed south from San Francisco. Her commanding officer, Surgeon Charles F. Stokes, the *New York Times* reported, had "the muzzles of his medicine bottles uncapped, and his crew of interns in readiness for whatever may arise."[11]

There might well have been some basis for press criticism of the *Relief*'s command arrangement, which had stirred such strong emotions just three months earlier, for as the ship approached Magdalena Bay it was discovered that the civilian sailing master had no chart of the harbor entrance and had never before entered the bay.[12] Assistant Surgeon Walter F. Schaller, the only officer on board who had ever been there, was called to the bridge and asked whether he knew of any reefs or shoals. He did not, and so the captain decided to "proceed cautiously." In this unseamanlike manner the *Relief* joined the fleet.[13]

She was undoubtedly a welcome sight to surgeons of the fleet. Surgeon Stone held a "house cleaning" of chronic cases in his sick bay, transferring two insane men, two consumptives, two cases of paralysis, and a few others to the hospital ship.[14] A total of 152 ailing crew members of the fleet were eventually taken on board the *Relief* and conveyed to the naval hospital at Mare Island, California.[15]

Although the *Relief* performed coastal duties adequately, she was in no condition for extended cruising. The voyage from San Francisco onward had been an uninterrupted litany of misfortune. Her refrigeration system broke down en route to Hawaii, resulting in the loss of all her frozen stores.[16] By the time she reached Pago Pago her boilers were acting up, a problem little helped by a "dangerously incompetent" civilian chief engineer.[17] These problems paled alongside displays of instability en route to Auckland: at one point during the storm the fleet had earlier encountered the *Relief,* which started her career as a Long Island ferry, was reported to have rolled a frightening fifty-five degrees. It was only with difficulty that patients were kept in their bunks.[18] More heavy weather was encountered in the Tasman Sea.

At Sydney Sperry ordered the *Relief* to proceed directly to Manila through the sheltered waters inside the Great Barrier Reef, with the *Yankton* as escort. A board of inspection and survey at Manila reported the hospital ship's condition to be "good and safe by only a narrow margin," an admission that she was barely seaworthy.[19] Sperry, who had "always considered her unseaworthy," advised the Bureau of Navigation that the ship was unfit to conduct a winter passage home via the Mediterranean but that a winter passage via Guam and Hawaii, after the typhoon season, would be acceptable.[20] As a result of these recommendations, the *Relief* was ordered to support the Pacific Fleet.[21]

On the battleship fleet's return from Yokohama, Sperry jubilantly recorded that he had finally shed himself of the hospital ship. He doubted that she could have survived the gale the fleet had experienced. She could easily "go up in a flash if she ever takes fire, or go to pieces like wet pasteboard in a gale."[22] Despite these privately expressed concerns, three days later Sperry inexplicably took no action when the *Relief,* under new orders, got under way from Manila for the U.S. West Coast at the height of the typhoon season. The result of this imprudent voyage nearly fulfilled both of his dire predictions. Storm warnings were already up when the *Relief* steamed out of Manila Bay. By the time she reached San Bernadino Strait, it was clear she was in the path of an approaching typhoon. The civilian sailing master requested permission to "lay to" in the lee of the land and wait out the storm. Surgeon Stokes, professionally unqualified to evaluate the situation effectively and undoubtedly still smarting from the debate over his ability to command, denied this request. "We'll show them that the Medical Corps is not afraid of a typhoon," he was reported to have said. "Out we go!"[23]

Once committed to the open sea, the *Relief*'s instability made retreat impossible. Heavy seas prevented a run to the south, and inevitably she passed right through the eye of the typhoon. Mountainous seas smashed her white pine deckhouses and short-circuited wiring, which started seven fires and left the ship in darkness.[24]

At the height of the storm an engine broke down and the civilian crew was forced to rig a sea anchor and makeshift sails. After three days a resourceful sick berth attendant made some temporary repairs and the storm-battered ship limped back to Manila.[25] A second board subsequently declared the *Relief* unseaworthy, and she was retained in the Philippines as a stationary hospital ship. Thus ended, rather ingloriously, the first cruise of a U.S. naval hospital ship under the command of a doctor.

Shortly after the *Relief* returned to Manila Bay the Atlantic battleship fleet completed its preparations for a return voyage. Departure day, 1 December 1908, dawned gray and drizzly over the bay, but the weather failed to dampen the spirits of the men. Promptly at 8:00 A.M. they began the final leg of their long voyage. This was accompanied by a traditional observance. each of the battleships flew a homeward-bound pennant over two hundred feet long.[26] As they slowly headed for the open sea, "nearly everyone looked at Corregidor over the port quarter with much pleasure and a sigh of relief," for after the death of the emperor and empress dowager of China the press had circulated rumors that the fleet was under orders to mobilize off the Chinese coast.[27]

Junior officers faced a dilemma more immediate than the uncertainties of the international situation. During the final weeks in Manila there had been a whole-sale transferring of officers between Atlantic Fleet battleships and ships of the Pacific Fleet's Third Squadron. Many were markedly reluctant to take up a new assignment to the Asiatic station after already passing almost a year away from home. Midshipman Louis Maxfield had worried about the possibility of being transferred and only felt safe when Corregidor was left astern. "This ship [the *Illinois*] may be old and a trifle passé," he wrote on the next evening, "but it is going home, and that means a lot."[28]

For the remainder of the week, as the fleet steamed southwest en route to the Strait of Malacca, the weather was fair and everyone enjoyed a rare respite from the daily routine of drills. On Sunday, 6 December, they passed within sight of Singapore without stopping. The *Connecticut* fired a twenty-gun salute to the British ensign, while a number of boats and yachts stood out to get a closer look at the fleet.[29] Then the ships altered course to the northwest and entered the Strait of Malacca. With a new work week drills began with renewed vigor. Individual ships' drills or range-finding exercises occupied morning hours, signal drills and maneuvers afternoon hours. The day's exercises normally came to a close with night signal drills. This schedule kept the fleet's signal officers busy from eight in the morning until ten or eleven at night.[30]

The trip to Colombo, the next port of call, was marred by an unfortunate incident. On 8 December, while approaching the northern end of the Strait of Malacca, the *New Jersey* reported a man overboard. All ships stopped, and search-lights illuminated the area as a lifeboat recovered him. The fleet resumed its course, whereupon the rescued man revived enough to ask whether another man had been retrieved. Only then was it discovered that two people had gone over. The *New Jersey* remained behind for several hours in an unsuccessful attempt to locate the second man.[31]

Late the next evening the *Georgia*'s surgeon diagnosed a case of smallpox. Permission was granted for the ship to proceed immediately to Colombo to land the sick man.[32] She hauled out of formation, slowly built up to maximum speed, and drew ahead of the fleet. The following morning all *Georgia* crew members who had been ashore at Manila were vaccinated. On 11 December the battleship established communication with the British authorities in Colombo informing them of her approach.[33] Next day at 9:00 A.M. she passed through the breakwater flying her yellow quarantine flag, fired a salute to the port, and then received a quarantine officer aboard. After the sick man was moved ashore the *Georgia* immediately began coaling from the Austro-Hungarian collier *Kobe,* an evolution that was not completed until 14 December, at which time normal liberty was granted.[34]

The remainder of the fleet conducted an uneventful run to Colombo. Weather remained favorable from the time the fleet "weighed anchor until it was cast again, . . . [with] a steady cool North Easter . . . of just enough force to scare the clouds away and keep the sea rippled."[35] These exceptional conditions made for an unusually fast passage. Although the fleet slowed to nine knots, and part of the time to eight, it passed Point de Galle, the southern tip of Ceylon, at about 11:00 P.M. on 12 December, a full day ahead of schedule.[36]

The ships arrived off Colombo next morning and awaited pilots to guide them to moorings inside the breakwaters that formed the harbor. There being only six pilots, the process of mooring took all morning. When the entire fleet finally came to rest, the battleships were moored bow and stern to buoys and "packed in like sardines."[37]

A full schedule of entertainment had been arranged for the visitors—receptions, concerts, smokers, and dinners, in many of which the colonial governor, Colonel Sir Henry E. McCallum, took part with his house guest, Rear Admiral Sperry.[38] Few personal accounts of these events survive, although everyone seems to have recorded their observations of the people of Colombo. The "lanky Hindus, merchants and fakirs" crowded the breakwater and swarmed about ships' gangways "like so many mother-carey's-chickens."[39] Men who went ashore found the shopkeepers "very obsequious, calling all white men 'Master,' " and they attracted all manner of people hoping to provide services in return for cash.[40] Midshipman Maxfield encountered rickshaw men, shopkeepers, tattooers, "and a whole rabble of other people telling [him] where the most beautiful Singhalese girls could be found very cheap. Poor girls!"[41]

At the colonial government's request, normal liberty was limited to eighty firstclass libertymen per ship, exclusive of organized tours, and was permitted only from 1:00 to 6:00 P.M.[42] This undoubtedly would be seen as a hardship by presentday sailors, but that was not the case in 1908. Watching the passing scene—bumboats crowded with colorful people selling everything imaginable, a harbor full of steamers, bustling shoreside activity—proved popular. Shipboard entertainment also helped pass the time when duties were completed. Archa Adamson recorded a visit to the *Louisiana* to attend a smoker and noted that a few days later the *Georgia*'s minstrel troupe performed in the *Nebraska,* to the great pleasure of her crew.[43]

The main purpose of the Colombo visit, of course, was neither cultural nor social. The distance from Manila to Suez was too great for ships to steam without coaling. Sperry had worried about this aspect of arrangements at Colombo during the Australasian portion of the cruise.[44] After the difficulties at Albany he had cabled Washington to emphasize that colliers bound for Colombo would have to sail by 14 October at the latest.[45] Despite his urgent appeal, only one of the chartered colliers sailed before Sperry's deadline—the Austro-Hungarian steamer *Kobe*, which began her journey from the U.S. East Coast on 11 October. The remaining two got under way on 18 and 20 October, so once again little margin for delay had been allowed.[46] Sperry was undoubtedly relieved to see, upon the fleet's arrival, that all three contracted colliers had arrived on time.

As the fleet visit drew to a close, presents arrived from Sir Thomas Lipton: five pounds of tea for each officer and one pound for each enlisted man. To this bounty were added many local purchases. The last evening in port Surgeon Stone recorded, like sailors from time immemorial, "Came back to the ship with my last cent spent, and loaded down with packages of tea and other plunder."[47]

The fleet departed on a Sunday. Though it was Christmas week the voyage across the Arabian Sea was not a pleasure cruise. The men endured several days of strenuous battle drills, range-finding exercises, signal drills, maneuvers, and searchlight exercises. That Friday was Christmas, and unlike the Christmas of 1907, when the newly departed fleet lay in Port of Spain, an atmosphere of optimism prevailed. "It makes all the difference in the world which way you are travelling," one midshipman recorded.[48]

On 26 December the fleet sighted Socotra at the mouth of the Gulf of Aden, which marked the end of the Arabian Sea crossing. It had been an enjoyable trip through smooth seas.[49] In the *Connecticut* splendid weather was complemented by orchestra music on the quarterdeck every evening from 8:00 to 9:00.[50]

One modern account of the cruise reports that "boredom, tension and fatigue" beset the men during this period, but Louis Maxfield recorded an incident that might belie this.[51] The enlisted men in the *Illinois* held a meeting to plan a ball that would take place when they reached their home port of Boston. "After the meeting the band played on the forecastle and the men had a great time dancing. Of course they [don't] dance every day but the ball has given an impetus to practice, so the deck was covered with waltzing couples. . . . You would naturally think they had had enough entertainment on this cruise and would want to rest," Maxfield concluded condescendingly, "but not so with a bluejacket."[52]

Another man went overboard on the voyage to Suez. In the course of a drill on 29 December the *Kansas* hoisted an incorrect signal. The *Missouri*, further down the line, hoisted the same signal, then realizing the mistake immediately hauled it down.[53] The *Illinois* saw only the flag N, which meant man overboard. Her captain reacted by launching a lifeboat. As crewmen climbed down to it a rung of the Jacob's ladder gave way and one man fell. Although the sea was calm and additional boats were promptly lowered, he was not recovered.[54]

The fleet steamed north through the Red Sea, encountering an increasing number of steamers and a British troop ship bound for India, its decks crowded with soldiers who gave the fleet three cheers as it passed.[55] On New Year's Eve 1909 it neared Suez and the men performed their New Year's "high jinks."[56] Without further incident the fleet completed the northward transit of the Red Sea and Gulf of Suez and anchored at the southern terminus of the Suez Canal at 8:00 A.M. on 3 January 1909, two days ahead of schedule.[57]

Planning for the Mediterranean portion of the voyage had commenced when the fleet was still in San Francisco. On 3 June 1908 Secretary of the Navy Metcalf had directed Sperry to propose an itinerary for the fleet's return from Manila.[58] Sperry recommended that the fleet leave Manila on 1 December, coal at Colombo, and arrive at Suez on 5 January 1909. After passing through the canal and coaling, the fleet would be divided into units for separate visits to French, Italian, and Algerian ports. This, Sperry reported, would give the men more liberty opportunities while at the same time free host governments from the obligation they might feel to offer expensive entertainment.[59] But Sperry's proposed itinerary did not find complete favor. The Fourth Division had been scheduled to visit Naples. Acting Secretary of the Navy Newberry pointed out that Italy prohibited the simultaneous visit of more than three warships to any of its ports, and the Navy Department was reluctant to seek an exception to the policy. Further, Newberry felt that some ships should stop at Gibraltar and perhaps Malta to take up the British government's invitation to these ports. He also recommended Phalerum Bay (Piraeus) and Athens as excellent places for liberty. With reference to the two battleships that Sperry had scheduled to visit Palermo, Newberry said that in a recent visit there the Armored Cruiser Squadron had "found conditions most unpleasant." In light of these reservations Sperry was requested to submit a revised itinerary.[60]

The admiral asked for a report on health conditions in Athens and temporarily set aside planning for this phase of the cruise.[61] Upon the fleet's arrival in Manila he cabled his revised itinerary proposals, which envisaged a total of eight battleships calling at Italian ports: three each at Genoa and Naples and two at Leghorn (Livorno). The First Division would be split between Villefranche and Marseilles. Two ships would visit Athens, while the remaining two would divide their time between Malta and Algiers. Forwarding this schedule to Secretary of State Root, Metcalf said the fleet's Mediterranean visits would be unofficial, intended for the recreation of officers and crew.[62]

American diplomats on the scene were quick to perceive the benefits of fleet visits, and countries to be visited seemed reluctant to treat them as unofficial. Gabriel Bie Ravndal, the U.S. consul-general in Beirut, complained that the chief political mission of the fleet was thought to be completed as soon as the battleships had left the Orient.[63] In fact the political situation in the Balkans and eastern Mediterranean gave increased political importance to its passage.

In Turkey liberal groups protesting the autocratic excesses of Ottoman Sultan Abdulhamit II had united in the summer of 1908 to form the Committee of Union and Progress (*Terakki Cemiyetinin Tesekkulu*), more commonly known as the Young Turks. In July this coalition forced the sultan to recall Parliament and restore constitutional rule. Elections were scheduled for November and December, but in the meantime the Ottoman Empire's neighbors took advantage of the temporary vacuum of power. Austria annexed Bosnia-Herzegovina outright; Bulgaria declared its independence; and Greece annexed Crete. Preoccupied with the institution of liberal policies at home, the Young Turks limited their reaction to these infringements to diplomatic protests. Elections swept the Young Turks to power with 287 of 288 seats in the new Parliament, but ethnic and religious divisions within the party that had formerly been suppressed now appeared. These and the greed of Turkey's neighbors threatened the liberal goals of the new regime.[64]

On 1 November Consul-General Ravndal cabled a suggestion that the two ships scheduled to visit Athens should also visit Beirut to express American support of the new government of Turkey.[65] Ravndal's request and a similar one from Chargé d'Affaires Louis Einstein failed to move Secretary Root to ask the navy for a change of itinerary.[66] The head of the American Presbyterian mission in Beirut addressed a powerful appeal to Oscar Strauss, secretary of commerce and labor, urging a Turkish visit on the grounds that it would be almost unfriendly to have the fleet pass without acknowledging the new government.[67] Strauss forwarded this appeal with his stamp of approval.[68] Apparently Root also approved, for he sent the correspondence to Secretary Metcalf, who responded by ordering the *Ohio* and *Missouri* to visit Smyrna (Izmir) for two days.[69]

At this point Acting Secretary Newberry notified Root that it was inadvisable to make further itinerary changes.[70] This protest was ineffective: eleven days later a two-day port visit to Salonika (Thessaloniki), then a part of European Turkey and a center of Young Turk strength, was added to the itinerary of the *Ohio* and *Missouri*.[71]

Another American diplomat in the Ottoman Empire was quick to see the potential of the fleet's Mediterranean visit. William Coffin, consul at Tripoli, inquired whether one or two battleships could pay a short visit there.[72] This request was favorably received, and in due course Coffin was informed that the *Kentucky* would visit on 13 and 14 January.[73]

Next the American ambassador to the Hellenic Court pointed out that the present schedule had the *Ohio* and *Missouri* arriving in Greece on that country's new year's day. He urged Root to have the navy speed up coaling or steam faster so the ships could reach Piraeus in time for the court ball, where the officers would be introduced to the royal family. The Navy Department acquiesced.[74]

While these scheduling problems were being dealt with in Washington, other diplomats made direct approaches to Admiral Sperry. From Colombo he complained of being pestered by ambassadors and consuls, whom he informed with well veiled temper that the Navy Department had declared the visits unofficial.[75]

During the fleet's voyage to Suez the itinerary was thrown into disarray. Early on 28 December a major earthquake and tidal wave struck the area of Messina, Sicily, and Reggio di Calabria. Initial estimates of 150,000 to 200,000 dead were believed to be low. There was little the fleet could do in the way of immediate relief; however, when the ships reached Suez, Sperry ordered the *Culgoa* to hasten to the scene of the disaster and deliver her remaining cargo of several hundred tons of foodstuffs. Similarly, battleships were canvassed for medical stores in excess of their immediate requirements; these and six surgeons were transferred to the *Yankton,* which followed the *Culgoa* through the canal en route to Messina. In other support efforts, the Mediterranean station ship USS *Scorpion* was sent from Constantinople, while at New York the supply ship *Celtic,* already loaded with stores for the fleet, received materials for a hastily prefabricated hospital and set sail for the earthquake zone on 31 December.[76]

Receptions for the fleet, out of deference to the Italian tragedy, would have to be subdued. Furthermore, another major itinerary change was required. American Ambassador Lloyd C. Griscom had cabled that the Italian prime minister feared the battleships would arrive too late to assist victims of the earthquake. Newberry ordered Sperry to proceed to Naples and offer the fleet's service, using his own discretion about port calls but counseling against sending ships to Italian ports for liberty. Newberry also directed that two ships be sent to Beirut and then to join the *Ohio* and *Missouri.* Finally, itinerary changes notwithstanding, the date of departure for home was to remain unaltered.[77] These new orders were received by the flagship at 8:00 A.M. on 5 January 1909, and by noon the sailing orders for every ship had been changed.[78]

Although Sperry and his staff were fully occupied with schedule changes and the Messina relief operation, diplomatic demands did not abate. On 29 December the American consular agent in Cairo cabled Root that the Khedive had invited a delegation of officers to a banquet and added, "Refusal would be regrettable, perhaps misunderstood."[79] Though this invitation, communicated directly to Sperry, aroused his ire, he complied.[80] Rear Admiral William P. Potter, three captains, and four other officers formed the official party that visited the Khedive and accepted the official hospitality of Egypt.[81] Several additional parties of officers and men made "flying" visits to Cairo to see the sights.

Meanwhile, arrangements were being made to handle the largest single-group transit in the Suez Canal's history. To accommodate the fleet the canal was closed to all other traffic and the battleships were sent through on three successive days in groups of four, five, and seven.[82] The first two groups sailed without incident, completing their transit in a single day. On 6 January the third and largest group, led by the Second Division flagship, the *Georgia,* started north. The trip proceeded without incident until about noon when the *Georgia* went aground just south of the Bitter Lakes.[83] The six battleships following her moored to pilings at the side of the canal, while she lowered boats and carried lines to pilings on the opposite bank. Using these lines she managed to work herself free after about two hours and resumed the northward transit.

Because of this delay the group did not reach the middle of the canal until about 7:00 P.M. The *Georgia, Nebraska,* and *New Jersey,* the three lead ships, were ordered to continue on to Port Said. The remaining four anchored off the canal company's headquarters at Ismailia, where the company president took the opportunity of the unanticipated delay to host a dinner party for the officers.[84]

Next morning the four battleships got under way. At one point the monotony of this final leg was interrupted by the appearance along the canal bank of the Cairo–Port Said train with American enlisted men "all over the cars, on the roofs, and apparently enjoying themselves." They were returning to their ships after a whirl-wind tour of the city and the pyramids.[85]

The only purpose of the fleet's stop at Port Said was to coal, and it was due to the limited harbor area that the battleships had been sent through in three groups.[86] It had been hoped that each group would coal expeditiously and clear the harbor before the arrival of the next group.[87] Unfortunately, problems developed in the coaling arrangements. The Navy Department had contracted with a company that lacked facilities to provide the coal in sufficient quantity. The contractor filled a single lighter, and the battleships had to "squabble for it."[88] Additional delays followed when it was discovered that the contractor was trying to cheat on the quantity of coal delivered. It was so dry, moreover, that shifting it raised clouds of dust which seeped everywhere.[89] On board the *Rhode Island*, coaling proceeded fitfully during the night and was not finished until near noon the next day.[90]

As individual ships completed coaling they departed Port Said en route to various ports. Despite many changes in the itinerary, it retained a certain cohesion. The First Division would go to Naples to offer earthquake assistance and thence to Villefranche on the French Riviera for liberty. The Second Division would proceed directly to Marseilles for liberty. The Third Division would break into two units to visit Greek and Turkish ports, the Fourth would split up to visit the North African littoral—Malta, Tripoli, and Algiers.

Sperry's orders had been to proceed to Naples with the four ships of the First Division. Before leaving Port Said, however, he had decided that the whole division would be unnecessary, confiding in a letter to his son that he intended to go to Naples in the *Connecticut* and send the other ships directly to Villefranche "to get on with their play day."[91] Sperry diverted his flagship to Messina after the *Culgoa* contacted him by wireless to say that Ambassador Griscom was there and wanted the *Connecticut* to transport him back to Naples.[92] After spending the day at anchor off Messina, the *Connecticut* embarked the ambassador and got under way in a "sharp rain squall, accompanied by blinding flashes of lightning." Against this stygian background the flagship left the scene of the tragedy, carefully feeling her way, constant soundings being made from the forward chains to detect any earth-quake-induced changes to the navigability of the Messina Strait.[93] In Ambassador Griscom Sperry found support for his plan to send the remainder of his division directly to Villefranche. He informed Washington that Griscom considered condi-tions at Naples unfavorable for a visit and that all the ships of the First Division except the flagship had been sent directly to Villefranche.[94]

The *Connecticut* arrived at Naples on 10 January without salutes or the usual honors and remained in port for ten days directing relief operations. The American effort was unobtrusive. The *Yankton* remained at Messina providing medical assist-ance, while the *Culgoa* delivered supplies to towns and villages on the Calabrian coast. The *Celtic*, with her cargo of stores and prefabricated hospital, arrived on 19 January, and as a result of coordination with the Italian Ministry of Marine, her cargo was being unloaded an hour after she moored.[95]

In Messina the small party put ashore by the *Scorpion* and *Yankton* had been unable to recover the bodies of the American consul and his wife, who had died in the earthquake. The American vice consul on the scene estimated that it would take two hundred men a week to excavate the bodies; therefore, on 13 January Sperry diverted the *Illinois,* then en route to Malta, to Messina.[96] The *Illinois* arrived the next morning and parties were promptly landed. They started removing the pile of debris that had formerly been the American consulate. While the men worked from the top a party led by Louis Maxfield tunneled in from the side, and after a relatively short time they located and recovered the bodies of the dead diplomat and his wife.[97] Mission completed, the *Illinois* got under way for Malta to rejoin the *Wisconsin* and *Kearsarge* and participate in the British reception.[98]

While Louis Maxfield and his shipmates were digging in Messina, Sperry was personally received by King Victor Emmanuel in Rome. The king expressed his appreciation of American assistance. After the *Connecticut* returned to sea, however, Sperry privately concluded that the earthquake victims did not need and could not use the tendered supplies, and that the Italian government had taken them "out of politeness."[99] This assessment was not shared by Commander H. P. Huse, skipper of the *Celtic,* who spent more than a month in Italy assisting in the relief effort. In a letter to Secretary Newberry, Huse forwarded a message from Marquis del Carretto, the mayor of Naples, who wrote of the great suffering that had been eased by American stores and the "excellent feeling" this assistance had produced in Italy. The mayor commended Admiral Sperry for the tactful manner in which he had placed supplies at the disposal of the Italian government.[100] In March 1909 Italy expressed a desire to decorate officers and surgeons who had lent "brotherly assistance to the sufferers of the earthquake," and although navy regulations at the time forbade acceptance of foreign awards, the fact that the offer was made indicated Italian appreciation.[101] The same can be said of the Italian Red Cross's award of silver medals and diplomas in 1911 to American relief workers.[102]

Meanwhile the Third Division was visiting ports in the eastern Mediterranean. The *Louisiana* and *Virginia* sailed on schedule for Beirut. However, plague had been reported there, and Consul-General Ravndal warned in advance that the ships should not communicate with the shore before he had conferred with Rear Admiral Schroeder.[103] At 10:00 A.M. on 8 January 1909 the *Louisiana* and *Virginia,* watched by multitudes under bright skies, arrived off Beirut and saluted the port by firing twenty-one guns. The consul-general and various medical authorities came "to within hailing distance" of the *Louisiana* and told Rear Admiral Schroeder that they could not provide a clean bill of health for the port, so he decided to depart. The battleships saluted the consular officer, returned a gun salute by a Turkish gunboat, then "stood off and sailed away" en route to Smyrna.[104]

No such problems confronted the captains of the *Missouri* and *Ohio* in Athens. Those ships arrived in time for officers to attend the Greek new year reception where the queen received them warmly. The visit was a rapid-fire round of festivities that included a tour of the battlefield of Marathon and the usual social engagements. Virtually the entire royal family visited the *Missouri.*[105] On 18 January Ambassador Richmond Pearson reported that the ships had sailed after "receiving conspicuous, extraordinary . . . honors."[106] One Athens paper found ample justification for the reception in the ties created through Greek immigration to the United States and in what it perceived to be American support for Greek annexation of Crete.[107]

From Athens the *Missouri* and *Ohio* paid a short visit to Salonika. The battleships arrived in late afternoon of 19 January and departed for Smyrna on the morning of 21 January.[108] At Smyrna the two ships rejoined the *Louisiana* and *Virginia,* participated in the standard round of unofficial receptions and dinners, and sent tour parties to the ancient ruins at Ephesus.[109]

Another attempt had been made to expand the Turkish itinerary. On 2 January the American chargé d'affaires at Constantinople cabled Secretary Root wanting to know whether an invitation for Sperry to visit Constantinople in one of his battleships would be agreeable. At this time international agreement forbade the passage of foreign warships through the Turkish Straits; therefore, Chargé Einstein reported, Sperry would be invited to the Sublime Porte if means could be found to do so without violating the Treaty of Paris.[110]

By the time this request reached the Navy Department, Sperry had already been ordered to proceed to Naples. As a result, Secretary Newberry responded that it would be impractical for the admiral to call at any Turkish port, but added that, should Turkey wish to extend the invitation to Rear Admiral Schroeder, they could communicate with him at Smyrna. There is no evidence that an invitation was sent.[111] On 18 January the American ambassador announced that it would not be possible for any American battleship to visit Constantinople, and there the issue rested.[112]

Chargé Einstein also forwarded Turkey's request that Turkish naval officers be invited to travel to the United States aboard the battleships.[113] To this request Newberry responded favorably, stating that if the State Department considered it advisable, accommodations could probably be made for ten officers.[114] He clearly identified the issue as resting within the State Department's domain, which may have alerted the State Department to the possibility that it would result in unanticipated expenditure of public funds and that more entertainment might be required in the United States. In forwarding Newberry's response to the American embassy in Constantinople, Secretary Root confidentially directed the staff there to make it known, politely, that American courtesy would be limited to transportation, and that the Turkish officers would not be the guests of the United States once they arrived there.[115]

The Navy Department accepted the ten passengers. Einstein forwarded this news, and on 11 January reported that Turkey's minister of foreign affairs had assured him a special fund amounting to 200 Turkish lire per officer would be appropriated for the visit.[116] When the Third Division's visit to Smyrna drew to a close, it was well prepared to embark the ten Turkish officers.[117]

To cheering crowds the *Wisconsin* and *Kearsarge* entered the Grand Harbor of Valetta, Malta, on 14 January.[118] The *Kentucky* was paying a two-day visit to Tripoli, and the *Illinois* had been diverted to Messina. Host for the visit was

Admiral Sir Assheton G. Curzon-Howe, commander in chief, Mediterranean Fleet, flying his flag from HMS *Exmouth*.[119] Despite her diversion, the *Illinois* managed to reach Malta on 17 January in time to attend a "pretty stiff and formal" ball given by the Duke and Duchess of Connaught.[120] On 19 January, after a series of social events and tours of the island fortress, the three battleships left Malta en route to their next port of call.

Forty-eight hours later, the *Wisconsin, Illinois,* and *Kearsarge* entered Algiers and joined the *Kentucky*, which had already been there three days. The ships were scheduled for a full week at this port, so plenty of opportunities arose to explore the city. The men found it generally interesting, although the natives' attitude toward casual prostitution made at least one midshipman comment "that our country is about the cleanest and most decent in the whole world." The ships each took on a few hundred tons of coal before getting under way on Saturday, 30 January 1909, in bright sunshine, with crowds lining le Boulevard de la République and bands playing the Marseillaise. They were treated to a pretty maneuver as the ships, building up to full speed as they left, executed a sharp turn around the harbor's breakwater before shaping course for Gibraltar.[121]

As a result of the Messina earthquake, French ports had become the focal point of the fleet's recreation in the Mediterranean, with a total of eight battleships divided evenly between Villefranche and Marseilles. Rear Admiral Wainwright arrived in Marseilles with the *Georgia* and *Nebraska* on Friday, 15 January, followed by the *Rhode Island* and *New Jersey* the next day.[122] Unofficial receptions were given by local civil and military officials and the American community. On Sunday, 17 January, thousands of French people visited the ships, swarming over the quays and holding up traffic.[123]

Many officers took leave in Marseilles and Villefranche to visit Paris and various destinations in Italy. Surgeon Stone toured Florence, and a party of officers visited Rome, where they had an audience with the Pope. Parties and sightseeing continued in French ports throughout the week of 17 January and into the next. The First Division departed Villefranche as scheduled on 27 January and proceeded to Gibraltar, while two ships of the Second Division, whose program had been subjected to further changes, got under way on 27 January, the remaining two on the following day.[124]

There were two reasons for the latest rescheduling. The original plan had called for the fleet to coal at Negro Bay, with only the First Division visiting Gibraltar. The coaling rendezvous had subsequently been shifted to Tetuan Bay because of the better anchorage there. Now, as the date of the fleet's arrival approached, Vice Admiral Sir James E. C. Goodrich, RN, the admiral superintendent at Gibraltar, insisted that as many battleships as possible be accommodated in the basin at Gibraltar rather than at the Tetuan Bay anchorage.[125] The other itinerary change was a matter of diplomacy. The United States had decided to recognize Mulai Hafid as the sultan of Morocco. Secretary Newberry therefore directed Sperry to send one flag officer and no less than two battleships to call at Tangier.[126] Rear Admiral Wainwright was assigned this duty. He sailed from Marseilles with the

Georgia and *Nebraska* on 27 January.[127] After a choppy but otherwise uneventful passage, they arrived off Tangier on 30 January and fired a twenty-one-gun salute to Morocco, officially recognizing the administration of Mulai Hafid.[128] After exchanging salutes with a couple of French cruisers and a Spanish gunboat, the battleships came to anchor and Wainwright and the two captains conducted official calls.[129]

The Tangier visit was just a stopover for the night, and only twenty-five enlisted men per ship were granted liberty.[130] The main feature of the visit, aside from the salute signifying American recognition, was a ball hosted by the American minister to Morocco, Samuel M. Gummeré.[131] On this occasion one of the senior officers committed a "gross breach of courtesy." Captain Edward F. Qualtrough had returned to his ship, the *Georgia,* after an afternoon "tea" in a state of apparent intoxication. Subsequently, at the ball, he appeared "in full view of the Admiral [Wainwright] and assembled guests, . . . reeling down the long carpet approach to the receiving line."[132] After returning to the ship that night he was suspended from his command for being drunk on duty. As a result of charges that Wainwright laid, Admiral Sperry ordered a court-martial convened while the fleet was at Gibraltar.[133]

Captain Qualtrough defended himself by claiming that the combination of long hours on the bridge bringing the ship through the Strait of Gibraltar and a day of social functions without food had made him ill. Six officers, including Admiral Wainwright and Captain Nicholson of the *Nebraska,* testified that he had been drunk and was, in their opinion, unfit for duty. The *Georgia*'s surgeon maintained that Qualtrough had been treated for "gastric catarrh" and was in bad physical condition. Qualtrough claimed that he had taken only one drink; it was a strong cigar he had smoked that had had such a sickening effect on him.[134] The court-martial board accepted this explanation and acquitted him; Admiral Sperry, however, reversed the decision.[135] Captain Qualtrough, who was restricted to the *Georgia* and forbidden to enter on the quarterdeck or bridge, completed the voyage a virtual prisoner in the ship he had formerly commanded.[136]

This incident brought home the fact that the old men in command of the fleet were not sufficiently strong to withstand the rigors of commanding a modern ship in foreign waters. As if to reinforce this point, another battleship commanding officer, Captain Hamilton Hutchins of the *Kentucky,* suffered a nervous breakdown and was relieved by Sperry while the fleet was in Gibraltar.

The final days of January saw the fleet reassembling at Gibraltar for the final leg of the long voyage. As usual, the main purpose of the stop was to coal and load provisions. This latter task met with an unanticipated snag. All surplus provisions carried aboard the fleet stores ship *Culgoa* had been distributed in Sicily and Calabria. The *Celtic,* originally scheduled to augment the *Culgoa* in the Mediterranean, had also been diverted to provide earthquake relief. To meet shortages in the fleet, the steamer *Republic* was loaded in New York with $61,000 of food supplies and sent to rendezvous with the *Culgoa* at Gibraltar. On 23 January the *Republic,* outbound from New York, collided with the steamer *Florida* in a fog off Nantucket. Both ships sank.[137]

The Atlantic Fleet paymaster moved rapidly to compensate for the loss. On 24 January he traveled from Villefranche to Marseilles, where he contracted for $36,670 of stores, which were loaded on board the *Culgoa* at that port. The stores ship left Marseilles on 29 January and started to deliver her cargo to the fleet in Gibraltar on 1 February.[138]

On Sunday, 31 January, the First Division, led by Rear Admiral Sperry in the *Connecticut,* approached Gibraltar. Indicative of the unusual interest the fleet cruise aroused, the citizens, though long accustomed to visiting ships, swarmed over the Rock's vantage points and the waterfront to watch. Waiting to greet the Americans were the British battleships *Albemarle* and *Albion,* the Second Cruiser Squadron of the Royal Navy, the Russian battleships *Tsarevitch* and *Slava* and protected cruisers *Bogatyr* and *Oleg,* and a French and a Dutch gunboat, all with sides manned and bands playing. Vice Admiral Goodrich of the Royal Navy, although Sperry's senior, brushed aside protocol and called on the American admiral to extend his greeting first.[139] Rear Admiral Wainwright, with the *Georgia* and *Nebraska,* arrived in the early evening, the other battleships the following day.[140]

Because the *Connecticut* arrived on Sunday, normal salutes were postponed until after the morning colors ceremony next day. The daily colors ceremony itself was a cacophony of national airs as, promptly at 8:00 A.M., within the narrow confines of the basin at Gibraltar, bands on ships of five nations played their own national anthems followed by those of the other four nations. Over a period of ten or fifteen minutes the groups were all playing different music. After the last national anthem, the *Connecticut* fired a twenty-one-gun salute to the colony, which was returned by shore batteries and HMS *Albemarle.* "The reverberations were incessant for an hour, and clouds of gray smoke blew over the waters" as the ships of each nation rendered gun salutes to Admiral Sperry's flag, each of which was returned gun for gun by the *Connecticut.*[141]

No shore leave was granted enlisted men at Gibraltar. Those not involved in coaling participated in a program of athletics, boxing, smokers, and rowing events. Officers, when they weren't attending receptions and balls, were free to explore the colony and many recorded their impressions. Surgeon Stone observed, as have many sailors over the years, that at Gibraltar he could have bought almost everything he had seen elsewhere on the cruise, and at a cheaper price.[142]

All this while the ships were coaling. The *Minnesota, Vermont,* and *Kansas* commenced immediately after the last gun salute on Monday morning.[143] It was an unusually burdensome task, as each ship required from 1,200 to 1,600 tons. The upper decks of the *Illinois* were so full of coal that there was no room for men to fall in at quarters.[144]

The fleet visit to Gibraltar came to an end on Saturday, 6 February. At 9:00 A.M., under cloudless skies, the *Georgia, Nebraska, New Jersey, Rhode Island,* and *Virginia* made their way out of the crowded harbor, trailed by the other ships. Bands in the British ships played "Auld Lang Syne" and "For He Is a Jolly Good Fellow" as the American ships passed.[145]

Within an hour, fifteen battleships had cleared harbor and formed a single column, awaiting the flagship. At 10:30 the *Connecticut* got under way and received an unusual twenty-one-gun national salute from Vice Admiral Goodrich, who was flying his flag on the *Devonshire*. She returned the salute, and then her band struck up "God Save the King" while she passed the British flagship and left port. Returning this courtesy, the *Devonshire*'s band played "The Star-Spangled Banner." The *Connecticut* steamed the length of the waiting battleship column and, upon reaching its head, hoisted the guide flag, ordered standard speed, and shaped a southerly course to clear Cape Tarifa. Strains of "Home, Sweet Home" were heard emanating from fleet bands as the ships left Gibraltar astern. The local signal tower finally lost sight of the fleet at 1:57 P.M., when the last of the battleships, now in line of squadrons, disappeared below the western horizons.[146]

"And now, at last, after all these weary months we are headed across the Atlantic bound for home," Surgeon Stone recorded in his diary that evening.[147]

Admiral Sperry had planned to use the final leg of the voyage as a period for extensive tactical drills and, weather permitting, the annual admiral's inspection, for which he would have to transfer by boat to each of the battleships in turn. Winter storms brought three days of high winds and seas and altered these plans. When the weather improved on 10 February, work started in earnest. Ships conducted the full range of day and night drills and prepared for inspection. Unfortunately the good weather was short-lived. On 14 February winds built in intensity to gale force, and that night the *Virginia, Illinois,* and *Kentucky* each lost a lifeboat, leading Surgeon Stone to record that "Neptune . . . did not want the cruise to finish without our finding out what [he] could do when [he] tried."[148]

News of the fleet's position and progress first reached Washington late on 11 February. In what was then a feat of radiotelegraphy, Sperry relayed his position via the *Yankton,* which was preceding the fleet, to the wireless station on Fire Island, a distance of over two thousand miles.[149] This contact was "the first harbinger of . . . the homeland."[150] The information signaled was most welcome, for several units were at sea attempting to rendezvous with the fleet, while ashore public interest in its return was keen.

With the Atlantic Fleet on its world cruise, the Navy Department had organized fighting units remaining in the Atlantic into a single command designated Third Squadron, Atlantic Fleet. Under Rear Admiral Conway H. Arnold, in the flagship *Maine,* this squadron had been formed around the new battleships *New Hampshire, Idaho,* and *Mississippi* after their commissioning. It also included two armored cruisers and three scout cruisers.[151] The Third Squadron had been ordered to rendezvous with the returning battleship fleet in a position approximately one thousand miles east of Cape Hatteras. To do this the battleships, except the *Idaho,* sailed from Guantanamo Bay, Cuba, on 10 February. The *Idaho* sailed from Philadelphia and joined the squadron on 16 February. On the afternoon of 17 February the four battleships came up with the fleet. On signal from Admiral Sperry they took position to starboard of the First Squadron, forming line of squadrons with that squadron in the center.[152]

The appearance of the Third Squadron struck many as peculiar. The decision to paint battleships and cruisers gray had already been put into effect for stateside units.[153] Additionally, the *Idaho* and *Mississippi* had been built with new lattice-cage masts that would soon replace solid military masts on all American battleships and that would be their most recognizable feature for the next four decades. Overall, the effect was foreign. The new masts looked like oil wells to Louis Maxfield; Surgeon Stone noted that they might be "a military improvement but they are certainly ugly."[154] On board the *Georgia* one sailor exclaimed, "Hey, look at those guinea ships!"[155]

The fleet's return to the United States was an event of major proportions. Although there had been some pressure to have the homecoming at New York, in October 1908 the president and his cabinet decided on Hampton Roads, where Roosevelt would review the battleships.[156] Elaborate entertainment plans had been made in Norfolk, Richmond, and Hampton, and while the *Connecticut* was still in Naples Secretary Newberry cabled Sperry with the order that under no circumstances should the fleet enter Hampton Roads early.[157] Sperry replied that the *Connecticut* would pass the Tail of the Horseshoe lightship at 11:00 A.M. on 22 February; having allowed a liberal amount of time for the Atlantic passage, he intended to arrive near the coast early and then occupy the remaining time with tactical exercises.[158]

This is precisely the plan that was followed. Despite rough weather, the fleet had not been significantly delayed. At noon on Saturday, 20 February, the ships slowed speed so as not to upset the schedule. The final full day at sea was beautifully clear, and although it was Sunday much time was spent applying a final coat of white paint before the presidential review the next morning. At 2:00 A.M. on Monday the fleet came to anchor fifteen miles off Cape Henry, there to await the grand entry nine hours later.[159]

Ashore, the scene was one of mounting excitement as the battleship fleet neared home. "NAVY-MAD THRONGS AT HAMPTON ROADS," headlined the *New York Times,* reporting events two days before the fleet's arrival. Every hotel and boarding house was crowded with large parties from all over the East Coast that had arrived for Fleet Week. The streets of Norfolk and Hampton were festive; public buildings and streets had been draped in bunting in a manner reminiscent of Australian ports. In Norfolk "patriotism of the best American type [was] bubbling over." Such was the anticipation that hundreds of people made the long trek to Virginia Beach and Cape Henry on the final day before the fleet's return in the vain hope of getting a glimpse of the battleships, which were reported to be maneuvering fifty miles offshore.[160]

The president's yacht, with Roosevelt, Secretary Newberry, and Commander Sims on board, left Washington at noon on Sunday and headed south. The *Mayflower* joined a stream of yachts and steamers en route to Hampton Roads, including the navy yacht *Dolphin,* carrying members of the Senate and House Naval Affairs committees. Noteworthy for their absence from the moving mass of officialdom were two of the nation's most prominent naval officers. Admiral of the Navy George Dewey had earlier informed the White House and Navy Department that he was suffering from sciatica and his physician had advised against the trip. Nor could Rear Admiral Evans attend. This caused some comment. The old admiral's health had improved following an operation in August, and he had subsequently undertaken a lecture tour whose object was, in part, to criticize Roosevelt's naval policies. When he refused to interrupt his tour to be present at Hampton Roads, speculation grew about friction between him and the president.[161]

Monday, 22 February 1909—George Washington's Birthday—dawned under overcast skies and squalls. The inclement weather, though, failed to extinguish the spirits of tens of thousands gathered to greet the returning ships. The most ambitious well-wishers managed to secure passage aboard one of the flotilla of small craft that headed out to the Tail of the Horseshoe for the presidential review. There seaborne crowds waited expectantly until a few minutes before 11:00 A.M., when a "whole forest of masts and fighting tops" appeared "from out of the seaward mists."[162]

On signal from the flagship, the twenty-six warships—twenty battleships, five cruisers, and the *Yankton* (which, having arrived at Hampton Roads earlier, had rejoined the fleet at anchor)—fired a simultaneous twenty-one-gun salute to President Roosevelt. Within a few minutes the long column, the *Connecticut* at its head and each ship flying huge American ensigns at the masthead, gaff, and flagstaff aft, approached the *Mayflower*. Each ship fired an individual twenty-one-gun salute to the president as it passed the yacht, while a flotilla of excursion steamers, tugs, and launches kept up a "continuous roar of salutes." The presidential review was "the apotheosis of Roosevelt, the one supreme, magnificent moment" in the career of the man who, more than any other, had made the world cruise possible.[163]

As Roosevelt received individual salutes, the head of the seven-mile-long column continued up the channel, altered course to port, and passed Old Point Comfort. There many thousands of spectators had gathered on the parapets of Fortress Monroe and facing the Chamberlin Hotel, where "under a sombre screen of dripping umbrellas, they looked like so many inedible fungi."[164] As the *Connecticut* steamed close to the point, people cheered loudly, then a band ashore played "There's No Place Like Home." The flagship continued into Hampton Roads, proceeding as far as Sewall's Point before countermarching and anchoring off Old Point Comfort. Having completed the review off the Tail of the Horseshoe, the *Mayflower* followed the last of the fleet into port.

After a brief reception for admirals and commanding officers in the *Mayflower*, Roosevelt went to each division flagship and to loud ovations addressed the assembled crews. He summarized his pride in the fleet's achievement by noting that this had been the first battle fleet ever to circumnavigate the globe. "Those who perform the feat again can but follow in your footsteps."[165] When he returned to the *Mayflower* in late afternoon, the review and the cruise were officially completed.

For some men the arrival at Hampton Roads was a joyous homecoming, but for most the normal routine continued.[166] A program of receptions, balls, dances, and dinners as demanding as any in foreign ports had been arranged, and the morning after the fleet's return half of the battleships began coaling. That endless, oncrous chore was made worse by a southeaster that brought pelting rain to the fleet anchorage.[167] For most enlisted men Hampton Roads was but another anchorage on a long voyage; home and loved ones would not be reached until individual ships returned to their home ports—Philadelphia, New York, and Boston.

Dispersal was delayed by a requirement to supply a landing force for President William H. Taft's inaugural parade on 4 March 1909. After that ceremony, the last of the battleships left Hampton Roads. A few of the oldest units were scheduled to go into reserve status. The remainder went to shipyards to have their new lattice masts installed and accumulated layers of white paint scraped away. Ornate gilded scrollwork would be removed from their bows, and they would assume a more warlike appearance after being painted the new "battleship gray." These measures, which permanently altered the appearance of the fleet, symbolized not just the end of the cruise and the Great White Fleet, but also the end of an era in American naval development.

FIFTEEN

Others Can But Follow

The world cruise of the Atlantic battleship fleet has traditionally been viewed as an outstanding example of Theodore Roosevelt's active foreign policy, a classic illustration of his forceful use of the Big Stick. This is a misconception, albeit one encouraged by Roosevelt himself. Rather than a textbook example of him brandishing his Big Stick to awe Japan, official records of the cruise reveal a prudent president attempting to get a good measure of the abilities of his battleship fleet before the need to use it arose.

Although diplomacy naturally takes precedence over technical considerations in the interpretation of peacetime developments between nations, the wholesale application of this priority to the battleship cruise has resulted in a distorted appreciation of its significance. Often forgotten is the fact that battleships of the period were far less reliable mechanically than modern warships. Planning a cruise posed important questions about technical capabilities that could be resolved only through experience. In what material condition would the fleet be at the end of a voyage to the Pacific? Would it be ready to fight? How would inadequate and virtually untested Pacific coast facilities respond to fleet requirements? And would a lengthy cruise help or hinder training?

The need to test the fleet was imperative. This was the all-important consideration behind the decision to conduct a cruise, and it was arrived at without reference to or advice from the State Department. The cruise was undertaken primarily as an exercise of naval and military plans to be carried out in the event of war with Japan. But when the fleet arrived at Magdalena Bay, its ability to endure a lengthy voyage and arrive at its destination prepared to fight had been proven; Roosevelt had measured his Big Stick, its strengths and limitations. From this point on, he was prepared to use the fleet in pursuit of foreign policy goals.

Fortunately, by this time Roosevelt understood the situation in Japan, where growing domestic dissatisfaction over the financial burden imposed by overly ambitious postwar military and naval expansion programs was threatening the position of the Saionji Cabinet. American diplomats had provided sound analyses of the Japanese government's financial situation, and from them it could easily be concluded that that country was neither prepared nor preparing for a conflict with the United States in the near future. Indeed, Japan's pressing need for retrenchment dictated a policy of rapprochement. Therefore Roosevelt's acceptance of Japan's invitation, while it may have appeared to be a grand flourish of his Big Stick, was a move that involved little actual risk.

The threatening and indiscreet behavior of Germany's kaiser in 1908 and continuing German naval expansion were significant factors leading to American rapprochement with Japan. Roosevelt's growing conviction that Wilhelm might plunge Europe into war gave added emphasis to the need for an arrangement permitting continued concentration of the American battleship fleet in the Atlantic.[1] By November 1909 the General Board had concluded that, as a result of accelerated dreadnought construction programs, Germany had displaced the United States as the world's second naval power. And although undecided as to whether Germany or Japan was the most probable enemy, the board was unanimous in labeling the former "the most formidable antagonist."[2]

While Americans following the cruise once again fixed their attention on Germany, Australians and New Zealanders chose to highlight the apparent similarity of American and Australasian concerns over defense in the Pacific. The main Australasian fear remained the presumed expansionist intentions of Japan.[3] The presence of the American battleship fleet in the Pacific, however temporary and for whatever reason, led Australasians to conclude that American naval strength would provide some of the protection no longer readily available from the British fleet. Debate over Australian defense, heightened by the fleet visit, also strengthened the desire for an Australian navy that would "more or less inevitably" be the instrument of the White Australia policy.[4]

After the excesses of "gorge, guzzle and gush" that characterized the visits to Australia and New Zealand, those nations settled back into their more familiar and comfortable relationship with Great Britain.[5] Their defense concerns, expressed as a result of the American war scare and the fleet visits, eventually translated into a hollow promise that the mother country would establish an imperial squadron in the Pacific with HMS *New Zealand*, the battle cruiser New Zealand donated to imperial defense in 1909, as flagship.

An intangible aspect of the cruise, difficult to assess, is the influence of personal contact—the importance of impressions made by the fleet as it visited various ports. State Department records show that American diplomats, men generally not slow to criticize the navy in their correspondence with Washington, were uniformly delighted with the behavior of enlisted men ashore. This is not to say that none of the men got drunk and rowdy; that none of them patronized houses of ill repute; that there was never an altercation with local people. But the number of men who engaged in these activities was relatively small and their hosts viewed such behavior in perspective. Discipline ashore was strict and well enforced by a shore patrol established specifically for the cruise.

The *New York Times* concluded that the "high class of the enlisted personnel" was a factor in "advertising the formidability of the fleet abroad."[6] But more importantly, as *Outlook* magazine suggested, personal contacts established by the men did "more than years of civil diplomacy . . . to cement international friendships with this country." This was not just the friendship of comrades in arms, because fleet personnel were "representative American citizens" and treated as such by citizens of the cities they visited.[7]

Their success may be judged by Japanese acclaim. In an article entitled "Banzai to the American Fleet," Tokyo's *Asashi Shimbun* reported that the Japanese people felt special friendship for the open-hearted, kind Americans. Their "irreproachable conduct" during the fleet visit had "considerably enhanced" their reputation.[8] That Japan should also derive some benefit from the visit was suggested in the newspaper *Jiji Shimpo,* which noted that the men of the returned battleship fleet appreciated better than most Americans the "goodwill of the Japanese people toward America."[9]

Citizens both of the countries visited and of America recognized the educational value of the cruise. The American public avidly followed the fleet's progress, and in newspapers and magazines tens of millions read detailed reports about the nations being visited. New Zealanders appropriately referred to the phenomenon as the advertising of New Zealand. For a nation like the United States, long accustomed to looking inward, long preoccupied with developing the vast resources and capabilities within its borders, the world cruise opened new vistas. No earlier episode in American history had so thoroughly stirred and sustained popular interest in international events or so convincingly identified the United States as a major actor on the world stage.

The cruise occurred at a time of unprecedented naval expansion throughout the world. Suggestions that it provided the impetus or quickened the pace of this expansion imply a level of influence on global events not achieved until later decades. During the period examined here one primary consideration drove the naval arms race: the Anglo-German naval confrontation in the North Sea. Of secondary considerations the world cruise was but one, and certainly not the most significant. Regional antagonisms in South America and the Mediterranean generated naval construction programs that predated and were entirely unrelated to the American cruise. Japan's naval program, a five-year plan incorporated in the 1906 budget, also predated it. Similarly, Australia's desire to develop an independent navy had first been officially mooted in 1902. All of these programs, it seems certain, would have gone ahead with or without the cruise.

Nevertheless, the cruise did add further popular appeal to battleships and navies in general. Certainly the arrival of sixteen first-class battleships in a foreign port— a display Admiral Sperry called "our greatest show on earth"—made a strong impression on the local populace and may well have given naval expansion a better name than it already enjoyed.[10] But added popularity contributed to the naval arms race only where the desire for expansion—spurred by technical developments, regional antagonisms, racial fears, and other factors—already existed. Clearly the world cruise of the Atlantic Fleet was a result of the worldwide naval expansion in the first decade of the century, not its cause.

Although the cruise exerted little long-term influence on international relations and was but a minor factor in the naval arms race, its effect on the American navy itself was great. Enforced absence from navy yards had thrown full responsibility for maintenance and repair on ships' crews. As the cruise progressed they became more efficient and the fleet experienced fewer breakdowns. Confidence and a marked increase in mechanical reliability were the inevitable results.

Rigorous fuel economy measures were initiated after the desperate shortage en route to Rio de Janeiro. Rear Admiral Sperry was immensely proud of the fleet's achievement in this respect. "Efficiency has increased 25 per cent by economy of coal consumption," he told the Confederate Club in Richmond one day after the fleet returned, "due to hard work and faithful men below decks."[11] The steaming competition had boosted the military value of the battleships, which gained more efficient engineering crews and increased steaming radii.[12]

The prolonged period of formation steaming with daily tactical drills added immensely to the skill of commanding and watch-keeping officers. When the fleet left Rio de Janeiro Sperry was reporting confidently on officers' station-keeping abilities.[13] This reaffirmed the oft-repeated adage that a sailor belongs on a ship and the ship belongs at sea. As Harry Yarnell wrote, "It is only on the bridge of the ship in fleet that the requisite skill and confidence necessary to perform evolutions successfully can be obtained."[14]

The gunnery practice, daily range-finding exercises, annual record target practice at Magdalena Bay, and annual battle exercises at Manila Bay paid off as well. "We made great improvement in the accuracy of our gun-fire," Admiral Sperry told an appreciative audience at the Lambs Club in New York. "When we left San Francisco we put 23 per cent of our shots through a target one-third the size of a battleship. When we reached home we could make 50 per cent of hits."[15] The highest-scoring ships of the fleet, the *Vermont* and *Illinois,* had achieved thirteen hits out of sixteen shots with their main battery guns, attaining an impressive battle practice grade of 81.26 percent.[16] This improvement made a considerable difference—doubling gunnery efficiency doubled a nation's naval power at no additional cost—and it was an important consideration in 1909, when many countries' naval appropriations were placing heavy burdens on their taxpayers.[17]

The cruise provided a rare opportunity for the bureaus of the Navy Department to estimate the fleet's coal and provisions requirements; to call for bids and let contracts for those supplies; and to arrange for their transportation to the locations—at great distances from home ports—where they would be required. The failure of the Bureau of Equipment to allow sufficient lead time for coal deliveries in Australasia was the one major logistic-support problem during the cruise. Admiral Sperry, noting that foreign colliers failed to deliver twenty-five thousand tons of coal while the fleet was in Australasia, wrote, "If we cannot have a suitable commercial marine of our own, then the government should own sufficient colliers."[18]

The weakness implied in American reliance on foreign-flag colliers was one of the most important technical lessons of the cruise. The strategic implications were inescapable. Had war broken out while the fleet was in distant waters, it would have been immobilized by lack of logistic support. "Undoubtedly," *Scientific American* concluded, "the greatest need of the navy to-day is a fleet of large and fairly fast colliers, built expressly for naval purposes."[19] This glaring deficiency was partially addressed in the 1909 naval program, which authorized construction of five naval colliers in addition to the two then under construction. These seven units constituted the entire modern collier force before World War I. The problem of fuel support was not effectively solved until liquid fuels replaced coal as the fleet's main source of energy.

Noteworthy improvements in engineering reliability and fuel conservation, with the concomitant increase in steaming radius and the fleet's now proven ability to maintain itself in a high state of combat readiness for an extended cruise, led to a strategic reassessment by the Navy Department. Before the battleship cruise, it was assumed that the fleet would need to call at the Philippine base for repairs and maintenance before meeting the Japanese fleet in battle. The cruise had demonstrated that the battleship fleet could steam to the Far East and arrive there combat ready. Based on this experience and data collected during the cruise, naval planners cut their estimates of time required to mount naval operations against Japan from 120 days to 90 days. Furthermore, the General Board felt less dependent on a base in the Far East—a change of attitude that conveniently supported the decision to develop America's main Pacific naval base at Pearl Harbor.[20]

"Nothing is more conducive to good administration and efficiency in any branch of public service," Harry Yarnell wrote, "than a wide-spread knowledge of its intimate details, and consequent criticism by the press."[21] The great debates that attended the progress of the fleet undoubtedly spread knowledge of details about naval administration. But interpretation of the significance of those details remained sharply divided along partisan lines. The Navy Department lost a lot of credibility when its indignant denials of all criticism, regardless of merit, came under sustained public examination. Concerning one of Henry Reuterdahl's initial complaints, about battleships being overdraft, the Admiral of the Navy and Rear Admirals Goodrich, Sperry, Schroeder, and Wainwright—the latter three senior officers when the battleship fleet was returning to the United States—had officially expressed their concurrence.

As the fleet conducted its return voyage from Manila, Rear Admiral Sperry completed a detailed list in order of priority of alterations and repairs necessary to "maintain cruising and battle efficiency."[22] When carried out, four of the first five jobs significantly reduced ships' weights and therefore tended to reduce overdraft. Two of the five top-priority jobs—removal of all upper bridges fore and aft, and of all lower aft bridges and emergency cabins on nonflagships—were performed exclusively for weight reduction, and weight reduction was a secondary effect of two other top-priority measures. However belatedly, steps were being taken to alleviate the overdraft problem that Rear Admiral Converse and Chief Constructor Capps insisted did not exist.

But paradoxically, the overwhelming success of the cruise tended to diminish the importance of battleship-design criticism and of the changes that had been wrought. Although debate at home raged, *American Review of Reviews* reported, "it must be acknowledged that the fairest and most conclusive test of a naval system is the actual results produced."[23] Even as Rear Admiral Schroeder and Wainwright's scathing appraisals of the defects in the ships they commanded were on their way to Washington, the London *Spectator* reported that the "prompt arrival" of the American fleet at Auckland "must have convinced all onlookers . . . that the rumors of grave defects . . . were quite unfounded."[24] And at the end of the cruise *Scientific American,* with a disingenuousness consistently employed in its support of the naval bureaucracy, interpreted the successful completion of the cruise as a "sharp rebuke" to critics of the navy.[25]

In effect, civilian observers watching the fleet's virtually incident-free voyage over fourteen months and nearly 45,000 miles concluded that the ships were sound. This was a valid conclusion. The ships had proven they could keep the sea, had proven the reliability of their engineering plants. The quality of their crews had been demonstrated. But no critic had suggested the ships were incapable of conducting a peacetime cruise. Defendants overlooked the fact that the cruise had only tested fleet units as ships, not as *battle*ships. The critics—and the fleet's admirals—held that what needed improvement was battle qualities. Faulty turret design could not be tested by 100,000 miles of peacetime steaming. That, and improper location of belt armor, could only be tested in actual combat. These, perhaps, were the considerations behind Secretary Newberry's remarkably guarded evaluation of the cruise in his annual report for 1908: "Whatever may be said in technical criticism of the navy, the American people . . . know, . . . at least, that the vessels will float; that their officers and men can handle them; and, so far as actual tests in time of peace can show, that the ships and the men are fit in every particular for any duty."[26]

The eleventh-hour appointment of the Moody Commission, postponed and manipulated as it was to assist the administration's campaign to gain congressional authorization for yet more dreadnoughts, suggests the relative priority President Roosevelt attached to effective Navy Department reorganization. The commission's findings would later form an important part of the Taft administration's legacy.

The reform cause suffered unnecessarily during the Roosevelt years because reformers insisted that satisfactory change could be brought about only through sweeping legislation. In effect, Sims and his associates sought total defeat of the firmly entrenched enemy when most of their goals might have been achieved through a more pragmatic and gradual approach.

Although Sims's frontal assault on the bureaucracy failed, the world cruise sparked increased interest in the navy and led American public opinion to conclude that some sort of reorganization was indeed necessary. When he assumed office in March 1909, Secretary of the Navy George von L. Meyer investigated and eventually accepted the findings of the Moody Commission. But rather than risk the inevitable legislative confrontation with Congress, Meyer implemented many of the Moody plan's broad aspects through changes in navy regulations. Sims, who

Above: The central feature of Auckland's decorations for the fleet visit was this elaborate arch at the foot of the city's main thoroughfare, Queen Street. (Auckland Public Library)

Left: Uncle Sam: "Shut your mouth and open your eyes and I'll show you something to make you wise." (*Literary Digest* 36:1908)

The *Virginia, Missouri, Ohio, Kansas, Minnesota, Vermont,* and *Kentucky* can be seen in this photo of the fleet at anchor in Auckland's Waitemata Harbor.

The U.S. Atlantic Fleet and cruisers of the Royal Navy's Australasian station at anchor in Auckland, New Zealand, August 1908. The presence of working sail serves as a reminder that although the navy had completed the shift from sail to steam, this was still an era of transition for merchant shipping. (Auckland Public Library)

Painting the World Brown
Will Our Turn Come?
(Auckland *Weekly Graphic*, April 1904)

In Sydney Rear Admiral Sperry parades
down Pitt Street, temporarily renamed
American Avenue. (National Archives)

Three portraits of enlisted men aboard the fleet flagship *Connecticut,* taken during the fleet visit to Sydney, August 1908. *Left·* A young and fresh-faced seaman sews canvas covering on the ship's railing. The clean-cut, youthful appearance of American bluejackets drew praise throughout the cruise. *Center:* A first-class boatswain's mate proudly shares the limelight with a canine crew member who strikes a military pose for the photographer. *Right:* A marine corporal displays the strict military bearing and meticulous attention to military appearance for which the Marine Corps has always been famous.

Sailors on board the *Connecticut* checking out Sydney's local newspaper.

Top: A Bid for the Belt (Sydney *Bulletin,* 5 March 1908)

Center: The fleet commanders, pictured while visiting the governor general of Australia. *Seated from left:* Rear Admiral William H. Emory, commander, Second Squadron; Rear Admiral Charles S. Sperry, commander in chief; Rear Admiral Seaton Schrocder, commander, Fourth Division; and Rear Admiral Richard Wainwright, commander, Second Division. (Naval Historical Center)

Bottom: U.S. Marines march during a review in the Domain, Sydney. (National Archives)

Top: The Modern American Dreadnought (*Literary Digest* 36:1908)

Center: The navy marches into Melbourne, pelted by dust. (USNI)

Bottom: The *New Jersey* weathering the typhoon en route to Yokohama. (Naval Historical Center)

Landing of the first liberty party in Yokohama. Strict discipline was enforced while the men were ashore to prevent
embarrassing incidents. (USNI)

A Japanese postcard commemorating the fleet visit to Yokohama, October 1908. The inset shows
Rear Admiral Sperry, his flag lieutenant, and a Japanese aide assigned for the visit. (Naval
Historical Center)

Indicating that there was social contact between Japanese and Americans during the fleet visit, officers of the USS *Missouri* and of HIJMS *Nisshin* pose under the former's forward turret. Standing in the back row directly under the port gun is Midshipman (later Admiral) H. Kent Hewitt. (USNI)

The American and Japanese fleets at anchor off Yokohama. Unlike the white American ships, the Japanese fleet was painted a businesslike gray. The American navy had decided on a similar color but would not make the change until after the battleships returned home. (USNI)

British and German political cartoons reflect different attitudes toward and hopes for the announced American fleet visit to Japan. (*Literary Digest* 36:1908)

Above: Happy Afterthoughts
Japan (to American Eagle): "But how sweet of you to come all this way on purpose to see me!"
Eagle: "Why, yes, I thought you'd be pleased!"
(Punch)

Above: In the Pacific
Each: "I'm too good a friend to begin; but if you begin, why, then—"
(*Wahre Jacob* [Stuttgart])

Getting Even with Teacher
(*Literary Digest* 36:1908)

That Congress Umbrella
U.S.: "An excellent umbrella, providing it doesn't rain."
(*Literary Digest* 36:1908)

Flattening Out the War-Scare
An International Squeeze
(*Literary Digest* 37:1908)

The entertainment center specially built to accommodate the fleet at Amoy, China. (USNI)

The First Battle (*Literary Digest* 36:1908)

When the Navy Puts Doctors in Command of Hospital Ships

Rear Admiral Willard H. Brownson, USN, resigned his position as chief of the Bureau of Navigation rather than issue orders for a surgeon to assume command of the *Relief*. (Naval Historical Center)

This situation, illustrated at the time of the command controversy in January 1908, almost occurred when in November of that same year the *Relief* sailed into the eye of a typhoon and nearly foundered. (*Literary Digest* 36:1908)

The *Relief* at anchor at Auckland. The former Long Island ferry displayed terrible instability at sea. (Auckland Public Library)

Three sailors pose atop camels at the base of the Sphinx. Two other members of the party have substituted fezzes for the more traditional flat hats.

Ship's shadow on bank of Suez Canal.

The *Maine* casts her shadow on the bank of the Suez Canal during the Atlantic Fleet's transit, January 1909.

Port Said from the forecastle of the *Maine*. The *Ohio* is to starboard.

President Theodore Roosevelt welcoming the fleet back to the United States, 22 February 1909. Sailors representing each ship assembled in the four flagships, which Roosevelt visited in turn. This is the scene aboard the *Connecticut*. (USNI)

Embroidered tapestry commemorating the cruise. It features a picture of the fleet and portraits of President Theodore Roosevelt and Rear Admirals Charles S. Sperry and Robley D. Evans. The space inside the life preserver was reserved for a personal photo—in this case, of three unidentified enlisted men. (USNI) had opposed this course of action in 1908, now hailed it as the fruition of Roosevelt's scheme for reorganization.[27] Rather than establishing grand division chiefs with statutory authority, as the Moody Commission had recommended, Meyer ordered senior line officers to Washington to serve as aides advising him on issues categorized along the general lines of the divisions. Although the system lacked the clarity statutory authority would have given, it proved reasonably effective and remained in force during the final years before World War I. The first "aid [sic] for operations" and ex officio principal advisor to the navy secretary was Rear Admiral Richard Wainwright, whose criticism of battleship designs has been noted.[28]

The Navy Department never conceded that significant defects existed in the design of the *North Dakota* and *Delaware;* the conservative majority at the Newport Conference forced a repetition of the *North Dakota* design in the *Utah* and *Florida* largely to save face. Several years would pass before the magnitude of the reformers' victory in obtaining a resolution requiring the development of several designs for all future battleships and the appointment of a board of line officers to review and approve the plans became apparent. But in April 1910, Sims confided to Former President Roosevelt that the next American battleships to be laid down would be much superior to their predecessors. The military characteristics of the new ships were established under Rear Admiral Wainwright's supervision; the first review board to consider American dreadnought designs was chaired by Rear Admiral Schroeder and included Commanders Key and Sims.[29]

Not surprisingly, in view of the membership of the body of line officers reviewing designs, the *Nevada* and *Oklahoma,* the dreadnoughts being considered, incorporated many of the features of the rejected Newport plan: increased displacement, fourteen-inch guns, and more properly placed armor. When the two dreadnoughts finally went into commission in 1914, *Jane's Fighting Ships* credited them as marking "a new era in naval construction."[30]

Although the cruise of the American battleship fleet presented a colorful international spectacle at a time when the world "was in an extremely belligerent mood," its impact on global events was minimal.[31] It touched on many American foreign relations issues of the day, but a tendency then and in subsequent times to attribute diplomatic successes to the cruise generally disregards underlying reasons. The cruise might be seen more validly as a catalyst for certain developments in American foreign relations.

Similarly, the naval arms race of the first decade of the century grew not out of the cruise but out of rapid industrialization on the part of European continental powers, the appearance of HMS *Dreadnought,* and the failure of the Second Hague Conference in 1907. The battleship cruise was a manifestation, a result, of that arms race, not one of its major causes.

The significance of the battleship fleet cruise, therefore, must be understood in the context of a developing American navy. It was the first effective test of the New Navy's sea legs, of its ability to respond to defense requirements in the Pacific. And the experience it provided paved the way for a reappraisal of America's Pacific defense capabilities. Unprecedented publicity encouraged critical examination of battleship design and navy organization. Both were found wanting. That examination is an integral, often overlooked, part of the story of the fleet cruise, and perhaps equally important, it illuminates the story of the navy's often painful process of modernization. The fleet that returned from the world cruise was a fleet that through long and sustained practice had been welded into a single, highly professional unit. The combined effect of cruise and debate was to set the American navy firmly on the road toward more rational, efficient, and professional development.

Notes

PREFACE

1. "The American Navy as a Factor in World Politics, 1903–1913," 863–79.
2. Howard K. Beale, *Theodore Roosevelt and the Rise of America to World Power*, 173, citing address at Mechanics Pavilion, San Francisco, 13 May 1903.

CHAPTER 1

1. Arthur J. Marder, *The Anatomy of British Seapower: A History of British Naval Policy in the Pre-Dreadnought Era*, 239, 428.
2. John R. Walser, "France's Search for a Battlefleet," 86–87, 105–6, 163–64.
3. Marder, *Anatomy*, 469.
4. Jonathan Steinberg, *Yesterday's Deterrent: Tirpitz and the Birth of the German Navy, 1888–1918*, 18.
5. Holger H. Herwig, *"Luxury" Fleet: The Imperial German Navy, 1888–1918*, 42.
6. Zara S. Steiner, "Great Britain and the Creation of the Anglo-Japanese Alliance," quoting Selborne memorandum, 4 Sep. 1901, British Foreign Office, 46/547.
7. Marder, *Anatomy*, 451.
8. Alfred Thayer Mahan, "The True Significance of the Pacific Cruise of the Battleship Fleet," 407.
9. The development of the American navy in the prewar years is well documented in Harold and Margaret Sprout, *The Rise of American Naval Power, 1776–1918*.
10. Theodore Roosevelt, *State Papers as Governor and President, 1899–1909*, 135.
11. Richmond P. Hobson, "America, Mistress of the Sea," 557.
12. The ten battleships were the *Connecticut, Louisiana* (1902), *Idaho, Mississippi, Kansas, Minnesota, Vermont* (1903), *New Hampshire, Michigan,* and *South Carolina* (1904). Sprout, *American Naval Power*, 259–61.
13. Roosevelt to Wood, 9 Mar. 1905, in Elting E. Morison, *The Letters of Theodore Roosevelt*, 4:1136.
14. Raymond A. Esthus, "The Taft-Katsura Agreement: Reality or Myth?" 46–51.

15. Roosevelt, *State Papers,* 361–62.

16. Roosevelt to Henry Cabot Lodge, 5 June 1905, in Morison, *Roosevelt Letters,* 4: 1202–6.

17. Carl-Axel Gemzell, *Organization, Conflict and Innovation: A Study of German Naval Strategic Planning, 1888–1940,* 73.

18. Braisted, *The United States Navy in the Pacific, 1897–1909,* 188, citing Secretary of the Navy Bonaparte to Rear Admiral Brownson, 14 Aug. 1906.

19. Dewey to Metcalf, 25 April 1907, in National Archives (hereafter cited as NA), Record Group (hereafter cited as RG) 80, General Board of the Navy, study 420–1.

Chapter 2

1. *New York Times,* 14 June 1907.

2. Louis Morton, "Military and Naval Preparations for the Defense of the Philippines during the War Scare of 1907," 95; Braisted, *United States Navy,* 206; Richard D. Challener, *Admirals, Generals, and American Foreign Policy, 1898–1914,* 246–47.

3. Challener, *American Foreign Policy,* 235, citing Joint Board minutes, meeting of 18 June 1907.

4. Ibid., 253.

5. Morton, "Defense of the Philippines," 95.

6. Wotherspoon to army chief of staff, 29 June 1907, AG 1260092, National Archives, quoted in ibid., 96–97. No stenographic record was kept. Fortunately Colonel Wotherspoon prepared a detailed memorandum shortly afterward.

7. *New York Herald,* 2 July 1907. This conclusion on the route to be taken was logical but premature. The final decision on the fleet's route had not yet been made.

8. *New York Times,* 2, 3 July 1907.

9. Ibid., 3 July 1907.

10. Ibid., 5 July 1907.

11. Ibid.

12. Ibid., 7 July 1907.

13. Ibid.

14. Hale's position is outlined in Hale to Newberry, 27 July 1907, Roosevelt correspondence.

15. Roosevelt to Newberry, 30 July 1907, in Morison, *Roosevelt Letters,* 5: 734.

16. Braisted, *United States Navy,* 211, citing Evans to Brownson, 17 Aug. 1907; Brownson to Roosevelt, 18 Aug. 1907, Roosevelt correspondence.

17. Rear Admiral Robley D. Evans, *An Admiral's Log,* 394.

18. *New York Times,* 24 Aug. 1907.

19. Roosevelt, *State Papers,* 624–25.

20. Theodore Roosevelt, *An Autobiography,* 624–25.

21. Morison, *Roosevelt Letters,* 7: 393.

22. Root to Beaupré, ciphered telegram, 20 Jan. 1908. NA, RG 59, 8258/64.

23. *New York Times,* 5 July 1907.

24. For examples, see Morison, *Roosevelt Letters,* 5: 688, 693–94, 709–10, 720, 725, 726, 728.

25. *New York Times,* 24 Aug. 1907.

26. Sprout, *American Naval Power,* 297. Great Britain, with a navy twice as large as the American navy, maintained only six navy yards, while the United States maintained eleven, only two of which were on the Pacific Coast. The eleven yards together contained fewer dry docks than the single largest British yard.

27. Dewey to Metcalf, 20 Jan. 1908, NA, RG 80, Records of the General Board, study 404.

28. George Kibbe Turner, "Our Navy on the Land: The Greatest Waste of National Funds in the History of the United States," 400.

29. *New York Times,* 7 July 1907; Dewey to Metcalf, 20 Jan. 1908, NA, RG 80, Records of the General Board, study 404.

30. H. A. Crafts, "American Docking Facilities on the Pacific Coast," 55. Depth of the new Mare Island dry dock was to be 30 feet over the sill; controlling depths of the access channel in 1909, after two years of dredging operations, were 21.0 feet at mean low water and 27.0 feet at mean high water (Gordon Carpenter O'Gara, *Theodore Roosevelt and the Rise of the Modern Navy,* citing U.S. 60th Cong., 2nd sess., House Committee on Naval Affairs, *Hearings on Estimates Submitted by the Secretary of the Navy, 1909,* 347).

31. "Our Naval Forces in the Pacific," 4.

32. *New York Times,* 9 July 1907. For an excellent detailed analysis of the Puget Sound Navy Yard's capabilities, see H. Cole Estep, "The Position and Equipment of the Puget Sound Navy Yard."

33. Crafts, "American Docking Facilities," 556.

34. Ibid.

35. *New York Times,* 13 Oct. 1907.

36. "Is Our Pacific Cruise Pacific?" 13.

37. *New York Times,* 29 Sep. 1907.

38. Rear Admiral George W. Melville, "The Important Elements in Naval Conflicts," 134–35.

39. Morison, *Roosevelt Letters,* 5: 759.

40. *New York Times,* 27 Aug. 1907.

41. Ibid., 28, 29 Aug., 1 Sep. 1907.

42. Ibid., 30 Aug. 1907.

43. Ibid., 27 Sep. 1907.

44. Ibid., 1 Oct. 1907.

45. Ibid., 14 Oct. 1907.

46. For details of the contracts, see Newberry to Rear Admiral Cowles, chief of the Bureau of Equipment, 16 Oct. 1907, NA, RG 80: 18768/50, and *New York Times,* 13 Oct. 1907.

47. *New York Times,* 20 Oct. 1907.

48. Ibid., 18 Dec. 1907.

49. Ibid., 21 Mar. 1908.

50. Rear Admiral George W. Melville, "Our Actual Naval Strength," 380.

CHAPTER 3

1. For details of the fleet's activities, see "Summer Plans for the Atlantic Fleet."

2. Evans, *Admiral's Log,* 400–401.

3. *New York Times,* 15 June, 6 Aug., 30 Sep. 1907.

4. Metcalf to commander in chief, Pacific Fleet, 5690-56-2107, 5 Dec. 1907, NA, RG 45, area 9.

5. Dayton to commanding officers, 25 May 1907, NA, RG 45, area 10.

6. Braisted, *The United States Navy,* 208, citing Newberry to Dayton, 1 Jul. 1907, NA, RG 24: BuNav Letterpress, CXLI, 194.

7. Dayton to Metcalf, cipher telegram, 29 June 1907, NA, RG 45: SecNav Cipher

Telegrams Received, vol. 4; Dayton memo to First Division, 3 July 1907, NA, RG 45, area 10.

8. Dayton to First Division, no. 231-F, 24 July 1907, NA, RG 45, area 10.

9. Acting Secretary of the Navy Cowles to Dayton, 20 July 1907, SecNav Cipher Telegrams Sent, vol. 3; Newberry to Dayton, 23 July 1907, NA, RG 45, area 10.

10. Dayton to First Division, 6 Aug. 1907, NA, RG 45, area 10.

11. Newberry to Dayton, 9 Aug. 1907, SecNav Cipher Telegrams Sent, vol. 3.

12. Dayton to Newberry, 10 Aug. 1907, ibid.

13. Brownson to Dayton, 10 Aug. 1907, ibid.

14. Dayton to First Division, 17 Aug. 1907, NA, RG 45, area 10; Braisted, *The United States Navy*, 208; *New York Times*, 3, 27 Sep. 1907.

15. *New York Times*, 9 Aug. 1907.

16. Commander in Chief Atlantic Fleet order no. 5885, 4 Nov. 1907, NA, RG 45: 00; *New York Times*, 2 Dec. 1907.

17. *New York Times*, 3 Dec. 1907.

18. Ibid., 2 Dec. 1907.

19. Louis Maxfield to his mother, 14 Dec. 1907, in Maxfield, Cathcart Family Papers.

20. *New York Times*, 14 Dec. 1907.

21. Barker to Dewey, 7 Aug. 1907, NA, RG 80, Records of the General Board, study 420–1.

22. Lieutenant Commander S. P. Fullinwider to Sims, 6 Dec. 1907, Sims correspondence.

23. *New York Times*, 14 Dec. 1907; London *Times*, 14 Dec. 1907.

24. *New York Times*, 14 Dec. 1907; *New York Herald*, 16 Dec. 1907. A review of the *Connecticut*'s log reveals she transferred seven Asians and received fourteen messmen with European names during the last week in port (NA, RG 24: *Connecticut* Log, Dec. 1907).

25. *New York Times*, 15 Dec. 1907.

26. Ibid., 11 Dec. 1907. Similar "incidents" were reported in many West Coast cities, Hawaii, and the Philippines.

27. *New York Times*, 15 Dec. 1907.

28. "Full dress" is a procedure whereby signal flags are strung on wires from the mastheads to the bow and stern. National ensigns are displayed at each masthead as well as at the ship's stern.

29. *New York Herald*, 17 Dec. 1907.

30. The second officer to board was Rear Admiral Thomas, who brought with him the correspondents Barry and Reuterdahl, both of whom were "anxious to have a few words with the President" (Thomas letter to his wife, 16 Dec. 1907, Charles M. Thomas correspondence).

31. Thomas correspondence, 16 Dec. 1907.

32. *New York Times*, 17 Dec. 1907.

33. Ibid.

34. *New York Times*, 16 Dec. 1907; *New York Herald*, 16, 17 Dec. 1907.

35. *New York Herald*, 17 Dec. 1907.

36. Ibid.

37. Ibid., 16 Dec. 1907.

38. *New York Times*, 18 Dec. 1907.

39. Ibid., 16 Dec. 1907.

40. Ibid., 19 Dec. 1907.

41. Ibid.

NOTES

CHAPTER 4

1. 19 Dec. 1907, Thomas correspondence.
2. *New York Times,* 8, 29, 30 Sep., 1, 23, 24, 29 Oct., 10, 21 Nov. 1907.
3. Ibid., 10 Nov. 1907.
4. Quoted in Carlyon Bellairs, "The Impending Naval Crisis," 311.
5. *New York Times,* 5 Sep. 1907.
6. Surgeon Eugene P. Stone, diary, 16 Dec. 1907.
7. *New York Times,* 19 Dec. 1907.
8. Ibid., 22, 23 Dec. 1907.
9. Archa A. Adamson, diary, 20 Dec. 1907.
10. Maxfield correspondence, 20 Dec. 1907; Adamson diary, 20 Dec. 1907.
11. *New York Times,* 21, 22 Dec. 1907; Maxfield correspondence, 20 Dec. 1907; Stone diary, 21, 22 Dec. 1907; Jones, *With the American Fleet,* 18, 28.
12. *New York Times,* 25 Dec. 1907.
13. Stone diary, 23 Dec. 1907.
14. *New York Times,* 25 Dec. 1907; Matthews, *With the Battlefleet,* 53–55.
15. Thomas correspondence, 23 Dec. 1907.
16. American Consul William Handley (Trinidad) to the assistant secretary of state, no. 56, 31 Dec. 1907, NA, RG 59: 8258/75.
17. Ibid.; *New York Times,* 25 Dec. 1907.
18. NA, RG 59: 8258/75.
19. American Consul Orrett (Kingston) to State Department, telegram, 16 Jan. 1907, NA, RG 59: 3892/2.
20. Orrett to State Department, telegram, 17 Jan. 1907, NA, RG 59: 4001/70.
21. Roosevelt to George Otto Trevelyn, 23 Nov. 1906, in Morison, *Roosevelt Letters,* 5: 499.
22. The official correspondence between Swettenham and Davis is contained in Great Britain, *Correspondence Relating to the Resignation of Sir A. Swettenham of His Office as Governor of Jamaica,* a copy of which is filed in NA, RG 38: reg. no. 1475, locker I-9-a, naval attaché reports. Additional correspondence is contained in NA, RG 59:4001. Much of the correspondence was subsequently published in *Foreign Relations of the United States, 1907,* part 1, 558–69.
23. British Cabinet memorandum, CAB 37/89, 1907, no. 73.
24. Matthews, *With the Battlefleet,* 38–39; Jones, *With the American Fleet,* 32–33.
25. Thomas correspondence, 24 Dec. 1907. Consul Handley's failure to mention this incident suggests his report was not entirely unbiased.
26. C. S. Sperry to C. S. Sperry, Jr., 25 Dec. 1907, Sperry correspondence.
27. *New York Times,* 4, 9 Feb. 1908.
28. Jones, *With the Atlantic Fleet,* 38–39.
29. Matthews, *With the Battlefleet,* 25.
30. *New York Times,* 23, 24, 25 Dec. 1907; Evans, *Admiral's Log,* 417.
31. *New York Times,* 25 Dec. 1907.
32. Matthews, *With the Battlefleet,* 44; Evans, *Admiral's Log,* 418.
33. Matthews, *With the Battlefleet,* 47, 49.
34. Handley to the assistant secretary of state, 31 Dec. 1907, NA, RG 59:8258/75.
35. Thomas correspondence, 29 Dec. 1907.
36. *New York Times,* 30 Dec. 1907.
37. Matthews, *With the Battlefleet,* 52–56; Stone diary, 1 Jan. 1908.

38. Sperry to Metcalf, 28 Jan. 1908, Sperry correspondence; Rear Admiral Seaton Schroeder, *A Half Century of Naval Service*, 313.

39. *New York Times*, 30 Dec. 1907.

40. Thomas correspondence, 7 Jan. 1908.

41. Ibid., 30, 31 Dec. 1907, 5, 6, 8, 11 Jan. 1908.

42. Evans, *Admiral's Log*, 422; Maxfield correspondence, 4 Jan. 1908.

43. Maxfield correspondence, 3, 4 Jan. 1908.

44. Thomas correspondence, 5 Jan. 1908. Emphasis in original.

45. Ibid., 7 Jan. 1908.

46. Sperry to Edith M. Sperry, 8 Jan. 1908, Sperry correspondence.

47. Thomas correspondence, 9 Jan. 1908.

48. See *New York Times*, 13 Jan. 1908; Matthews, *With the Battlefleet*, 61–63; Captain Henry C. Davis, "Leaves from the Log," 16; Richard Barry, "One Night with the Big Fleet: An Incident of the Great Cruise," 460–65; Stone diary, 10 Jan. 1908.

CHAPTER 5

1. Graham H. Stuart and James L. Tigner, *Latin America and the United States*, 679.

2. *Jornal do Comercio*, 13 Jan. 1908.

3. *New York Times*, 23 Dec. 1907.

4. *Jornal do Comercio*, 13 Jan. 1908.

5. Ibid.; *New York Times*, 13 Jan. 1908.

6. Matthews, *With the Battlefleet*, 88.

7. *New York Times*, 13 Jan. 1908; *Jornal do Comercio*, 13 Jan. 1908; Stone diary, Maxfield correspondence, 12 Jan. 1908.

8. *Jornal do Comercio*, 13 Jan. 1908.

9. *New York Times*, 13 Jan. 1908.

10. Ibid., 14 Jan. 1908; *Jornal do Comercio*, 14, 17 Jan. 1908.

11. Gleaves, *Emory*, 289; Schroeder, *Naval Service*, 314–15; *Jornal do Comercio*, 14 Jan. 1908.

12. Matthews, *With the Battlefleet*, 111; Hart, *Great White Fleet*, 89.

13. *New York Times*, 15 Jan. 1908; Matthews, *With the Battlefleet*, 105–6; Wainwright to Evans, 14 Jan. 1908, NA, RG 24: 6072/15.

14. *New York Times*, 15 Jan. 1908.

15. Sperry to Edith M. Sperry, 8 Jan. 1908, Sperry correspondence.

16. Evans to Pillsbury, no. 194, 21 Jan. 1908, NA, RG 24: 6072/62.

17. Sperry to Edith M. Sperry, 14 Jan. 1908, Sperry correspondence.

18. Undated letter postmarked Toronto, Canada, 5 Dec. 1907, signed "American", Captain Rogers telegram to Lieutenant Commander W. L. Howard, naval attaché (Berlin), 7 Dec. 1907, Howard telegrams to Rogers, 11, 13 Dec. 1907, Naval History Division, Operational Archives, all in unmarked folder in war portfolio no. 1, reg. no. 4–15, "Formosa-Pescadores-Japan," NA folder no. 139, OpNav folder no. 4, Naval History Division (hereafter cited as Plot Folder).

19. Howard to Rogers, 13 Dec. 1907, Plot Folder.

20. Captain John C. Fremont to Rogers, no. 87, 19 Dec. 1907; no. 88, 19 Dec. 1907; and no. 89, 19 Dec. 1907, Plot Folder.

21. Fremont telegram to Rogers, 21 Dec. 1907, Plot Folder.

22. Metcalf to Evans, 24 Dec. 1907, and Evans to Thomas, 25 Dec. 1907, Thomas correspondence.

23. Root telegram to Dudley, 23 Dec. 1907, NA, RG 59: 10799.

24. Thomas correspondence, 24 Dec. 1907.

25. Evans telegram to BuNav, 26 Dec. 1907, Plot Folder.

26. White to Root, 23 Dec. 1907, and Root to Dudley, 24 Dec. 1907, NA, RG 59: 10799/1.

27. Treasury Agent Gottschalk to Assistant Secretary of Treasury Reynolds, 29 Dec. 1907, NA, RG 59: 10799/5–7.

28. Dudley telegram to Root, 7 Jan. 1908, NA, RG 59: 10799/10.

29. *New York Times,* 20, 21 Jan. 1908; *Jornal do Comercio,* 20 Jan. 1908.

30. *New York Times,* 20 Jan. 1908.

31. Ibid., 21 Jan. 1908.

32. Evans, *Admiral's Log,* 425.

33. *New York Times,* 10, 19 Jan. 1908; U.S. Minister Edward C. O'Brien to Root, no. 378, 2 Feb. 1908, NA, RG 59: 8258/224; and O'Brien telegram to Root, 3 Feb. 1908, NA, RG 59: 8258/300.

34. *New York Times,* 4 Jan. 1908.

35. Ibid., 13 Jan. 1908.

36. "A Friend of America" to Rogers, 6 Jan. 1908, Plot Folder.

37. Rogers to Commander J. A. Dougherty, 6 Jan. 1908, ibid., no. 8791.

38. Metcalf to Evans, 2 Jan. 1908, ibid.

39. Evans to Cone, no. 172, 19 Jan. 1908, NA, RG 45, area 4.

40. *New York Times,* 18 Jan. 1908.

41. For a detailed examination of Argentine relations, see Harold F. Peterson, *Argentina and the United States, 1810–1960,* 290–99.

42. To be built in British yards. An amount of $31,250,000 had been appropriated for these ships in 1904; however, contracts were not let until after HMS *Dreadnought* revolutionized battleship design. For further detail, see Seward W. Livermore, "Battleship Diplomacy in South America, 1905–1925," 32–33.

43. Livermore, "Battleship Diplomacy," 32.

44. Peterson, *Argentina and the United States,* 292.

45. Wilson to Bacon, 9 Jan. 1908, NA, RG 59: 8258/64.

46. Secretary of the Navy letter 2974–173, 13 Jan. 1908, NA, RG 59: 8258/68. See also Metcalf telegram to Evans, 13 Jan. 1908, Plot Folder.

47. Penna to Roosevelt and Loeb to Bacon, 14 Jan. 1908, Roosevelt to Penna, 15 Jan. 1908, all in NA, RG 59: 8258/69; *New York Times,* 16 Jan. 1908.

48. Wilson to Root, no. 671, 22 Jan. 1908, NA, RG 59: 8258/163.

49. Zeballos to Portela and Portela to Root, 16 Jan. 1908, NA, RG 59: 8258/83–4; Peterson, *Argentina and the United States,* 292.

50. Dudley to consul general (Rio), 18 Jan. 1908, NA, RG 59: 8258/151–8; encl. 5 of Dudley to Root, no. 123, 25 Jan. 1908, NA RG 59: 8258/151–8.

51. Dudley to Argentine minister to Brazil, 20 Jan. 1908, NA, RG 59: 8258/151–8; encl. 7 of Dudley to Root, no. 123, 25 Jan. 1908, NA, RG 59: 8258/151–8. Evans cipher telegram to Metcalf, 19 Jan. 1908, NA RG 45: SecNav Ciphers Received; Evans to Cone, no. 172, 19 Jan. 1908, NA, RG 45, area 4.

52. Maxfield correspondence, 15 Jan. 1908.

53. "Miscellaneous Notes Regarding the Brazilian Navy, U.S. Atlantic Fleet, January 1908," NA, RG 38: 08–187, 0-4-a.

54. *Jornal do Comercio,* 22 Jan. 1908. This presidential visit and review had, of course, been scheduled well in advance and the fleet was prepared to render the appropriate honors. See Thomas correspondence, 19 Jan. 1908.

55. Stone diary, 22 Jan. 1908.

56. Ibid. See also Matthews, *With the Battlefleet,* 127–31.

57. *Jornal do Comercio,* 22 Jan. 1908; *Revista da Semana,* 28 Jan. 1908, in Dudley to Root, no. 129, 27 Jan. 1908, NA, RG 59: 8258/164–84.

58. *A Noticias,* 22 Jan. 1908, in Dudley to Root, no. 129, 27 Jan. 1908, NA, RG 59: 8258/164–84.

59. Stone diary, 21 Jan. 1908; Adamson diary, 21 Jan. 1908.

60. *New York Times,* 27 Jan. 1908.

61. Ibid. See also Wilson to Root, 27 Jan. 1908, NA, RG 59: 8259/89.

62. Figuera Alcortes to Roosevelt, 27 Jan. 1908, NA, RG 59: 8258/93; Estanislao Zeballos to Root, 27 Jan. 1908, NA, RG 59: 8258/90.

63. Root to Wilson, 28 Jan. 1908, NA, RG 59: 8258/89.

64. Wilson to Root, 29 Jan. 1908, NA, RG 59: 8258/92; Root to Zeballos, 29 Jan. 1908, NA, RG 59: 8258/90; Roosevelt to Alcorte, 29 Jan. 1908, NA, RG 59: 8258/93.

65. Peterson, *Argentina and the United States,* 293.

66. Matthews, *With the Battlefleet,* 117–18; Evans, *Admiral's Log,* 432–33.

67. Matthews, ibid., 118–21; *New York Times,* 29 Jan. 1908; "A Beautiful Sea Spectacle," *Outlook,* 667–68; Evans, *Admiral's Log,* 433. A national salute was not normally fired at sea; it was intended and understood as an unusual honor.

68. Sperry to Metcalf, 27 Jan. 1908, Sperry correspondence. Although Hart has reported that Sperry's plea for war paint was rejected (*Great White Fleet,* 125–26), in fact, the recommendation, which reached Washington in mid-March, was approved by the chief of the Bureau of Navigation and endorsed by the General Board on 26 May. After extensive testing by the Bureau of Construction and Repair, Secretary Metcalf selected the shade to be used and on 23 October 1908 directed the painting of the fleet (with certain exceptions) slate grey (NA, RG 80: 22328/3–4; see also NA, RG 80, General Board Proceedings, 25 May 1908, endorsement to BuNav letter 5543-2 of 16 May 1908, and *New York Times,* 14 Aug. 1908).

69. Sperry to Metcalf, 27 Jan. 1908, Sperry correspondence. Sperry's letter reached Washington in March, was sent to President Roosevelt, and was then read to the Cabinet, whose members "highly appreciated" it (Roosevelt to Sperry, 21 March 1908, Sperry correspondence).

CHAPTER 6

1. Stuart and Tigner, *Latin America and the United States,* 627–28. The *Baltimore* incident occurred on 16 Oct. 1891, when the commanding officer of the USS *Baltimore,* Captain Winfield S. Schley, unwisely granted liberty to his men at Valparaiso. At the time anti-American feeling was running high as a result of perceived American bias in the Chilean civil war. Two enlisted men were killed in anti-American rioting. Chilean reluctance to accept responsibility for the actions of the rioters led the two countries to the brink of war. The gunboat *Yorktown,* Commander Robley D. Evans commanding, remained in Valparaiso after the *Baltimore*'s departure. Evans's firm handling of the situation was credited with reducing Chilean-American tensions (see Erwin Johnson, *Thence Around the Cape: The Story of United States Naval Forces on Pacific Station 1818–1923,* 144–47).

2. Stuart and Tigner, ibid.

3. *"La escuadra norteamericana en aguas chileanas,"* Zigzag.

4. *New York Times,* 8, 10 Jan. 1908; Hicks to Root, 10 Jan. 1908, NA, RG 59: 8258/64.

NOTES

5. *New York Times,* 10, 29 Jan. 1908; *El Comercio,* 28 Jan. 1908; Hicks to Root, 20 Jan. 1908, NA, RG 59: 8258/91. Rear Admiral Simpson's report to Chilean Minister of Marine Admiral Jorge Montt contained a detailed report of the *Chacabuco*'s voyage (see Hicks to Root, no. 204, 2 March 1908, NA, RG 59: 8258/325-9, hereafter cited as Simpson Report).

6. *El Comercio,* 31 Jan. 1908.

7. Hart, *Great White Fleet,* 131.

8. Sperry to C. S. Sperry, Jr., 9 Feb. 1908, Sperry correspondence.

9. Maxfield correspondence, 31 Jan. 1908.

10. Stone diary, 1 Feb. 1908.

11. *"Escuadra norteamericana."*

12. *El Comercio,* 2 Feb. 1908.

13. *"Escuadra norteamericana."*

14. Midshipman H. Kent Hewitt to his parents, 1 Feb. 1908, Hewitt correspondence.

15. Hicks to Root, 21 Feb. 1908, NA, RG 59: 8258/301-2.

16. *"Escuadra norteamericana";* Simpson Report.

17. Hewitt correspondence, 7 Feb. 1908; Evans, *Admiral's Log,* 436; Matthews, *Battlefleet,* 141.

18. *El Comercio,* 4 Feb. 1908; Hicks to Root, 21 Feb. 1908, NA, RG 59: 8258/301-2; Sperry to C. S. Sperry, Jr., 9 Feb. 1908, Sperry correspondence.

19. Adamson diary, 4 Feb. 1908; Maxfield correspondence, 2, 3 Feb. 1908; Stone diary, 3 Feb. 1908. Malcolm F. Willoughby, *Yankton: Yacht and Man of War,* 93; Roman J. Miller, *Around the World with the Battleships,* 36–38.

20. Hicks to Root, 21 Feb. 1908, NA, RG 59: 8258/301-2; Simpson Report; *New York Times,* 4 Feb. 1908.

21. Hart, *Great White Fleet,* 132.

22. Falk, *Evans,* 431–32. Falk refers only to officers; Hart writes officers "of high rank."

23. Adamson, "Impressions."

24. Marine Corps History Center, Muster Roll, p. 454.

25. Hart, *Great White Fleet,* 132. In his detailed report of the visit, Minister Hicks made no mention of this incident. Had it actually been a diplomatic catastrophe, he could hardly have failed to report it (Hicks to Root, no. 200, 21 Feb. 1908, NA, RG 59: 8258/301-2).

26. Simpson Report.

27. Thomas correspondence, 31 Jan. 1908; Hicks to Root, 7 Feb. 1908, NA, RG 59: 8258/107, and 21 Feb. 1908, NA, RG 59: 8258/301-2, no. 200.

28. Hicks to Root, 7 Feb. 1908, and Root to AmLeg Santiago, 7 Feb. 1908, NA, RG 59: 8258/107; Montt's reply to Roosevelt, 8 Feb. 1908, NA, RG 59: 8258/110-1.

29. Hicks to Root, 21 Feb. 1908, NA, RG 59: 8258/301-2.

30. *El Comercio,* 8 Feb. 1908.

31. Maxfield correspondence, 8 Feb. 1908; Jones, *With the Atlantic Fleet,* 225–26.

32. Sydney Brooks, "The Voyage of the American Fleet," 201.

33. Hicks to Root, 12 Feb. 1908, NA, RG 59: 8258/126; *New York Times,* 14 Feb. 1908; Evans, *An Admiral's Log,* 438. The Chilean destroyers were the *Capitan Thompson, Muñoz Gambera,* and *Capitan O'Brien* (Evans to Metcalf, 15 Feb. 1908, NA, RG 45, area 9, no. 409).

34. *New York Times,* 11, 14 Feb. 1908.

35. *El Comercio,* 15 Feb. 1908.

36. *"Escuadra norteamericana."*

37. Thomas correspondence, 14 Feb. 1908.

38. *"Escuadra norteamericana."*

39. Thomas correspondence, 14 Feb. 1908.

40. Ibid.

41. *"Escuadra norteamericana."*

42. Maxfield correspondence, 16 Feb. 1908.

43. Stone diary, 19 Feb. 1908; Maxfield correspondence, 19 Feb. 1908.

44. *New York Times,* 18, 29 Dec. 1907.

45. Combs to Root, 4 Dec. 1907, NA, RG 59: 8258/66.

46. *New York Times,* 9 Dec. 1907.

47. Combs to Root, no. 72, 22 Jan. 1908, NA, RG 59: 8258/112.

48. *New York Times,* 20 Feb. 1908.

49. Thomas correspondence, 21 Feb. 1908; Hewitt correspondence, 22 Feb. 1908.

50. Hewitt correspondence, 22 Feb. 1908.

51. Thomas correspondence, 21 Feb. 1908. See also Sperry to Edith M. Sperry, 23 Feb. 1908, Sperry correspondence and Schroeder, *Half Century of Naval Service,* 327.

52. Hewitt correspondence, 23 Feb. 1908; Stone diary, 20 Feb. 1908; Matthews, *With the Battlefleet,* 202.

53. Gleaves, *Emory,* 298–99.

54. Ibid., 298.

55. Hewitt correspondence, 23 Feb. 1908.

56. Pardo to Roosevelt, 24 Feb. 1908, and Roosevelt to Pardo, 24 Feb. 1908, NA, RG 59: 8258/148–9.

57. Roosevelt to Kermit Roosevelt, 4 Mar. 1908, in Morison, *Roosevelt Letters,* 6: 958.

58. Stone diary, 24 Feb. 1908.

59. Robert S. Dunn, "On Liberty," 15–16.

60. Stone diary, 24 Feb. 1908; Hewitt correspondence, 27 Feb. 1908.

61. *New York Times,* 28 Feb. 1908; Maxfield correspondence, 21 Feb. 1908; Stone diary, 22, 24, 27, 28 Feb. 1908; Hewitt correspondence 23, 27 Feb. 1908.

62. *New York Times,* 24, 25, 26, 28 Feb. 1908.

63. Thomas correspondence, 23 Feb. 1908.

64. Combs to Root, no. 78, 5 March 1908, NA, RG 59: 8258/271–3.

65. Thomas correspondence, 26 Feb. 1908.

66. Combs to Root, no. 78, 5 March 1908, NA, RG 59: 8258/271–3.

67. Stone diary, 29 Feb. 1908.

68. Hewitt correspondence, 10 March 1908.

69. Gleaves, *Emory,* 301. Archa Adamson also claimed that the man had tried to desert (Adamson diary, 29 Feb. 1908).

70. Metcalf to Evans, 13 Feb. 1908, SecNav Confidential Ciphers Sent; Ingersoll to Lieutenant W. R. Gherardi, 25 Feb. 1908, no. 540, NA, RG 45, area 9. A detailed account of the stranding is contained in *New York Times,* 14 Feb. 1908.

71. *New York Times,* 13 Feb. 1908.

72. Gherardi to secretary of the navy, 6 March 1908, NA, RG 45, area 9. Willoughby, *Yankton,* 100–113, gives the most detailed published account of the expedition.

73. Maxfield correspondence, 6 March 1908; Hewitt correspondence, 10 March 1908.

74. Hewitt correspondence, 10 March 1908.

75. Stone diary, 11 March 1908.

76. Evans, *Admiral's Log,* 442; *New York Times,* 22 Dec. 1907.

77. *New York Times,* 18 Nov. 1907.

78. Ibid., 26 Feb. 1908, 13 March 1908.

79. Thompson to Root, 11 Feb. 1908, NA, RG 59: 8258/113.

80. Root to Thompson, 19 Feb. 1908, ibid.

81. Thompson to Root, 13 March 1908, NA, RG 59: 8258/235.

82. Evans to the Bureau of Navigation, 12 March 1908, NA, RG 45, area 9.

83. *New York Times,* 13 March 1908.

84. Thomas correspondence, 6 March 1908. Emphasis in original.

85. *New York Times,* 14 March 1908.

86. Maxfield correspondence, 18 March 1908; Stone diary, 18 March 1908.

87. Maxfield correspondence, 20 March 1908. For a detailed description of these exercises, see Matthews, *With the Battlefleet,* 228–53, and Jones, *With the Atlantic Fleet,* 97–111.

88. Maxfield correspondence, 22 March 1908.

89. Metcalf to Evans, 6072–108, 10 March 1908, NA, RG 45, area 9.

90. *New York Times,* 17 March, 3 May 1908.

91. Ibid., 7 Jan. 1912. This was the admiral's obituary.

92. Evans to C. S. Sperry, 14 April 1907, Sperry correspondence.

93. Naval History Division, General Board Proceedings, 26 March 1907.

94. Sims to Anne Hitchcock Sims, 6 April 1907, Sims correspondence.

95. *New York Times,* 11, 14, 15 Oct., 14, 15 Dec. 1907.

96. Thomas correspondence, 20 Dec. 1907.

97. Ibid., 16 Dec. 1907.

98. Ibid., 24 Dec. 1907.

99. Ibid., 14 Jan. 1908.

100. Ibid.; Sperry to Edith M. Sperry, 14 Jan. 1908, Sperry correspondence.

101. Thomas correspondence, 14 Jan. 1908.

102. Ibid.

103. Ibid., 4 Feb. 1908.

104. Ibid., 13 Feb. 1908.

105. Ibid., 6 March 1908.

106. Combs telegram to Root, 5 March 1908, and Combs letter to Root, 5 March 1908, both NA, RG 59: 8258/217.

107. Sperry to Edith M. Sperry, 19 Jan. 1908, postscript dated 21 Jan. 1908, Sperry correspondence.

108. Evans to Sperry, 11 April 1907, ibid.

109. Sperry to Metcalf, 27 Jan. 1908, Sperry correspondence.

110. Sperry to Porter, 22 Feb. 1908, 13 March 1908, ibid.

111. Sperry to Edith M. Sperry, 23 Feb. 1908, ibid.

112. Sperry to Porter and Sperry to Edith M. Sperry, 13 March 1908, Thomas correspondence; *Army & Navy Journal,* 21 March 1908, 774.

113. Thomas correspondence, 13 March 1908. Emphasis in original.

114. Sperry to Porter, 13 March 1908, Sperry correspondence.

115. Roosevelt to Sperry, 17 March 1908, ibid.

116. Sperry to Edith M. Sperry, 16, 27 March 1908, and Sperry to C. S. Sperry, Jr., 5 April 1908, ibid.

117. Sperry to Edith M. Sperry, 27 March 1908, ibid; Evans cipher telegram to Pillsbury, 31 March 1908, NA, RG 45, Confidential Ciphers Received. *New York Times,* 1, 2, 3 April 1908.

118. Roosevelt to Evans, 23 March 1908, in Morison, *Roosevelt Letters,* 6: 981.

119. Sperry to Edith M. Sperry, 25 March 1908, Sperry correspondence.

120. *New York Times,* 2 April–3 May 1908.

CHAPTER 7

1. *New York Times,* 12 April 1908.
2. Maxfield correspondence, 10 April 1908.
3. *New York Times,* 15 April 1908.
4. Ibid., 13, 15 April 1908.
5. Jones, *With the Atlantic Fleet,* 258–59; *New York Times,* 16 April 1908.
6. Hewitt correspondence, 18 April 1908.
7. Stone diary, 16 April 1908.
8. Hewitt corresondence, 18 April 1908; *New York Times,* 18 April 1908.
9. Jones, *With the Atlantic Fleet,* 259; Stone diary, 18 April 1908.
10. Stone diary, 18 April 1908.
11. *New York Times,* 19 April 1908.
12. Stone diary, 18, 19 April 1908.
13. *New York Times,* 24, 25 April 1908; Maxfield correspondence, 24 April 1908.
14. *New York Times,* 24, 26 April 1908.
15. Stone diary, 25 April 1908.
16. *New York Times,* 26 April 1908.
17. Maxfield correspondence, 25–29 April 1908; Stone diary, 25–29 April 1908.
18. *New York Times,* 28, 30 April 1908.
19. Stone diary, 1 May 1908; *New York Times,* 1 May 1908.
20. *New York Times,* 5 May 1908.
21. Ibid., 6 May 1908.
22. *Japan Weekly Mail,* 28 April, 2 May 1908.
23. *New York Times,* 21, 28 Feb. 1908.
24. Ibid., 17 May 1908.
25. Ibid.
26. Ibid., 7, 17 May 1908; Stone diary, 6 May 1908.
27. *New York Times,* 7 May 1908.
28. Ibid., 8 May 1908. Metcalf and the governor of California were in the lead carriage.
29. Ibid., 9 May 1908.
30. Ibid., 9, 10 May 1908.
31. Ibid., 10 May 1908.

CHAPTER 8

1. Navy secretary letter, 5690-7-2449, 27 Feb. 1907, NA, RG 45, area 9. "Pacific Fleet Organized," *The Navy,* 9; Robert Erwin Johnson, *Thence Around Cape Horn: The Story of United States Naval Forces on Pacific Station, 1818–1923,* 162–65.

2. Metcalf to commander in chief, Pacific Fleet, 5690-56-2107, NA, RG 45, area 9; *New York Times,* 22 Dec. 1907.

3. Rear Admiral George W. Melville, "Is our Naval Administration Efficient?" 46–47.

4. Quoted in Vice Admiral Edwin B. Hooper, *The Navy Department: Evolution and Fragmentation*, 7.

5. O'Gara, *Roosevelt and the Rise of the Modern American Navy*, 21, citing "Evils of Our Naval Bureaucracy," *Literary Digest*, 37 (1908): 875.

6. "Arrangement of Magazine, Ammunition Supply, and Installation of Battery, USS *Kentucky*," 2 Feb. 1901, cited in Morison, *Sims*, 79.

7. Morison, *Sims*, 79–80.

8. Letter, 28 Sep. 1901, Sims correspondence.

9. Paul T. Heffron, "Secretary Moody and Naval Administrative Reform, 1902–1904," 30.

10. Commander Daniel J. Costello, "Planning for War: A History of the General Board of the Navy, 1900–1914," 24.

11. O'Gara, *The Modern American Navy*, 25, citing the Navy Department's *Annual Report of the Secretary of the Navy, 1906*, 5.

12. "Our Blunders in Warship Construction," *The Navy*, 13–5.

13. That is, at least since receipt of Sims's letter cited in footnote 6 above.

14. "More Truths About Our Battleships," *The Navy*, 8–11. See also *New York Times*, 12 July 1907.

15. *New York Times*, 14 July 1907.

16. New York *Nation*, vol. 85, 19 July 1907, 45.

17. *New York Times*, 16 July 1907.

18. Ibid., 19 July 1907.

19. "Battleship Georgia Disaster," *Scientific American*, 58.

20. *New York Times*, 7 Oct. 1907, quoting *The Navy*, vol. 1, no. 10, Oct. 1907.

21. Navy Department, *Annual Report of the Secretary of the Navy, 1907*, 437.

22. Reuterdahl to Sims, 4 Oct. 1907, Sims correspondence.

23. Sims to Anne Hitchcock Sims, 22 June 1907, Sims correspondence.

24. Reuterdahl to Sims, 4 Oct. 1907, Sims correspondence.

25. Henry Reuterdahl, "The Needs of Our Navy," 251–61.

26. Ibid., 252–53.

27. Ibid., 262.

28. Ibid., 258.

29. Ibid., 259.

30. Naval Historical Foundation, *Admiral Brownson*, 23.

31. *New York Times*, 25 Dec. 1907.

32. Ibid., 26 Dec. 1907; Naval Historical Foundation, *Admiral Brownson*, 24–26.

33. *New York Times*, 28 Dec. 1907.

34. Ibid., 6 Jan. 1908.

35. Ibid.; Naval Historical Foundation, *Admiral Brownson*, 31.

36. "Our Navy Under Fire," *Current Literature*, 126. See also "The President and the Admiral," *Literary Digest*, 71–73; "The Navy Quarrel," *Independent*, 691; and "Gagging an Admiral," *Army and Navy Journal*, 491.

37. Thomas correspondence, 23 Jan. 1908. Copies of the official correspondence relating to Brownson's resignation were published in 60th Cong., 1st sess., House doc. 502, a copy of which is contained in NA RG 80: 15285/59:1.

38. Morison, *Roosevelt Letters*, 6: 891–92fn.

39. *New York Times*, 8 Jan. 1908.

40. "The Reuterdahl Attack on Our Navy Answered," *Scientific American* (18 Jan. 1908): 38–39, (25 Jan. 1908): 60–62.

NOTES

41. Ibid., 25 Jan. 1908, 60–62.
42. *McClure's Magazine* 30, no. 6 (Feb. 1908): 517, letter to the editor.
43. Plunkett to Sims, 3 Jan. 1908, Sims correspondence.
44. *Scientific American* 98 (22 Feb. 1908): 122.
45. Dewey to Metcalf, 14 June 1907, in NA, RG 80, Records of the General Board, study 420–2.
46. Hill to Metcalf, 15 June 1907, NA, RG 80: 24667.
47. Ibid., Converse endorsement to Hill, 20 June 1907, and to Metcalf, 15 June 1907.
48. Ibid., Converse to Metcalf, 25 June 1907.
49. Goodrich to Metcalf, 12 Aug. 1907, quoted in Metcalf to Goodrich, 18 Feb. 1908, NA, RG 80: 26000/1.
50. *New York Times,* 31 Dec. 1907. Converse had earlier served as chief of the Bureau of Ordnance, of the Bureau of Equipment, and of the Bureau of Navigation.
51. Converse to Metcalf, "Statement Regarding Criticisms of Navy," 5 Feb. 1908, NA, RG 80: 26000/1; Benjamin to Sims, 5 March 1908, Sims correspondence.
52. Sims to Roosevelt, "Comments upon the Report by Admiral Converse, Concerning Criticism of Defects in Our Naval Organization and Materiel," 14 Feb. 1908, Sims correspondence.
53. Sims to Roosevelt, 14 Feb. 1907, Sims correspondence.
54. Quoted in *New York Times,* 20 Feb. 1908.
55. Morison, *Sims,* 185. Morison's account of the Senate hearings remains the most thorough published treatment of the topic (see 184–99).
56. Metcalf to Sims, 15 Feb. 1908, NA, RG 80: 26000/2 (enclosed in this file with the letter was an unsigned three-page memorandum comparing Reuterdahl's article with Sims's reports to the Bureau of Navigation, 7 Aug. and 23 Aug. 1903); Metcalf to Hill, 15 Feb. 1908, and Hill to Metcalf, 24 Feb. 1908, NA, RG 80: 26000/3. The Admiral of the Navy was also asked to identify the author of his letter of 14 June 1907, which criticized the department's armor placement policy (Metcalf to Dewey, 25742/2, 15 Feb. 1908, in NA, RG 80, Records of the General Board, study 420–6).
57. *New York Times,* 21 Feb. 1908.
58. Sims, "Roosevelt and the Navy," 62; Morison, *Sims,* 184–85.
59. This term was used to describe Metcalf's search (*New York Times,* 21 Feb. 1908).
60. Navy Department memo, 19 Feb. 1908 (4:00 P.M.), NA, RG 80: 26000.
61. Metcalf to Goodrich, 18 Feb. 1908, NA, RG 80: 26000/1.
62. Goodrich to Metcalf, 27 Feb. 1908, NA, RG 80: 26000.
63. Morison, *Sims,* 186, citing *U.S. Senate, Hearings Before the Committee on Naval Affairs, on Bill S.335,* 1908, 3.
64. Ibid., 187, citing *Hearings,* 13ff and 16ff.
65. Ibid., citing *Hearings,* 102–3.
66. Goodrich to Metcalf, 27 Feb. 1908, NA, RG 80: 26000.
67. Evans to Metcalf, no. 883, 22 March 1908, NA, RG 24: 6072/195.
68. Morison, *Sims,* 192–93.
69. *New York Times,* 3 March 1908.
70. Ibid.
71. Ibid., 6 March 1908.
72. Morison, *Sims,* 196, citing *Hearings,* 309–10.
73. Ibid., 197, citing *Hearings,* 311.
74. Ibid., 199.
75. Thomas correspondence, 8 March 1908; Hart, *The Great White Fleet,* 174.
76. Thomas correspondence, 25 Jan. 1908.

NOTES

77. Sperry to Edith M. Sperry, 23 Feb., 12 March 1908, Sperry correspondence.
78. Sims to Roosevelt, 14 April 1908, Sims correspondence.
79. Cone to Sims, 22 April 1908, Sims correspondence.
80. "Admiral Evans on Naval Armor," *Literary Digest,* 469.
81. Evans to Metcalf, no. 910, 17 March 1908, and Robinson to Evans, 4 March 1908, NA, RG 80: 25107/21:1.
82. Key to Senate Naval Committee, 21 March 1908, NA, RG 80: 26000/10.
83. Key to Sims, 30 March 1908, Sims correspondence.
84. Hale to Metcalf, 9 April 1908, NA, RG 80: 26000/7.
85. Ibid., Converse endorsement of Hale to Metcalf.
86. Metcalf to Hale, 13 April 1908, NA, RG 80: 26000/7.
87. Key to Sims, 3 April 1908, Sims correspondence.
88. Roosevelt to Metcalf, 23 March 1908, in Morison, *Roosevelt Letters,* 6: 980.

Chapter 9

1. Sydney *Morning Herald,* 20 Aug. 1908.
2. Deakin to Bray, 24 Dec. 1907, NA, RG 59: 8258/124; Bray to Bacon, 24 Dec. 1907, no. 398, NA, RG 59: 8258/123.
3. Chargé d'Affaires *ad interim* Carter to Root, no. 229, 8 Feb. 1908, NA, RG 59: 8258/109.
4. Root to American embassy, London, 13 Feb. 1908, and copy to Bray, 14 Feb. 1908, NA, RG 59: 8258/109.
5. Root to Roosevelt, 21 Feb. 1908, NA, RG 59: 8258/143-5.
6. William S. Sims, "Roosevelt and the Navy," 62.
7. Root to Roosevelt, 21 Feb. 1908, NA, RG 59: 8258/143-5.
8. *New York Times,* 22 Feb. 1908.
9. Neville Meany, *The Search for Security in the Pacific, 1901–1914,* 164–66.
10. *New York Times,* 14 March 1908.
11. Bryce to Bacon, 14 March 1908, NA, RG 59: 8258/241.
12. Ibid., Root to Bryce, 14 March 1908; Root to Bryce, no. 264, 14 March 1908, NA, RG 59: 8258/215.
13. Sydney *Morning Herald,* 20 Aug. 1908; Melbourne *Argus,* 13 March 1908. See also Melbourne *Age,* 16 March 1908.
14. *New York Times,* 16 March 1908.
15. Donald C. Gordon, "Roosevelt's 'Smart Yankee Trick,' " 353.
16. Melbourne *Herald,* 16 March 1908.
17. Ward to Prickitt, 4 Mar. 1908, NA, RG 59: 8258/330.
18. Prickitt to Bacon, no. 39, 4 March 1908, NA, RG 59: 8258/330.
19. Prickitt to Bacon, 15 March 1908, NA, RG 59: 8258/237.
20. G. P. Taylor, "New Zealand, the Anglo-Japanese Alliance and the 1908 Visit of the American Fleet," 56, citing prime minister to governor, 16 March 1908, governor's files, telegrams to and from secretary of state, 1908, New Zealand National Archives, Wellington.
21. Bryce to Root, 21 March 1908, NA, RG 59: 8258/254.
22. Metcalf to Root, 28 March 1908, 6072–167, NA, RG 59: 8258/288.
23. Raymond Esthus, *Roosevelt and Japan,* 262, quoting Oscar King Davis, *Released for Publication* (Boston: 1925), 87–88.
24. J. A. LaNauze, *Alfred Deakin: A Biography,* 490, quoting Deakin correspondence, Deakin to Amory, 16 May 1908.

NOTES

25. Donald C. Gordon, *The Dominion Partnership in Imperial Defense, 1870–1914*, 213.

26. Sydney *Morning Herald*, 10 Aug. 1908.

27. New Zealand, *Parliamentary Debates*, 30 Sep. 1908, 709.

28. *Auckland Weekly News*, 9 July 1908.

29. Taylor, "The Anglo-Japanese Alliance," 59.

30. Takahira to Root, no. 21, 18 March 1908, NA, RG 59: 8258/252.

31. *New York Times*, 21 March 1908.

32. Bacon to Takahira, 20 March 1908, NA, RG 59: 8258/252. See also Metcalf to Root, 6072–137, 20 March 1908, Root to Takahira, 25 March 1908, and Takahira to Root, 23 March 1908, NA, RG 59: 8258/253.

33. *Bristol Times and Mirror*, 21 March 1908.

34. *Journal de St. Petersbourg*, 13, 26 March 1908, trans. in Montgomery Schuyler to Root, no. 238, 1 April 1908, NA, RG 59: 8258/322-3.

35. *Japan Weekly Mail*, 28 March 1908.

36. Ibid.

37. Bacon to O'Brien, no. 103, 24 March 1908, NA, RG 59: 8258/252; O'Brien to Root, no. 290, 16 April 1908, NA, RG 59: 8258/356.

38. Takahira to Root, 15 May 1908, NA, RG 59: 8258/356.

39. Bacon to O'Brien, no. 149, 21 May 1908, NA, RG 59, 8258/356. O'Brien to Root, 20 May 1908, NA, RG 59: 8258/404; O'Brien to Root, no. 352, NA, RG 59: 8258/425. By this time O'Brien had reached the conclusion that his advice had been incorrect.

40. Wu Ting-fang to Root, no. 4, 23 March 1908, NA, RG 59: 8258/255.

41. Root to Wu Ting-fang, no. 106, 24 March 1908, NA, RG 59: 8258/255.

42. Bacon to Metcalf and Bacon to Rockhill, 25 March 1908, NA, RG 59: 8258/255. Curiously, the acceptance was not forwarded to the Navy Department, although on the same day both documents were sent to the American minister in Peking, William W. Rockhill.

43. Metcalf telegram to Evans, 24 March 1908, and Evans telegram to Metcalf, 24 March 1908, Sperry correspondence.

44. Sperry to Edith M. Sperry, 27 March 1908, Sperry correspondence.

45. Metcalf to Root, 6072–168, 28 March 1908, NA, RG 59: 8258/289.

46. Metcalf to Evans, 27 March 1908, NA, RG 24: 6072/173; Pillsbury telegram to Sperry, 28 March 1908, referred to in Sperry to Metcalf, 2-203-WFD, 3 April 1908, NA, RG 45: 00.

47. Wu to Root, 27 March 1908, NA, RG 59: 8258/287.

48. Newberry to Root, 6072–188, 31 March 1908, NA, RG 59: 8258/308.

49. Rockhill to Root, 18 April 1908, NA, RG 59: 8258/335; Rockhill to Root, no. 911, 21 April 1908, NA, RG 59: 8258/386.

50. Loeb to Newberry, 27 April 1908, NA, RG 45: 00.

51. Root to Rockhill, 28 April 1908, NA, RG 59: 8258/355.

52. Bryce to Root, no. 74, 4 April 1908, NA, RG 59: 8258/318.

53. Metcalf to Root, 6072–220, 9 April 1908, and Bacon to Bryce, no. 293, 15 April 1908, NA, RG 59: 8258/320.

54. Secretary to Admiralty to commander in chief, no. 154, 5 May 1908, RNAS correspondence. Despite the detailed itinerary reported by the Admiralty, some confusion apparently still prevailed. The London *Times* on 1 June reported that it had been "decided that the cruisers *Cambrian* and *Prometheus* should meet the United States Fleet at Suva . . . " (Rogers to Bureau of Navigation, memo 8075, 14 June 1908, NA, RG 45, area 10).

55. Vice-Consul Leslie E. Brown (Suva) to Bacon, no. 23, 18 May 1908, and Bacon to

Metcalf, 18 June 1908, NA, RG 59: 8258/409; Pillsbury to Root, 6072–367, 22 June 1908, and Carr to Brown, 27 June 1908, NA, RG 59: 8258/417.

56. Bryce to Root, no. 77, 10 April 1908, NA, RG 59: 8258/321; Metcalf to Root, 6072–233, 15 April 1908, and Root to Bryce, no. 296, 17 April 1908, NA, RG 59: 8258/332.

57. Consul General Amos P. Wilder (Hong Kong) telegram to Root, 5 June 1908, NA, RG 59: 8258/402; Wilder letter to Bacon, 4 June 1908, NA, RG 59: 8258/420; Wilder to Bacon, 12 May 1908, NA, RG 59: 8258/411-3; Root telegram to Wilder, 5 June 1908, NA, RG 59: 8258/402; Carr to Wilder, no. 131, 23 June 1908, NA, RG 59: 8258/411-3. Wilder reported to Bacon the surprise of the governor, who then obtained confirmation from London (10 June 1908, NA, RG 59: 8258/430).

58. Bryce to Root, no. 72, 2 April 1908, NA, RG 59: 8258/310; Metcalf to Root, 6072–224, 10 April 1908, and Bacon to Bryce, no. 298, 18 April 1908, NA, RG 59: 8258/324.

59. Bryce to Root, no. 73, 2 April 1908, NA, RG 59: 8258/311; Consul Henry D. Baker (Hobart) telegram to Root, 17 March 1908, NA, RG 59: 8258/240; Baker to Bacon, no. 12, 19 March 1908, NA, RG 59: 8258/369-75; Metcalf to Root, 6072-216, 9 April 1908, and Bacon to Bryce, no. 29, 11 April 1908, NA, RG 59: 8258/319.

60. Consul T. Edwin Dudley (Vancouver) to Bacon, no. 909, 12 March 1908, NA, RG 59: 8258/248-50; Newberry to Root, 6072-176, 23 March 1908, and Carr to Dudley, no. 545, 4 April 1908, NA, RG 59: 8258/299.

61. Bryce to Root, no. 93, 1 May 1908, NA, RG 59: 8258/353; Newberry to Root, 6072-282, 6 May 1908, and Root to Bryce, no. 318, 8 May 1908, NA, RG 59: 8258/357.

62. Kiao-chow: Hill (Berlin) to Root, 14 July 1908, Newberry memo to Bacon, 14 July 1908, Newberry to Root, 6072-392, 15 July 1908, and Bacon to Hill, 15 July 1908, NA, RG 59: 8258/431; Hill to Root, 30 Sep. 1908, NA, RG 59: 8258/500; Metcalf to Root, 6072-458, 5 Oct. 1908, and Root to Hill, 6 Oct. 1908, NA, RG 59: 8258/513; Natal: Chargé Howard to Adee, 13 Aug. 1908, NA, RG 59: 8258/461; Pillsbury to Root, 6072-411, 18 Aug. 1908, NA, RG 59: 8258/463; Tandjong-Priok: Netherlands legation in Washington to Bacon, 29 Aug. 1908, NA, RG 59: 8258/469; Metcalf to Root, 6072-421, 8 September 1908, NA, RG 59: 8258/485.

63. *New York Times,* 29 March 1908.

64. Edwin A. Falk, *From Perry to Pearl Harbor: The Struggle for Supremacy in the Pacific,* 199–200.

65. *Boston Transcript,* 20 May 1908.

66. *New York Times,* 10, 12 April 1908.

67. Ibid., 16 May, 20 July 1908.

68. Gleaves, *Emory,* 316.

69. Thomas correspondence, 18 Feb. 1908.

70. Gleaves, *Emory,* 316.

71. *New York Times,* 4 July 1908.

72. Ibid., 18, 27 Sep. 1907.

73. Ibid., 1 Apr. 1908; U.S. Atlantic Fleet circular letter no. 10, 16 April 1908, NA, RG 45: 00.

74. *New York Times,* 20 May 1908.

75. Bureau of Navigation letter, 29 May 1908, NA, RG 59: 8258/494-5.

76. See, for example, *New York Times,* 20 May, 9, 27 June, 1, 2, 4, 7, 16, 17, 18, 27 Sep., 1, 5, 11, 18, 19, 20 Oct. 1908.

77. Pillsbury memo to Newberry, 19 May 1908, NA, RG 45, area 9. The destroyer

tender *Solace* accompanied the fleet. For a summary of this cruise, see Rear Admiral Bradley A. Fiske, *From Midshipman to Rear Admiral,* 417–26.

78. *New York Times,* 21, 25, 29, 30 Aug., 2, 4, 23, 24, 28 Sep., 12, 13, 23 Oct. 1908.

79. Hatzfeldt to Bacon, 12 June 1908, Newberry to Roosevelt, 13 May 1908, Root to Hatzfeldt, 17 June 1908, and Hatzfeldt to Root, 28 July 1908, NA, RG 59: 8258/310. The ships that called at Apia were the cruisers *Tennessee* and *Washington* and the destroyers *Whipple* and *Hopkins.*

80. Fiske, *From Midshipman to Rear Admiral,* 419.

81. Metcalf to Dayton, 5690/108, 27 May 1908, and Metcalf to the commanding officer of the *Solace,* 5690/108, 27 May 1908, NA, RG 45, area 9.

82. Metcalf to Dayton, 30 July 1908, NA, RG 45, area 9. This information was widely publicized. See, for example, Sydney *Morning Herald,* 20 Aug. 1908, quoting London *Daily Telegraph,* 19 Aug. 1908.

83. *New York Times,* 14 Oct. 1908.

84. Fiske, *From Midshipman to Rear Admiral,* 423.

85. E. T. Constein to Sims, 20 Aug. 1908, Sims correspondence.

86. Commander in chief, Atlantic Fleet, circular letter no. 10, 16 April 1908, NA, RG 45: 00.

87. For some copies of the many requests, see NA, RG 45: 00 and NA, RG 24: 6072.

88. Newberry to commander in chief, Atlantic Fleet, 1 May 1908, NA, RG 24: 6072/ 279.

89. Humboldt Chamber of Commerce to Metcalf, 11 April 1908, NA, RG 45: 00.

90. Maxfield correspondence and Stone diary, 18 May 1908; Maxfield correspondence, 19, 20 May 1908.

91. Stone diary, 21 May 1908.

92. These visits only partially fulfilled the earnest request of Senator S. M. Piles that the fleet visit Port Angeles, Port Townsend, Anacortes, Everett, Seattle, Bremerton, Tacoma, Olympia, Blaine, Bellingham, Hoquiam, Aberdeen, South Bend, "and other towns in the vicinity of each of these places" (Piles to Metcalf, 21 Feb. 1908, NA, RG 24: 6072/ 90).

93. *New York Times,* 27 May 1908; Jones, *With the American Fleet,* 290.

CHAPTER 10

1. Caswell Saufley to Sallie Rowan Saufley, 3 July 1908, Sallie Rowan Saufley correspondence.

2. Stone diary, 4 July 1908.

3. *New York Times,* 8 July 1908.

4. Hewitt correspondence, 15 July 1908; Maxfield correspondence, 12 July 1908.

5. *New York Times,* 15 July 1908.

6. Maxfield correspondence and Stone diary, 14 July 1908.

7. *New York Times,* 14, 17 July 1908.

8. Stone diary, 15, 16 July 1908.

9. Ibid., 16 July 1908.

10. *New York Times,* 17 July 1908.

11. Ibid.

12. Saufley correspondence, 19 July 1908.

13. *New York Times,* 18 July 1908.

14. Maxfield correspondence [19] July 1908.

15. Saufley correspondence, 19 July 1908.

16. Ibid.

17. Schroeder, *Half-Century of Naval Service*, 338.

18. *New York Times*, 20 July 1908.

19. Naval History Division, Operational Archives, *Proposed Routes Between the Pacific Coast and the Philippines*, War Portfolio no. 3, ref. no. 7-c NA folder no. 142, OP-29 folder no. 7.

20. *New York Times*, 23 July 1908.

21. Ibid., 21 July 1908.

22. Ibid., 22 July 1908.

23. Stone diary, 22 July 1908.

24. Maxfield correspondence, 24 July 1908.

25. Sperry to Edith M. Sperry, 1 Aug. 1908, Sperry correspondence.

26. Stone diary and Maxfield correspondence, 1 August 1908.

27. Thomas A. Bailey, "The World Cruise of the American Battleship Fleet," 412.

28. *Weekly Graphic*, 2 April 1904.

29. M. P. Lissington, *New Zealand and Japan, 1900–1941*, 7; Bernard K. Gordon, *New Zealand Becomes a Pacific Power*, 20. G. P. Taylor concluded that "there was little or no anti-Japanese feeling" before 1908 ("The Anglo-Japanese Alliance," 72).

30. Alfred Thayer Mahan, "The True Significance of the Pacific Cruise," 407.

31. Arthur J. Marder, *Fear God and Dread Nought: The Correspondence of Admiral of the Fleet Lord Fisher of Kilverstone*, vol. 2, 168.

32. Review of *The World's Awakening*, in Sydney *Bulletin*, 23 April 1908.

33. Sydney *Bulletin*, 14 May 1908.

34. Sydney *Morning Herald*, 11 Aug. 1908.

35. Wellington *Evening Post*, 23 Mar. 1908.

36. Will Lawson, "The White Squadron," Sydney *Bulletin*, 16 July 1908.

37. Sperry to Oscar Strauss, 4 Feb. 1907, Sperry correspondence.

38. Sperry to Edith M. Sperry, 16 Aug. 1908, ibid.

39. Sperry to Edith M. Sperry, 9 Sep. 1908, ibid.

40. Challener, *American Foreign Policy*, 260.

41. *New Zealand Herald*, 7 Aug. 1908; Wellington *Evening Post*, 8 Aug. 1908.

42. J. Barr, *The Ports of Auckland: A Souvenir of the Jubilee of the Auckland Harbour Board*, 132.

43. For a stirring contemporary description of the maneuver, see *Weekly Graphic and New Zealand Mail*, 12 Aug. 1908.

44. Ship's log, the USS *Rhode Island*, 9 Aug. 1908, NA, RG 24; Stone diary, 9 Aug. 1908.

45. Prickett to Bacon, 1 Sep. 1908, NA, RG 59: 8258/501-5.

46. *New Zealand Herald*, 11 Aug. 1908; *Auckland Star*, 10 Aug. 1908; *Weekly Graphic*, 12 Aug. 1908; *New York Times*, 10 Aug. 1908.

47. *Weekly Graphic*, 12 Aug. 1908.

48. *Weekly Graphic*, 12 Aug. 1908; *New Zealand Herald*, 11 Aug. 1908; *New York Times*, 11 Aug. 1908; Hewitt correspondence, 16 Aug. 1908.

49. *New Zealand Herald*, 11 Aug. 1908; *Weekly Graphic*, 12 Aug. 1908; Stone diary, 10 Aug. 1908.

50. Maxfield correspondence, 11 Aug. 1908.

51. The best summary of all these events is contained in the *Weekly Graphic*'s two "Fleet Week Specials," 12, 19 Aug. 1908.

52. Peter J. Coleman, "New Zealand Liberalism and the Origins of the American Welfare State," 372–91.

53. *Weekly Graphic*, 12 Aug. 1908.

54. Matthews, *Back to Hampton Roads,* 30.

55. Maxfield correspondence, 14 Aug. 1908.

56. Saufley correspondence, 20 Aug. 1908.

57. Gleaves, *Emory,* 321; Maxfield correspondence, 12 Aug. 1908.

58. Eugene Stone, Louis Maxfield, and H. Kent Hewitt all participated in the Rotorua trip and recorded their impressions (Stone diary, 12–14 Aug. 1908; Maxfield correspondence 11, 12, 14 Aug. 1908; Hewitt correspondence, 16 Aug. 1908).

59. *Weekly Graphic*, 12 Aug. 1908; *New Zealand Herald*, 17, 18 Aug. 1908.

60. Sydney *Morning Herald*, 13 Aug. 1908.

61. *Auckland Star* and *New York Times*, 14 Aug. 1908.

62. Saufley correspondence, 20 Aug. 1908.

63. See, for example, *Auckland Star,* 15 Aug. 1908.

64. *New Zealand Herald*, 15 Aug. 1908.

65. *New York Times*, 15 Aug. 1908.

66. *Auckland Star* and *New York Times*, 15 Aug. 1908.

67. *Auckland Star,* 15 August 1908.

68. *New Zealand Herald*, 17 Aug. 1908.

69. Ibid., 15 Aug. 1908.

70. New York *Nation*, vol. 87, 13 Aug. 1908, 127; London *Daily Telegraph*, 11 Aug. 1908, quoted in *New York Times*, 11 Aug. 1908.

71. London *Daily Chronicle*, 15 Aug. 1908, quoted in *New York Times*, 15 Aug. 1908.

CHAPTER 11

1. *New York Times*, 20 Aug. 1908.

2. Ibid.; Sydney *Morning Herald*, 21 Aug. 1908.

3. *New York Times*, 20 Aug. 1908; Sydney *Morning Herald,* 21 Aug. 1908.

4. *New York Times*, 21 Aug. 1908.

5. Sydney *Morning Herald*, 21 Aug. 1908.

6. Ibid., 19 Aug. 1908.

7. *New York Times*, 21 Aug. 1908.

8. Sydney *Morning Herald*, 22 Aug. 1908.

9. Maxfield correspondence, 23 Aug. 1908; American consul (Newcastle) to Bacon, 17 Sep. 1908, no. 63, NA, RG 59: 8258/538.

10. Sydney *Morning Herald*, 24 Aug. 1908.

11. Ibid. This passage was omitted in the *New York Times* report of the banquet (24 Aug. 1908).

12. Sydney *Morning Herald*, 24 Aug. 1908.

13. Sydney *Bulletin*, 27 Aug. 1908.

14. Sydney *Morning Herald*, 25 Aug. 1908.

15. Ibid., 26 Aug. 1908.

16. Ibid., 27 Aug. 1908.

17. Ibid., 28 Aug. 1908. *New York Times* reports only fifty stragglers recovered on 27 Aug. 1908 (28 Aug. 1908).

18. Sydney *Morning Herald*, 28 Aug. 1908.

19. Ibid., 29 Aug. 1908; *New York Times,* 29 Aug. 1908.

20. Hewitt correspondence, 30 Aug. 1908.

21. Sydney *Morning Herald,* 29 Aug. 1908.

22. Ibid.

23. A copy of the official program is preserved in NA, RG 45: 00 and summarized in the *New York Times* and Sydney *Morning Herald,* 29 Aug. 1908.

24. Maxfield correspondence, 29 Aug. 1908.

25. Stone diary, 29 Aug. 1908.

26. Sydney *Morning Herald,* 31 Aug. 1908.

27. *New York Times,* 31 Aug. 1908.

28. Sydney *Morning Herald,* 1 Sep. 1908.

29. Ibid.

30. Hewitt correspondence, 14 Sep. 1908.

31. Sydney *Morning Herald,* 2, 3 Sep. 1908.

32. Ibid., 4 Sep. 1908.

33. Ibid., 26, 29 Aug., and 3, 4 Sep. 1908.

34. Ibid., 4 Sep. 1908.

35. Sydney *Bulletin,* 10 Sep. 1908.

36. Ibid.

37. Sydney *Morning Herald,* 7, 8 Sep. 1908; *New York Times,* 7 Sep. 1908.

38. Sydney *Bulletin,* 10 Sep. 1908.

39. Sydney *Morning Herald* and *New York Times,* 5 Sep. 1908. The name of the ship was incorrectly reported as *Laura* in Navy Department, Bureau of Navigation, *Information Relative to the Voyage of the Atlantic Fleet,* 10, and in all subsequent treatments.

40. A board of marine inquiry investigated the accident and found the master of the *Leura* guilty of careless navigation (Sydney *Morning Herald,* 30 Sep. 1908).

41. Sydney *Morning Herald,* 7 Sep. 1908.

42. Navy Department, Bureau of Navigation, *Information Relative to the Voyage of the Atlantic Fleet,* 10.

43. Sydney *Morning Herald,* 26 Sep. 1908.

44. Sydney *Bulletin,* 10 Sep. 1908.

45. Hewitt correspondence and Stone diary, 15 Sep. 1908.

46. *New York Times,* 11 Sep. 1908; Sydney *Morning Herald,* 11 Sep. 1908.

47. Sydney *Morning Herald,* 8 Sep. 1908.

48. Saufley correspondence, 15 Sep. 1908.

49. Sydney *Morning Herald,* 18 Sep. 1908.

50. Stone diary, Maxfield correspondence, 9 Sep. 1908.

51. Sydney *Morning Herald,* 12 Sep. 1908.

52. For a good contemporary description of Albany, see Stone diary, 11 Sep. 1908.

53. Prickitt to Bacon, 15 April 1908, NA, RG 59: 8258/376-9.

54. Metcalf to Root, 25 May 1908, 6072-332, and Metcalf to Root, 1 June 1908, NA, RG 80: 18768/74; Carr to Prickitt, no. 36, 5 June 1908, NA, RG 59: 8258/398.

55. Sperry to Pillsbury, 17 Aug. 1908, Sperry correspondence; Sperry telegram to Pillsbury, 11 Sep. 1908, NA, RG 24: 6072/426.

56. Lieutenant Commander Fullinwider memo, enclosure to Bray to Bacon, no. 13, 7 Sep. 1908, NA, RG 59: 8258/526-7 (hereafter cited as Fullinwider memo).

57. Ibid.; Sydney *Morning Herald,* 23 Aug. 1908.

58. Sydney *Morning Herald,* 24 Aug. 1908.

59. Ibid., 25, 26 Aug. 1908.

60. Fullinwider memo; Sydney *Morning Herald,* 25, 26 Aug. 1908.

61. Fullinwider memo.

62. Sperry to master of the *Usher,* 22 Aug. 1908, NA, RG 45, area 10.

63. Sydney *Morning Herald,* 25 Aug. 1908.

64. Sperry telegram to Pillsbury, 1 Sep. 1908, NA, RG 45, area 10.

65. Sperry telegram to Pillsbury, 11 Sep. 1908, NA, RG 45, area 10. The *Tottenham,* which arrived on 7 September, the *Teviotdale,* which arrived on 28 August 1908, and the *Kildale* had a total of 16,313 tons of cargo coal (NA, RG 59: 8258/468).

66. Gleaves, *Emory,* 324.

67. Ibid.

68. *New York Times,* 16 Sep. 1908.

69. Harris (commander, naval station Cavite) to Pillsbury, 15 Sep. 1908, NA, RG 45, Confidential Ciphers Received; Sperry to Edith M. Sperry, 16 Sep. 1908, Sperry correspondence.

70. Sperry to C. S. Sperry, Jr., 13 Oct. 1908, Sperry correspondence; Sydney *Morning Herald,* 16 Sep. 1908; Stone diary, 17 Sep. 1908; Maxfield correspondence, 16 Sep. 1908; *New York Times,* 16 Sep. 1908.

71. *New York Times,* 17 Sep. 1908, dateline Albany, 16 Sep.; Consul (Melbourne) to State Department, 12 Nov. 1908, NA, RG 59: 8258/550.

72. Vice Admiral Poore to Sperry, 6 Aug. 1908, citing chief harbormaster letter of 14 July 1908, Sperry correspondence.

73. *New York Times,* 19 Sep. 1908.

74. Ibid.

75. Hart, *Great White Fleet,* 198.

76. Newberry to Roosevelt, 10 Feb. 1909, contains many details about contracts and the movements of the *Usher, British Monarch,* and *Baron Minto* (NA, RG 80: 18768/107).

77. Ibid.

78. Sperry to Pillsbury, 18 Aug. 1908, Sperry correspondence.

79. Ibid., Sperry to C. S. Sperry, Jr., 13 Oct. 1908.

80. *New York Times,* 19 Sep. 1908.

81. Stone diary, 18 Sep. 1908.

82. Sydney *Morning Herald,* 18 Sep. 1908; *New York Times,* 18, 19 Sep. 1908.

83. *New York Times,* 19 Sep. 1908.

84. Stone diary, 20 Sep. 1908.

Chapter 12

1. *Banzai!* was reviewed in the *New York Times,* 28 June 1908. See also the New York *Nation,* 23 July 1908, 73–74.

2. A review of *Der Kreig von 1908: Um die Vorherrschaft in Stillen Meer* in the New York *Nation,* 23 July 1908, 74.

3. "Firm Policy in the Far East," *New York Times,* 16 Aug. 1908.

4. The most detailed work on this topic is Luella J. Hall, "The Abortive German-American-Chinese Entente of 1907–8," but for a more balanced treatment of the subject, see Melvin Small's dissertation, "The American Image of Germany, 1906–1910," 192–204.

5. Hall, "The German-American-Chinese Entente," 221, quoting *Die Gross Politik* (*DGP*), vol. 21, 465.

6. Ibid., citing von Tschirschky to von Sternburg, 15 Sep. 1907, *DGP,* vol. 25, 71.

7. Ibid., von Sternburg to von Bülow, 8 Nov. 1908, *DGP,* vol. 25, 78–79.

NOTES

8. Raymond A. Esthus, *Theodore Roosevelt and the International Rivalries*, 124.

9. Von Sternburg to Roosevelt, 14 July 1907, Roosevelt correspondence.

10. Ibid., von Sternburg to Roosevelt, 19 July 1907.

11. G. P. Gooch and Harold Temperley, *British Documents on the Origins of the War, 1898-1914*, 8: 459.

12. Roosevelt to Root, 8 Aug. 1908, in Morison, *Roosevelt Letters*, 6: 1163-64.

13. Ibid., Roosevelt to Whitelaw Reid, 6 Jan. 1909, 1466-67.

14. William Harlan Hale, "Thus Spoke the Kaiser: The Lost Interview Which Solves an International Mystery," 513-23.

15. Interview, *Daily Telegraph*, 28 Oct. 1908; Arthur J. Marder, *From Dreadnought to Scapa Flow*, 1. 144-85.

16. Roosevelt to Lee, 17 Oct. 1908, in Morison, *Roosevelt Letters*, 6: 1293-94.

17. *Japan Advertiser*, 20 Aug. 1908.

18. A. Maurice Low, "Japan and the Saxon," 312.

19. Schroeder, *Half Century of Naval Service*, 351-55.

20. Maxfield correspondence, 23 Sep. 1908; Stone diary, 22 Sep. 1908.

21. Hewitt correspondence, 27 Sep. 1908.

22. Stone diary, 26 Sep. 1908.

23. Maxfield correspondence, 26 Sep. 1908; Schroeder, *Half Century of Naval Service*, 354.

24. Maxfield correspondence, 27 Sep. 1908.

25. Ibid., 28 Sep. 1908.

26. Maxfield correspondence, 29, 30 Sep. 1908; Stone diary, 30 Sep. 1908; Schroeder, *Half Century of Naval Service*, 355.

27. Hewitt correspondence, 30 Sep. 1908.

28. Maxfield correspondence; *New York Times*, 3 Oct. 1908.

29. *New York Times*, 23 Sep. 1908.

30. Metcalf to Sperry, 24 Sep. 1908, NA, RG 45, Confidential Ciphers Sent.

31. Mrs. M. K. Hewitt to Metcalf, 24 Sep. 1908, NA, RG 24: 6072/448.

32. *New York Times*, 27, 29 Sep. 1908.

33. Ibid., 1 Oct. 1908.

34. Hewitt correspondence and Stone diary, 30 Sep. 1908; Sperry telegram to Pillsbury, 3 Oct. 1908, NA, RG 24: 6072/465.

35. Secretary of War Wright to Metcalf, 8 Oct. 1908, and Metcalf to Wright, 10 Oct. 1908, NA, RG 24: 6072/469.

36. Stone diary, 6, 7 Oct. 1908.

37. Ibid., 7 Oct. 1908; Maxfield correspondence, 8, 9 Oct. 1908.

38. Maxfield correspondence and Stone diary, 4 Oct. 1908; Hewitt correspondence, 8 Oct. 1908; *New York Times*, 7 Oct. 1908.

39. Gleaves, *Emory*, 326; Stone diary, 9 Oct. 1908.

40. *New York Times*, 10 Oct. 1908.

41. Ibid.

42. Schroeder, *Half Century of Naval Service*, 356.

43. Maxfield correspondence, 11 Oct. 1908.

44. Maxfield correspondence and Stone diary, 12 Oct. 1908; Hewitt correspondence, 10 Oct. 1908; Schroeder, *Half Century of Naval Service*, 356-59.

45. Saufley correspondence, 20 Nov. 1908.

46. Hewitt correspondence, 16 Oct. 1908.

47. Stone diary, 12, 13 Oct. 1908; Schroeder, *Half Century of Naval Service*, 356;

Hewitt correspondence, 16 Oct. 1908; *New York Times,* 17 Oct. 1908; Sperry to secretary of the navy, no. 4837, para. 7, 17 Feb. 1909, NA, RG 45: 00.

48. Stone diary, 12 Oct. 1908.

49. *Japan Weekly Mail,* 24 Oct. 1908, byline, 16 Oct.; *New York Times,* 17 Oct. 1908; O'Brien to Root, 30 Oct. 1908, NA, RG 59: 8258/619–29; Sperry to Newberry, no. 4837, 17 Feb. 1909, NA, RG 45: 00.

50. Hart, *Great White Fleet,* 202–3, 217.

51. *Japan Weekly Mail,* 17 Oct. 1908.

52. Ibid., 28 Mar. 1908.

53. Ibid., 4 July 1908; "Japanese Navy: Fall Maneuvers, 1908," attaché report W. 128, 7 Aug. 1908, NA, RG 38: 08-655, F-9-c.

54. Maxfield correspondence, 18 Oct. 1908.

55. *Japan Weekly Mail,* 24 Oct. 1908; *New York Times,* 18 Oct. 1908. Interestingly, the *Japan Weekly Mail* reported that the protected cruiser *Soya* preceded the fleet bearing the message, "The Great White Fleet is coming." This is the first instance encountered in this research in which the Great White Fleet is used as a proper name.

56. Maxfield correspondence, 18 Oct. 1908. One of the ships, the *Riojun Maru,* carried over a thousand schoolgirls; they provided the singing Maxfield heard (*Japan Weekly Mail,* 24 Oct. 1908).

57. *New York Times,* 19 Oct. 1908.

58. Ibid.

59. *Japan Weekly Mail,* 15 Aug. 1908.

60. Ibid., 17 Oct. 1908.

61. Ibid., 1 Aug. 1908.

62. Chargé Jay (Tokyo) to Root, no. 440, 12 Sep. 1908, NA, RG 59: 8258/508-9.

63. Sperry to Denison, 19 June 1908, Sperry correspondence; H. J. Jones, *Live Machines: Hired Foreigners and Meiji Japan,* 43, 98–101.

64. Sperry to C. S. Sperry, Jr., 30 Oct. 1908, and Sperry to Denison, 19 June 1908, Sperry correspondence.

65. Ibid., Sperry to Roosevelt, 28 Oct. 1908.

66. Ibid., Roosevelt to Sperry, 21 March 1908.

67. Sperry to Roosevelt, 7 April 1908, Sperry correspondence; Roosevelt to Metcalf, NA, RG 24: 6072/676.

68. Commander in chief, Atlantic Fleet, to commanding officers, no. 2813, 19 Oct. 1908, NA, RG 45: 00.

69. Babbit to Bacon, 30 Oct. 1908, NA, RG 59: 8258/619-29.

70. *Japan Weekly Mail,* 24 Oct. 1908.

71. Maxfield correspondence and Stone diary, 18 Oct. 1908.

72. Stone diary, 18 Oct. 1908.

73. Sperry to C. S. Sperry, Jr., 30 Oct. 1908, Sperry correspondence.

74. Roosevelt telegram to Sperry, 17 Oct. 1908, NA, RG 24: 6072/472 (copy also in NA, RG 45, area 10).

75. Sperry to Roosevelt, 28 Oct. 1908, Sperry to C. S. Sperry, Jr., 30 Oct. 1908, Sperry to Edith M. Sperry, 1 Nov. 1908, and Sperry to Porter, 14 Dec. 1908, Sperry correspondence.

76. Text of emperor's reply in Sperry to Metcalf, 20 Oct. 1908, NA, RG 45, area 10.

77. Sperry to C. S. Sperry, Jr., 30 Oct. 1908, Sperry correspondence. See also Sperry to Edith M. Sperry, 1 Nov. 1908, and Sperry to Roosevelt, 28 Oct. 1908, Sperry correspondence.

78. Ibid., Sperry to Porter, 14 Dec. 1908.

79. Ibid., Sperry to Denison, 15 Oct. 1908.

80. Ibid., Sperry to Denison, 15 Oct. 1908, and Sperry to Roosevelt, 28 Oct. 1908.

81. Ibid., Sperry to Roosevelt, 28 Oct. 1908.

82. *New York Times,* 28 Nov. 1908; Sperry to C. S. Sperry, Jr., 30 Oct. 1908, Sperry correspondence.

83. Stone diary, 24 Oct. 1908.

84. Maxfield correspondence, 25 Oct. 1908.

85. Stone diary, 24 Oct. 1908.

86. *New York Times,* 28 Nov. 1908. Only $7,500 had been authorized for entertainment in New Zealand, Australia, Japan, and China (Sperry to Metcalf, no. 683, 10 June 1908, NA, RG 24: 6072/365).

87. Maxfield correspondence, 20 Oct. 1908; *New York Times,* 25 Oct. 1908.

88. Sperry to Roosevelt, 24 Oct. 1908, Sperry correspondence.

89. Ibid., Roosevelt to Sperry, 22 Oct. 1908.

90. Roosevelt to Whitelaw Reid, 4 Dec. 1908, in Morison, *Roosevelt Letters,* 6: 1411.

91. Ibid., Roosevelt to Lee, 20 Dec. 1908, 1432.

92. "Arrangement between the United States and Japan concerning their relations in the Orient," with notation, "Handed to the President by the Japanese Ambassador on Oct. 26, 1908," NA, RG 59: 16533/1.

93. *New York Times,* 1 Dec. 1908; *Japan Weekly Mail,* 5 Dec. 1908.

94. Hart, *Great White Fleet,* 235.

95. Raymond A. Esthus, review of Hart, *Great White Fleet.*

96. Sperry to Edith M. Sperry, 1 Nov. 1908, Sperry correspondence.

97. Ibid., Sperry to C. S. Sperry, Jr., 9 Jan. 1909.

98. Ibid., Sperry to Edith M. Sperry, 1 Nov. 1908.

99. Ibid., Sperry to C. S. Sperry, Jr., 9 Jan. 1909.

100. *Japan Times,* 17 Jan. 1907; *Japan Daily Mail,* 17, 19 Jan. 1907; Wright to Root, no. 148, 19 Jan. 1907, NA, RG 59: 4080/9-13. The current exchange rate was ¥ 1 = US$ 0.498.

101. O'Brien to Root, no. 154, 22 Jan. 1908, NA, RG 59: 4080/31-8.

102. Roger F. Hackett, *Yamagata Aritomo in the Rise of Modern Japan, 1838–1922,* 239; Consul-General Henry B. Miller (Yokohama) to Bacon, 22 Jan. 1908, NA, RG 59: 4080/29.

103. *Japan Weekly Mail,* 2 May 1908.

104. Esthus, *Theodore Roosevelt and Japan,* 251–52.

105. Ibid., 252, citing Takahira to Roosevelt, 20 July 1908, NA, RG 59: 2542/691-2.

106. Strauss to Root, 51931/1, 3 Oct. 1908, NA, RG 59: 2542/744-49.

107. Statistics in Strauss to Root, 51931/1, 12 Oct. 1908, NA, RG 59: 2542/756; Root telegram to American ambassador (Tokyo), 19 Oct. 1908, NA, RG 59: 2542/761.

108. New, *Uncertain Friendship,* 158.

109. James B. Crowley, "National Defense and the Consolidation of Empire." 227.

110. *Japan Weekly Mail,* 31 Oct. 1908.

111. Ibid., 14 Nov. 1908.

112. Crowley, "National Defense," 231.

113. *New York Times,* 27 July 1908.

114. Ibid.; Consul Julian A. Arnold (Amoy) to Bacon, no. 341, 6 Oct. 1908, NA, RG 59: 8258/551-2.

115. Arnold to Bacon, no. 342, 27 Nov. 1908, NA, RG 59: 8258/614-5.

116. Ibid.; *New York Times,* 18, 21 Oct. 1908.

117. Arnold to Bacon, no. 342, 27 Nov. 1908, NA, RG 59: 8258/614-5.

118. Ibid.; *New York Times,* 25 Oct. 1908.

119. *New York Times,* 26, 27 Oct. 1908.

120. Rockhill to Arnold, no. 1711, 7 Oct. 1908, NA, RG 59: 8258/614-5.

121. Rockhill to State Department, no. 986, 27 Aug. 1908, NA, RG 59: 8258/516.

122. Rogers to Pillsbury, no. 948a, 3 Oct. 1908, NA, RG 24: 6072/468, quoting Gillis to Rogers, 21 Aug. 1908.

123. Arnold to Bacon, no. 342, 27 Nov. 1908, NA, RG 59: 8258/614-5.

124. Maxfield correspondence, 30 Oct. 1908.

125. *New York Times,* 1 Nov. 1908.

126. Maxfield correspondence, 3 Nov. 1908.

127. *New York Times,* 12 Nov. 1908.

CHAPTER 13

1. *New York Times,* 27 Aug. 1907.

2. Ibid., 3 Oct. 1907.

3. Ibid., 4 Oct. 1907.

4. Ibid., 2 Dec. 1907.

5. Roosevelt, *State Papers,* 554.

6. Sprout, *Rise of American Naval Power,* 264.

7. *New York Times,* 11 Feb. 1908.

8. Ibid., 22 Feb. 1908.

9. L. W. Busby, *Uncle Joe Cannon,* 224–25.

10. *New York Times,* 15 April 1908.

11. "The United States and the World," *Spectator,* 606–7.

12. Bowers, *Beveridge and the Progressive Era,* 278.

13. *New York Times,* 22 April 1908.

14. Ibid., 23 April 1908.

15. Ibid., 24 April 1908.

16. Ibid., 25 April 1908.

17. Ibid., 26, 27 April 1908.

18. Ibid., 28 April 1908.

19. Meadows, "Eugene Hale and the American Navy," 192, quoting "The New Reporter," *Saturday Evening Post,* 180 (23 May 1908): 18–19; Bowers, *Beveridge,* 282, quoting Beveridge to George W. Perkins, 28 Apr. 1908.

20. Meadows, "Eugene Hale," 193.

21. "Circular Defining the Chief Characteristics of Battleship Nos. 28 and 29," in NA, RG 80, Records of the General Board, study 420-6.

22. Hill to Metcalf, 15 June 1907, NA, RG 80: 24667.

23. Ibid., Board on Construction endorsement to Hill's letter, 20 June 1907.

24. *New York Times,* 17 Dec. 1907.

25. Key to Sims, 10 June 1908, Sims correspondence.

26. Sims to Anne Hitchcock Sims, 23 June 1908, Sims correspondence.

27. Ibid., Sims to Roosevelt, 23 June 1908.

28. Key to Metcalf, 9 June 1908, in Newberry to General Board, 1159–212, 2 July 1908, and Dewey to Metcalf, 420–2, 11 Nov. 1908, in NA, RG 80, Records of the General Board, study 420-6.

29. Sims to Roosevelt, 23 June 1908, Sims correspondence.

30. Ibid., Sims to Anne Hitchcock Sims, 26 June 1908.

31. Metcalf to Dewey, 1159-212, 2 July 1908, in NA, RG 80, General Board Records, study 420-6.

32. Sims to Anne Hitchcock Sims, 10 July 1908, Sims correspondence.

33. Ibid., Sims to Roosevelt, 10 July 1908.

34. Ibid., Sims to Anne Hitchcock Sims, 22 July 1908, and Sims to Whittlesy, 22 July 1908.

35. *New York Times,* 23 July 1908.

36. The requirement to record and report all votes was made formal in Newberry to Morrell, 29 July 1908, NA, RG 80: 26887.

37. Sims to Anne Hitchcock Sims, 21 July 1908, Sims correspondence.

38. Morison, *Sims,* 213.

39. Ibid.; Sims to Roosevelt, 2 Aug. 1908, Sims correspondence.

40. Sims to Roosevelt, 13 Aug. 1908, Sims correspondence; Dewey to Newberry, GB 420-2, 11 Nov. 1908, NA, RG 80, General Board Records, study 420-6.

41. Sims to Anne H. Sims, 27, 28 July 1908, and to Whittlesy, 27 July 1908, Sims correspondence.

42. Ibid., Sims to Anne H. Sims, 31 July 1908.

43. Ibid.

44. Goodrich quoted in William S. Sims, "Theodore Roosevelt at Work," 100.

45. Sims to Roosevelt, 13 Aug. 1908, Sims correspondence. On 31 July 1908, the *Delaware* was 35.3% and the *North Dakota* 45.7% complete.

46. Sims to Roosevelt, 13 Aug. 1908, Sims correspondence.

47. Roosevelt telegram, 15 Aug. 1908, in Newberry to Roosevelt, 26 Aug. 1908, NA, RG 80: 26887/3.

48. Sims to Roosevelt, 8 Aug. 1908, Sims correspondence.

49. Ibid., Sims to Roosevelt, 22 Aug. 1908.

50. Bureau of Ordnance memo 22140/5, 17 Nov. 1908, NA, RG 80, General Board Records, study 420-6.

51. Sims to Roosevelt, 22 Aug. 1908, Sims correspondence; Newberry to Roosevelt, 26 Aug. 1908, NA, RG 80: 26887/3.

52. Roosevelt to Newberry, 28 Aug. 1908, Sims correspondence.

53. Dewey to Metcalf, 11 Nov. 1908, NA, RG 80, General Board Records, Study 420-6.

54. E. T. Constein to Sims, 20 Aug. 1908, Sims correspondence.

55. Ibid., Vogelgesang to Sims, 1 July 1908; Bureau of Navigation letter 2036-69, 6 July 1908, copy in Sims correspondence.

56. Schroeder to secretary of the navy, no. 3/706-WFM, 29 July 1908, Sims correspondence.

57. Ibid. See also ibid., Wainwright to Pillsbury, 228-WFD, 5 Aug. 1908.

58. Ibid., Sperry to Metcalf, no. 00-WJF, 29 Aug. 1908.

59. Ibid., Sims to Roosevelt, 30 Aug. 1908.

60. *New York Times,* 11 Oct. 1908.

61. Ibid., 9 Nov. 1908.

62. "That Newport Conference," *Scientific American,* 294.

63. "Newport Conference Approves Designs of New Battleships," *Scientific American,* 426.

64. *New York Times,* 24 Nov. 1908.

65. Ibid.

66. Ibid., 28 Nov. 1908.
67. Sims to Lieutenant Commander Whittlesy, 22 July 1908, Sims correspondence.
68. Ibid., Goodrich to Sims, 25 June 1908, and Sims to Roosevelt, 10 Aug. 1908.
69. Ibid., Roosevelt to Sims, 13 Aug. 1908.
70. Ibid., Key to Sims, 12 Nov. 1908.
71. Newberry to Roosevelt, 31 Aug. 1908, NA, RG 80: 26887/3.
72. See, for example, Luce to Sims, 29 Dec. 1908, Sims correspondence.
73. Ibid., Luce to Sims, 1 Jan. 1909.
74. Morison, *Sims,* 222–23.
75. Sims to Roosevelt, 30 Dec. 1908, Sims correspondence.
76. Department of the Navy, *Annual Report of the Secretary of the Navy, 1908,* 472.
77. Ibid.
78. Roosevelt to Newberry, 29 Dec. 1908, in Morison, *Roosevelt Letters,* 6: 1453.
79. Ibid., Roosevelt to Newberry, 2 Jan. 1909, 6: 1456.
80. Ibid., Roosevelt to Arthur H. Lee, 7 Feb. 1909, 6: 1508.
81. Ibid., 1457fn, and Roosevelt to Kermit Roosevelt, 23 Jan. 1909, 1480.
82. Ibid., Roosevelt to Mahan, 27 Jan. 1909, 1487. See also 60th Cong., 2 sess., Senate Doc. 740, 25 Feb. 1909.
83. Sixtieth Cong., 2 sess., Senate Doc. 740, 25 Feb. 1909, and Doc. 743, 27 Feb. 1909.
84. Ibid., Doc. 743, 27 Feb. 1909, 4.
85. Morison, *Roosevelt Letters,* 6: 1488fn.

Chapter 14

1. Sperry to Newberry, no. 4837, 17 Feb. 1909, NA, RG 45: 00.
2. Sperry to Pillsbury, 21 Nov. 1908, NA, RG 24: 6072/503.
3. *New York Times,* 22 Nov. 1908.
4. Sperry to Edith M. Sperry, 27 Nov. 1908, Sperry correspondence; Newberry to Sperry, 22 Nov. 1908, NA, RG 24:6072/503.
5. Sperry to Edith M. Sperry, 27 Nov. 1908, Sperry correspondence; Newberry to Sperry, 23 Nov. 1908, NA, RG 24: 6072/607.
6. Sperry to Edith M. Sperry, 27 Nov. 1908, Sperry correspondence; Sperry to Newberry, 24 Nov. 1908, NA, RG 24: 6072/503. The complete set of correspondence on granting leave is in NA, RG 24: 6072/607, "Report of Board on Advisability of Granting Leave in Manila."
7. Sperry to commanding officers, no. 3482, 25 Nov. 1908, NA, RG 45: 00.
8. Hewitt correspondence, 6 Dec. 1908.
9. Maxfield correspondence, 27 Nov. 1908.
10. Sperry to Edith M. Sperry, 27 Nov. 1908, Sperry correspondence.
11. *New York Times,* 6 March 1908.
12. Stone diary, 27 March 1908.
13. Commander Walter F. Schaller, "Naval Command at Sea: The Story of Hospital Ship *Relief* #1," 12–13.
14. Stone diary, 27 Mar. 1908, 1 Apr. 1908.
15. Milt Riske, "A History of Hospital Ships," 7.
16. Schaller, "Naval Command at Sea," 14.
17. Sperry to Edith M. Sperry, 27 Nov. 1908, Sperry correspondence.
18. Schaller, "Naval Command at Sea," 14.

19. Sperry to Edith M. Sperry, 1, 27 Nov. 1908, Sperry correspondence.

20. Ibid., Sperry to Edith M. Sperry, 1 Nov. 1908.

21. Secretary of the Navy to commander in chief, Pacific Fleet, 6118/31, 29 Oct. 1908, NA, RG 45, area 10.

22. Sperry to Edith M. Sperry, 13 Oct. [Nov.] 1908, Sperry correspondence.

23. Schaller, "Naval Command at Sea," 15, citing diary of Howard P. Strine. Understandably, this comment did not appear in Stokes's official report (Stokes to Sperry, 26 Nov. 1908, NA, RG 80: 15285).

24. Sperry to Edith M. Sperry, 27 Nov. 1908, Sperry correspondence.

25. Schaller, "Naval Command at Sea," 15.

26. Maxfield correspondence, 1 Dec. 1908; Hewitt correspondence, 6 Dec. 1908.

27. Maxfield correspondence, 6 Dec. 1908; *New York Times*, 18 Nov. 1908.

28. Maxfield correspondence, 1, 2 Dec. 1908.

29. Hewitt correspondence and Stone diary, 6 Dec. 1908; Saufley correspondence, 14 Dec. 1908.

30. Hewitt correspondence, 15 Dec. 1908.

31. Stone diary, Maxfield correspondence, and Adamson diary, 8 Dec. 1908.

32. Stone and Adamson diaries, 9 Dec. 1908; Maxfield correspondence, 12 Dec. 1908.

33. Adamson diary, 10, 11 Dec. 1908.

34. Consul William C. Teichmann (Colombo) to Bacon, no. 23, 11 Feb. 1909, NA, RG 59: 8258/693-6, Adamson diary, 12, 13, 14 Dec. 1908.

35. Saufley correspondence, 14 Dec. 1908.

36. Stone diary, 10 Dec. 1908; Maxfield correspondence, 12 Dec. 1908.

37. Maxfield correspondence, 13 Dec. 1908.

38. Sperry to commanding officers, no. 3852, 13 Dec. 1908, NA, RG 45: 00.

39. Saufley correspondence, 14 Dec. 1908. Mother Carey's chickens is nautical slang for stormy petrels.

40. Stone diary, 14 Dec. 1908.

41. Maxfield correspondence, 13 Dec. 1908.

42. Sperry to commanding officers, no. 3852, 13 Dec. 1908, NA, RG 45: 00; Teichmann to Bacon, no. 11, 14 Nov. 1908, NA, RG 59: 8258/603-4, and no. 13, 19 Nov. 1908, NA, RG 59: 8258/605-6.

43. Adamson diary, 14, 19 Dec. 1908.

44. Sperry to Pillsbury, 17 Aug. 1908, Sperry correspondence.

45. Sperry telegram to Pillsbury, 11 Sep. 1908, NA, RG 24: 6072/426.

46. Metcalf to Root, 27 Oct. 1908, NA, RG 80: 18768/89; NA, RG 59: 8258/532. The colliers arrived on 26 November and 1 and 6 December (Teichmann to Bacon, no. 14, 21 Dec. 1908, NA, RG 59: 8258/1645).

47. Stone diary, 19 Dec. 1908.

48. Hewitt correspondence, 29 Dec. 1908.

49. Stone diary, 26 Dec. 1908; Maxfield correspondence, 26 Dec. 1908.

50. Sperry to Edith M. Sperry, 1 Jan. 1909, Sperry correspondence.

51. Hart, *Great White Fleet*, 261.

52. Maxfield correspondence, 27 Dec. 1908.

53. Hewitt correspondence, 29 Dec. 1908.

54. Maxfield correspondence, Hewitt correspondence, and Adamson diary, 29 Dec. 1908.

55. Maxfield correspondence, 30 Dec. 1908.

56. Stone diary, 1 Jan. 1909.

57. Ibid., 3 Jan. 1909.

58. Metcalf to Sperry, 6072/345, 3 June 1908, NA, RG 45: 00.

59. Ibid., Sperry to Metcalf, no. 820, 16 June 1908.

60. Newberry to Sperry, 13 June 1908, NA, RG 24:6072/346.

61. Sperry to Pillsbury, 30 June 1908, Sperry correspondence.

62. Metcalf to Root, 3 Oct. 1908, NA, RG 24: 6072/455.

63. Ravndal to Bacon, no. 201, 6 Nov. 1908, NA, RG 59: 8258/574.

64. For a detailed discussion of the Young Turk movement and policies of the period, see Stanford J. Shaw and Ezel Kural Shaw, *History of the Ottoman Empire and Modern Turkey,* vol. 2, 255-80, from which this summary has been drawn.

65. Ravndal telegram to Root, 1 Nov. 1908, NA, RG 59: 8258/537.

66. Einstein to Root, 15 Nov. 1908, NA, RG 59: 8258/561.

67. Jessup to Strauss, 5 Nov. 1908, NA, RG 59: 8258/564–5.

68. Ibid., Strauss to Root, 21 Nov. 1908.

69. Newberry to Root, 4067-46, 2 Dec. 1908, NA, RG 59: 8258/586.

70. Newberry to Root, 4 Dec. 1908, NA, RG 59: 8258/591.

71. Newberry to Sperry, 15 Dec. 1908, NA, RG 45, Ciphers Sent; Newberry to Root, 6072/523, 15 Dec. 1908, NA, RG 59: 8258/600.

72. Coffin to Bacon, no. 12, 23 Oct. 1908, NA, RG 59: 8258/542; Newberry to Root, 17 Nov. 1908, 6072/496, NA, RG 59: 8258/560.

73. Newberry to Root, 6072/496, 19 Nov. 1908, and Carr to Coffin, 28 Nov. 1908, NA, RG 59: 8258/562; Newberry to Sperry, 17 Nov. 1908, NA, RG 45, Ciphers Sent; Sperry telegram to Bureau of Navigation, 19 Nov. 1908, NA, RG 45, area 10.

74. American legation (Athens), no. 59, 20 Oct. 1908, NA, RG 59: 8258/558; Newberry to Root, 6072/497, 20 Nov. 1908, NA, RG 59: 8258/563.

75. Sperry to Edith M. Sperry, 18 Dec. 1908, Sperry correspondence; Sperry to Pillsbury, 31 Dec. 1908, NA, RG 45, area 10.

76. Sperry to C. S. Sperry, Jr., 9 Jan. 1909, Sperry correspondence; Newberry telegram to Sperry, 4 Jan. 1909, NA, RG 24: 6072/536; *New York Times,* 4 Jan. 1909.

77. Newberry telegram to Sperry, 4 Jan. 1909, NA, RG 24: 6072/536.

78. Sperry to C. S. Sperry, Jr., 9 Jan. 1909, Sperry correspondence.

79. Iddings telegram to Root, 29 Dec. 1908, NA, RG 59: 8258/608.

80. Sperry telegram to Bureau of Navigation, 2 Jan. 1909, NA, RG 24:6072/562.

81. Iddings to Bacon, no. 424, 22 Jan. 1909, NA, RG 59: 8258/665; Potter to Newberry, 13 Jan. 1909, in Newberry to Root, 6072/597, 30 Jan. 1909, NA, RG 59: 8258/651-2.

82. Sperry to Edith M. Sperry, 4 Jan. 1909, Sperry correspondence.

83. Stone diary, Adamson diary, and Maxfield correspondence, 6 Jan. 1909.

84. Maxfield correspondence and Stone diary, 6 Jan. 1909.

85. Stone diary, 7 Jan. 1909.

86. Maxfield correspondence, 7 Jan. 1909.

87. Stone diary, 4 Jan. 1909.

88. Ibid., 8 Jan. 1909.

89. Maxfield correspondence, 9 Jan. 1909.

90. Stone diary, 9 Jan. 1909.

91. Sperry to C. S. Sperry, Jr., 6 Jan. 1909, Sperry correspondence.

92. Ibid., Sperry to Edith M. Sperry, 11 Jan. 1909, and Sperry to C. S. Sperry, Jr., 17 Jan. 1909.

93. *New York Times,* 11 Jan. 1909.

94. Sperry telegram to Bureau of Navigation, 11 Jan. 1909, NA, RG 24: 6072/559.

95. Sperry to Edith M. Sperry, 20 Jan. 1909, Sperry correspondence; *New York Times,* 20 Jan. 1909.

96. *New York Times,* 7, 15 Jan. 1909; Maxfield correspondence, 13 Jan. 1909.

97. Maxfield correspondence, 15 Jan. 1909.

98. Ibid., 18 Jan. 1909.

99. Sperry to Edith M. Sperry, 22 Jan. 1909, Sperry correspondence.

100. Huse to Newberry, 16 April 1909, NA, RG 45, area 4.

101. Willoughby, *Yankton,* 129.

102. Assistant chief of the Bureau of Navigation to Lieutenant Commander C. B. McVay, 6392/80, 31 March 1911, McVay correspondence.

103. *New York Times,* 6 Jan. 1909; Ravndal telegram to Sperry, 6 Jan. 1909, in Ravndal to Bacon, no. 224, 9 Jan. 1909, NA, RG 59: 8258/653-7.

104. Ravndal to Bacon, no. 224, 9 Jan. 1909, NA, RG 59: 8258/653-7.

105. *New York Herald* (Paris edition), 7 Jan. 1909.

106. Pearson telegram to Root, 18 Jan. 1909, NA, RG 59: 8258/639.

107. *Proine* (Athens), 7 Jan. 1909.

108. E. E. Young to Bacon, no. 17, 22 Jan. 1909, NA, RG 59: 8258/664.

109. *New York Times,* 23, 25 Jan. 1909.

110. Einstein telegram to Root, 2 Jan. 1909, NA, RG 59: 8258/611.

111. Newberry to Root, 6072/542, 5 Jan. 1909, NA, RG 59: 8258/618.

112. *New York Times,* 19 Jan. 1909.

113. Einstein to Root, 2 Jan. 1909, NA, RG 59: 8258/611.

114. Ibid., Newberry to Root, 6072/542, 5 Jan. 1909.

115. Root telegram to American embassy (Constantinople), 9 Jan. 1909, NA, RG 59: 8258/618.

116. Einstein telegram to Root, 11 Jan. 1909, NA, RG 59: 8258/632.

117. *New York Times,* 19, 24 Jan. 1909.

118. Ibid., 15 Jan. 1909.

119. Potter to Newberry, 21 Jan. 1909, NA, RG 45, area 4; Gale to Bacon, no. 8, 23 Jan. 1909, NA, RG 59: 8258/662-3.

120. Maxfield correspondence, 19 Jan. 1909.

121. Ibid., 22, 28, 29, 30 Jan. 1909.

122. Horace Lee Washington to Bacon, 16 Jan. 1909, NA, RG 59: 8258/649.

123. *New York Times,* 17 Jan. 1909.

124. Washington to Bacon, 29 Jan. 1909, NA, RG 59: 8258/668.

125. *New York Times,* 27 Jan., 1 Feb. 1909.

126. Newberry to Sperry, 9 Jan. 1909, NA, RG 45, Ciphers Sent.

127. Adamson diary, 27 Jan. 1909.

128. *New York Times,* 31 Jan. 1909.

129. Adamson diary, 30 Jan. 1909; *New York Times,* 31 Jan. 1909; Gummeré to Root, no. 415, 1 Feb. 1909, NA, RG 59: 8258/619.

130. Adamson diary, 30 January 1909.

131. *New York Times,* 1 Feb. 1909.

132. Cummings, *Wainwright,* 191.

133. The court-martial board was comprised of Rear Admiral Schroeder and Potter and five captains (*New York Times,* 3, 4 Feb. 1909).

134. Ibid., 4 Feb. 1909.

135. Ibid., 5 Feb. 1909.

136. Upon his arrival in the United States, Qualtrough successfully appealed the decision (Cummings, *Wainright*, 191).

137. *New York Times*, 1, 20, 24, 25 Jan. 1909; Newberry telegram to Sperry, 23 Jan. 1909, NA, RG 24: 6072/585.

138. *New York Times*, 25 Jan. 1909; Consul Washington to Bacon, 29 Jan. 1909, NA, RG 45, area 4.

139. *New York Times*, 1 Feb. 1909.

140. Adamson diary, 31 Jan. 1909; *New York Times*, 1 Feb. 1909.

141. *New York Times*, 2 Feb. 1909.

142. Stone diary, 1 Feb. 1909.

143. *New York Times*, 2 Feb. 1909.

144. Maxfield correspondence, 3 Feb. 1909.

145. Ibid., 6 Feb. 1909.

146. *New York Times*, 7 Feb. 1909.

147. Stone diary, 6 Feb. 1909.

148. Maxfield correspondence, 7–10, 14 Feb. 1909; *New York Times*, 18 Feb. 1909; Stone diary, 15 Feb. 1909.

149. *New York Times*, 13 Feb. 1909.

150. Stone diary, 12 Feb. 1909.

151. Arnold to secretary of the navy, 31 May 1909, NA, RG 45: 00.

152. Arnold to secretary of the navy, no. 95-AE, 4 March 1909, NA, RG 45: 00. The *Salem* joined the fleet shortly after the battleships, the *Chester* on 18 February, the *North Carolina* and *Montana* on the night of 20–21 February, and the *Birmingham* on 21 February.

153. *New York Times*, 26 Oct. 1908.

154. Maxfield correspondence, 17 Feb. 1909; Stone diary, 17 Feb. 1909.

155. Adamson, "Log and Diary of Cruise Around the World," undated recollections at end.

156. *New York Times*, 10 Feb. 1909.

157. Newberry telegram to Sperry, 18 Jan. 1909, NA, RG 24: 6072/576.

158. Sperry telegram to Newberry, 22 Jan. 1909, NA, RG 24: 6072/583.

159. Stone diary, 20–22 Feb. 1909.

160. *New York Times*, 21, 22 Feb. 1909.

161. Ibid., 22 Feb. 1909.

162. Ibid., 23 Feb. 1909.

163. Ibid.

164. Ibid.

165. Ibid.; Roosevelt, *Autobiography*, 624–25.

166. Stone diary, 22 Feb. 1909.

167. *New York Times*, 24 Feb. 1909.

Chapter 15

1. Braisted, "The United States Navy's Dilemma," 242.

2. Small, "The American Image of Germany," 95–96; Braisted, *United States Navy in the Pacific*, 239.

3. Sperry to Roosevelt, 12 Sep. 1908, Sperry correspondence.

4. "Australian Problems," *Spectator*, 352.

5. Meaney, *The Search for Security in the Pacific*, 167.

NOTES

6. *New York Times*, 14 Jan. 1909.

7. "The Return of the Fleet," *Outlook*, 425.

8. *Asahi Shimbun*, 25 Feb. 1909.

9. *Jiji Shimpo*, 25 Feb. 1909.

10. Sperry to C. S. Sperry, Jr., 9 Feb. 1908, Sperry correspondence.

11. *New York Times*, 24 Feb. 1909.

12. "The Cruise of the Atlantic Fleet," undated, unsigned, Harry E. Yarnell papers, 6.

13. Sperry to Metcalf, 27 Jan. 1908, Sperry correspondence.

14. "The Cruise of the Atlantic Fleet," Yarnell papers, 8.

15. *New York Times*, 15 March 1909.

16. Sperry to Porter, 14 Dec. 1908, Sperry correspondence

17. "The Cruise of the Atlantic Fleet," Yarnell papers, 13.

18. "Cruise of the Atlantic Fleet," undated, Sperry correspondence.

19. "Lessons and Results of the Battleship Cruise," *Scientific American*, 146.

20. Challener, *Admirals, Generals and American Foreign Policy*, 40.

21. "The Cruise of the Atlantic Fleet," Yarnell papers, 3.

22. Sperry to Newberry, no. 4165, 4 Jan. 1909, NA, RG 24: 6072/583.

23. Winthrop L. Marvin, "Greatest Naval Cruise," 462.

24. "The United States Fleet," *Spectator*, 218–19.

25. "Lessons and Results of the Battleship Cruise," *Scientific American*, 146.

26. *Annual Report of the Secretary of the Navy, 1908*, 7.

27. Sims to Roosevelt, 30 April 1910, Sims correspondence.

28. These senior officers were officially designated "aids," not "aides."

29. Sims to Roosevelt, 30 April 1910, Sims correspondence.

30. Quoted in Morison, *Sims*, 214, and Cummings, *Wainwright*, 221.

31. Charles Edward Jefferson, "The Delusion of Militarism," 379.

Bibliography

UNPUBLISHED GOVERNMENT DOCUMENTS

U.S. National Archives. Record Group 24. Bureau of Navigation General Correspondence, 1903–13. File 6072. General Correspondence, World Cruise of the Battleship Fleet.
    ———. Record Group 38. Intelligence Division, Naval Attaché Reports, 1886–1939.
———. Record Group 45. Bureau of Navigation Correspondence. SecNav Confidential Ciphers Sent. Vol. 3, 17 Sep. 1906–18 Jan. 1910. SecNav Confidential Ciphers Received. Vol. 4, 6 Jan. 1905–18 May 1909. SecNav Confidential Letters Received, Vol. 4, 16 June 1904–16 Oct. 1908.
———. Record Group 45. Area Files of the Naval Record Collection, 1775–1910. Area 4, Eastern Atlantic, Southeastern Atlantic, Mediterranean. Area 8, Caribbean. Area 9, Eastern Pacific. Area 10, Western Pacific, Australasia, Indian Ocean.
———. Record Group 59. General Records of the Department of State: Numerical and Minor Files, 1906–10. File 2542, Japanese Immigration. File 3892, Kingston, Jamaica, Earthquake. File 4001, Kingston, Jamaica, Earthquake. File 4080, Financial Policy of Japan. File 8258, World Cruise of the Battleship Fleet. File 10799, Precautions for Safety of the Fleet. File 12611, Relations Between the United States and Japan. File 16533, Root-Takahira Negotiations.
———. Record Group 80. General Records of the Navy Department: General Correspondence, 1897–1915. File 15285, USS *Relief.* File 18768, Bureau of Equipment Correspondence: Shipping Coal in Foreign Ships. File 20392, Post-Cruise Repairs. File 22328, Painting of Naval Vessels. File 24667, Relative Distribution of Waterline Armor on Battleships (especially nos. 28 and 29). File 25107, Atlantic Fleet: Supply of Coal While in Eastern Waters. File 26000, Comments on Alleged Defects, Waterline Armor, Freeboard, etc. File 26887, Newport Conference.
———. Record Group 80. General Records of the Navy Department and Records of the General Board of the Navy. Proceedings, 1900–12. Letterbooks, 1904–10. Studies.
Naval History Division, Operational Archives, Washington, D.C. War portfolios 1, 2, and 3.

BIBLIOGRAPHY

Marine Corps History Center, Washington, D.C. Muster Roll of Officers and Enlisted Men of the U.S. Marine Corps on Board USS *Louisiana,* Feb. 1908.

Published Government Documents

U.S. Congress. House. *Letter from the Secretary of the Navy Transmitting Letters, etc., Relating to the Appointment of Surgeon Charles F. Stokes to Command of the Hospital Ship Relief . . . etc.* 60th Cong., 1st sess. H. Doc. 553.

———. Senate. *Message from the President Transmitting Two Preliminary Reports of the Commission Appointed to Consider Certain Needs of the Navy.* 60th Cong., 2d sess. S. Doc. 740.

———. *Message from the President Transmitting the Final Report of the Commission on Naval Reorganization with Accompanying Letter from Mr. Justice Moody.* 60th Cong., 2nd sess. S. Doc. 743.

U.S. Department of the Navy. *Alleged Structural Defects in Battleships.* Washington: GPO, 1908.

———. *Annual Report of the Secretary of the Navy, 1907, 1908,* and *1909.* Washington: GPO, 1907, 1908, 1909.

———. Bureau of Navigation. *Information Relative to the Voyage of the United States Atlantic Fleet Around the World, December 16, 1907 to February 22, 1909.* Washington: GPO, 1910.

———. Bureau of Navigation. *Men on Board Ships of the Atlantic Fleet Bound for the Pacific December 16, 1907: With Home Addresses in the United States.* Washington: GPO, 1908.

U.S. Department of State. *Foreign Relations of the United States, 1907, 1908,* and *1909.* Washington: GPO, 1910.

Great Britain. *British Documents on the Origins of the War, 1898–1914.* Vol. 8, *Arbitration, Neutrality and Security.* Gooch, G. P. and Harold Temperley, eds. London: HMSO, 1932.

Jamaica. *Correspondence Relating to the Resignation by Sir A. Swettenham of His Office as Governor of Jamaica.* London: HMSO, 1907.

New Zealand. *Parliamentary Debates.* Wellington: GPO, 1907, 1908.

Unpublished Works

Adamson, Archa A. "Log and Diary of Cruise Around the World, 1906–1910. USS *Georgia,* Flagship 2nd Division, Atlantic Fleet." Navy Department Library, MIC 66-B.

Braden, Charles Johnson. Correspondence. Illinois State Historical Society Library.

Cheevers, James W. "Henry Reuterdahl." Unpublished, n.d., U.S. Naval Academy Museum.

Costello, Commander Daniel J. "Planning for War: A History of the General Board of the Navy." Ph.D. diss., Fletcher School of Law and Diplomacy, 1968.

Emory, Rear Admiral William Hemsley. Correspondence. Library of Congress.

Hewitt, Admiral H. Kent. Correspondence. Naval Historical Foundation.

McNeeley, Robert Whitehead. Correspondence. South Caroliniana Library, University of South Carolina.

Maxfield, Midshipman Louis. Correspondence. Cathcart Family Papers, Minnesota Historical Society.

Mustin, Henry C. Papers. Library of Congress.

Reckner, James R. " 'Stars and Stripes, If You Please . . . ': New Zealand and the Great

BIBLIOGRAPHY

White Fleet." Master's research essay, University of Auckland, 1983. Copy in Navy Department Library.

Roosevelt, Theodore. Correspondence. Library of Congress.

Saufley, Midshipman Caswell. Correspondence. Part of Sallie (Rowan) Saufley Papers, M2867, Southern Historical Collection, University of North Carolina at Chapel Hill.

Sims, Admiral William Snowden. Correspondence. Library of Congress.

Small, Melvin. "The American Image of Germany, 1906–1914." Ph.D. diss., University of Michigan, 1965.

Sperry, Rear Admiral Charles Stillman. Correspondence. Library of Congress.

Stone, Eugene Potter. Diary. Naval History Division, Navy Department.

Thomas, Rear Admiral Charles Mitchell. Correspondence. Library of Congress.

Walser, John R. "France's Search for a Battlefleet: French Naval Policy, 1898–1914." Ph.D. diss., University of North Carolina at Chapel Hill, 1976.

Yarnell, Admiral Harry E. Diaries and Papers. Naval History Division, Navy Department.

BOOKS

Around the World with the Fleet, 1907–1909: A Pictorial Log of the Cruise. Annapolis: Naval Institute Press, 1929.

Bailey, Thomas A. *Theodore Roosevelt and the Japanese-American Crises.* Stanford: Leland Stanford Jr. University, 1934.

Barr, J. *The Ports of Auckland: A Souvenir of the Jubilee of the Auckland Harbour Board, 1871–1921.* Auckland: United Press, 1926.

Beale, Howard K. *Theodore Roosevelt and the Rise of America to World Power.* Baltimore: Johns Hopkins Press, 1956.

Bowers, Claude G. *Beveridge and the Progressive Era.* New York: Literary Guild, 1932.

Braisted, William Reynolds. *The United States Navy in the Pacific, 1897–1909.* Austin: University of Texas Press, 1958.

Busby, L. W. *Uncle Joe Cannon.* New York, 1927.

Carter, S. *The Incredible Great White Fleet.* New York: Collier's Press, 1971.

Challener, Richard D. *Admirals, Generals, and American Foreign Policy, 1898–1914.* Princeton: Princeton University Press, 1973.

Clinard, Outen James. *Japan's Influence on American Naval Power.* Berkeley: University of California Press, 1947.

Crowley, James B. "Creation of an Empire, 1896–1910," and "National Defense and the Consolidation of Empire, 1907–13." In Jon Livingston, Joe Moore, and Felicia Oldfather, comps., *The Japan Reader.* Vol. 1, *Imperial Japan, 1800–1945.* New York: Pantheon, 1973.

Cummings, Captain Damon E. *Admiral Richard Wainwright and the United States Fleet.* Washington: GPO, 1962.

Davis, George Theron. *A Navy Second to None.* New York: Harcourt, Brace, 1940.

Department of Defence. Navy. *An Outline of Australian Naval History.* Canberra: Australian Government Printing Service, 1976.

Esthus, Raymond A. *Theodore Roosevelt and the International Rivalries.* Waltham, Massachusetts: Ginn-Blaisdell, 1970.

———. *Theodore Roosevelt and Japan.* Seattle: University of Washington Press, 1966.

Evans, Rear Admiral Robley D. *An Admiral's Log: Being Continued Recollections of Naval Life.* New York: Appleton, 1910.

Falk, Edwin A. *Fighting Bob Evans.* New York: Cape and Smith, 1931.

BIBLIOGRAPHY

Falk, Edwin A. *From Perry to Pearl Harbor: The Struggle for Supremacy in the Pacific.* Garden City: Doubleday, Doran, 1943.

Fiske, Rear Admiral Bradley A. *From Midshipman to Rear Admiral.* London: T. Werner Laurie, 1919.

Gemzell, Carl-Axel. *Organization, Conflict and Innovation: A Study of German Naval Strategic Planning, 1888–1940.* Lund, Sweden: Esselte Studium, 1973.

Gleaves, Rear Admiral Albert, ed. *The Life of an American Sailor: Rear Admiral William Hemsley Emory, United States Navy: From His Letters and Memoirs.* New York: Doran, 1923.

Gordon, Bernard K. *New Zealand Becomes a Pacific Power.* Chicago: University of Chicago Press, 1960.

Gordon, Donald C. *The Dominion Partnership in Imperial Defense, 1870–1914.* Baltimore: Johns Hopkins Press, 1965.

Griswold, A. Whitney. *The Far Eastern Policy of the United States.* New Haven: Yale University Press, 1962.

Hackett, Roger F. *Yamagata Aritomo in the Rise of Modern Japan, 1838–1922.* Cambridge: Harvard University Press, 1971.

Harrod, Frederick S. *Manning the New Navy: The Development of a Modern Naval Enlisted Force, 1899–1940.* Westport, Connecticut: Greenwood Press, 1978.

Hart, Robert A. *The Great White Fleet: Its Voyage Around the World, 1907–1909.* Boston: Little, Brown, 1965.

Herwig, Holger H. *"Luxury" Fleet: The Imperial German Navy, 1888–1918.* London: Allen and Unwin, 1980.

Hooper, Vice Admiral Edwin B. *The Navy Department: Evolution and Fragmentation.* Washington: NHF, 1978.

Iriye, Akira. *Pacific Estrangement: Japanese and American Expansion, 1897–1911.* Cambridge: Harvard University Press, 1972.

Johnson, Robert Erwin. *Thence Round Cape Horn: The Story of United States Naval Forces on Pacific Station, 1818–1923.* Annapolis: Naval Institute Press, 1963.

Jones, H. J. *Live Machines: Hired Foreigners and Meiji Japan.* Vancouver: University of British Columbia Press, 1980.

Jones, Robert D. *With the American Fleet from the Atlantic to the Pacific.* Seattle: Harrison, 1908.

La Nauze, J. A. *Alfred Deakin: A Biography.* 2 vols. Melbourne: Melbourne University Press, 1965.

Lissington, M. P. *New Zealand and Japan, 1900-1941.* Wellington: A. R. Shearer, 1972.

——. *New Zealand and the United States, 1840–1944.* Wellington: A. R. Shearer, 1972.

Lowe, Peter. *Great Britain and Japan, 1911–1915: A Study in Far Eastern Policy.* London: Macmillan, 1969.

Marder, Arthur J. *The Anatomy of British Sea Power: A History of Naval Policy in the Pre-Dreadnought Era, 1880–1905.* Hamden, Connecticut: Archon, 1964.

——, ed. *Fear God and Dread Nought: The Correspondence of Admiral of the Fleet Lord Fisher of Kilverstone.* 2 vols. London: Jonathan Cape, 1956.

——. *From Dreadnought to Scapa Flow: The Royal Navy in the Fisher Era, 1904–1919.* London: Oxford University Press, 1961.

Matthews, Franklin, *With the Battlefleet: Cruise of the Sixteen Battleships of the United States Atlantic Fleet from Hampton Roads to the Golden Gate, December 1907–May 1908.* New York: B. W. Huebsch, 1908.

——. *Back to Hampton Roads: Cruise of the United States Atlantic Fleet from San*

BIBLIOGRAPHY

Francisco to Hampton Roads, July 7, 1908–February 22, 1909. New York: B. W. Huebsch, 1909.

Meaney, Neville. *The Search for Security in the Pacific, 1901–14.* Sydney: Sydney University Press, 1976.

Miller, Chief Turret Captain Roman J. *Around the World with the Battleships.* 3rd ed. Chicago: A. C. McClurg, 1910.

Morison, Elting E. *Admiral Sims and the Modern American Navy.* Boston: Houghton Mifflin, 1942.

———, ed. *The Letters of Theodore Roosevelt.* 8 vols. Cambridge: Harvard University Press, 1951–54.

Naval Historical Foundation. *The Resignation of Admiral Brownson.* Washington: NHF, 1976.

Neu, Charles. *An Uncertain Friendship: Theodore Roosevelt and Japan, 1906–1909.* Cambridge: Harvard University Press, 1967.

Nish, Ian H. *The Anglo-Japanese Alliance: The Diplomacy of Two Island Empires, 1894–1915.* London: Athlone, 1966.

O'Gara, Gordon Carpenter. *Theodore Roosevelt and the Rise of the Modern Navy.* Princeton: Princeton University Press, 1943.

Peterson, Harold F. *Argentina and the United States, 1810–1964.* New York: State University of New York, 1964.

Reilly, John C., Jr., and Robert L. Scheina. *American Battleships, 1886–1923: Pre-Dreadnought Design and Construction.* Annapolis: Naval Institute Press, 1980.

Roosevelt, Theodore. *An Autobiography.* New York: Scribner's, 1925.

———. *State Papers as Governor and President, 1899–1909.* New York: Scribner's, 1925.

Schaller, Commander Walter F. *United States Naval Hospital Ships.* Washington: NIIF, 1973.

Schroeder, Rear Admiral Seaton. *A Half Century of Naval Service.* New York: Appleton, 1922.

Shaw, Stanford J., and Ezel Karal Shaw. *History of the Ottoman Empire and Modern Turkey.* Vol. 2, *Reform, Revolution, and Republic: The Rise of Modern Turkey, 1808–1975.* Cambridge: Harvard University Press, 1977.

Sprout, Harold and Margaret. *The Rise of American Naval Power, 1776–1918.* Princeton: Princeton University Press, 1944.

Steinberg, Johnathan. *Yesterday's Deterrent: Tirpitz and the Birth of the German Navy, 1888–1918.* London: Macdonald, 1965.

Stuart, Graham H., and James L. Tigner. *Latin America and the United States.* 6th ed. Englewood Cliffs, New Jersey: Prentice-Hall, 1975.

Taylor, T. D. *New Zealand's Naval Story.* Wellington: A. H. and A. W. Reed, 1948.

White, John A. *The Diplomacy of the Russo-Japanese War.* Princeton: Princeton University Press, 1964.

Willoughby, Malcolm F. *"Yankton": Yacht and Man-of-War.* Cambridge: Crimson, 1935.

ARTICLES

"Admiral Evans and the Armor Belt Problem." *Outlook* 88 (4 April 1908): 758.

"Admiral Evans on Naval Armor." *Literary Digest* 36, no. 14 (4 April 1908).

"Admiral Evans's Report on the Needs of Our Ships." *Scientific American* 98 (13 June 1908): 422–23.

"America and the Command of the Sea." *Spectator* 102 (22 May 1909): 804–5.

204

BIBLIOGRAPHY

"The American Fleet at Melbourne." *Collier's Magazine* 42, no. 5 (24 October 1908): 4.
"The American Fleet in Australia." *American Review of Reviews* (Aug. 1908): 150.
"The American Pacific Fleet." *Spectator* 99 (21 December 1907): 1037–38.
Andrews, Lieutenant Commander Philip. "As the Executive Officer Saw It." *Harper's Weekly* 52, no. 2678 (18 April 1908): 12.
———. "From Whites to Blue: The Changes of Clime and Clothes with the Fleet." *Harper's Weekly* 52, no. 2679 (25 April 1908): 10–11.
———. "With the Fleet: Whiling Away the Endless Miles and Hours." *Harper's Weekly* 52, no. 2674, (21 March 1908): 20–21.
"Answers to *The Navy*'s Criticisms of Our Fleet." *The Navy* 1, no. 8 (August 1907): 12–15.
"Australian Problems." *Spectator* 101 (12 Sep. 1908): 352.
Bailey, Thomas A. "The Root-Takahira Agreement of 1908." *PHR* 9, no. 1 (March 1940): 19–36.
———. "The World Cruise of the American Battleship Fleet." *PHR* 1 (December 1932): 389–423.
Barnes, James. "Robley D. Evans, Rear Admiral." *Outlook* 87, no. 12 (23 November 1907): 674–86.
Barry, Richard D. "One Night with the Big Fleet: An Incident of the Great Cruise." *Cosmopolitan* 46 (March 1908): 460–65.
"The Battleship Fleet in Australian Waters." *Collier's Magazine* 42, no. 3 (10 October 1908): 16–17.
"The Battleship Fleet in Japan." *Collier's Magazine* 42, no. 10 (28 November 1908): 16–17.
"Battleship Fleet to the Pacific." *Independent* 63 (11 July 1907): 57.
"Battleship *Georgia* Disaster." *Scientific American* 97 (27 July 1907): 58.
"The Battleships That Are Going to the Pacific." *Literary Digest* 35, no. 18 (2 November 1907).
"A Beautiful Sea Spectacle: The Argentine Squadron and the Fleet." *Outlook* 78 (28 March 1908): 667–68.
"Behind the Guns in Magdalena Bay." *Harper's Weekly* 52, no. 2679 (25 April 1908): 14.
Bellairs, Carlyon. "The Impending Naval Crisis." *National Review* 50 (1908): 308–17.
Benjamin, Park. "The Prevention of Battleship Disasters." *Independent* 63 (18 July 1907): 190–93.
———. "Warships as Playthings." *Independent* 64 (2 April 1908): 737–40.
Braisted, William Reynolds. "The United States Navy's Dilemma in the Pacific, 1906–1909." *PHR* 26 (1957): 235–44.
Brooks, Sydney. "The Real 'Pacific Question'." *Harper's Weekly* 51, no. 2651 (12 October 1907): 1484.
———. "The Voyage of the American Fleet." *Fortnightly Review* 83 (1908): 201–15.
Buell, R. L. "The Development of Anti-Japanese Agitation in the United States." *Political Science Quarterly* 37 (December 1922): 605–38.
Chay, Jongsuk. "The Taft-Katsura Memorandum Reconsidered." *PHR* 37 (1968): 321–26.
"China's Welcome to the Fleet." *Collier's* 42, no. 15 (2 February 1909).
"Coaling the Pacific Fleet with Foreign Ships." *Literary Digest* 35, no. 15 (12 October 1907): 514–15.
Coleman, Peter J. "New Zealand Liberalism and the Origins of the American Welfare State." *JAH* 69, no. 2 (September 1982): 372–91.
"Composition of the Fleet Which Sailed Around the World." *Scientific American* 100 (22 Feb. 1909): 156.

BIBLIOGRAPHY

"Condition of the Battleships After the Long Cruise." *Scientific American* 100 (22 May 1909): 386.

"A Costly Naval Experiment." *Litarary Digest* 31 (21 October 1905): 562.

Crafts, H. A. "American Docking Facilities on the Pacific Coast." *Cassier's Magazine* 33, no. 5 (March 1908): 555–59.

"Criticisms of Our Navy Answered." *Literary Digest* 36, no. 6 (8 February 1908): 176–78.

"The Cruise of Our Battleships to the Pacific." *Scientific American* 97 (7 September 1907): 162.

"The Cruise of the American Fleet to the Pacific." *Living Age* 255 (16 November 1907): 440–42.

"The Cruise of the American Fleet to the Pacific." *Spectator* 99 (12 October 1907): 517–18.

"The Cruise of the Atlantic Fleet: A Condensed Log of the Cruise." *The Navy* 3, no. 3 (March 1909): 8–10.

"The Cruise of the Battlefleet." *Outlook* 87 (21 December 1907): 839–40.

"The Cruise of the Great Fleet." *Cassier's Magazine* 40, no. 11 (7 December 1907): 16–17.

Davis, Captain Henry C. "The Dawn Comes Up Like Thunder: Magdalena Bay." *Harper's Weekly* 52, no. 2679 (25 April 1908): 11–12.

———. "The First Page of the Battle Fleet's Log." *Harper's Weekly* 52, no. 2665 (18 January 1908): 10–13.

———. "Leaves from the Log." *Harper's Weekly* 52, no. 2671 (29 February 1908): 16–17.

———. "Reaping the Honors: With the Fleet on Its Triumphal Return to the United States After Its 14,000-Mile Cruise." *Harper's Weekly* 52, no. 2682 (16 May 1908): 16.

"A Defense of the Naval Bureaucracy." *Literary Digest* 38, no. 2 (9 January 1909): 43–44.

"The Departure of the Fleet." *Independent* 63 (26 December 1907): 1521–23.

Dunn, Robert. "Crossing the Line with the Fleet." *Harper's Weekly* 52, no. 2670 (22 February 1908): 10–12.

———. "The End of the Voyage." *Harper's Weekly* 52, no. 2686 (13 June 1908): 13.

———. "On Liberty: Adventures in a Friendly Port with the Shore Patrol During the Homecoming Run of the Battleship Fleet." *Harper's Weekly* 52, no. 2681 (9 May 1908): 13–16.

———. "Through the Straits of Magellan." *Harper's Weekly* 52, no. 2678 (18 April 1908): 10–12.

———. "The Work and Play of the Fleet." *Harper's Weekly* 52, no. 2666 (25 January 1908): 10–12.

"End of the Battleship Cruise." *Current Literature* 46 (March 1909): 238–43.

"La escuadra norteamericana en aquas chileanas." Zigzag 156 (16 February 1908).

Estep. H. Cole. "The Position and Equipment of the Puget Sound Navy Yard." *Engineering Magazine* 33, no. 5 (August 1907): 753–65.

Esthus, Raymond A. Review of Robert A. Hart's *Great White Fleet.* In *JAH* 53, no. 1 (June 1966): 151.

———. "The Taft-Katsura Agreement: Reality or Myth?" *IMH* 31 (1959): 46–51.

"The Ethics of Criticism." *Scientific American* 99 (5 December 1908): 392.

"European Expert Opinion on the Pacific Cruise." *Literary Digest* 35, no. 26 (28 December 1907): 979.

"Evolutions in Sydney Harbor." *Current Literature* 45 (October 1908): 369–73.

"An Expert View of the Cruise." *Outlook* (21 December 1907): 840–41.

"The Fleet at Honolulu." *Cassier's Magazine* 41, no. 22 (22 August 1908): 10.

"The Fleet Enroute to Japan." *American Review of Reviews* (October 1908): 411.

BIBLIOGRAPHY

"The Fleet in Australian Waters." *American Review of Reviews* (September 1908): 275–76.

"The Fleet in Home Ports." *American Review of Reviews* 37 (May 1908): 529.

"The Fleet in South American Waters." *American Review of Reviews* 37 (February 1908): 147.

"The Fleet in the Pacific." *Current Literature* 44 (May 1908): 476–77.

"The Fleet's Return." *Literary Digest* 38, no. 9 (27 February 1909): 326–27.

"The Fleet's Triumphs." *World's Work* 16, no. 1 (October 1908): 10743–44.

"The Fleet to Visit Japan." *Literary Digest* 36, no. 13 (28 March 1908): 430–31.

"Gagging an Admiral." *Army and Navy Journal* 45 (11 January 1908): 491.

Gordon, Donald C. "Roosevelt's 'Smart Yankee Trick.' " *PHR* 30 (1961): 351–58.

"A Grave Indictment of Our Navy." *Literary Digest* 35 (1907): 971–73.

Hale, William Harlan. "Thus Spoke the Kaiser: The Lost Interview Which Solves an International Mystery." *Atlantic Monthly* 153, no. 5 (May 1934): 513–23.

Hall, Luella J. "The Abortive German-American-Chinese Entente of 1907–8." *JMH* 1, no. 2 (June 1929): 219–35.

Hazeltine, Mayo W. "Would England Side with Japan Against the United States?" *North American Review* 183 (1907): 1280–84.

Heffron, Paul T. "Secretary Moody and Naval Administrative Reform, 1902–1904." *American Neptune* 29 (1969): 30–53.

Hewitt, Admiral H. Kent. "The Around the World Cruise, December 1907–February 1909." *Shipmate* 21, no. 7 (July 1958): 12–13, and no. 8 (Aug. 1958): 2–3.

Hobson, Captain Richmond Pearson. "America Mistress of the Sea." *North American Review* 175 (October 1902): 544–57.

"How Chile Received Our Fleet." *American Review of Reviews* 37 (May 1908): 609–10.

"How Japan Regards the United States." *Harper's Weekly* 51, no. 2657 (23 November 1907): 1715–16.

Howland, H. J. "The Return of the Fleet." *Outlook* 91 (27 February 1909): 424–26, and 91 (6 March 1909): 541–47.

"How Our Pacific Cruise Looks to Europe." *Literary Digest* 35, no. 16 (19 October 1907): 561.

Hurd, Archibald S. "The American Fleet from an English Point-of-View." *Cassier's Magazine* 32 (October 1907): 467–77, and 33 (December 1907): 256–67.

"Is Our Pacific Cruise Pacific?" *Current Literature* 44 (January 1908): 12–17.

"The Itinerary of the Cruise." *Scientific American* 100 (20 February 1909): 157.

"Japan, America and the Anglo-Saxon World." *Spectator* 99 (13 July 1907): 40–41.

"The Japanese Navy of Today." *Scientific American* 99 (24 October 1908): 279–82.

"Japan's Great Welcome to the Fleet." *American Review of Reviews* (November 1908): 539–40.

Jefferson, Charles Edward. "The Delusion of Militarism." *Atlantic Monthly* 103 (1909): 379–88.

"The Joys of Target Practice." *Cassier's Magazine* 41, no. 6 (2 May 1908): 8.

"Lessons and Results of the Battleship Cruise." *Scientific American* 100 (20 February 1909): 146.

Livermore, Seward W. "The American Navy as a Factor in World Politics, 1903–1913." *AHR* 63, no. 4 (July 1958): 863–79.

———. "Battleship Diplomacy in South America, 1905–1925." *JMH* 16 (March 1944): 31–48.

Low, A. Maurice. "The Anglo-Japanese Alliance." *The Forum* 33 (April 1902): 196–206.

Luce, Rear Admiral Stephen Bleeker. "The Fleet." *North American Review* 185 (October 1908): 564–76.

BIBLIOGRAPHY

Mahan, Alfred Thayer. "The True Significance of the Pacific Cruise of the Battleship Fleet." *Scientific American* 97 (7 December 1907): 407.

———. "The Value of the Pacific Cruise to the Fleet." *Cassier's Magazine* 41, no. 23 (24 August 1908).

Marvin, Winthrop L. "The Greatest Naval Cruise of Modern Times." *American Review of Reviews* 37 (April 1908): 456–63.

Maurer, John H. "Fuel and the Battle Fleet: Coal, Oil and American Naval Strategy, 1898–1925." *Naval War College Review* 34 (September–October 1981): 60–72.

Maxey, Professor Edwin A. "The Anglo-Japanese Treaty." *Arena* 27 (May 1902): 449–54.

Meadows, Martin. "Eugene Hale and the Navy." *American Neptune* (July 1962): 187–93.

"The Meaning of the Pacific Cruise." *Literary Digest* 35, no. 25 (21 December 1907): 946–47.

Melville, Rear Admiral George Wallace. "The Important Elements in Naval Conflicts." *Annals of the American Academy of Political and Social Science* 26 (July 1905): 123–36.

———. "Is Our Naval Administration Efficient?" *North American Review* 189 (1909): 46–47.

———. "Our Actual Naval Strength." *North American Review* 176 (March 1903): 376–90.

Minger, Ralph Eldin. "Taft's Mission to Japan: A Study in Personal Diplomacy." *PHR* 30 (1961): 279–94.

Moore, John Hammond. "The Eagle and the 'Roo': American Fleets in Australian Waters." *USNIP* 97, no. 11 (November 1971): 43–51.

"More Truths About Our Battleships." *The Navy* 1, no. 7 (July 1907): 8–11.

Morton, Louis. "Military and Naval Preparations for the Defense of the Philippines During the War Scare of 1907." *Military Affairs* 13, no. 2 (Summer 1949): 95–104.

———. "War Plan Orange: Evolution of a Strategy." *World Politics* 11 (January 1959): 221–50.

"The Naval Conference at Newport." *The Navy* 2, no. 6 (July 1908): 16–20, and 2, no. 7 (August 1908): 6–8.

"The Naval Investigation." *Outlook* 88, no. 12 (21 March 1908): 613.

"Naval Questions." *American Review of Reviews* 37 (Feb. 1908): 137–38.

"The Naval Review at San Francisco." *American Review of Reviews* 37 (June 1908): 661.

"The Navy and Its Critics." *Literary Digest* 36, no. 1 (4 January 1908): 1–3.

"*The Navy* and Naval Criticism." *Scientific American* 98 (1908): 122.

"The Navy and the Pacific Coast." *Outlook* 87, no. 4 (28 September 1907): 139–41.

"The Navy Defended." *Outlook* 88, no. 9 (29 February 1908): 470.

"The Navy Quarrel." *Independent* 64 (9 January 1908): 69.

Neu, Charles E. "Theodore Roosevelt and American Involvement in the Far East, 1901–1909." *PHR* 35 (1966): 433–50.

"The Newport Conference." *Scientific American* 99 (31 October 1908): 294.

"Newport Conference Approves Designs of New Battleships." *Scientific American* 99 (12 December 1908): 426.

Nish, Ian H. "Australia and the Anglo-Japanese Alliance, 1901–1911." *Australian Journal of Politics and History* 9, no. 2 (November 1963).

"Official Answer to the Navy's Critics." *Literary Digest* 36, no. 9 (27 February 1908): 290.

"Official Synopsis of the Newport Conference: General Order No. 78." *The Navy* 2, no. 10 (November 1908): 28–39.

O'Laughlin, J. C. "The American Fighting Fleet: Its Strategic Disposition." *Cassier's Magazine* 27 (1903): 375–92.

"Our Blunders in Warship Construction." *The Navy* 1, no. 6 (June 1907): 13–15.

"Our Fleet in the Pacific." *American Review of Reviews* 37 (March 1908): 266.

"Our Naval Forces in the Pacific." *Scientific American* 97 (6 July 1907): 4.

"Our Navy Under Fire." *Current Literature* 44 (February 1908): 124–36.

"Our Rank as Second Naval Power." *Scientific American* 98 (30 May 1908): 386.

"Our Ships Under Criticism." *American Review of Reviews* 37 (March 1908): 267–68.

Palmer, Frederick. "The Best of Cruises." *Cassier's Magazine* 41, no. 12 (13 June 1908): 17.

———. "Bluejacket Stories." *Cassier's Magazine* 41, no. 25 (12 September 1908): 19.

———. "The Bull-Fight at Lima." *Cassier's Magazine* 41, no. 6 (2 May 1908): 18.

———. "The Fleet Comes Home." *Cassier's Magazine* 42, no. 22 (20 February 1909): 16–17.

———. "The Fleet's First Step." *Cassier's Magazine* 40, no. 17 (18 January 1908): 9.

———. "The Fleet's Longest Run." *Cassier's Magazine* 40, no. 22 (22 February 1908): 9–12.

———. "The Fleet's Respects to Chile." *Cassier's Magazine* 41, no. 5 (25 April 1908): 23–24.

———. "The New 'Old Man' of the Fleet." *Cassier's Magazine* 41, no. 4 (27 June 1908): 19.

———. "The Sailing of the Great Fleet." *Cassier's Magazine* 40, no. 11 (7 December 1907): 13–14.

"The President and the Admiral." *Literary Digest* 36, no. 3 (18 January 1908): 71–73.

"The Progress of Our Fleet." *American Review of Reviews* 37 (March 1908): 276–77.

"The Proposed Despatch of Sixteen Battleships to the Pacific." *Harper's Weekly* 51, no. 2639 (22 July 1907): 1047.

Putnam, George P. "San Francisco's Welcome to the Fleet." *Outlook* 89, no. 4 (23 May 1908): 149–52.

Ray, Thomas W. "The Bureaus Go on Forever . . . " *USNIP* 94, no. 1 (January 1968): 50–63.

"The Recent Criticisms of Our Navy." *Scientific American* 98 (1908): 95.

Reid, George H. "An After-Glance at the Visit of the American Fleet to Australia." *North American Review* 189 (March 1909): 404–9.

"A Remarkable Cruise." *American Review of Reviews* (April 1908): 402.

"The Return of the Fleet." *Outlook* (27 February 1909): 424–26.

Reuterdahl, Henry. "The Needs of Our Navy." *McClure's Magazine* 30, no. 1 (January 1908): 251–63.

———. "President Roosevelt and the Navy's Renaissance." *Pearson's Magazine* 20, no. 6 (December 1908): 566–86.

"The Reuterdahl Attack on Our Navy." *Scientific American* 98 (18 January 1908): 38–39, and (25 January 1908): 60–62.

Riske, Milt. "A History of Hospital Ships," in Naval History Foundation, *United States Naval Hospital Ships*. Washington: Naval History Foundation, 1973.

"The Sailing of the Fleet." *American Review of Reviews* (December 1907): 661.

Schroeder, Rear Admiral Seaton. "America's Welcome Abroad." *Independent* (March 1909): 478–80.

"Scraping Off the Naval Barnacles." *Literary Digest* 38, no. 6 (6 February 1909): 195–97.

"The Senate Hearings on the Alleged Defects of Our Navy." *Scientific American* 98 (4 April 1908): 238.

"The Senate, the Scientific American, and the New York Sun." *Scientific American* 98 (2 May 1908): 306, 310.

BIBLIOGRAPHY

"Sending the Fleet to the Pacific." *Literary Digest* 35, no. 10 (7 September 1907): 313–14.

"Should We Send a Fleet to the Pacific?" *Literary Digest* 35, no. 2 (13 July 1907): 40–41.

Sims, William S. "Roosevelt and the Navy: Letters from President Roosevelt, Never Before Published, Throw New Light on the Gunnery Question." *McClure's Magazine* 54, no. 10 (December 1922): 56–62, 78.

———. "Roosevelt and the Navy: Recollections, Reminiscences and Reflections." *McClure's Magazine* 54, no. 9 (November 1922): 32–41.

———. "Theodore Roosevelt at Work." *McClure's Magazine* 54, no. 11 (January 1923): 61–66, 95–101.

"Steady Improvement in Naval Gunnery." *Scientific American* 97 (20 July 1907): 42.

Steiner, Zara S. "Great Britain and the Creation of the Anglo-Japanese Alliance." *JMH* 31 (1959): 27–36.

"The Story of Magdalena Bay." *American Review of Reviews* 37 (April 1908): 477–78.

"Strengthening of the Pacific Fleet." *Scientific American* 100 (27 February 1909): 167.

"Summer Plans for the Atlantic Fleet." *The Navy* 1, no. 6 (June 1907): 13–15.

Taylor, G. P. "New Zealand, the Anglo-Japanese Alliance and the 1908 Visit of the American Fleet." *Australian Journal of Politics and History* 15, no. 1 (April 1969): 55–76.

"That Newport Conference." *Scientific American* 99 (31 Oct. 1908): 294.

"That Pacific Cruise." *The Navy* 1, no. 9 (September 1907): 10–11.

"Training Bluejackets for the Battleship Cruise to the Pacific." *Harper's Weekly* 51, no. 2651 (12 October 1907): 1485.

"The Travels of the Fleet." *The Navy* 2, no. 6 (July 1908): 27–33.

"The True Significance of the Pacific Cruise." *American Review of Reviews* 37 (January 1908): 88–89.

Turner, George Kibbe. "Our Navy on Land: The Greatest Waste of National Funds in the History of the United States." *McClure's Magazine* 32 (1909): 397–411.

"The United States and the World." *Spectator* 100 (18 April 1908): 606–7.

"The United States Fleet." *Spectator* 101 (15 Aug. 1908): 218–19.

"United States Navy Battleships at Auckland." *Nation* 87 (13 August 1908): 127.

NEWSPAPERS

Age (Melbourne)
Argus (Melbourne)
Asahi Shimbun (Tokyo)
Auckland Star
Auckland Weekly News
Boston Transcript
Bristol Time and Mirror
El Comercio (Punta Arenas)
Japan Advertiser
Japan Daily Mail
Japan Times
Japan Weekly Mail (Tokyo)
Jiji Shimpo (Tokyo)
Jornal do Commercio (Rio de Janeiro)
London *Daily Chronicle*
London *Daily Telegraph*

BIBLIOGRAPHY

London *Times*
Melbourne *Herald*
New York *Nation*
New York Times
New Zealand Herald (Auckland)
New Zealand Weekly Graphic
Proine (Athens)
Revista do Semana
Sydney *Bulletin*
Sydney *Morning Herald*
United States Army and Navy Journal and Gazette of the Regular and Volunteer Forces
  (Army and Navy Journal)
Weekly Graphic and New Zealand Mail
Wellington Evening Post

Index

INDEX

INDEX

INDEX

INDEX

INDEX

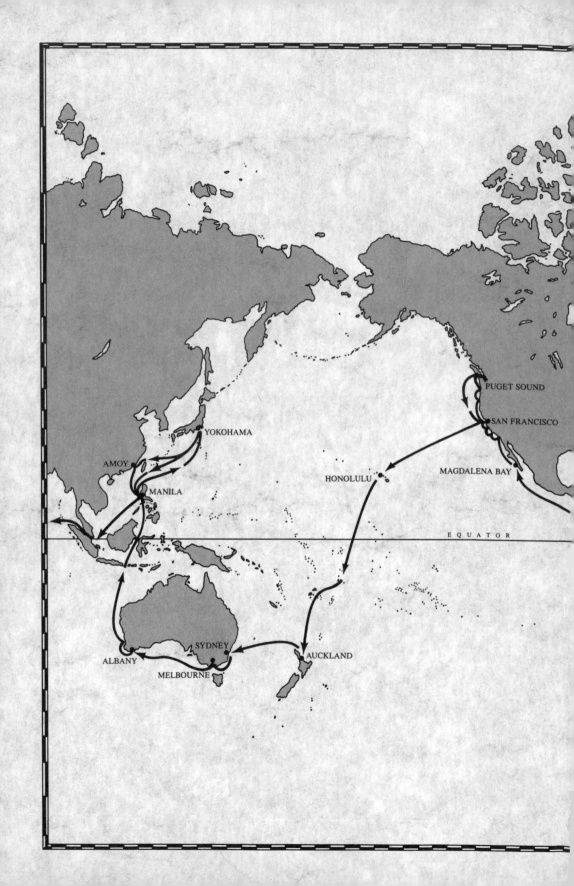

PUGET SOUND

SAN FRANCISCO

YOKOHAMA

AMOY

HONOLULU

MAGDALENA BAY

MANILA

EQUATOR

SYDNEY

ALBANY   AUCKLAND

MELBOURNE